Mental Health of the
Industrial Worker

Mental Health of the

Industrial Worker

A Detroit Study

Arthur Kornhauser Wayne State University

With the collaboration of **Otto M. Reid**

John Wiley & Sons, Inc., New York · London · Sydney

To Mary, Ruth, and Bill

Preface

This book is concerned with the psychological condition of workers in modern mass-production industry. I have attempted to assess and compare the mental health of men at higher and lower skill levels, with special attention to the human effects of routine production jobs. As noted in the opening chapter, despite the continuing sweep of automation vast numbers of these low level jobs are destined to remain—and they will persistently confront industrial society with deeply troublesome human problems.

My first aim is to weigh the conflicting contentions regarding urban factory workers: that they are miserable, alienated, psychologically impoverished; or that they are happy and self-confident, fully alive, and unprecedentedly well off, psychologically as well as materially. As anticipated, the truth lies at neither of these extremes. More significant, however, is the clear evidence of differential psychological effects corresponding to the positions men hold in the occupational structure. Insofar as our evidence indicates adverse effects, particularly at lower skill levels, it becomes important to depict the nature of the effects and to analyze specific influences that help account for the impairment. Finally, on the basis of my inquiry, I suggest possible directions of social change to be considered and evaluated in the search for remedies.

I have used the term mental health, unsatisfactory as it is, simply because I have been unable to find a good substitute. It is to be emphasized that the study is concerned with *positive* mental health, not mental *illness*. The meaning I attach to "positive mental health of workers" will be set forth in some detail. I shall also explore its relations to job satisfaction and to a range of attitudes and orientations toward other aspects of life as well.

The research reported here is broadly exploratory rather than directed to the testing of specific hypotheses. The results are based on a single intensive interview study at one point in time and predominantly in one industry and one city. Statistical analysis of the interview responses yields useful descriptive information and suggestive clues in regard to explanations, but causal interpretations based on such data necessarily remain tentative. Hopefully, my conclusions will be checked and extended by studies in other industries, under other conditions—and by *longitudinal* studies that will trace psychological changes occurring among workers during the course of their careers in different types of jobs. Nevertheless, despite the limitations of the present study, I believe that the results add significantly to existing knowledge concerning the vital problems of what is happening to the quality of life of industrial man.

The book is addressed not only to social scientists interested in the human problems of industry and the impact of socioeconomic influences, but equally to all thoughtful citizens concerned with wise social policy affecting the welfare of working people. Increasingly, in this age of affluence, it is recognized that appraisals of the industrial system must balance intangible personal and social effects against the traditional imperatives of economic efficiency. Among the intangibles are the matters studied here: the brute facts of unchallenging routine jobs; passive, goalless orientations to life; frustrating failure to achieve the goals of "success" instilled by our culture. These are problems for *society*, in my opinion, not primarily the responsibilities of industrial managements. The answers must be hammered out by all concerned, utilizing the most valid knowledge available. This study represents an effort to augment such knowledge, to add a little to the growing body of information which may help guide social decisions.

Readers who wish to skip technical procedures and details of supporting evidence may obtain the essentials of my results and conclusions from the several chapter summaries and from Chapter 12. The first two chapters present my orientation and procedures. Chapters 3 and 4 describe the overall results of the mental-health assessments, first for the entire sample of factory workers, then for subgroups by occupational level and for comparison groups of nonfactory men. Chapters 5 and 6 are more analytical; they attempt to ascertain characteristics of low-level occupations that may be responsible for the poorer mental health observed among workers in these jobs. Chapter 7 analyzes personality characteristics associated with mental-health differences. The remainder of the book, going beyond the mental-health assessments, provides a more detailed picture of factory workers' orientations toward their work, their nonwork lives, and their world. In the last half of the final chapter I frankly "take off" from the research findings to propose questions and interpretations in regard to social policy.

Many persons have contributed valuably to this book. Though I shall name only a few, I am deeply grateful to all the others as well. Special thanks go to Dr. Otto M. Reid who shouldered a large share of responsibility for the conduct of the study. The later stages of analysis, interpretation, and writing, which have been entirely in my own hands, have benefited particularly from criticisms and fruitful suggestions by Louis Ferman, Ruth and William Kornhauser, James Reed, Gerald Rosenbaum, Richard Shore, and Charles Solley. Most of all I am indebted to my wife, both for many editorial improvements and for the thousand thoughtful ways in which she freed my time and gave encouragement that helped bring the book to completion.

Principal support for the investigation was provided by a research grant, M–460, from the National Institute of Mental Health. Grateful acknowledgment is made to that agency and, for other assistance, to Wayne State University College of Liberal Arts, the Computing Center, and the Wayne State Fund; also to the Institute of Labor and Industrial Relations of Wayne State University and the University of Michigan. I wish to thank the several University administrators who generously provided assistance and facilitation for the research: particularly Lloyd Allen Cook, Edward L. Cushman, Ronald Haughton, Walter Hoffman, Victor A. Rapport, and Ross Stagner.

ARTHUR KORNHAUSER

Detroit, Michigan
December 1964

Contents

1.

Psychology and the study

of working people

Year after year, from the beginning of the industrial revolution to the present day, thoughtful observers have expressed deep concern over the harmful effects believed to result from the specialized, routinized work of the factory. The "assembly line" has become a symbol of the alleged evils of impersonal, dehumanized, goalless, robotlike performance. Other semiskilled manufacturing operations are considered only a trifle less onerous. The consequences of years spent in such jobs, it is asserted, range from mild boredom and discontent to passive resignation and stunted personal development or to bitter despair, violent revolt, severe psychoneuroses, and even outright psychotic breakdown.

There is, of course, a contrary body of opinion that argues against these pessimistic conclusions. The opposed views emphasize the contentment of most employees. They point out that the modern factory worker is unbelievably well off compared to the general run of mankind, past and present; that his vastly improved conditions of life and work afford him opportunities for enjoyment and self-realization beyond the dreams of previous generations. Production workers by the millions are living full, well-adjusted lives, we are told. Sometimes, in fact, the writing in this vein grows almost lyrical in its celebration of the enviable position of the "happy worker" in modern industry.

These obviously are complex issues that permit no simple answers. Yet the questions are so important for our industrial society that we are impelled to seek the best answers we can find, however far short of finality. In view of this vital need and the widespread recognition of the problem, there remains a remarkable dearth of evidence, especially of facts collected by careful systematic inquiries. Al-

1

though research-minded psychologists and other social scientists have increasingly turned their attention in this direction, knowledge is still extremely scanty.[1] The study reported in this book represents a further attempt to help fill the gaps and to draw whatever conclusions appear justified.

The psychology of industrial work has devoted itself for the most part to problems of productivity and organizational effectiveness. Working people have been studied primarily as means to the ends of efficiency, whether of the single enterprise or of the larger society. Even when attention is directed to attitudes, feelings, and morale, interest usually centers on how these subjective states affect work performance and the functioning of the industrial organization.[2]

An alternative orientation focuses on working people as themselves the significant ends. Interest attaches to the personal development and well-being of the men and women in industry, the improvement of their individual and social health, especially their "mental health." The present study belongs to this second category. It inquires about the impact of modern economic organization, particularly the demands of mass-production manufacturing, on the people involved. What does the industrial way of life do to, and for, the men who man the machines? What does their work mean to them and what are the effects of their factory occupations on their spirit and their life adjustments?

Are factory workers happy and well adjusted in the main? Or are they predominantly bitter or depressed or anxious or apathetic? Are they enthusiastic, idealistic, self-reliant, zestful? Or cynical, alienated, disspirited? One can find assertions, that they are all these contradictory things and many more. Evidence to support the assertions is scarce indeed. Even less is known about subgroups, for example, by job levels, age, income, and education. Are assembly-line jobs peculiarly monotonous, frustrating, deadening—and hated? Do simple unchallenging tasks tend to produce poor mental health? On all these questions violent disagreement continues despite the debates that go on decade after decade.

The present project aimed to secure evidence bearing on these issues. It is not a book on mental *illness*. It deals with the psychology of normal working people, not with psychiatric cases. Its principal concern is with employed, successful factory workers exemplified by those in the automobile plants of Detroit. Attention focuses on an overall assessment of the mental *health* of these men.

Many other more specific characterizations of individuals are also analyzed, however, in an effort to gain better understanding of the industrial worker and the influences favorable or unfavorable to his development and effective functioning as a person.

The changing character of factory work and composition of the work force

The accelerating rate of industrial change, the "new industrial revolution," has been so dramatic and so greatly publicized that many persons have been led to believe that the problems just referred to are about to disappear, that they will soon be dead issues.   There can be no doubt that enormous changes in the nature and conditions of work have taken place over the years and that even more profound transformations are now in process, particularly the technological innovations popularly encompassed by the term automation.   To say this, however, is by no means to declare that low-skilled routine types of work are on the point of vanishing.

A glance at historical trends will help put the matter in perspective. Over the half century from 1900 to 1950, the number of semiskilled workers in the United States increased from fewer than four million to some twelve million.   As a proportion of the total labor force they moved from 13 per cent to 20 per cent.   In manufacturing alone, the "operatives and kindred workers" (to adopt the census designation) went from less than one and a half million in 1900 to approximately six million in 1950.[3]   But the past decade has witnessed an important change.   The rapid upward trend has been interrupted by the advent of automation.   How drastically this alters the dimensions of the factory worker problem we shall consider later, after a brief note to recall important changes other than the growth in numbers of persons affected.

Qualitatively, the outstanding trend has been the vast improvement of the factory worker's condition.   Through recent generations and continuing to the present time, real incomes and standards of living, health, and life expectancy have risen at spectacular rates.   Home ownership, automobiles, savings accounts, and undreamed-of comforts have come to large sections of the working class as well as to the middle class.   For the less fortunate, social security benefits, minimum-wage laws, unemployment compensation, and other welfare measures provide a floor where none existed before.   Steady advances in the workshop have paralleled the gains of workers as consumers.

The worst features of the early factory system have disappeared. Heavy, back-breaking drudgery is rare in present-day industry. Men—and women and children—no longer labor long hours in dark and filthy surroundings; they no longer live in constant fear of unreasonable speed-ups, wage cuts, arbitrary discipline and dismissal. Both employment policies and relationships and the physical and social conditions of work are immeasurably improved. Modern personnel administration, enlightened supervision, an established role for labor unions as protector and champion of workers' interests —these clearly mark the change. No need here for tracing these changes in detail or for probing into the varied forces responsible. Whatever the causes, the fact of widespread and striking improvements is everywhere apparent.

Yet even the most enthusiastic admirers of the human achievements of contemporary industry recognize that serious problems remain. Unemployment and irregular employment, substandard and inadequate wages and working conditions, strains imposed by outmoded skills, by blocked occupational progress, job transfers and need for retraining and relocating—such economic and human difficulties have persistently plagued the course of industrial development. However, it is not to the problems of displacement, substandard conditions, or rapid changes that we shall direct attention but rather to the day-in and day-out adjustments of men steadily employed in factory jobs with above-average pay and relatively good employment conditions. Here, too, there are challenging questions —in regard to the meaning of work and the satisfactions it offers, the effects of jobs in which the worker is an atom in a large aggregation, lacking individuality and independence, subjected to disciplined routine and the unending execution of prescribed operations planned in detail by "higher-ups." These are still the characteristic features of factory work, in greater or less degree, despite the many changes for the better.

Indeed the extreme subdivision and tight control of operations has sometimes so robbed the worker of motivation and sense of responsibility that a reverse process of "job enlargement" has commended itself to managers. Fascinating cases are now on record demonstrating the gains for production and morale that have been achieved by recombining elementary operations into larger units.[4] Experiments of this kind offer significant testimony in respect to the negative human effects of extreme simplification of tasks and the benefits of restoring *meaning* to work.

The exciting new development bearing on these problems is *automation*. Hailed by some as a blessing and lamented by others as a curse, this latest technological phase of the industrial revolution is undeniably destined to eliminate or transform vast numbers of industrial jobs—above all, simple repetitive machine operations. It is already producing far-reaching consequences on employment and unemployment, changes of skill levels and occupational distribution, knotty problems of training and retraining, of work satisfaction and motivation, needs for new management and union structures and methods, and an array of additional direct and indirect effects. It would take us too far afield from our present purpose to comment on these developments. The single issue of critical importance in reference to our study is how generally and how rapidly routine semiskilled jobs will be eliminated. If almost all such work is about to disappear, then the whole problem of the mental health and attitudes of the average factory worker is outdated. The idea has its appeal, but before one accepts it a cautious second look is in order.

These days when technological reality outdistances science fiction, and thus provides some substance for uninhibited fears and hopes, it is all too easy to accept highly exaggerated predictions of completely automatic production in a world run by electronic brains. Automation unquestionably has displaced many factory workers and will displace many more. The impact on employment, both of those displaced and those unhired, is serious and calls for all-out national effort to provide better answers. But the facts of unemployment by no means signify that there will soon be no low-skilled jobs. Indeed, the absolute number of semiskilled "operatives" has held constant during this decade of automation.

Census figures on the United States labor force reveal that from 1950 to 1963 the total number of operatives did not change much; in both years it was approximately 12 million.[5] Since the labor force as a whole was increasing, particularly in professional, subprofessional, technical, and service occupations, the *proportion* in semiskilled work did decline—from slightly over 20 per cent to slightly over 18 per cent. Furthermore, the Department of Labor projections, based on all available information, have forecast substantial increases in the number of operatives to a total of 13.6 million in 1970 and 14.2 million in 1975 (though their *percentage* of the larbor force will drop further to approximately 16 per cent).[6]

In *manufacturing* industry, other tabulations show that the total of "production workers" (nonsupervisory blue-collar workers of all grades) rose during the mid-1950's and then fell back so that the numbers in 1950, 1960, and 1963 are nearly identical. Semiskilled operatives in manufacturing actually increased in number from 1950 to 1960.[7]

The present study deals with these millions of industrial workers who are *not* about to be displaced. For a great many years to come, society will continue to worry about what routine semiskilled industrial jobs are doing to and for employees as human beings. Although the advance of automation will surely continue, it is well to recognize that it is not all encompassing. It encounters technical and economic limitations and counter-considerations which mean that many operations will remain in human hands. Even though large numbers of machine-tending and product-inspecting types of work are abolished and many other jobs are transformed, sober appraisal indicates that immense numbers of men will continue to be engaged in low-level industrial jobs that retain the basic characteristics with which our study is concerned.[8]

Views congruent with the foregoing are tellingly expressed by two foremost research authorities on these matters.

Even in a highly developed industrial country like the United States, the automatic sector of industry is likely to continue a great deal smaller in its number of gainfully employed than the non-automatic sector. (Walker, 1962, p. 78)

For anyone unwilling to delude himself, to become engrossed in dubious speculations about a distant future . . . , it must seem highly probable that for several generations yet there will remain a multitude of jobs in which the worker can find no outlet for his tastes, his deeper wishes, or his personality. (Friedmann, 1961, p. 121)

Finally, from a leader in science and technology comes this perhaps too sanguine conclusion.

The assertion that automation is producing a very spectacular rise in productivity, and thereby causing an unusually severe and widespread unemployment problem, is not borne out by the facts. The nature of the technological changes being introduced into industrial manufacturing processing has altered, but the trend has been continuous. Thus, in spite of spectacular improvements in productivity in certain industrial processes, the overall picture is not essentially different in recent years from that of the last forty years. (DuBridge, 1962, p. 31)

The place of work in the lives of industrial workers

The giant strides of industrial technology with its promise of material abundance have caused our society as never before to ask searching questions regarding the meaning and psychological value of work in men's lives. There is growing recognition that it is no longer necessary for so much of life to be absorbed in work; that more and more we have a choice between increasing production and decreasing the time and effort we devote to our jobs. Yet we know that this way of posing the issue is a grave oversimplification. For clearly work not only serves to produce goods and services; it also performs essential psychological functions. It operates as a great stabilizing, integrating, ego-satisfying central influence in the pattern of each person's life. If the job fails to fulfill these needs of the personality, it is problematic whether men can find adequate substitutes to provide a sense of significance and achievement, purpose and justification for their lives.

We strongly incline to the view that work will continue, in one form or another, to hold a most important place in meeting people's social and psychological needs; furthermore, that workers will have constantly rising expectations of what the job should offer in the way of intangible as well as tangible rewards. At the same time, increasing freedom from the demands of work will permit nonwork activities to become a source of vital additional gratifications and means to enhanced fullness of life—but not as a *substitute* for the job. This view contrasts with the contention that work will soon be obsolete and that even now it has so lost meaning for great numbers of men that they must learn to center their lives rather in expanded and enriched leisure pursuits.

Some of the findings from our own research give evidence of the psychological salience of the job within the factory population studied. In order to throw light on how important the job looms in the total life picture of auto workers, we opened our interviews with broad questions asking how the individual feels about his life and the way it has been working out. The men were interviewed at home and no hint was given that we had any special interest in the work area of their lives. They were as free to talk about their families, gardens, hunting trips, church activities, and gratifications and frustrations as consumers as they were about their jobs. We employed a series of nondirective probing questions to encourage them to range widely in comments about themselves, their problems, hopes, worries, and satisfactions—past, present, and future. All the ideas they volunteered were then classified to yield a measure of the relative frequency with which different subjects were referred to. This classification of responses tells us something interesting about the importance of the job compared to other life interests. When we group all the ideas mentioned into broad categories, the proportions come out as shown in Table 1-1 (first column). More of the volunteered comments referred to the man's job than to his family, his leisure and social activities, or any other sector of his life interests.

We next obtained a measure of the topics most salient for the respondents by counting those that they particularly stressed or mentioned repeatedly. The proportions by this count are shown in the second column above. The job is again a prominent interest and becomes strikingly so if we add the references to personal economic conditions. This may be justifiable since the latter ideas pertain to earnings and personal finances closely dependent on the job. Indeed, a number of ideas classified under health and personal competence might also be added since many of them have some reference to the job. A final comparison was made, this time by counting the number of *individuals* for whom each topic was a salient one. Personal economic concerns, job, and family prove to be salient for the largest proportions (61, 58, and 55 per cent

Table 1-1   Factory workers' life interests as indicated by volunteered responses

	All Ideas	Salient Ideas
The job	26%	22%
Family relations; wife and children	18	22
Leisure and social activities	16	11
Own health, age, competence, etc.	13	13
Personal economic condition	10	17
Social conditions, war, politics, people, etc. (with no clear personal reference)	10	8
Life experiences and relationships (other than current economic)	7	7
	100%	100%
Number of ideas (base of percentages)	3704	1419

respectively) while all other interests are salient for less than 40 per cent.

In short, the foregoing results indicate that the job and its direct economic consequences are very much in the forefront of working people's thinking, at least on a par with family interests and decidedly more prominent than other segments of their lives.[9]

Are they satisfied with their jobs and their lives?

Intertwined with the preceding issue of how important work is in the lives of industrial workers is the equally crucial question of how *satisfying* they find their jobs and life conditions.   A large body of evidence is now available on these matters though the conclusions to be drawn are still in dispute.   Many observations to be reported in this book have direct bearing on this issue and will be discussed in some detail.   Although job satisfaction is certainly not equivalent to good mental health, the two are positively correlated and the analysis of their interdependence constitutes one of our major objectives.

Our own results are in substantial agreement with hundreds of other studies in finding that workers express predominantly favorable feelings toward their jobs and life situation.   At the same time there are many important negative reactions; it is apparent that large numbers of men are not *well* satisfied and that their positive responses to general questions must be cautiously accepted and heavily discounted.   But negative interpretations can likewise easily be exaggerated.   Not a few industrial workers, particularly those in more skilled jobs that offer variety and responsibility, experience their work as thoroughly interesting and enjoyable.   More typically, the general run of working people are *moderately* contented, often in a passive, unenthusiastic, accepting fashion.   Although they reveal numerous elements of discontent, they usually come out with a net balance of feelings on the positive side.

To describe such findings is not, of course, to pronounce them good or bad.   One may well believe that workers *should* be either better satisfied or more dissatisfied than they are.   One may argue, for example, that liking for a simple, unchallenging job, or even passively accepting it, signifies dwarfed aspirations, absence of perceived alternatives, and a general deadening of spirt that are deplorable.   These problems of social evaluation, too, we shall have to weigh as we proceed.

Finally, lest the emphasis on preponderantly favorable job feelings imply more than is warranted, we call attention to a few facts showing how far factory work is from being viewed by workers as an enviable way of life.   When workers in the automobile plants were asked how factory work compares with other types of work, almost twice as many gave unfavorable as favorable evaluations.   Further questioning as to what effects "production jobs" have on men elicited a flood of negative comments.   Even allowing for the fact that the form of question probably suggested ill effects, the intensity and volume of the negative answers convincingly portrays the low esteem and unpleasant feelings attached to these jobs.   In line with such reactions we also found, as have others, that only a small minority of factory workers feel their jobs attractive enough that they would willingly go into the same kind of work if they could "go back to the age of 15 and start all over again."

In this introductory section we conclude simply that the industrial worker has diverse and even contradictory feelings toward work.   Nevertheless, the daily job, with all its drawbacks, still serves as a major means by which men strive to realize the values, tangible and intangible, which our culture emphasizes.   Most men manage to secure enough such gratifications from their work to consider it on the whole somewhat satisfying.   In later chapters we shall deal in detail with the varied results pertaining to these job attitudes and motivations.   The analysis will include attention to the important differences among individuals and occupational groups.

Other parts of our inquiry among auto workers lead to tentative assessments of their satisfactions and personal adjustments in *nonwork* spheres of life.   Here, too, and more markedly than in respect to the job, favorable attitudes predominate.   Most of these working people have come to terms with their world as it is; they feel reasonably well satisfied, mildly optimistic about the future, and preponderantly positive in their volunteered comments about themselves, their homes and families, leisure pursuits, and their lives generally.   Judged by broader standards of what life can mean, however—in terms of personal development, range of interests, richness and fullness of life—their condition may be perceived by students of society as leaving much to be desired.   Not a few of the workers themselves share these less sanguine appraisals.   There are those, both within and outside the working class, who are impressed by the relative emptiness, narrowness, and impoverishment of the nonwork as well as work sectors of their life.

Surely there is no demonstrably "right answer" to such value-laden questions. It is nonetheless necessary for everyone concerned to ascertain and weigh whatever facts he can insofar as they have bearing on his evaluative judgments. Each of us according to his own lights, and all of us collectively through ongoing discussions, may then proceed more intelligently to support or oppose particular features of existing industrial organization, work relationships, and social conditions affecting working people.

The core purpose of the present study lies precisely at this point. It attempts to add a little to present knowledge and interpretations that may help guide public opinion and the policies of industry, labor, and government in respect to the well-being and fullest possible development of industrial workers.

Psychological guidelines

Research *procedures* of the study will be described in the next chapter. Here we sketch the general framework within which the inquiry is oriented.

(*a*) The focus is on broad *occupational groupings of workers;* not on individual differences, interpersonal relations, or the functioning of organizations or small groups. Interest centers on psychological effects common to large numbers of persons similarly situated; we are concerned with attitudes and adjustments characteristic of entire categories of men who share specified conditions of work and life.

(*b*) The central concern is with "mental health": those behaviors, attitudes, perceptions, and feelings that determine a worker's overall level of personal effectiveness, success, happiness, and excellence of functioning as a person. The concept clearly is evaluative and it is multidimensional. It concerns complex combinations of inner and outer behavior which result in what is judged to be more satisfactory or less satisfactory psychological and social functioning. Furthermore, it is to be definitely understood that we are not dealing with *mental illness* nor do we assume that the indicators of positive mental health which we employ have any known relationship to serious disorders or "psychoses." Finally, it is noted that our assessments of mental health are based solely on interview responses from the working people studied.

(c) Most important in this introductory chapter is a suggested *frame of reference* and *way of thinking* about the problem of how men's occupations and associated life conditions make for better or poorer mental health and consequently what kinds of changes may be advisable in the interests of better mental health. Empirical research findings cannot take the place of theoretical orientation. The research can hopefully add a little useful knowledge here and there that serves to check and revise previous interpretations and to suggest new leads. But generalized conclusions are never demonstrated or proved by studies such as the present one; they are merely made more plausible or probable insofar as the empirical findings are compatible with certain theoretical expectations. There are always possible alternative interpretations that also "fit the facts," and the choice among the alternatives turns on assumptions and on conclusions from wider bodies of knowledge that transcend the special circumstances of the given research. In the present connection the wider body of knowledge has to do especially with the "psychology of personal adjustment." An understanding of the mental health of working people cannot be divorced from more general formulations of how people interact with the world about them as they strive to satisfy their inner needs in an environment not always indulgent and by means for which their resources are not fully adequate.

In the following few pages we suggest the outlines of such guiding conceptualizations. The picture is painted in broad strokes and does not pretend to represent a consensus among psychologists. It simply states the working conceptions of this study, conceptions that we believe are consonant with observations and research data accumulated over the years by students of human nature working on widely varied problems in diverse settings. In essence it is a dynamic or motivational theory which places major emphasis on the goal-seeking and need-satisfying character of behavior, especially on the central importance of needs and desires that are salient in each person's efforts to maintain and enhance his positive feelings of self-identity and self-worth.

The highlights of our theoretical orientation are the following.

1. A person's behavior, regardless of whether it is satisfactorily adjustive or maladjustive, is always determined jointly by the total make-up of the individual at the time (his total "personality") and by the situation in which he finds himself. His personality is a complex, more or less unified result of everything that has been part

of his life history, beginning with his inheritance and earliest child-hood experiences and continuing to the present.   What he *is*, in this sense, governs what he *does* (and perceives, thinks, feels) *in given circumstances*.   What he "is," in reference to potential behavior, may be usefully divided into those inner processes that direct be-havior toward ends or goals ("motives") and those processes that provide the means or instrumentalities of action ("mechanisms"—perceptual and thought habits, knowledge, skills, etc.).

Our interest here is not in ephemeral bits of action by this or that person but in enduring, repeated forms of behavior common to many individuals of similar background and personal make-up.   We shall focus, that is, on differences of behavior and attitudes (and "mental health") that occur in *contrasting situations* (occupations) among groups of persons whose motives and mechanisms of action are as-sumed to be fundamentally alike.   For this purpose a key concept is that of widely shared motives or common goal values.

2. The proposed concept of social motivation, in brief, is this: Thought and action are directed toward goals by internal states and processes variously referred to as motives, wants, needs, purposes, desires, drives, preferences, attitudes, and equivalent terms.   We shall use "motives" or "wants" as the general designation.   Motives develop from the biological nature of man but are largely a product of social learning so that the most significant, generally held motives can be viewed as internalized norms and values of the culture. These socially shaped motives that men strive to satisfy, in their work as elsewhere, vary to some extent with social-class and group influences, particularly in regard to their relative intensity and in regard to the specific subgoals that are sought.   Nevertheless, certain major, underlying goals remain fairly constant and dependable.

Prominent among the motives widely shared in our culture are desires for material acquisitions, personal well-being and security, "success" with its accent on money, social esteem, and influence. But there are powerful motives aimed at less obvious gratifications as well—desire for simple companionship, for affection, for apprecia-tion and approval by one's associates; wants for personal freedom and independence; for interesting, challenging activities and effective performance; a sense of accomplishment, completion, and signifi-cance through either individual or collective efforts; desires to help and protect others; to remove or destroy whatever interferes with movement toward one's goals; above all, general goals of self-esteem and feeling of personal worth, and groping for peace of mind, for secure beliefs to hang onto, for acceptable goals to make life meaningful.   The basic problem of men's relationship to work is found in the question of how far these varied and insistent motives are gratified, and how far thwarted, by the opportunities, conditions, and demands of their jobs.   Additional questions have to do with how success-fully men redefine their goals, raise or lower their expectations and desires, to accord better with the realities of their own social situation.

3. *All* the motives function in relation to the "ego," as part of the individual's concept of himself, his self-image and self-ideal de-veloped throughout his lifetime.   This contrasts with attempts by some psychologists to split off a special set of ego motivations—de-sires for achievement, status, growth, power, and so on—as distin-guished, for example, from security and economic goals.[10]   In our view the latter motives involve the ego no less than the former; witness workers' intense personal concern for safe working condi-tions, for protection against unemployment, and for income enough to enjoy life and provide food for the children.   Each person struggles, through *all* his activities, to maintain his favorable self-feelings and to defend his sense of personal identity and worth when threatened by failures, frustrations, and painfully irreconcilable wishes.   An elaborate superstructure of motivations develops to pro-tect the feelings of self-regard (the so-called "defense mechanisms" like rationalization, projection, regression, reaction formation, and many others).   Mental health depends above all else on the develop-ment and retention of goals that are neither too high nor too low to permit realistic, successful maintenance of belief in one's self as a worthy, effective human being, a useful and respected member of society.

4. Insofar as conditions of life and work offer opportunity and en-couragement for fulfillment of important desires, or for perceived movement *toward the goals*, people tend to carry on their activities happily, effectively, in good mental health.   On the other hand, if their wants and expectations are thwarted, especially if they en-counter prolonged frustration in their striving for self-expression, achievement, and feelings of personal worth in line with their self-conception and aspirations, then symptoms of impaired mental health are likely to appear.

Research and speculation concerning working people's adjustment have taken different directions at this point.   Each theory tends to emphasize certain aspects of the whole environment, resulting in partial and sometimes misleading interpretations.   For example frustration, low morale, and unsatisfactory mental health may be attributed solely to economic deprivation and insecurity; or to class differences in opportunity for success, personal growth, and self-realization; or the emphasis may be on the simplicity and robotlike character of work, or poor human relations on the job; or status inferiority, aspiration-achievement disparity, or a congeries of variables pertaining to characteristics of mass society and large-scale bureaucratic organization. We believe that an adequate frame of reference must be comprehensive enough to include all such factors and many others, not only in the industrial setting itself but in the nonwork world as well. Questions also arise whether the impact of industrial jobs may be due to variations in personal make-up among men who go into different kinds of work as well as to differences in situational factors like those just mentioned. We shall consider these various possibilities in regard to problems of worker adjustment, alienation, and morale in the framework of the foregoing concepts and, in our conclusions, we shall try to indicate how a broadly inclusive motivational approach may usefully bring the separate emphases into perspective.

5. In sum, the proposed psychological orientation views mental health as determined by the *total* personality and the *total* environment as it impinges on the person. Mental health is not so much a matter of freedom from specific frustrations as it is an overall balanced relationship to the world which permits a person to maintain realistic, positive belief in himself and his purposeful activities. Insofar as his entire job and life situation facilitate and support such feelings of adequacy, inner security, and meaningfulness of his existence, it can be presumed that his mental health will tend to be good. What is important in a negative way is not any single characteristic of his situation but *everything* that deprives the person of purpose and zest, that leaves him with negative feelings about himself, with anxieties, tensions, a sense of lostness, emptiness, and futility.

Our research data cover only very limited parts of this extensive theoretical canvas, though less limited than is typical in empirical psychological inquiries. But precisely because empirical studies deal with restricted portions of the complex reality, it becomes most important to think in terms of the larger framework within which the parts may be interpreted. Throughout the book we shall have occasion to consider findings in reference to these motivational concepts. In the final chapter we shall attempt a general interpretation of our results in these terms and shall ask what implications the conclusions carry for organizations and for social policy.

2.

The assessment of mental health:

methods of the study

In this chapter we shall describe the procedures of the study, the people studied, and especially our methods for assessing mental health and the justification for the use of the obtained measures. Later chapters will focus on what these measures indicate regarding Detroit automobile workers, their differences by occupational level, and an analysis and interpretation of the differences.

A working conception of mental health

The paramount requirement for carrying out the aims of the study was the adoption of procedures for specifying and assessing "mental health." We decided to follow two guiding principles: (1) we would begin with a variety of simple, commonly accepted ideas as to what constitutes good versus poor mental health[1] and would proceed in subsequent steps to interrelate, test, and in some sense "validate" these ideas; and (2) we would rely primarily on data obtainable by means of interviews with the working people themselves.

The rationale of our mental-health measures is this: we conceptualize mental health not as representing any psychodynamic unity but as a loose descriptive designation for an overall level of success, personal satisfaction, effectiveness, and excellence of the individual's functioning as a person. It refers to a *combination* of psychological and behavioral attributes some of which the person must possess above a required minimum and others of which signify better mental health the more they are present. No single process or entity is hypothesized as underlying mental health; rather we are interested in any and all parts of the person's behavior from the

16

standpoint of their positive or negative significance for his total happiness, adjustment, and effectiveness. That elements of good mental health may exist side by side with bad components in the same person is a matter of everyday observation. The idea that a common core will eventually be discovered which constitutes the essence of psychological health or illness appears to be extremely doubtful. We proceed, then, on the assumption that mental health is multidimensional though this is not at all to imply that there are not certain dimensions of especially great importance relative to others. Our search is not for any peculiarly crucial key measures of mental health but for useful indicators chosen from innumerable possible ones. The purpose is to select indicators which, taken in combination, are representative enough of important parts of a person's total behavior to provide useful estimates as to the satisfactoriness of his general level of psychological and social functioning.

This somewhat vague formulation will assume greater definiteness in terms of the specific content of our interviews and the indexes derived from them. The choice of these component variables will represent our working definition of mental health. It is not an arbitrary definition, of course; it must be shown to have some correspondence with usual conceptions, particularly with those of qualified experts (psychiatrists and clinical psychologists). Moreover, the fuller meaning of the assessments will need to be developed and enriched by exploring the relationships among the indicators and between them and a variety of other personal and situational variables.[2] In later sections of this chapter and in following chapters we shall deal at some length with data bearing on both these requirements.

There remains the large and troublesome problem of subjective value standards which enter into the definition and assessment of mental health. The culture-bound, normative character of the concept cannot be gainsaid. There are no objective, value-free judgments of "good" and "not so good" mental health. With lively awareness of this fact, we nevertheless believe it useful to attempt such assessments. However, it is necessary to recognize the evaluative nature of the judgments, to see them for what they are and not to confuse them with the empirical "indicators" obtained from the interview responses. The first research step is to specify and measure those features of the individual's condition and behavior thought to be indicative of good or poor mental health (e.g., high self-esteem or self-derogation, degree of freedom from anxiety, general trust or distrust of people). Then, as a separate operation, it can be decided whether these measures do indeed furnish valid appraisals of "mental health" as one defines it for his present purposes. By the same token, the separate empirical measures can be used with whatever other meanings one finds it intellectually defensible to attribute to them. The safeguard against arbitrary judgments about mental health lies in explicit description of the factual bases of the assessments.[3]

Research methods

Data for the study were obtained by means of detailed interviews with samples of employed men in the Detroit area. The interviewing was carried on during the second half of 1953 and the early months of 1954.[4] Since the research focus is on occupational comparisons, men were selected from specified job categories by a systematic sampling procedure using the personnel files of a number of companies. The persons selected were subsequently interviewed at their homes. Usable interviews were secured with 655 men. Among these, our analysis concentrates on a core sample of 407 Detroit factory workers.[5] All the information from each interview was coded and entered on punch cards for tabulation, construction of indexes, and analyses of relationships. Supplementary data came from interviewers' ratings and reports on each respondent, from interviews with wives (402 completed interviews), and from company records of absences and visits to plant medical clinics. The most important features of these processes are summarized in the next paragraphs.

THE SAMPLE

Names for the core sample of Detroit manual workers were drawn from the files of 13 large and medium-sized automotive manufacturing plants in metropolitan Detroit. Supplementary samples for comparison purposes consist of the following: manual workers from 6 Detroit nonmanufacturing companies (2 of the 6 are aggregates of several companies); factory workers from 8 plants in small towns outside metropolitan Detroit; office workers (in relatively low salary brackets, comparable to those of manual employees) from 6 Detroit automotive companies and from 3 nonmanufacturing companies.

Lists were prepared by going through company personnel files and selecting every *n*th name which satisfied certain predetermined criteria (prescribed job categories; white, native-born men on payroll at least three years, and in one of two age categories, 20 to 29 or 40 to 49). The original lists totaling more than one thousand names were found to contain a number of wrong or out-of-date addresses and persons who did not satisfy our selection criteria, leaving a potential sample of 875. Interviews were completed for 75 per cent of these men (655 individuals). Of the remainder, 15 per cent represent firm refusals to be interviewed; others could not be found at home despite repeated call-backs, proved unwilling to continue the long interview, or were unavailable for other reasons. The numbers and characteristics of the respondents in different categories of those interviewed can best be introduced at a later point when we report results of the study.

THE INTERVIEW

In line with our earlier comments about mental health, the purpose of the interview was to secure information about the respondent's usual feelings, attitudes, and behavior which would indicate how he is "getting along psychologically," his "mental health" as viewed in the value context of contemporary American culture. In addition, the interview sought other types of data to be studied in relation to the mental-health indicators. Altogether, the content of the interview might be classified as follows.

Life satisfactions; attitudes toward self, accomplishments, other persons; aspirations and values.

Job characteristics and work relationships; attitudes and satisfactions pertaining to work, employing organization, and union.

Life history, including adjustments and attitudes in preworking years and as a child.

Current nonjob conditions, activities, and attitudes; use of leisure time.

Emotional adjustment, neurotic symptoms.

Social attitudes and "philosophy."

It is possible, of course, to sample only limited parts of each of these six areas. The interview aimed especially to secure indications of the way in which the worker perceives himself and his personal situation; features of both his job and his life away from work that are experienced as most satisfying and least so; his chief sources of tension and insecurity and the forms of expression they take; in general, the pattern of life adjustment he has adopted and how satisfactory he finds it.   A distinctive characteristic of the present project lies in the effort to combine areas of inquiry ordinarily studied separately.   We are attempting to *interrelate* the evidence turned up by several lines of questioning that have been noted.

The interview followed a long, carefully structured schedule of questions.[6]   These were asked exactly as phrased and in fixed sequence.   Many of these questions were of a form that required the interviewee to answer freely in his own words.   Interviewers recorded the replies as fully and as nearly verbatim as possible.   In addition, we obtained check responses to other questions and to lists of typical personal adjustment items of the kind used in personality inventories.   The average interview required three and a half to four hours, divided into two sessions, and in most instances a supplementary interview was held with the respondent's wife for something over half an hour.   The usual precautions of sound survey procedures were observed—in the matter of wording, pretesting, and revising questions and in respect to selection, training, and supervision of interviewers.[7]

CODING, INDEXES, AND ANALYSIS

In order to prepare the wealth of qualitative data obtained in the interviews for systematic quantitative analysis, rather elaborate coding operations were necessary.   Response data were coded not only by separate questions but also for blocks of related items.   Code classifications were developed partly through logical analysis and anticipation of dimensions and categories likely to prove promising in the context of our research purposes and partly through groupings of ideas that emerged from the empirical material itself.   Usually the code resulted from a combination or interaction of these two processes.   Code categories were designated as unambiguously as possible, usually by means of specific illustrations to guide coders.   Classifications were revised or redefined when necessary, and in a number of instances very specific categories were merged to form more inclusive categories.   The content of the codes will be described when useful in the reporting of results.

Some thirty "indexes" or "scores" derived from the original codes will likewise be introduced at appropriate places throughout the report. It is these derived summary figures on which the major portion of our analysis will be based. The indexes refer largely to personal qualities, attitudes, and behavioral tendencies thought either to indicate mental health or to bear potentially enlightening relationships to it.

The "reliability" and "validity" of the classifications and indexes —or, more generally and significantly, their justification and usefulness—will be examined by searching for meaningful relationships among the available variables. Literally hundreds of cross-relationships have been tabulated in order to test and illuminate the meaning of mental health as here assessed and to draw inferences regarding the questions posed at the beginning of the study.[8]

A few cases

To make the research undertaking more concrete, we insert here a few thumbnail sketches which illustrate the kind of information the interviews make available regarding each worker. The basic initial question is whether "normal" men like these can be meaningfully and validly classified as to the level of their mental health by means of quantitative indexes derived from their interview responses.

* * *

B.N.: 46 years of age; boyhood on farm and in small town of a northern state; eighth grade schooling; married and two children; 23 years on same job, driving cars from final assembly to lot or repair shop (10 to 15 minutes per car). Well satisfied with his life, his job, and his leisure. Not interested in promotion; would like to work for himself ("I have plans but I haven't put them into operation yet.") In recent years he built a home all by himself which he speaks of repeatedly with pride. Hopes now to build some overnight cabins. "I like to build things." He sees relatives and friends on occasion but has very little social life and no participation in organizations; says "Oh, I like to have friends but I can do without them." As to his spare time: "I like all sports, everything about them"; also hunting and traveling. A little dissatisfied with his home and family life: "My wife is always nagging at me. My son won't help me in my work." However, he does not seem to take this too seriously. Earlier he volunteered: "My wife and I don't fight" and when asked in what ways his life is not just the way he would want it, his answer was: "I am satisfied with everything." He reports his health fairly good though he is bothered by sinus trouble, colds, headaches. Other response indications: strong pro-labor orientation though no active participation; says he does not worry; feels in good spirits almost all the time; self-confident and high self-esteem; expresses some moderate hostility. (Mental-health classification in comparison with all factory workers studied: highest one-third. The basis for these quantitative assessments is explained in the following section of the chapter.)

* * *

S. T.: 25 years of age; unmarried; ninth grade schooling; boyhood on farm in South; holds a repetitive factory job feeding pieces into a machine, two per minute. He expresses general dissatisfaction with his life and especially toward his job. "I dread the very fact of going in day after day to the same routine." He had a boyhood interest in radio and electronics and would like to get such work but has done nothing at all about it. "I've had bad breaks all my life and financial troubles and I more or less take it for granted that it always will be that way. I've given up thinking I'll get ahead." Has great variety of spare-time activities and says his leisure time "probably gives me more satisfaction than anything else"—being with his girl and seeing relatives; swimming, picnics, parties, and going to athletic games; working on his car, rebuilding and refinishing furniture; playing music; Bible study (Jehovah's Witnesses, twice a week). "Since I met my girl I dropped most of my old friends." As to health, "I have a tired feeling all the time and weakness and hyperthyroid trouble"; has been seeing a doctor every two weeks. Also mentions indigestion ("I take things all the time for upset stomach") and high blood pressure. Check-response questions indicate distrust of people, feelings of self-blame, and a great deal of worry and nervousness. (Mental-health classification: lowest one-third.)

* * *

D. M.: 47 years of age; entire life in Detroit; son of Polish immigrants; three years of high school; married and has six children; repetitive assembly-line job. Neither well satisfied nor dissatisfied with his life as a whole but a realistic acceptance without bitterness. "What more can you expect out of life than I got; it isn't much but no use crying and hollering. So I try and live and do all right. . . . In many ways I am well off; I have good children and they work hard at school and I am proud of them. . . . I would like to put all of them through college." Dissatisfied with his job—"it's just a job; OK but not very exciting; just the same old stupid thing, there's nothing to it"—but he is making no attempt to change. Likes his fellow workers and foreman ("He's a good man; not much upstairs but good-natured and easy-going"). Well satisfied with his leisure and feels completely happy about his home and family life ("My life at home compensates me for the disappointments I have had"). Great interest in sports, especially actively helping his son's football career; son was elected captain and received scholarship to college. Sees relatives occasionally and has friends from the shop and church; one close friend with whom he goes fishing; picnics and outings with his family. Fixes things around the house; has built addition to it and "now working on a room in the attic." Strong interest in church and in union; attends both regularly. Health is excellent; no ailments. Responses to check items indicate very little hostility, worry or nervousness; in good spirits almost all the time; trusts people. (Mental-health classification: highest one-third.)

* * *

R. M.: Age 46 ("I'm getting old; I've realized that lately"). Grew up in small Michigan town; parents born in Michigan. Married and two children; only eighth grade schooling though both parents had gone to high school ("I wanted to get out and go to work"). Now, for past ten years, inspects and repairs crankshafts in large auto plant. Rates himself as "completely satisfied" with his life in general; as principal sources of enjoyment mentions TV, sociable card games, sports like swimming, and "my work—mostly the money." Later, however, speaks of the job as interesting and using his abilities, the satisfaction of "doing a good job" and "getting good work OK'd." Also works around the house; "I've got a tool bench in basement and I build things"; hobby is boats ("building one now"); not enough time to get caught up with home repairs (yet at another point: "I'd like to have more spare time but then I wouldn't know what to do with it"). Little ambition or future planning; "I've turned down promotion to job-setting because that's too rough, too much grief"; speaks vaguely of going into business for himself but has done nothing about it; says he takes life as it comes since "you can't stop the way things come." "My wife does all my worrying; I don't worry, generally." Complains of sinus trouble and headaches; health good otherwise. Check responses indicate neither high nor low standing in self-esteem, sociability, and most other personality traits and social attitudes. (Mental-health classification: middle one-third.)

* * *

T. H.: 24 years old; born and grew up in Detroit; married and two children; high school followed by incomplete trade school course; now electrician apprentice in auto plant. Well satisfied with life, his job, home, and spare-time activities. Ambitious for success and confident he is on the way—in his main job and "on the side I'm working and investing money to open a business with my dad." He is enthusiastic about his present electrical and electronic work and its opportunities—"there's a whole variety of skills you learn; it's interesting, it's amazing work . . . , can't think of anything I don't like about it . . . ; when you design circuits you have to fall back on your schooling; you have to know what you're doing." Likes his fellow workers, foreman, company, and union. Away from the job, he does part-time work repairing trucks and rebuilding motors; and also preparing the new store. "I'd say I work all the time." However, he occasionally goes visiting with his wife, goes to the lake, reads, and watches TV. Would like to go fishing but finds no time. No health troubles except some indigestion. His check responses indicate optimism and good spirits, no worries, self-confidence, and positive accepting attitudes toward people. (Mental-health classification: highest one-third.)

* * *

F. O.: 43 years of age; boyhood on farm; high school graduate; married and three children; assembly-line job. Somewhat dissatisfied with life in general; very dissatisfied with his job ("it is just a living; just peanuts; it doesn't mean anything to me personally"). Also dissatisfied with home and family life and spare-time activities. "I've always tried to live a good Christian life but things haven't gone so well; it's very strange." He wanted to be a clergyman—but "dad didn't help me." "My father never treated me right all my life. And then my uncle went and cheated me . . . and I haven't been able to quite find myself. I'm weak. I don't have confidence in myself. I've always been the nervous type; that's my father's fault." "I've had my miseries: my daughter has committed a sin . . . She went and done just what my mother had done before (had an illegitimate child)." Later in the interview he admits that he himself was illegitimate and in boyhood

"the fellows all made fun of me because I was conceived in sin."
Says his own marriage is unhappy—"too many family troubles and
inherited weaknesses." In spare time he does shop work in the
garage, takes trips with his children, reads, goes to church (strong
religious interest), etc. Personal relationships are strained. "I
don't seem to fit in with the other men at work; we don't get along
with each other." Criticizes his foreman, company, union, boyhood
school teachers, etc. Sees relatives infrequently. "I don't have any
friends; I stay to myself. I'd like to have friends but I can't." Says
his health is good in general but complains of trouble with his
feet and with constipation. (Mental-health classification: lowest
one-third.)

* * *

By means of lengthy, intensive interviews with several hundred
men like the foregoing we have sought to obtain data to help answer
the questions suggested in the introductory chapter.

Indexes of mental health

Six component indexes were combined to provide a general
measure of mental health. The six parts are the following.

1. An index of manifest anxiety and emotional tension.
2. An index of self-esteem, favorable versus negative self-feelings.
3. An index of hostility—versus trust in and acceptance of people.
4. An index of sociability and friendship versus withdrawal.
5. An index of overall satisfaction with life.
6. An index of personal morale—versus anomie, social alienation,
despair.

These indexes were chosen as ones possessing "face validity" in
reference to mental health. Each is considered a partial indicator.
Taken together, they represent an operational definition of mental
health for purposes of the study. Each index in turn is defined
by the content of the items on which it is based. The composition of
the indexes is described in Appendix B. Most of the items are also
listed in abbreviated form in Table 3-5.

When we speak of better versus poorer mental health we shall
mean the personal condition that expresses itself in responses of
greater self-esteem, morale, and trust in people, friendly interpersonal relations, relative satisfaction with life, emotional security

and freedom from interfering manifestations of anxiety. It is not assumed that the six measures are independent of one another; on the contrary there is considerable overlap as will become evident when we look at their intercorrelations.

One particularly difficult decision had to be made whether to include an additional component index covering active purposive striving. We incline to the view that this characteristic of positive, effortful problem-solving orientation belongs in a rounded appraisal of mental health; that the usual "adjustment" concept is open to serious question insofar as it implies passive acceptance and conformity as the desirable patterns of behavior to the neglect of active attempts to change one's world. At the same time it must be recognized that good adjustment, even if of a somewhat passive contented type, is clearly superior to the opposite condition with which it is being contrasted. The contrast is not with vigorous, purposive orientations but with despair, bitterness, hostility, negative self-feelings, anxiety, and social withdrawal. In any event we decided that more would be gained by treating the "purposive striving" variable separately and examining its relationships independently, since its inclusion does involve controversial value judgments and is sometimes criticized for introducing an unwarranted middle-class bias.[9] We shall return to the issue in the last section of this chapter.

The first four of the foregoing indexes were initially combined to provide an "adjustment index"; this score was then used along with "life satisfaction" and "personal morale" to yield an overall "mental-health" index. Although many of our later analyses will employ the separate indexes as well as the composite one, the latter has the virtue of being more representative of the varied aspects of mental health and it possesses greater stability than the limited partial indexes. The adjustment index is a mere additive combination of the four part-indexes. The mental-health index was constructed in a more complex manner which classifies individuals into five categories (excellent to poor mental health). The procedure is described in Appendix B. Actually, it turns out that a simple addition of the six component indexes yields almost identical mental-health scores; the two sets of scores have a correlation of .95 with each other (Pearson correlation coefficient).

As would be expected, the several component indexes correlate substantially with one another. The specific responses on which they are based obviously do not tap separate and distinct psychological factors; predominantly positive correlations occur between items in different indexes as well as between those in the same index. Agreement between items of the same index is decidedly greater, however, than for a sample of items taken at random from different indexes. Using items from the check-list inventory portion of the interview, the comparison shows a median interitem tetrachoric correlation of .35 within the indexes versus a median of .17 across indexes.

A summary of intercorrelations among the eight indexes (six component indexes plus the two composites) is shown in Tables 2-1 and 2-2. The tables are based on the part of our sample which consists of 407 cases of manual workers in Detroit automotive manufacturing plants. Since the figures are tetrachoric correlation coefficients, subject to fairly large fluctuations depending on the cutting points used in dividing the variables into two-by-two tables, they are to be viewed

*Table 2-1 Interrelations among component and composite indexes of mental health—young factory workers** *(Tetrachoric correlation coefficients)†*

	Freedom from Anxiety	Self-esteem	Freedom from Hostility	Socia-bility	Life Satis-faction	Personal Morale	Adjust-ment
Freedom from anxiety	. . .						
Self-esteem	.40	. . .					
Freedom from hostility	.27	.49	. . .				
Sociability	.02	− .05	.33	. . .			
Life satisfaction	.34	.69	.35	.34	. . .		
Personal morale	.26	.37	.52	.30	.48	. . .	
Median correlation with 5 other indexes	.27	.40	.35	.30	.35	.37	
Adjustment (composite of first 4 indexes)	.80	.57	.70	.51	.55	.43	. . .
Mental health (composite of 6 indexes)	.62	.72	.66	.59	.78	.71	.90+

* N = 109.

† Each cell entry is an average of two to four tetrachoric coefficients of correlation computed with different cutting points.

Table 2-2   Interrelations among component and composite indexes of mental health—middle-aged factory workers *
(*Tetrachoric correlation coefficients*)

	Freedom from Anxiety	Self-esteem	Freedom from Hostility	Socia-bility	Life Satis-faction	Personal Morale	Adjust-ment
Freedom from anxiety	...						
Self-esteem	.41	...					
Freedom from hostility	.38	.47	...				
Sociability	.15	.34	.43	...			
Life satisfaction	.48	.70	.36	.21	...		
Personal morale	.30	.33	.56	.37	.25	...	
Median correlation with 5 other indexes	.38	.41	.43	.34	.36	.33	
Adjustment (composite of first 4 indexes)	.81	.68	.65	.67	.60	.52	...
Mental health (composite of 6 indexes)	.78	.72	.71	.61	.77	.66	.95+

* N = 298.

† Each cell entry is an average of two to four tetrachoric coefficients of correlation computed with different cutting points.

as approximations only.   As a safeguard against extreme variations, however, each reported figure is an average of two to four coefficients computed with different cutting points.

The correlations with only a single minor exception are positive and most are large enough to indicate considerable interdependence (20 of the 30 coefficients for pairs of component indexes are between .30 and .50).   Close correspondence is particularly apparent between the composite indexes and their components.   The indexes of adjustment and of overall mental health are so highly correlated with each other as to signify near-identity; in all later analyses we shall use only the latter.

Special explanations account for the few coefficients in Tables 2-1 and 2-2 that are notably high or low relative to others.   Thus the unusually high correlation of self-esteem with life satisfaction is an artifact produced by the inclusion of three items common to these two indexes. This is the only pair of indexes with more than one item in common.[10] It is seen that the four smallest coefficients, the only ones below .25, all involve the sociability index. The explanation lies partly in the ambiguity of this index (it shows the poorest internal consistency) and partly in the contrasting (hence counteracting) positive and negative psychological relationship which sociability bears to other components of mental health. Low sociability sometimes reflects negative traits of anxiety and inadequacy with consequent withdrawal; for other persons the lower sociability rating represents the opposite: high self-sufficiency, self-esteem, and nondependence (a number of our cases fit the latter description, particularly in the young group). Negative self-feelings and anxiety may thus be associated with either high or low degrees of social participation. Individuals manifesting these reverse relationships tend to offset one another in a correlation table, resulting in low coefficients of the kind our data exhibit for these particular indexes.

Apart from the foregoing, the correlations are all positive ones of moderate size. The differences among them do not appear to warrant special attention or attempts at interpretation for present purposes. This is especially true in view of the relatively crude indexes and correlational procedure involved. The important question here is what implications the figures as a whole carry in respect to the use of a general index of mental health. Within the limits of our data, the evidence points to a considerable degree of interrelatedness among the several indexes; they do not fly off in different directions.[11] This does not mean that we have established a single general factor of mental health; rather that the separate measures have enough interrelationship to permit their combination into a total score which, tentatively on the basis of the "face validity" of the data, we are labeling mental health.

Confidence in the genuineness of the relationships is enhanced by finding that they hold true at separate educational levels. The reason for this test is the following: since persons of greater schooling tend to score higher on all indexes it appeared possible that the index interrelationships are spurious, merely reflecting different amounts of education. Examination of tabulations for separate educational groups indicates that this is not the case. The relationships are maintained consistently, with only very minor exceptions.

Critical questions of some seriousness may still be asked, of course, regarding the assessment of mental health by the procedures used.

First, all the indexes are based on the respondents' own reports of their attitudes, feelings, and behavior—and at a single point in their lives.   Second, the interviews were relatively direct and without psychological subtlety, conducted for the most part by interviewers lacking professional psychological or psychiatric training and with no use of projective tests or similar diagnostic tools.   Third, the indexes represent only a fraction of all the information obtained in the interviews; other response material will be introduced later, to be compared with the measures reported here to see whether it, too, fits into a structure of positively interrelated aspects of overall mental health.   Finally, it is to be noted that, extensive though our interviews were, their coverage was necessarily of limited scope; consequently we have no way of answering whether similar positive correlations would occur if additional measurements were included, dealing, for example, with such personality traits as rigidity-flexibility, spontaneity, problem-solving orientation, long versus short time perspective, freedom from need distortion of perceptions, and many other characteristics that have been proposed as indicators of mental health.

In the light of such cautionary questions as the foregoing, it becomes specially important to ask whether our measures do assess mental health in a way that agrees with its definition by qualified experts.   The conclusion thus far is simply that a rather wide variety of attitudes and behavior symptoms ordinarily thought to be associated with "adjustment," "neuroticism," or "mental health" do hang together in a cluster which enables us to classify people into categories according to the degree to which they report these characteristics.   The value and meaning of the resulting classification must be judged by exploring its "relational fertility" and congruence with other variables.[12]   It seems clear that our indexes are crude measures of *something*.   If they were merely chance scores, aggregates of random responses, they could not show the consistently significant intercorrelations that were found.   But do they measure *mental health?*   It is to this crucial question that we now turn.

Validity of the mental-health indexes

Do the proposed indexes of mental health actually measure what the experts mean by mental health?   Before proceeding to use the indexes we set up a small-scale validation study to answer this question. We arranged to have several experienced, highly qualified clinical psychologists and psychiatrists read the complete interview records of 40 cases and give their overall evaluation of each individual's mental health.[13] Comparison of our quantitative indexes with these independent global ratings reveals that the indexes do, in fact, agree decidely well with the clinicians' judgment. If the objection is advanced that clinical opinions are themselves subjective and based on unknown standards, the only reply is that we possess no better criterion, nothing more objective to fall back on. Judgments of mental health are by their nature normative; they necessarily depend on the definitions and the values employed. It may be hoped that by working back and forth between such global estimates on the one side and series of specified quantitative indicators on the other side, greater degrees of agreement and more uniform definitions and assessments of mental health will gradually be achieved. Certainly this is one major aim of research efforts such as the present study.

The rating and validation procedures are set forth in Appendix C. The results, summarized in Table 2-3, show close agreement between scores on the index of mental health and the composite ratings by clinicians. The Pearson correlation coefficient is .76; the tetrachoric coefficient is .84. Only 1 of 14 persons high on the index receives

Table 2-3   Relationship between scores on mental-health index and clinicians' estimates of mental health based on the interview records*

Index of Mental Health

Composite Ratings by Clinicians		Low		Average	High		Total
		1	2	3	4	5	Total
High	A			1	2	4	7
	B		1	3	3	1	8
Average	C		2	1	2	1	6
Below	D	2	6	3	1		12
average	E	6		1			7
Total		8	9	9	8	6	40

* Pearson r = .76.   Tetrachoric r = .84.

a rating below average; 14 of 17 persons having low scores receive such ratings. It is apparent from these results that the meaning of mental health as represented by our index corresponds to what the clinicians also conceive to be better or poorer mental health.

The degree of agreement represented by this comparison may be exaggerated, however, since we constructed the overall index in a manner that might increase its correspondence with the ratings. To eliminate this source of bias, we made similar comparisons using the separate indexes. These component indexes were obtained in entire independence of the clinical judgments; the scores had all been computed long before the ratings were secured and the raters had no knowledge concerning the indexes. The adjustment index, which is a simple sum of the first four of the six separate indexes, provides a test of the agreement between the scores and the clinicians' estimates, entirely free of any possible spurious effect. This relationship, shown in Table 2-4, is seen to be approximately the same as that for the total mental-health index. The Pearson correlation coefficient is .67; the tetrachoric is .87. All 11 individuals with poorest adjustment scores were rated below average by the clinicians and 12 of 14 with highest scores were rated average or above.

Viewing the clinicians' rating study as a whole, we conclude that it offers encouraging support for the use of our indexes as measures

Table 2-4   Relationship between scores on adjustment index and clinicians' estimates of mental health based on the interview records*

Index of Adjustment

Composite Ratings by Clinicians		Low		Average		High		Total
		1–2	3	4	5	6	7	
High	A			2	1	1	3	7
	B		2	2	1	2	1	8
Average	C			3	2		1	6
Below	D	6	2	2	1	1		12
average	E	5	1	1				7
Total		11	5	10	5	4	5	40

* Pearson r = .67.   Tetrachoric r = .87.

of mental health. Whatever the crudity and limitations of the indexes, they do successfully indicate approximately the same assessments as would be returned by experienced psychologists and psychiatrists basing their judgments on similar interview material. The people whom we classify as having better or poorer mental health, with few exceptions, are classified in like manner by the independent experts. In the light of this knowledge, we may proceed more confidently into our subsequent analyses and interpretations.

Another check on the validity of the indexes deserves brief mention at this point since it adds a further element of reassurance. We compared scores obtained on the indexes with testimony given by the wives of the respondents. These reports by wives, unlike what was true of the ratings by clinicians, have the virtue of being truly independent of the interview material from which the indexes were derived. The wife's estimates are based on her own observations of her spouse over long periods of time and over a wide variety of life situations. They provide a crucial test of the procedure which attempts to assess a man's mental health by means of his own responses to questions asked in a single interview. The results are definitely favorable.

Two questions in the interview with wives can most clearly be compared with the husbands' responses: one question asked her opinion regarding her spouse's overall satisfaction with life; the other inquired whether he "is ever nervous or irritable." Responses to both questions agree rather well with the husbands' own reports. For example, ratings of the man's life satisfaction by himself and by his wife correlate .79 for the young group and .51 for the middle-aged (all figures here are tetrachoric coefficients). Estimates of his "nervousness" similarly correlate .48 and .66. When the wives' estimates are compared with the more general indexes of the husbands' mental health, the relationships are still strongly positive, as the following correlation figures illustrate.

	Young	Middle-aged
Wife's estimate of husband's life satisfaction compared with his "mental health" score	.50	.53
Wife's estimate of husband's nervousness compared with:		
His "mental health" score	.26	.44
His "anxiety" score	.65	.66

In more readily grasped percentage terms, correlations like those in the last line represent the following relationships.

	Young	Middle-aged
Percentage of men considered nervous by wife who have high anxiety scores	48%	44%
Corresponding percentage of men *not* considered nervous by wife	10%	8%

Earlier comparisons using clinicians' ratings supported the conclusion that within the limits of the interview content our indexes measure roughly the same thing as the panel of psychologists and psychiatrists mean by mental health. However, this gave no answer to the question whether the interview material itself is trustworthy, whether it represents the respondent's behavior and attitudes with some reality beyond his own verbal responses. The evidence from wives' reports now partially answers that question. Assessments based on the interview are encouragingly congruent with the reports of another set of observers who know the men in real life. Taking the two bodies of results together, there appears to be considerable justification for accepting our indexes as usable, even if crude, measures of mental health.

Purposive striving as a component of mental health

We return here to an important question which was laid aside at an earlier point. It has to do with the controversial issue whether assessments of mental health need to incorporate an additional component beyond the ones thus far dealt with—a component more explicitly representing purposive striving, personal independence and self-determination, active adaptation that seeks to change and master the environment rather than merely adjust to it. Or is this dimension too ambiguous as to its mental-health implications, sometimes being a manifestation of serious inner conflict and anxiety— a neurotic type of compulsiveness and *excessive* coping behavior— rather than an indication of superior mental health? Question is also raised at times whether the striving is a reflection of the Protestant ethic, an internalization of middle-class values, and consequently whether it distorts mental-health assessments in a class-biased direction.[14]

These questions obviously have important bearing on any effort to define and assess mental health. They call for further examination. To this end we kept our basic mental-health index relatively free of items which might emphasize the active striving aspects of behavior in order that we could treat this purposive dimension separately, with subsequent weighing of the case for and against its inclusion. We wish now to make this further analysis, to decide whether an expanded definition of mental health that specifically includes the positive striving dimension will produce results of greater—or less—value.

To help arrive at a decision, we have asked ourselves these questions: (1) Are the original mental-health assessments changed significantly by the addition of indicators of purposiveness? (2) If the addition of such measures does make a difference, is there evidence that favors or opposes the use of the expanded index rather than the original one? (3) Aside from specific evidence, do considerations of theory or dictates of value judgments argue for inclusion of the measures of active adaptation?

To answer the first question we obtained three measures of purposiveness and examined their relationships to the previously described mental-health indexes. The three new measures (further described in Appendix B) are as follows.

Index of active life orientation—for example, does the man feel that he can do much to make his future what he wants; does he push to change things or is he content to take life as it comes; does he care about advancement, etc.

Rating of "life style"—does the man give evidence of active, purposeful attitudes and goal-oriented conduct. (This rating and the following one are coder's estimates based on extensive blocks of interview responses.)

Rating of "purposefulness" in work and nonwork activities separately.

The question before us is whether these measures of purposive striving add anything significant to the previously described indexes of adjustment and mental health. In the first place, are they merely duplicating what we have already measured? The answer to this question is clearly negative. We find that the correlations of the new measures with the general indexes of adjustment and mental health are positive but not particularly high (average coefficients are .32 for the young and .27 for the middle-aged). Consequently, it is possible to combine the two sets of indexes to yield a mental-health assessment somewhat different from the original as a result of the incorporation of the active adaptation component.

To determine the effect of the reclassification, we checked those cases for which the assessment is changed in order to see whether they appear to be either more accurately or less accurately classified when measures of purposiveness are used. This is the second of the three questions proposed at the beginning of this section. The answer is that according to our present evidence the additional variables make no significant difference. This is simply to say that the clinicians' judgments of mental health, which we employed as a criterion, agree no better (if anything, a trifle worse) with the modified classification than with the original. Although this surely furnishes no conclusive basis for rejecting the revised mental-health rating, it does give rise to serious question concerning the usefulness of any such revision.

The question is also germane here whether the purposive striving aspect of mental health should be omitted because of the alleged likelihood that it would introduce a middle-class bias into the assessments. The argument is that we must avoid assigning high mental-health scores to people merely because they hold certain middle-class values. The problem becomes a difficult one of deciding whether any given behavior—for example, purposive striving in the sense of active attempts at mastery of the environment—is distinctively a middle-class attribute not to be expected of persons with working-class views or a generally approved value in our society which is properly included in a concept of good mental health. As a partial check on the correct answer to this question, we analyzed the relationship between measures of purposive striving and an index of middle-class versus working-class viewpoint. The latter index (see pp. 213–221 and Appendix B) is composed of responses to several questions having to do with beliefs about individual initiative and success, social-political change, and the role of government in relation to business and social welfare. If the purposive dimension reflects a characteristically middle-class orientation, we would expect a substantial degree of agreement between the measures of active purpose and the index of "middle-classness." Actually, for the sample of Detroit factory workers, there is little or no correlation. The coefficients with different measures of purposive striving range from .00 to .20 with an average of .07. The same absence of correlation is found between middle-class orientation and the original index of mental health. These results strongly suggest that within the factory population dealt with here we can dismiss the contention that middle-class sociopolitical values constitute a distorting influence on either the original mental-health assessments or the measure of purposive striving.

If other "middle-class characteristics" such as better education and superior jobs, and psychological accompaniments of these advantages, prove to be associated with both mental health and purposiveness (as they do), this signifies not a bias to be avoided but a significant social fact to be understood and dealt with.

The important final question in the present discussion of purposive striving is whether, in the absence of evidence that mental-health ratings are improved by inclusion of the purposive variable, other considerations may nevertheless argue against neglecting this dimension of behavior. Since the available results are neither clearly favorable nor unfavorable, an obvious compromise is to retain our original measures of mental health as the basic ones but to supplement these from time to time with separate analyses of purposefulness whenever this seems promising.

Illustrative of the evidence which justifies further use of the indexes of purposeful striving as having bearing on the study of mental health is the fact that these measures are significantly associated with the clinicians' estimates of mental health (correlations of .18 to .57, averaging .38). Simple correlations, however, tell only part of the story. For example, although the "active life orientation" index correlates poorly with clinicians' ratings (.18), individuals rated very high or very low differ markedly: of those considered in poor mental health by the clinicians, only 1 of 7 is actively oriented to life; of the high mental-health group, 5 of 7 exhibit an active orientation. Among those of intermediate mental health, it is interesting that this relationship does not hold at all; in fact, active striving tends to be more characteristic of those of doubtful mental health than of the moderately healthy, the latter being persons who have happily, if somewhat passively, adjusted to their life situation while the former more often express a spirit of restless dissatisfaction.

Our findings as a whole are congruent with the theoretically plausible interpretation that presence or absence of striving may signify either good mental health or the reverse, depending on the constellation of associated traits. In other words, we detect signs of both healthy and neurotic striving. The fact that our indexes of purpose reflect both these tendencies may account for their failure to contribute when merely added to the original mental-health indexes.

The important general point must not be lost. An adequate conceptualization of good mental health refers to something more than passive adjustment, contentment, "homeostatic balance," and freedom from inner tensions. Few persons would accept the healthy vegetable as a model. The more positive aspects of mental health, the active efforts of people to cope with their world, surely deserve attention. Although this dimension is by no means absent from our original indexes, it is important enough to call for separate, supplementary analyses when we later come to deal with mental differences among occupational groups. Consequently, we shall employ the measures of purposive striving introduced in this section along with the principal indexes described earlier.

Summary

This chapter has presented an account of the guiding conceptions and procedures adopted in an effort to assess the mental health of factory workers. The method relies primarily on a lengthy, detailed interview and questionnaire with 407 auto workers and 248 men in comparison groups. Our guiding conception of mental health views it as a designation for the overall level of effectiveness and satisfaction with which an individual carries on his psychological and social functioning as a person. The more precise meaning is described by reference to the content of the responses on which the appraisals are based. Several tests checked on the internal consistency of these components, on their validity by comparison with the wife's testimony, and on the validity of the total assessments as judged by agreement with estimates of independent experts. The evidence from all these comparisons appears satisfactory.

Particularly close agreement was demonstrated when the overall assessments were compared with composite ratings of mental health by experienced psychiatrists and clinical psychologists. This result argues strongly that we are measuring qualities very similar to what the clinicians also mean by mental health.

Consideration of purposive striving and active efforts to change things as proposed elements of mental health leads us to a working compromise that accepts these qualities as important but sees advantages in treating them separately instead of incorporating them into the general index. The dimension of purposiveness is not alone, however, in having significance as an aspect of mental health deserving separate consideration. The subindexes and specific responses constituting the global assessments need also to be studied in their own right. Even if one were to reject the idea of measuring "mental health" as a whole, the several parts would remain meaningful.

3.

The mental health of automobile workers

Employing the concept of mental health and the indexes that have been described, we can now sketch a rough composite portrait of the working people studied.   We shall begin with a few facts about who the men are—their age, education, and occupations—and shall then summarize what we have learned concerning their mental health.   In this chapter we deal with the sample of Detroit factory workers as a whole; the following chapters will analyze the results by occupational categories, education, and a number of additional characteristics, and will also compare the factory workers with other occupational groups.

Detailed data are available for 407 Detroit auto workers.[1]   They constitute a sample of white, native-born males holding hourly paid jobs and meeting our specifications as to occupation, age, and length of employment.   Two age groups were used: men 20 to 29 inclusive and 40 to 49 inclusive, to be designated "young" and "middle-aged" respectively.   A minimum length of employment of three years with the present company was specified, though a few cases were later discovered who reported less than this minimum. The numbers by age and by four occupational levels (in terms of skill and variety of work operations) are shown in Table 3-1.

Table 3-1   Age and skill level of Detroit factory workers in sample

Skill Level	Young Age 20–29	Middle-aged Age 40–49
Skilled	10	45
High semiskilled	23	98
Ordinary semiskilled	46	82
Repetitive semiskilled	30	73
Total	109	298

Table 3-2   Length of employment of Detroit factory workers in sample

Years with Company	Young	Middle-aged	Years in Present Job	Young	Middle-aged
Less than 3	5	2	Less than 1	22	17
3–4.9	11	13	1–1.9	18	23
5–9.9	72	49	2–4.9	33	41
10–14.9	18	61	5–9.9	28	90
15–19.9	1	77	10–14.9	5	53
20 or more	. . .	96	15 or more	1	71
Not ascertained	2	. . .	Not ascertained	2	3
Total	109	298	Total	109	208
Median	7.6 yrs	16.6 yrs	Median	3.3 yrs	8.7 yrs

Table 3-3   Amount of schooling of Detroit factory workers in sample

Grades Completed	Young	Middle-aged
Less than 8	3	55
8	12	79
9–11	56	110
12	34	42
Beyond 12	4	12
Total	109	298
Median	11.1 grades	9.4 grades

Tables 3-2 and 3-3 contain information on length of employment and education.

Our interest centers on the mental health of these men. For present purposes we divided scores on the index of mental health to constitute the five categories listed in Table 3-4. Despite the close similarity of scores shown in the table for younger and older workers taken as a whole, the age groups do differ when compared within separate occupational categories, as will appear later.

Mental health defined by component response items

The first all-important question is what the labels of high and low mental health signify. What meaning attaches to the com-

Table 3-4   Percentage distribution of mental-health scores of Detroit factory workers in sample

Classification of Mental-Health Scores	Young	Middle-aged
High	9%	13%
Above average	26	25
Average	32	27
Below average	19	21
Low	14	14
Total	100%	100%
Number of cases	109	298

parisons? Inasmuch as we have no absolute scale (as for light-heavy) or independent standards (as for hot-cold), the best we can do is to give meaning to the degrees of mental health by descriptions of attitudes and behavior characteristic of persons classified as possessing better or poorer mental health.[2] Accordingly, we shall look at the high and low mental-health groups to see in what ways they differ on the six component indexes and the specific responses that compose and define these indexes. In a word, the *meaning* of the mental-health assessment is to be inferred from the contents of the variables that correlate well with it. The appropriate data are assembled in Tables 3-5 and 3-6.[3]

The tables are to be understood as follows: for the two age groups separately, each line contains a pair of percentages; one tells what proportion of workers in roughly the highest one-third of mental-health scores (top two categories of Table 3-4) have the characteristic or give the response shown for that line, the other percentage does the same for the lowest one-third (lowest two categories of Table 3-4). The greater the difference between the two percentages the more closely that item is associated with our mental-health assessment. Those traits and responses that show sizable differences thus provide an "operational definition" of mental health. For example, the first line of Table 3-5 tells us that 16 per cent of the young group having high mental health manifest considerable anxiety, contrasted with 64 per cent of the group which constitutes the lowest one-third in mental health. This indicates that a large amount of "manifest anxiety" is an important aspect of the mental-health measurement among these young workers—though, reading across

Table 3-5   *Comparison of high and low mental-health groups on component indexes and items of the mental-health score*

| | Percentage of High and Low Groups Giving Specified Responses* | | | |
| | Young | | Middle-aged | |
Component Indexes and Items	High M.H. (N = 38)	Low M.H. (N = 36)	High M.H. (N = 115)	Low M.H. (N = 103)
1. Anxiety index: High anxiety	16%	64%	3%	69%
Low anxiety	53	6	52	2
Anxiety responses:				
Often worried and upset (G9)†	13	53	3	62
Ever bothered by nervousness (G20	16	67	14	62
Worry much re your future (G19)	5	49	6	42
Do not wake up rested (G2)	3	39	3	39
Health complaints—any named (C7b)	37	69	32	71
Possibly psychosomatic	18	42	16	50
Report 2 or more listed ailments (C8)	40	75	40	76
Report *none*	26	8	34	6
Have any health problems (G13)	18	36	7	49
Have trouble sleeping (G14)	11	31	6	42
Use special foods or tonics (C7c)	5	27	7	24
Medicines oftener than once a mo. (C9)	38	51	27	51
Occasional heavy drinking (F7e)	19	37	12	27
Seek help re personal problems (C6)	16	22	6	28
2. Self-esteem index: High	66	8	73	13
Low	3	75	7	67
Self-esteem responses:				
Ever so blue nothing worth while (G16)	13	82	4	60
Hard time making up mind (G7)	34	63	24	58
Accomplishing things want to (C5)	82	51	84	53
People often hurt your feelings (G18)	3	28	8	38
Can do much to make own future (A7d)	84	56	69	44
Often blame self for things done (G6)	18	36	37	70
Volunteered feelings of inadequacy (A2 to 7)	16	33	21	26
3. Hostility index: High hostility	5	53	3	47
Low hostility	74	11	72	13
Hostility responses:				
People get on nerves; do opposite (G31)	5	56	5	53
Many people unreasonable (G15)	11	60	20	60
Boil inside without showing it (G10)	47	88	42	83
Tell people to mind own business (G28)	3	35	8	38
Feel like smashing things (G17)	8	31	7	31
Stress bad vs. good traits of men (C2)	26	44	19	47
4. Sociability index: High	45	14	41	7
Low	8	44	17	59
Sociability responses:				
Not know whom can count on (D3)	19	69	22	69
Prefer being by self (G29)	11	46	12	49
Important to have friends (F11)	94	74	87	70
Belong to 2 or more organizations (F16)	71	47	76	64
Have more than 2 good friends (F9b,c)	63	44	56	46
Together oftener than once a month (F9i,k)	68	53	60	42
If things wrong, leave to others (G4)	11	23	7	17

Table 3-5   Comparison of high and low mental-health groups on component indexes and items of the mental-health score (continued)

Percentage of High and Low Groups
Giving Specified Responses*

Component Indexes and Items	Young		Middle-aged	
	High M.H. (N = 38)	Low M.H. (N = 36)	High M.H. (N = 115)	Low M.H. (N = 103)
5. Life satisfaction index: High	66%	0%	70%	9%
Low	11	86	5	70
Life satisfaction responses:				
Restless; not know what want (G1)	37	86	27	77
Preponderantly favorable ideas re life (A2 to 7)	82	33	81	42
Well satisfied with life (A3)	95	39	82	55
Well satisfied with leisure (F6a)	95	53	89	60
Almost always in good spirits (G12)	89	64	92	65
Chance to enjoy life is O.K. (G30)	81	69	83	59
Optimistic re own future (A7c)	55	44	60	36
6. Personal morale index: High	60	8	54	7
Low	5	64	3	49
Personal morale responses:				
Most people can be trusted (G8)	84	46	89	55
People out for themselves only (D5)	32	69	37	68
Officials not care re average man (D15)	16	43	22	55
Hardly fair to have children (D8)	0	28	3	31
Lot of average man getting worse (D2)	13	43	5	29
Success due to luck and pull (D1)	40	54	23	52
Have to live for today (D13)	16	36	22	43

* The "high" group in this table includes both the "high" and "above average" of Table 3-4; similarly "low" includes both "low" and "below average."
† Numerals in parentheses identify the place of the items in the interview schedule reproduced in Appendix A.

the same line, we see it is even more closely related among the middle-aged.

In order to simplify the tables, percentages for the middle one-third in mental health are omitted. Quite generally they fall between the two figures shown and for the most part they lie closer to the high group than to the low. The low one-third, in other words, is more markedly differentiated from others than is the high one-third.

With these tabulations before us, now, what substantive conclusions can be drawn regarding the content and meaning of the final mental-health assessments? Consider first the six component indexes listed as the initial entries of the numbered sections of Table 3-5. Since these six indexes were combined to produce the mental-health measurements, they naturally exhibit positive relationships to the resulting classification. In general, men who have high mental-health scores are also high on each of the component indexes; correspondingly, those in the low mental-health group tend to have unfavorable scores on each component.

Of the six indexes, life satisfaction and self-esteem are most closely associated with mental health (i.e., they show largest percentage differences between high and low groups, considering both young and middle-aged). Sociability-withdrawal shows least relationship. Among the middle-aged, but not among the young, anxiety is associated especially closely with mental health. The order of the relationships by percentage differences corresponds on the whole with the correlations between indexes and composite scores noted earlier (pp. 27–28). Actually, the percentage comparisons are merely another way of measuring the same relationship in order to make it more directly meaningful.

If we look at the smaller, more extreme groups of high and low mental health (the top and bottom groups of Table 3-4), more striking associations with the subindexes appear. For example, the extremely high and low, in both age groups, are *totally* separated on life satisfaction scores, 100 per cent being in the high and low satisfaction categories respectively. For high self-esteem the percentages are again 100 per cent to zero for the young; 88 per cent to 5 per cent for the middle-aged. It is to be emphasized that all these relationships are artificially close, resulting from the way the mental-health scores were derived. They are not presented to demonstrate anything remarkable or exciting; they simply help make clear the content of the mental-health assessments and thus define their meaning.

What we can say thus far on the basis of the percentage comparisons for the several indexes is this: good mental health, as measured here, means that the persons so labeled have high probability of feeling well satisfied with their lives, definitely positive and favorable in their self-feelings, relatively free of nervousness and anxiety (especially true of middle-aged). With probabilities slightly lower, they also tend to have high morale (trust in people and society, freedom from "anomie" or social alienation) and little manifestation of strong hostility. They are likewise somewhat less socially withdrawn. Mental health that is "not good" or "low" implies the opposite of these characteristics.

The more precise meaning of the six indexes is defined, in turn, by the specific responses on which they are based. It is these specific items, in the end, which tell what the mental-health assessments mean. The items are arranged under each index in Table 3-5 with the ones exhibiting largest percentage differences first (i.e., ones most intimately associated with mental health) and those having weakest associations last. The original questionnaire, of course, did not group the items by indexes; they were scattered through the interview. In the interests of brevity, too, it has been necessary drastically to abbreviate the wording of items in the tables.

Without exception the items show percentage differences in the expected direction and consistently for young and middle-aged. Almost all the differences are large enough to make it extremely improbable that they could occur by chance.[4] Inspection of the response figures under each index leads to the following summary of characteristics distinguishing men of high mental health.

Anxiety. Those in good mental health tend to be free of excessive worry, reports of nervousness, insomnia, psychosomatic ailments, heavy drinking, concern about health.

Self-esteem. They are free from extreme discouragement and lack of confidence in their own judgment; they have positive feelings of accomplishment and control of their future; they are infrequently oversensitive or given to self-blame.[5]

Hostility. People do not antagonize them ("get on your nerves so that you want to do the opposite . . . "; "often have to tell people to mind their own business"); they less frequently report "boiling inside," feeling "like smashing things for no good reason"; they less often volunteer bad qualities as the "things you have learned about people."

Sociability (versus Withdrawal). Persons of high mental health reject the view that one does not know whom he can count on (also a "personal morale" indicator); they do not prefer being by themselves; they consider it important to have friends and are more likely to have good friends, to belong to organizations, and to see friends more often.

Life Satisfaction. Mental health is associated with less feeling of restlessness ("wanting to be doing something but not knowing what"); with predominantly favorable comments concerning their life situation, self-ratings of being well satisfied, in good spirits, optimistic about their own future; with belief that they have "as much chance to enjoy life as [they] should have."

Personal Morale. Those in good mental health believe that most people can be trusted and that people are not "out for themselves" alone; relatively free from generalized pessimism and despair represented by such thoughts as "the lot of the average man is getting worse," "it is hardly fair to bring children into the world," "getting ahead is mostly a matter of luck and pull," and that "a person has to live pretty much for today and let tomorrow take care of itself."

Whether or not one chooses to use the mental-health label, there can be little question that differences of response represented by the foregoing table and resumé tell something important about the respondents. The picture of automobile workers that emerges—and presumably most other factory workers are not greatly different—is not to be lightly dismissed. As we study the column of percentages for the "low mental health" group (one-third of all workers), it is apparent that very substantial numbers report feelings, habits, and beliefs that must seriously impair their personal happiness and social effectiveness.

Corresponding percentages for the entire population of workers, though much reduced of course, nevertheless underscore the far from satisfactory psychological condition of mid-twentieth century "industrial man." To illustrate this type of evidence, a list follows with the proportions of all Detroit auto workers giving specified responses.

	Percentage of Auto Workers (N = 407)
Most people are out for themselves and don't care what happens to others. *Agree*	53%
Do you often feel restless, wanting to be on the move doing something but not knowing what? *Yes*	52%
How do you expect things to turn out for you in the future? *Not optimistic* (i.e., pessimistic, doubtful, or neither optimistic nor pessimistic)	51%
These days a person doesn't really know who he can count on. *Agree*	45%
Getting ahead in this world is mostly a matter of luck and pull. *Agree*	40%
Do you find that many people are so unreasonable that it is hard to talk to them? *Yes*	36%

Are you ever bothered by nervousness? *Yes*	35%
Self-rating of "how you feel about your life in general" on five-point scale. *Rating below "well satisfied"* (i.e., dissatisfied or "neither satisfied nor dissatisfied")	32%
Do you ever get so blue and discouraged that you wonder whether anything is worthwhile? *Yes*	27%
Are you often worried and upset? *Yes*	26%
Do people often get on your nerves so that you want to do just the opposite of what they want you to do? *Yes*	26%
On the whole, do you usually like to be by yourself rather than with other people? *Yes*	26%
Would you say that you have as much chance to enjoy life as you should have? *No*	26%
Do people often hurt your feelings? *Yes*	20%

The question here is not whether these findings compare unfavorably, or how unfavorably, with other sections of the general population. Such comparisons are needed and we shall do a little along this line in later chapters. We stress here, however, that the foregoing results, in and of themselves, offer evidence of "psychological problems," regardless of whether similar or more serious conditions of personal and social morale may exist in other groups.

Additional response items related to mental health

Thus far this analysis has considered only the variables that directly entered into the mental-health measurements. It remains, now, to give attention to additional correlates that can throw light on the meaning of the assessments. A number of these are brought together in Table 3-6, in a form identical with that of Table 3-5. The differences between the high and low mental-health groups are again in the expected direction, with minor exceptions which we shall mention. Even where the differences are relatively small, moreover, they are suggestive of attributes that may rationally be associated with better or poorer mental health.

The first part of the table deals with the measures of purposive striving discussed in Chapter 2. The percentage comparisons confirm the marked tendency for good mental health to mean greater purposiveness, more strongly among younger workers as would

Table 3-6   *Comparison of high and low mental-health groups on selected indexes and items which are* not *components of the mental-health score*

	Young		Middle-aged	
	High M.H.	Low M.H.	High M.H.	Low M.H.
Indexes and Items	(N = 38)	(N = 36)	(N = 115)	(N = 103)

*Percentage of High and Low Groups Giving Specified Responses**

1. Measures of purposive striving

Indexes and Items	Young High M.H.	Young Low M.H.	Middle-aged High M.H.	Middle-aged Low M.H.
Active life orientation index: High	76%	39%	45%	37%
Illustrative responses:				
Push hard to change things (C4)†	64	47	43	43
Want most in life: to get ahead (A8)	21	6	5	7
One of things want: to get ahead (A8)	47	22	22	30
Rating of life style: purposeful	42	19	30	14
Rating of purposefulness:				
Re work: High	40	17	22	9
Re nonwork. High	0	0	17	7
High or medium	45	50	68	52
Combined work and nonwork: High	68	36	68	35

2. Behavior and attitudes in personal life

Interpersonal relations: rated good	58	28	51	19
Family relations: rated good	95	64	87	71
Satisfied re home and family (F24a)	94	68	94	78
Family satisfaction index: low	18	44	20	35
Marriage happier than most (F29)	58	38	67	49
Likes living in Detroit (F2)	76	47	66	49
TV-radio: 15 hrs. or more (F13)	35	36	23	40
Reading: 3 hrs. or more (F14)	74	64	64	52
Never go to sports events (F7a)	34	36	27	52
Often to bar or tavern (F7b,c)	18	42	17	30
Never votes (F20b)	14	45	6	11
Belongs to a church (F16,18)	58	42	60	52
Not nervous etc. (wife's report)	47	30	50	18

3. Attitudes toward job

Job satisfaction index: High	40	11	47	19
Low	8	53	14	33
Well satisfied with job (B4)	79	39	81	64
Job is interesting (B9a)	87	34	80	52
Chance to use abilities on job (B10)	84	46	72	47
Want to go to work each day (B8a)	68	36	71	54
Thoughts at work mostly happy (B9e)	82	44	82	51
Worry about work (B7)	30	58	20	49
Into same work if starting over (E15)	41	14	30	17
Company is good or very good (B19)	60	47	76	55
Supervisor best or very good (B18c)	34	16	32	28
Like fellow workers (B17a)	63	53	75	59
Care much about promotion chances (B15)	72	54	51	65
Absent 4 days or more in year (B21a)	31	65	23	42

4. Attitudes on social issues

Labor orientation index: High	39	64	40	53
Subindexes:				
More gov't. control of business	42	64	37	58
More gov't. aid for needy	34	50	30	44
Authoritarian attitude index: High	13	28	23	51
Illustrative responses:				
Teach child absolute obedience (D6)	42	46	49	66
Need strong leaders, not talk (D14)	26	40	28	44
Against racial equality (H11)	58	69	50	66
Permit political free speech (H9a)	47	50	41	38
Free inquiry in colleges (H9d)	62	63	59	56
"Isolationist" foreign policy (H12a)	38	42	38	53
Fully favor U.N., no reservations (H12b)	68	52	64	56

* See first note of Table 3-5.
† See second note of Table 3-5. Indexes and ratings which have no identifying numbers are described in Appendix B.

reasonably be expected.   Of interest, too, is the closer association of mental health with purposiveness in *work activities* for the young than for the middle-aged and the closer correspondence in *nonwork activities* for the middle-aged than for the young.   Apparently many of the purposive older workers have abandoned their vocational ambitions and turned to more attainable goals in their private and social worlds.   Consistent with this is the fact that mental health is linked to responses like "push hard to change things" and "strong desire to get ahead" only for the young men but not for the middle-aged.

The second section of Table 3-6 contributes further to a constellation of coherent characteristics of the mentally healthy.   Most evident is the tendency for the high group to have more effective and satisfying interpersonal relations, both in their family situation and with other persons.   Another finding is that the mentally healthy resort less to passive, "escapist" activities like television (middle-aged only) and drinking at bars; and they devote more time to reading.   The tendency toward passivity and nonparticipation of the low mental-health groups is further reflected in the large number who do not vote (among the young) and the somewhat smaller amount of church membership.

Job-related attitudes are also associated with mental health in a consistent manner.   The men classified as having good mental health, both young and middle-aged, are much more commonly satisfied with their jobs and find the work interesting, enjoyable, affording opportunity for use of abilities, and not a source of worry. Moreover, they express more positive feelings about the company, their bosses, and their fellow workers.   Notably, too, they report considerably less absence from work (company records confirm this).   The importance men attach to opportunities for advancement bears a contrasting relationship to mental health among the young and the middle-aged.   For men in their twenties, interest in promotion goes with high mental health; for those in their forties the reverse is true, those who still crave advancement tend to be in poorer mental health.   This relationship and the cognate items under purposiveness are the only instances throughout these comparisons where a reversal of significant size occurs.   The fact that these isolated exceptions make excellent sense adds a note of reassurance regarding the procedures and findings as a whole.

Finally, in the last part of Table 3-6, we have included a sample of attitude measures pertaining to questions of general social outlook and orientation.   Here two divergent trends may be noted.

Economic liberalism of a prolabor, New Deal type is more popular among the working people of lower mental health. Since men of poorer mental health tend also to be of lower socioeconomic position, it is not unnatural that they more commonly favor economic reforms aimed at equalization of incomes and influence. Liberalism with respect to race relations, international relations, and antiauthoritarian attitudes is quite another matter. More liberal orientation on these issues is associated with *higher* mental health, due in part at least to the better education of the men with higher mental-health scores. The questions on freedom of speech are puzzling in this regard since, contrary to expectation, they show no consistent difference between high and low mental-health groups. We shall inquire further into all these relationships in later chapters. The results as a whole are congruent with those from other studies which report that economically and educationally limited groups are likely to be liberal on economic issues dealing with equalization of incomes, control of business, governmental help for the underprivileged, and similar reforms while remaining somewhat illiberal on issues which they do not perceive as affecting their own economic welfare or that of people with whom they feel closely identified.

Before leaving Table 3-6 it again seems appropriate to call attention to certain negative social implications of the findings. Items selected from the table are listed below in the same manner as previously done for Table 3-5. The percentages show the proportion of all Detroit auto workers who give the answers indicated.

	Percentage of Auto Workers (N = 407)
Social Issues	
What do you think ought to be done about race relations in this country—that is, between whites and Negroes? *For segregation, against full equality*	58%
The *most important* thing to teach children is absolute obedience to their parents. *Agree*	56%
Should people be allowed to speak in public against our democratic form of government? *No*	48%
What do you think should be America's position in world affairs—what should this country do about the way things are going in the rest of the world? *Isolationist direction*	43%
What do you think the United States should do about working with the United Nations? *Not work with it, or serious reservations*	37%

A few strong leaders could do more for this country than all the laws and talk. *Agree*   34%

Do you think that it is a good thing to have colleges where people study all kinds of ideas even if many of these are ideas that most of us believe are untrue and harmful? *No*   34%

Attitudes toward Job

If you could start all over, would you choose the same kind of work? *No*   75%

On the whole would you say that your job is (3 choices: really interesting; not very interesting; dull and monotonous)? *Last 2 choices*   35%

Self-rating of "how you feel about your job" on 5-point scale. *Rating below "well satisfied"* (i.e., dissatisfied or "neither satisfied nor dissatisfied")   31%

Personal Life apart from Job

Rating of life style. *Rated other than strongly purposeful*   77%

Do you push hard to change things [and make your life more like what you want] or are you content to take life as it comes? *The latter*   51%

Rating of purposefulness. *Very weak purpose evident re work*   26%

Very weak re nonwork activities   43%

Rating of interpersonal relations, whether satisfying and effective. *Rated very slightly so*   26%

Rating of adjustment to family and home life. *Unsatisfactory or questionable*   21%

Personal values and temperament will doubtless determine each person's reaction to these figures. Objectively, they support the indications of the items from Table 3-5 to the effect that substantial numbers of industrial workers are discontented and poorly adjusted. In addition, the items from Table 3-6 also reveal rather widely held social attitudes contrary to those of a healthy democratic society. Surely a problem worthy of attention exists when these significant proportions of urban industrial workers entertain the feelings and beliefs listed.[6]

Summary

This completes our present consideration of evidence bearing on the two-pronged question: what do our measures of mental health mean and how good is the mental health of Detroit auto workers? To answer the first question we compared specific responses of men with high and with low mental-health scores. They are found to differ in many ways which form a pattern of traits and attitudes reasonably interpretable as an operational definition of mental health. The descriptive rabbit thus pulled out of the tabulations is, of course, one that our premises and procedures first put into the hat. Nothing new has been created save an increased definiteness as to the qualities most clearly associated with the mental-health assessments. But this empirical clarification of the concept represents an important gain. The most characteristic types of responses associated with mental health, it turns out, are those expressing personal life satisfaction; high self-esteem (no strong feeling of inadequacy, discouragement, and self-blame), freedom from marked anxiety symptoms, worry, and nervous tensions. The mentally healthy also tend to have relatively positive, trusting, and non-hostile attitudes toward people and life relationships generally and decidedly greater interest and satisfaction in their work. In addition, they are more purposeful and ambitious, have better interpersonal adjustments, and more liberal and optimistic social views.

It *could* have happened that elements selected by guess or "hypothesis" as indicators of mental health would fail to hang together in a meaningful way. The men in good mental health *could* have turned out to be passive, frequent patrons of bars, often absent from work, especially inclined to antidemocratic sentiments. Or, contrary to our findings, mental health might have shown closer relations to purposiveness, ambitions, and desire for achievement among older than among younger workers. Fortunately, we encountered no disconcerting results such as these. To that extent, the statistical findings have value: they support and further specify the meanings of mental health that guided our assessment procedure.

One must avoid oversimple interpretations of these relationships. They serve to define mental health as the concept is used here; they do not offer explanations. The need for further analysis can be quickly illustrated. Consider, for example, the fact that the mentally healthy find their jobs more interesting. Is this because they actually hold better, more interesting jobs or because of subjective differences in attitude toward identical jobs? Is the superior mental health a cause or a result of experiencing work as interesting? What part is played by a complex of other variables— education, temperament, nonjob social milieu, and so on? Similar challenging questions arise in respect to each element of content associated with mental health. Our purpose will be to probe a little further into these problems as the analysis proceeds.

The remaining question dealt with in this chapter inquired how "satisfactory" the mental health of auto workers appears to be. Do the assessments point to any problems or matters for social concern? A partial basis for judgment is represented in the findings of Tables 3-5 and 3-6 and in the added lists of items showing proportions of all auto workers who responded in specified ways. Although widely divergent opinions may legitimately be held as to the seriousness of any particular characteristics indicated by these figures, few thoughtful persons can view the aggregate evidence with complacency. On their face, the findings raise important questions concerning the personal happiness and the psychological and social health of the factory workers. But these results, too, call for analyses which may contribute to their proper interpretation. However, the subsequent treatment will not alter the basic fact that large numbers of more or less typical working people like those in our sample manifest attitudes and behavior which by no stretch of imagination can be considered conditions of *good* mental health.

Following chapters will explore differences of mental health associated with occupations and other conditions. We shall seek clues concerning influences that produce more favorable or less favorable mental health. It is hoped that this analysis of determinants may help point the way to promising meliorative steps.

4.

Mental-health differences
by occupational level

This study focuses on differences in mental health among workers. We are particularly interested in determining how their mental health is affected by the nature of the jobs they hold. The necessary first step of the inquiry is to find whether there are, in fact, consistent differences of mental health between men in different types of occupations.

This question carries special interest in regard to differences among men in factory work. From the beginning of the factory system to the present, constant criticism and agitation have been directed against the alleged adverse psychological effects of specialized, repetitive production jobs. Yet remarkably little evidence has been brought to bear on the issue. No one knows how much truth there is to the common charges.

If it is once established that there are significant mental-health differences, it will then be imperative to search for explanations of how the differences come about and how they may be modified by changed conditions. If differences are not found, we are confronted with the equally challenging problem of why not, in view of what appear to be the greater deprivations and interferences with healthy psychological growth and self-expression at lower occupational levels. In terms of theoretical considerations as well as empirical evidence, the case is far from settled. Two broadly opposed possibilities exist: (a) that conditions of routine occupations do, indeed, impose special frustrations and psychological deficits which produce poorer mental health, and (b) that, contrariwise, "better" jobs create equal or greater problems of mental health both because of the expanded expectations and aspirations of their incumbents and because of additional stresses due, for example, to increased job responsibilities.

55

As we weigh the evidence from the present inquiry we shall want to consider these problems of interpretation along with the more simple but important direct question whether men in the lower ranges of the factory job hierarchy do manifest relatively unfavorable conditions of mental health.

Occupational differences in mental health

Our principal comparisons deal with hourly paid, "blue collar" Detroit factory workers. The sample consists of 298 middle-aged and 109 young men, all in automotive companies. Their jobs range from highly skilled to the lowest semiskilled. Supplementary comparisons will also be reported with three other occupational groups —semiskilled men in nonfactory work, factory workers in small towns outside metropolitan Detroit, and clerical or white-collar male employees at relatively low salary levels.

We begin by comparing occupational groups within the sample of Detroit auto workers. The overall results are clear and striking. When workers are classified into job levels by reference to skill and variety of work operations, responsibility, and pay, mental-health scores show consistent and significant correlation with the occupational hierarchy. *The higher the occupation the better mental health on the average.*

One simple set of figures will make this evident. In Table 4-1 we compare occupations by the percentages of workers enjoying good mental health—that is, having "high" mental-health scores. The cutting point for "high" is of course arbitrary, but constant; it corresponds to that used in Chapter 3 and represents the upper one-third of all workers. Jobs were assigned to the levels or categories by reference to three criteria: the official job title (clarified when necessary by consultation with automotive "insiders"); the worker's own description of his duties, job operations, and training time required; and the rate of pay.[1] The occupational classification of workers and the derivation of mental-health scores were completely independent operations, each carried out with no reference to the other. Consequently, nothing in the procedure could have spuriously contributed to the obtained mental-health differences by occupation. Inevitably there were borderline cases and ambiguities but since these occasional errors of occupational classification would tend to reduce rather than exaggerate the relationship to

*Table 4-1   Mental-health differences between
factory occupational groups*

	Young		Middle-aged	
Occupational Category	Proportion with High Mental Health	Number of Workers*	Proportion with High Mental Health	Number of Workers*
Skilled workers	58%†	33	56%	45
High semiskilled			41	98
Ordinary semiskilled	35	46	38	82
Repetitive semiskilled	10	30	26	73
(Repetitive, machine-paced only—*subdivision of preceding category*)	(7)	(15)	(16)	(32)
Total		109		298

* Totals on which the percentages are based.
† The two top categories are combined here because of the very small number of skilled and absence of significant difference between them and the high semiskilled.

mental health, the differences reported between occupations may be considered minimum figures.

The results summarized in the table deserve several further comments. Among middle-aged workers, one group is decidedly high —the skilled; and one group is decidedly low—those on "the line" or on machine-paced jobs (jobs where the worker has to conform to the speed of the machine or conveyor). Other differences are not great. Among the young, unlike the middle-aged, the high semiskilled have mental-health scores equal to the small group of skilled with whom they are combined in the tabulation. In the young group the large contrast occurs between the upper semiskilled and the ordinary semiskilled. At the lower end of the occupational scale, another large difference exists between the repetitive production workers, both paced and unpaced, in comparison with the ordinary semiskilled. Despite these variations between the two age groups, both show a gradient of descending proportions of good mental health from the most skilled to the most routine jobs. Even where the differences between adjacent categories are small, they are uniform in direction. Men on specialized repetitive jobs are consistently lowest.

Along with the overall consistency, however, we have noted that there is a suggestive difference of pattern between the age groups. One feature of the difference is that at the high semiskilled level the middle-aged have poorer mental health than the young while in routine low-level jobs they have *better* mental health than the young. The divergent findings in respect to the upper semiskilled group may be reconciled by an interpretation like the following. An essential aspect of mental health is a feeling of achievement, personal worth, and status among one's peers, or at least a sense of progress toward these goals. For the middle-aged factory worker, a skilled job carries these rewards; he has arrived. By contrast, even a fairly high semiskilled job leaves much to be desired; it fails to fulfill earlier aspirations stimulated by the man's rise to some what varied and responsible work above the general run of production jobs. The typical factory worker in his forties sees little to hope for beyond his present attainment. The lower percentage of these men enjoying high mental health presumably reflects this realization of severely limited opportunities for improvement of their work and life situation and for further personal growth. Among *young* men, on the other hand, high semiskilled jobs do represent considerable early achievement which commands respect and offers bright promise for the future as compared with the more common semiskilled positions. Subjectively, this evidence of early success may support positive self-esteem and personal morale just about as well as do skilled positions. This is what our data seem to imply.

Along parallel lines it may be possible to account for the contrasting results between age groups at the lowest job level. Two features of the findings call for explanation. One is the fact that larger numbers of the middle-aged than of the young are in good mental health (though there is extremely small difference in the proportions of *low* mental health). The superior mental health of the older group compared with the young is especially pronounced for men in nonmachine-paced types of work (the difference among machine-paced is negligible since the middle-aged have decidedly more of poor mental health as well as more with high ratings). The second fact is that there is a much greater difference between the mental health of middle-aged workers on machine-paced and nonpaced jobs than is found in the case of young workers. In fact, if we consider low mental-health scores as well as high, the relationship is slightly inverse for the young; the paced have *fewer* of poor mental health. These comparisons of paced and unpaced work are suggestive only, however, due to the small numbers in the subgroups of young workers.

Interpretations of these results might run as follows: among middle-aged men who have remained in low-level jobs, aspirations for more agreeable and rewarding work have not been aroused or encouraged and hence many of the workers have tended to make positive, accepting adjustments to their life as it is. This would be the more feasible for those holding nonproduction-line jobs. Older men are likely to feel their failure and the unsatisfying, objectionable character of their work particularly keenly if they have been unable or unwilling to get "off the line" despite its undesirable features and its uneviable reputation of being the worst place of all, even compared with other "unpaced" semiskilled work. *Younger* men are more likely to experience frustration, impending defeat, and resentment in *any* routine factory job, little caring whether it is paced or not. Over a longer period of years, as they approach middle-age, some of them will presumably also find new orientations to life and to themselves with associated improvement of their mental health.

Along quite different lines, it may be that the mental-health differences referred to are attributable to *selection* influences which have changed over the years—that is, to the kinds of men who have entered and remained in the lower occupations. More about this shortly. These and other alternative possibilities present important questions which call for longitudinal studies that would map the workers' changing mental health from the time of employment until they leave, change jobs, or continue indefinitely where they started. Though the present research can do relatively little toward offering definitive answers, some clues will be explored as we examine additional relevant data in subsequent sections.

Returning to the central conclusion that mental health is poorest among factory workers on repetitive production jobs, additional support is forthcoming from fully concordant results based on a small sample outside the Detroit metropolitan area. The first two lines of Table 4-2 give percentages parallel to those in Table 4-1 in regard to our main sample. The occupations are more coarsely grouped here because of small numbers. The proportions of high

Table 4-2   Mental health of comparison groups

	Young		Middle-aged	
Occupational Groups	Proportion with High Mental Health	Number of Workers*	Proportion with High Mental Health	Number of Workers*
Small-town factory workers				
High and ordinary semiskilled†	50%	18	62%	21
Repetitive semiskilled	33	18	46	22
Nonfactory workers in Detroit				
High and ordinary semiskilled†	69	48	39	46
White-collar employees	75	28	54	40

* Totals on which the percentages are based.
† Categories are combined because of small numbers.

mental health are seen to be above those of corresponding Detroit factory groups; but the point of chief interest is the fact that the results agree in finding lower mental health among holders of routine jobs than among those having jobs above that level. In more detailed breakdowns not shown because of the very limited numbers of individuals, the data also exhibit the same consistent tendency for the high semiskilled to have higher mental health than the ordinary semiskilled—and with a larger gap between the two for the younger than for the older men.

Table 4-2 also contains figures for two other comparison groups: semiskilled workers in nonmanufacturing industry in Detroit and white-collar employees at roughly comparable wage levels.[2] The percentages must be viewed as suggestive only since the samples of nonfactory and white-collar workers were not chosen in a manner to make them representative of the total population in those occupations. Nevertheless, within the limits of the sample, it is apparent that these groups, too, exhibit markedly better mental health than do men at the lowest levels of factory production jobs. The nonfactory sample consisted principally of warehouse workers and deliverymen, construction workers, truck and bus drivers, and public utility service and repairmen. The middle-aged men in this sample differ little as to mental health from the corresponding "ordinary semiskilled" factory workers; both stand well above the repetitive semiskilled, especially above those on machine-paced jobs. The nonfactory *young* men are far superior to their factory counterparts.

This finding is doubtless dependent in part on the unintentional selection of particularly favorable and well-educated groups of young men, principally from public utilities and the communications industry. This factor of selection accounts at the same time for the striking difference between the two age groups of nonfactory workers.

The white-collar sample comprises clerical and varied nonsupervisory salaried male employees, approximately two-thirds from automobile companies, the others from public utilities and mercantile establishments. These two parts of the sample did not differ significantly and hence are combined. The young white-collar workers prove decidedly high in mental health, well above most of the other groups studied. Among the middle-aged, white-collar men are approximately equal to the skilled in Detroit; they stand above all the Detroit semiskilled of similar age, but are lower than young groups of white-collar and nonfactory manual workers.

Once again one may speculate that the results are related to perceived "life chances," to the belief by these young white-collar and nonfactory workers that they are worthwhile persons who are "on their way." By contrast, one can guess that many men in their forties who remain in semiskilled work or in the low range of white-collar positions are likely to entertain a sense of failure and disappointment with life, conducive to poorer mental health. At the same time, white-collar men of middle-age as well as the younger do enjoy certain advantages over the semiskilled that make for better mental health, presumably in spite of their higher aspirations that are partially unfulfilled. At any rate explanations of this kind appear to fit the findings thus far reported.[3]

Occupational differences on specific questions related to mental health

While the preceding comparisons of occupational groups in terms of total mental-health scores portray the relationship in broad outline, the picture takes on additional meaning as we fill in details. What is the *content* of the mental-health differences? What are the concrete attitudes and behavior in respect to which the groups are dissimilar? A consideration of subindexes and specific responses should help answer these questions and in doing so should shed light on the central problem of how men's work relates to their psychological well-being.[4]

The main part of this analysis again deals with the sample of Detroit factory workers. In general we find that although the occupational groups differ on the component indexes in a way that corresponds with the results on the total mental-health scores, some of the separate indexes bear significantly closer relationship to job level than do others. The clearest occupational differences occur on the indexes of personal morale, sociability (or nonwithdrawal), and self-esteem. On these three indexes the top occupational category stands best and the low-level repetitive jobs stand worst without exception for both age-groups and for comparisons using both high and low scores on the indexes. The percentage differences among occupations are approximately the same as those on overall mental health. Although occupational differences on the other three indexes are somewhat smaller and less consistent, they definitely point in the same direction. Among young workers anxiety bears least relationship to job level; among middle-aged, life satisfaction and hostility are least related to the occupational hierarchy.

Analysis of the response items on which occupational groups differ yields even more specific information than does comparison of indexes. Although a large majority of the items differentiate between occupational groups, many differences are small and a number of items even show reversals from the main trend. Consequently, the content of those responses that do differ markedly by job level assume special importance since they indicate concretely the nature of the occupational mental-health variations.

Table 4-3 brings together examples of such differences of responses by factory groups. Pronounced differentiation occurs on a number of items that express discouragement, defeat, pessimism, distrust of people, feeling of personal inadequacy and futility—responses associated with the measures we have called personal morale or social alienation, self-esteem, and sociability or social withdrawal. The first 12 items are of this kind. The remaining 9 items from the mental-health index reflect feelings of dissatisfaction, frustration, and resulting restlessness, nervousness, and other symptoms of tension—response taken from our indexes of anxiety, hostility, and life satisfaction.

At the end of Table 4-3 we also list a few measures that were not part of the mental-health indexes. It is of interest to observe that the indexes of purposive striving that were previously discussed reveal occupational differences quite similar to those of the best differentiating mental-health items. The occupational groups like-

Table 4-3 Occupational differences among factory workers on selected items related to mental health

Percentage of Each Occupational Group Giving Specified Responses

	Young			Middle-aged			
	Skilled and High Semi-skilled (N = 33)	Ordinary Semi-skilled (N = 46)	Repetitive Semi-skilled (N = 30)	Skilled (N = 45)	High Semi-skilled (N = 98)	Ordinary Semi-skilled (N = 82)	Repetitive Semi-skilled (N = 73)
Items in Mental-Health Index							
Not know whom can count on (D3)*	34%	43%	60%	28%	45%	42%	56%
Have to live for today (D13)	22	30	43	22	32	29	34
Success is due to luck and pull (D1)	36	43	53	26	32	41	48
Ever so blue nothing worthwhile (G16)	22	34	46	9	23	31	29
People out for themselves only (D5)	42	61	63	37	57	45	62
Officials not care re average man (D15)	28	28	41	26	32	36	47
Can do much to make own future (A7d)	81	73	57	77	50	60	46
People often hurt your feelings (G18)	6	15	17	11	19	23	31
Prefer being by self (G29)	17	24	31	23	27	26	33
Things wrong, leave to others (G4)	6	13	20	9	7	11	17
Have more than 2 good friends (F9b,c)	66	52	43	56	52	46	48
Belong to more than 2 organizations (F16)	30	20	23	42	28	23	22
Often worried and upset (G9)	11	28	28	9	26	31	32

* Numerals in parentheses identify the place of the items in the interview schedule reproduced in Appendix A. Indexes and ratings which have no identifying numbers are described in Appendix B.

Table 4-3 (continued)

Percentage of Each Occupational Group Giving Specified Responses

	Young			Middle-aged			
	Skilled and High Semi-skilled (N = 33)	Ordinary Semi-skilled (N = 46)	Repetitive Semi-skilled (N = 30)	Skilled (N = 45)	High Semi-skilled (N = 98)	Ordinary Semi-skilled (N = 82)	Repetitive Semi-skilled (N = 73)
Items in Mental-Health Index (cont.)							
Ever bothered by nervousness (G20)	25%	46%	43%	27%	35%	28%	39%
Have any health problems (G13)	17	26	23	20	20	23	32
Do not wake up rested (G2)	11	17	20	7	17	22	26
Boil inside without showing it (G10)	53	65	80	56	63	66	63
Many people unreasonable (G15)	17	44	27	27	36	38	44
Preponderantly favorable ideas re life (A2 to 7)	67	67	35	73	64	58	52
Optimistic re own future (A7c)	69	48	37	59	43	48	47
Restless; not know what want (G1)	44	65	67	36	49	51	58
Other Items							
High "active life orientation" score	76	57	43	49	41	37	30
"Purposefulness" re work—high or medium	91	76	63	91	91	76	52
Combined re work and nonwork	67	48	43	76	57	52	34
Interpersonal relations rated good	57	35	37	53	34	38	29

wise differ in congruent fashion on a global rating of social adjustment based on the entire interview.

Although differences on the listed items are not at all spectacular in size or even thoroughly consistent in direction, the trends are clearly apparent. Nevertheless, since these are selected items and a number of others show no such trend or even occasionally run counter to expectations, a suspicion might arise that the discordant results could possibly lead to conclusions at variance with those we have stressed. That this is unlikely is evidenced by the fact that total index scores, based on all the items, reveal the same tendencies. The item results themselves afford further justification. For example, in 92 separate comparisons of the 46 items of Table 3-5 for the two age groups separately, 82 per cent of the differences between the top occupation and the next highest are in the favorable direction; similarly, 67 per cent of the differences between the lowest occupational group and the next lowest are in the expected direction. Furthermore, in almost all instances of percentage reversals, the predominant gradient between lower and higher occupations persists. Only 7 of the 92 comparisons show the high or low occupation failing to score as expected relative to the group at the opposite extreme of the occupational scale. Four of these 7 exceptions pertain to anxiety responses of the young workers, a result in line with the absence of differences on the total anxiety index for this group. Apart from this cluster of anxiety items, scrutiny of all the discordant proportions reveals no other consistent or meaningful tendency for some aspects of mental health to relate to occupation in a manner divergent from that we have described. At the same time, the considerable number of responses which show no relation to occupation or slight reversals from expected relationships do dictate caution. Interpretations of occupational mental-health differences will need to recognize that the testimony from different questions is far from unanimous.

The main trend of the foregoing results from comparisons of Detroit factory workers again receives support from congruent findings in the samples of small-town factory groups and white-collar employees in Detroit. In the small-town factories, workers in routine repetitive work also return more "unhealthy" responses than do the men on relatively varied semiskilled jobs. For all 46 mental-health items, considered separately for the two age groups, 61 per cent of the comparisons of small-town repetitive workers with other semiskilled are in the expected direction versus 26 per cent in a reverse direction (13 per cent show no difference). Data for the white-collar workers show them responding in the "better" direction more often than the high semiskilled in 75 per cent of the comparisons versus 23 per cent in the reverse direction (2 per cent with no difference). This agreement with expectations on most items, using totally different samples of workers, argues that we are dealing with relationships of some generality.

The tendency for so many men in routine production types of work to answer the varied questions in a less "healthy" direction is a significant and challenging social fact, regardless of whether one employs the mental-health concept. It is tempting, popularly, to assert that unhappiness and unfavorable psychological effects generally are the lot of mankind; they can be charged to the "human condition," to the state of man in the modern world. They are dismissed with the vernacular pronouncement "such is life." The foregoing comparative figures of occupational groups make these blanket explanations difficult to maintain without serious reservations. Persons differently situated in the economic system tend to enjoy better mental health or suffer poorer mental health according to their position. They do not undergo identical strains or experience identical consequences. It is these variations, particularly those associated with different kinds of factory employment, that we seek to account for and understand a little better.

More detailed inquiry concerning the occupational differences and especially concerning the factors responsible for favorable or unfavorable psychological effects will be our central preoccupation through the following analyses. We shall focus particularly on job-related variables and shall find that the occupational groups differ strikingly in their reactions to their work, in a manner that can scarcely fail to have important effects on their broader subjective states and life adjustments. But causal explanations other than those pertaining to influences of the work itself must likewise be carefully considered. It is these to which our immediate analysis turns.

Occupational differences: selection effects or job effects

A vital first question is whether the occupational mental-health differences are due to *effects of the jobs* and their associated conditions or, alternatively, whether the differences result from *selection of certain kinds of persons* who go into and remain in the several types of work. Is a man's job level a *result* of his condition of mental health rather than a cause? Are people in routine jobs, that is, because of personal characteristics associated with less satisfactory life adjustments? If occupational mental-health differences are in fact consequences of personality characteristics people bring to their jobs, it should be possible to detect differences among these people in the prejob period of their lives and to show that these personal differences can account for the occupational results.

A clear example, one that presents a good test case, is amount of schooling. Can the occupational results be "explained away" as due to educational differences between men who secure better jobs in contrast to those in less skilled work? Since substantial educational differences do occur between occupations and since education is also associated with better mental health, it appears plausible that the occupational mental-health differences might be attributable to the relationship of job level to education. The essential test is whether groups having *equal* education still show mental-health differences depending on their occupation. Do the occupational differences persist apart from the influence of education—that is, when only persons of like amounts of education are compared? Our findings show that they do. Proportions of workers having good mental health consistently decrease from higher- to lower-level occupations *for each of three educational categories separately.* Moreover, the magnitude of the differences between occupational levels is very nearly the same as when education is not controlled but is permitted to add its influence (see Table 4-4).

For the middle-age group (in which there are enough cases to permit more adequate analysis) occupation and education show a small additive effect on mental health as may be noted in Table 4-4. Mental health is best among those high in education *and* occupation, poorest for those low in both education and occupation. This is contrary, of course, to the psychologically plausible hypothesis that mental health is adversely affected by lack of congruency between educational status and occupational status—the view that poorest mental health occurs among persons of better education in low-level jobs (and perhaps also among those of low education in high-level jobs). This hypothesis receives no support at all from our data, either for the middle-age group or the younger workers. In fact, the percentage of good mental health in lower-level jobs

Mental Health of the Industrial Worker

*Table 4-4   Percentage of high mental-health scores by groups of
specified occupational and educational levels*

A. Middle-aged Factory Workers
Education

Occupation	Grade School	Some High School	High School Graduate	Total
Skilled	43% (7)*	45% (20)	72% (18)	56% (45)
High semiskilled	33 (46)	45 (33)	53 (19)	41 (98)
Ordinary semiskilled	31 (35)	39 (36)	55 (11)	38 (82)
Repetitive semiskilled	24 (46)	29 (21)	33 (6)	26 (73)
Total	30% (134)	40% (110)	57% (54)	39% (298)

B. Young Factory Workers†
Education

Occupation	Some High School or Less	High School Graduate	Total
Skilled and high semiskilled	57% (14)	58% (19)	58% (33)
Ordinary semiskilled	33 (36)	40 (10)	35 (46)
Repetitive semiskilled	10 (21)	11 (9)	10 (30)
Total	31% (71)	42% (38)	35% (109)

* Figures in parentheses show the number of cases in each cell on which the
accompanying percentage is based.
† Because of small numbers, we here combine the two lower educational groups
and the two upper occupational groups.

is *greater* for persons having more schooling. If we combine the two low occupational categories and take the medium and high mental-health scores together in order to have somewhat larger, more stable numbers, the better-educated man in low-level jobs of both age groups show *larger* proportions, not smaller, having moderately good mental-health scores (percentages from low to higher schooling run, for the young: 47, 60, and 68 per cent; for the middle-aged: 52, 65, and 82 per cent).

The analysis of our data as a whole leads to the conclusion that *educational differences, either by themselves or in interaction with job level, are not sufficient to account for the observed mental-health variations by occupation.* To the extent that this conclusion is confirmed and to the extent that other prejob personal characteristics (possible job-*selection* factors) yield similar findings, the probability increases that significant influences determining occupational mental health among factory workers are to be found in the jobs themselves and their associated life conditions. Certainly this does not mean that personal characteristics are not also important; on the contrary, in a later chapter we discuss their considerable influence on mental health. At this point, however, we are concerned only with the question whether occupational differences occur independently of selection effects.

Clearly the general question cannot be answered by reference to education alone. Men in the several job categories may differ in many other personal attributes that are possibly more crucial determinants of the observed mental-health variations. It may be, for example, that the better educated men in low-level positions are not equivalent to others of like education in higher positions in respect, say, to their intellectual competence, their ambitions and aspirations, their early home backgrounds, and similar favorable or unfavorable influences. Although an exhaustive check on such possibilities would be an endless undertaking, we have attempted to sample a number of the more important prejob characteristics that might account for the observed occupational differences. The analysis parallels that employed in respect to schooling.

A list of these further characteristics follows.[5] Results of the analyses are summarized in Table 4-5.

School success (an index using grade reached, good marks or not, whether liked school, and reason for leaving).

Income level of boyhood family (respondent's estimate on a five-point scale).

Table 4-5 *Percentage of high mental-health scores by groups of specified occupational level and prejob personal characteristics*

Prejob Personal Characteristics	Young			Middle-aged			
	Skilled; High Semiskilled	Ordinary Semiskilled	Repetitive Semiskilled	Skilled	High Semiskilled	Ordinary Semiskilled	Repetitive Semiskilled
Education							
Above average*	58% (19)†	40% (10)	11% (9)	58% (38)	48% (52)	43% (47)	30% (27)
Below average	57 (14)	33 (36)	10 (21)	43 (7)	33 (46)	31 (35)	24 (46)
School success							
Above average	61 (23)	44 (18)	15 (13)	57 (30)	53 (45)	45 (38)	11 (18)
Below average	50 (10)	29 (28)	6 (17)	53 (15)	30 (53)	32 (44)	31 (55)
Income level in boyhood							
Average or above	73 (22)	42 (33)	11 (19)	61 (31)	45 (64)	42 (52)	30 (40)
Below average	36 (11)	15 (13)	0 (10)	46 (13)	30 (33)	30 (30)	25 (32)
Childhood deprivation							
Below average (favorable)	57 (21)	50 (22)	6 (17)	63 (27)	47 (47)	48 (40)	32 (31)
Above average (unfavorable)	58 (12)	21 (24)	15 (13)	44 (18)	35 (51)	29 (42)	21 (42)

* For the young, "above average" means high school graduation and below average is everything less; for the middle-aged, above average means more than eighth grade and below average is eighth grade or less.
† Figures in parentheses show the number of cases in each cell on which the accompanying percentage is based.

Table 4-5 (*Continued*)

Prejob Personal Characteristics	Young			Middle-aged			
	Skilled; High Semiskilled	Ordinary Semiskilled	Repetitive Semiskilled	Skilled	High Semiskilled	Ordinary Semiskilled	Repetitive Semiskilled
Childhood anxiety							
Below average (favorable)	60% (15)	55% (20)	0% (11)	73% (22)	60% (47)	53% (45)	43% (28)
Above average (unfavorable)	56 (18)	19 (26)	16 (19)	39 (23)	24 (51)	19 (37)	16 (45)
Childhood happiness							
Above average	62 (13)	50 (18)	8 (13)	65 (23)	60 (48)	46 (39)	35 (31)
Below average	55 (20)	25 (28)	12 (17)	45 (22)	22 (50)	30 (43)	19 (42)
Childhood self-confidence							
Above average	65 (23)	45 (20)	8 (12)	59 (17)	53 (47)	50 (32)	26 (23)
Below average	40 (10)	27 (26)	11 (18)	54 (28)	29 (51)	30 (50)	26 (50)
Boyhood hopes							
Success, status, etc.	64 (22)	43 (21)	0 (14)	56 (27)	37 (49)	36 (45)	20 (40)
Other (including "none")	45 (11)	28 (25)	19 (16)	56 (18)	45 (49)	41 (37)	33 (33)
Boyhood work aspirations							
White collar or skilled	58 (19)	30 (23)	7 (15)	57 (21)	45 (49)	38 (37)	19 (26)
Other	57 (14)	39 (23)	13 (15)	54 (24)	37 (49)	38 (45)	30 (47)

Table 4-5 (*Continued*)

Prejob Personal Characteristics	Young			Middle-aged			
	Skilled; High Semiskilled	Ordinary Semiskilled	Repetitive Semiskilled	Skilled	High Semiskilled	Ordinary Semiskilled	Repetitive Semiskilled
Boyhood values Emphasis on social approval, prestige	73% (15)	35% (23)	7% (15)	57% (21)	41% (41)	33% (40)	19% (31)
Other	44 (18)	35 (23)	13 (15)	54 (24)	40 (57)	48 (42)	13 (42)
Boyhood values Emphasis on work using abilities, etc.	67 (15)	30 (20)	0 (14)	59 (29)	44 (36)	27 (29)	19 (27)
Other	50 (18)	38 (26)	19 (16)	50 (16)	39 (62)	43 (53)	30 (46)

Childhood deprivation (an index using responses to 12 questions pertaining to such matters as whether respondent lived with own or foster parents; their occupation, education, country of birth, and happiness; family income, childhood health; and why he left school).

Childhood anxiety and maladjustment (an index using responses to 10 questions asking about such matters as respondent's biggest problems as a child, his fears and worries, feeling toward friends, and speech difficulties).

Childhood happiness (an index based on 5 items asking about the way his life was in childhood, his problems, feeling about school, and a five-point estimate of his happiness).

Childhood self-confidence (an index using 10 items asking what kind of things he liked to do, what he did best, whether he took the lead, and about his aspirations).

Boyhood hopes ("main hopes and wishes as you grew up"; "what did you want to get out of life"—coded into 18 categories).

Boyhood work aspirations ("ideas and wishes about what kind of work you wanted to do"—coded into 8 categories).

Boyhood values (coder's estimate based on all responses concerning early life—14 categories).

Taken as a whole, the results of the analyses support the conclusions reached in regard to amount of schooling. The statistical relationship for education is repeated here in simplified form, as the first section of Table 4-5, for convenience in making comparisons with the other variables. The outstanding finding bearing on the question at hand is the fairly consistent decrease of percentages reading across each line of the table, from the more skilled and varied occupations to the most routine. In general, that is, regardless of men's standing above or below average on a variety of prejob characteristics, they still show group differences of mental health corresponding to their occupational level—differences roughly comparable in size to those for the total occupational groups. Even when we make the comparisons using more extreme groupings on the prejob characteristics, the results are much the same though with greater irregularity due to the small numbers. All these additional analyses further strengthen the conclusion that mental-health effects are directly associated with occupational levels independently of the personal characteristics of the job incumbents.

Since the evidence in regard to prejob characteristics is based on retrospective reporting of a remote period of life by our respondents, it must be viewed with caution. Responses concerning childhood conditions, feelings, and behavior are bound to be affected by complex distorting influences of later years, particularly by efforts to maintain and justify one's current self-conception. It is difficult to estimate the extent to which recollections are a product of such biasing tendencies. It could be, for example, that men of poor mental health in routine jobs are most likely to exaggerate unfavorable childhood factors since they need to justify *both* their low occupational level and their unsatisfactory adjustment. This is tenuous speculation at best, however. Equally plausibly, perhaps, one might argue the contrary: that these men can readily attribute their poor personal adjustment to their employment status, with no need to blame their childhood characteristics, whereas maladjusted men at higher job levels cannot so easily blame their current life conditions and consequently may overemphasize early sources of their difficulties. In the face of such uncertainties as to how the biases operate, we have chosen to use the results as they stand, with appropriate warnings inherent in what has just been said.

An important reason for taking the findings seriously is the fact that relatively objective indicators of prejob circumstances, such as respondents' education, family income in childhood, and objective parts of the deprivation index,[6] are in essential agreement with the indexes representing subjective responses that are more susceptible to distortion. No matter which of the varied objective and subjective indexes are used to classify workers in respect to their prejob personal and social characteristics, the same substantial differences in mental health according to job level remain. This persistence of mental-health variations by occupation, even when we take men similar in regard to factors of personal background, argues that the psychological differences between occupational groups are not accounted for by the *kinds of persons* in the several types of work. Consequently, it may be inferred that the differences are due in important degree to effects of the jobs themselves.

An additional word of caution is called for in another direction. Although our analysis demonstrates that the relationship between occupational level and mental health does not disappear when the influence of any one of the childhood variables is removed, it still does not rule out the possibility that if the combined influence of all these factors were removed the occupational effects would disappear. Although this is a logical possibility, the probability of any large effect of this kind seems remote in view of the small and irregular effects traceable to the characteristics separately, and because of the extensive overlap or duplication of persons classified favorably and unfavorably on the several childhood variables. To be sure, the possibility remains that other prejob factors, not indicated by any of our measures, may play a crucial role in causing the observed differences in mental health between occupational groups. Until evidence is forthcoming to support such alternative explanations, however, the foregoing conclusions appear to be the most reasonable ones.

One minor departure from the earlier results dealing with education should be noted. Contrary to the finding in respect to amount of schooling, there is indication that certain of these new variables in Table 4-5 do manifest a slight tendency for those persons in lowest-level jobs who have superior ability and higher aspirations to be in poorer mental health than those of lower ability and aspirations. Using school success as a measure of competence and ambition, for example, we detect that among middle-aged men in repetitive jobs only 11 per cent of those above average in school success have high mental health while 31 per cent of those below average in school success have high mental health. Another such relationship is illustrated by the frequency of *low* mental health (figures for low scores are not shown in the table) among young workers in repetitive jobs who reported boyhood hopes of sucess and achievement (64 per cent of them have low mental-health scores versus 31 per cent of other young workers in repetitive jobs). Although the numbers involved in this and similar comparisons are small and the results for different variables are irregular, it appears that some of the favorable prejob personal attributes do tend to make for poorer adjustment in low-level jobs. To a limited extent, then, the data lend support to the hypothesis that incongruence between aspirations and achievement may lead to poor mental health. We shall deal further with these relationships in Chapter 7.

This analysis of the way prejob variables may interact with low occupational status does not alter the main conclusion stated previously in regard to selection effects. In fact, *selection* decreases the number of persons affected by such incongruity and consequently *reduces* occupational differences of mental health; hence it clearly does not help to account for the observed occupational differences.

Summary

In sum, then, the indications from our present data are: (*a*) that mental health is poorer among factory workers as we move from skilled, responsible, varied types of work to jobs lower in these respects, and (*b*) that the relationship does not appear to be caused in any large degree by differences of prejob background or personality of the men who enter and remain in the several types of work. The relationship of mental health to occupation, in other words, seems to be genuine, not dependent merely on selection effects.   Thus, the evidence argues that mental health is intimately associated with the nature of the work in which men are engaged.

The strength of the foregoing inferences is enhanced by the fact that they are derived from a relatively homogeneous sample in which we have eliminated or controlled most variables that might otherwise be thought responsible for the occupational mental-health differences. The controlled factors include sex, race, country of birth, range of occupations (automotive factory workers only), length of employment, size of community—and our analysis adds such controls as age (and hence stage in the life cycle) and education.   To the extent that these potential influences are held constant, there is much less likelihood that the observed relation of mental health to occupational skill level is produced by variables other than those directly linked to occupation.

All of this attention to occupational factors as determinants of mental health must not mislead anyone into thinking that other influences are not also important.   Our sole purpose has been to find whether occupations and their associated life conditions are accompanied by differences of mental health among industrial workers and whether the differences are accounted for by extraneous factors. The conclusion that occupation is genuinely influential does not at all imply that other influences are not likewise significant.   We assume that mental health has *many* roots and, indeed, our data strongly support this expectation.   It is particularly clear that advantages of education and favorable early economic conditions make for better mental health.   In a later chapter we shall turn attention explicitly to these personal and social, nonoccupational determinants to compare them with the influence of occupation.   But the primary aim of the study remains the exploration of *occupational* effects.

It might be thought that in the foregoing analysis we have neglected an obvious and seemingly more direct type of evidence on the question of job effects versus selection effects.   If, as we have argued, adverse job influences are operative at lower occupational levels, it might be expected that the effects would be cumulative over the years and consequently that they should be observable by comparing older with younger workers and men with longer versus shorter periods of time on the job. We have made these comparisons and, in fact, no evidence is found in support of such expectations. On further reflection, however, it is clear that this type of analysis is most inconclusive; the relationships are much too complex to permit any safe inferences. In the first place, continued exposure to the job may not have cumulative ill effects but may lead to "immunization" or adaptation. More importantly, we have no data on *selective leaving* of the jobs; it may be that men of especially high or especially low mental health are most likely to quit this work for other employment; a good case can be argued for either hypothesis. Since these unknowns of selective turnover and long-run personal adjustments can operate in varied combinations, it is patently impossible to draw definite conclusions from the type of data available.

Actually, the only discernible tendency is for men in the young group who have long service on low-level jobs to number fewer than average in poor mental health. The temptation is to attribute this to selective job leaving by workers most frustrated in such work. If we assume, as appears reasonable, that these would be men of above-average aspirations and abilities, then the long-service group remaining should be comparatively low in respect to education, school success, boyhood aspirations, and present desire for promotion and belief in their chances for promotion. No differences of this kind are found, however, in respect to any of these variables. This result suggests that the better mental health of the group longer on the job occurs not because others, who would have shown ill effects, have moved up or have fled from the low jobs, but because unfavorable psychological reactions during early years on the unrewarding jobs gradually become dulled or stilled. According to this interpretation, men in the routine types of work come, over the years, to accept and make the best of their situation. Our findings suggest that this adaptive lowering of expectations affects young men of better and poorer education about equally and likewise those of varying degrees of school success and ambitions. This explanation is congruent with the earlier conclusion that selection into lower-level jobs on the basis of personal characteristics is not very important in accounting for the observed differences of mental health among occupations.

All that can be said for these last thoughts is that they appear, in the light of our data, to be plausible speculations. Only detailed longitudinal studies can adequately disentangle the variables. In the absence of such studies we are left with the conclusions arrived at more indirectly through the preceding pages.

5.

Job satisfaction

in relation to mental health

The evidence presented shows that there are substantial occupational differences of mental health as defined and measured by our indexes. Men in routine production jobs on the average have less satisfactory mental health; those in more skilled and varied types of work have better mental health. Moreover, the findings indicate that the differences of mental health result in large degree from the jobs themselves and their associated conditions quite apart from differences due to the kind of men employed in the different occupations.

This conclusion at once presents the challenging question of what aspects of occupations are important. Which of the myriad characteristics and higher- and lower-level jobs and associated life conditions are the salient determinants of better or poorer mental health? *Why* do we find poorer mental health in low-level occupations?

One can readily offer a long list of plausible explanatory factors— from lower pay, economic insecurity, and disagreeable working conditions to the more intangible influences of status, promotion opportunities, type of supervision and work-group relations, simplicity and repetitiveness of job operations and lack of personal control over them, nonuse of abilities with consequent feelings of futility, and many more such possible influences on and off the job. Some of these obviously may be more significant than others. In the following chapter we attempt to estimate the saliency of a number of these variables. In the present chapter we deal with the prior, more basic question whether job-level conditions *as a whole* produce differences of satisfaction and dissatisfaction which are associated with corresponding differences of mental health.

It would surely be a mistake to think in terms of this *or* that

78

causal factor as important. Mental health is a product of complex combinations of influences, varied and shifting, dependent on the values currently emphasized and the expectations aroused as well as on the existing conditions of gratification and deprivation. The attitudes, feelings, and behaviors that indicate better or poorer mental health are reactions of a person to his entire life situation; his relationship to the world permits him to maintain realistic, positive, satisfying belief in himself and his purposeful activities or it does not. The key question for our inquiry is whether lower-level factory jobs do, in fact, offer generally less favorable circumstances than do better jobs for the development and maintenance of good mental health.

The occupations we are comparing clearly present markedly dissimilar opportunities for satisfying self-actualizing lives. It is not simply the objective conditions, however, but the subjective meaning of these that is crucial for mental health. To what extent are the advantages and deprivations perceived and felt as such? We shall focus on the *experienced* gratifications and frustrations of working life in the quest for explanations of occupational differences in mental health. Our central conception is that *job feelings* are crucial intervening processes between the type of work men do and their level of mental health. We expect satisfaction with the job to be associated with better mental health, dissatisfaction with poorer mental health. Beginning with this broad formulation, we shall subsequently suggest more specific interpretations regarding the kinds of job characteristics which produce the satisfactions and dissatisfactions that foster or impair mental health.

A vast body of unsystematic observation and literary reporting has called attention to the unsatisfying and allegedly dehumanizing effects of specialized production work. The frustrations, the oppressive goalless boredom and stultification of the assembly line have been repetitiously commented on, deplored, and denounced. The conjunction of these prevalent complaints with the pronouncedly poorer mental health at lower occupational levels can scarcely be fortuitous. Rather, it would seem, the expressions of job dissatisfaction mark the scars of unfulfilled desires and expectations that are particularly common at lower skill levels.

Although most of the literature of protest against the factory comes from intellectuals, working people themselves also speak out. When they do, their bitter complaints and emotional reactions to the machine, the "line," and production jobs as a whole more vividly convey a sense of the inner connection between job feelings and personal adjustment than can any compilation of statistics. In our own interviews, for example, when we asked production workers about the effects of factory work and of production jobs, not a few gave vent to such feelings as these.

It gets them in a rut; they just plug along and never get out of it. It's not very healthy for a man to work in the smoke and dust and dirt. It's made me feel like I'm in a rut, like I never did anything with my life that I could have done.

Factory work is so monotonous. You are always being told where to go and what to do. It slows them up; they can't think for themselves; they are like machines or robots. A man does the same thing over and over again so many times he just doesn't care any more. It seems I just don't care any more; I am there and that's all.

It weakens their mind. Many men when they first come here were sharp and alert; after a few years they are not the same; their mind is dull. It sure has weakened me; it has taken the life out of me. Some days I feel I'm 70 years old [actually 43].

It's dirty work and monotonous. Everyone is your boss. The work doesn't require any thinking. You more or less lose individuality; you're just part of a machine. It burns you out. When I was on production it made me too tired to enjoy anything; I couldn't even enjoy reading the newspaper.

It's just work. There are some good jobs in the factory, too, I guess but none that are really enjoyable. Most men I talk to on production work want to get off it; they are always looking for some other job. It's very tiring work; it makes you nervous. I've seen men just shake after working 10 hours on the line; they get so tired they can't control it. Also they get more jumpy and they get irritated easier. I can't put my finger on it but it brings out the nervousness in me; my stomach tightens up and my legs ache so that I get home and I can't sleep. I haven't really felt well for the last 3 or 4 years.

Production, production, production is their thought; they want to get as much out of a man as they can. Shortens a man's life. The work is hard; you're working under tension all the time; must not fall behind. The men are on edge all the time so when they get home they are crabby. Took a lot of my good health; my nerves began going even before I went in service—from the work.

I think it takes a lot of initiative out of a person; have less confidence in your ability to get out and do other kinds of work. It's just automatic, same thing over and over; gets pretty monotonous. That kind of work takes something out of you; lose initiative to try something new; get into a rut and stay there.

It affects his nerves, his home life sometimes. The continuous grind, listening to growling of machines—you are broken up, shaken. You are tired, worn down at home, start arguing. The way they work, you have to have cast-iron system. . . . If I can't fix things, I destroy them; I blow up.

To be sure, there are other workers, particularly ones on some-what more varied and responsible jobs, who find the work interesting and satisfying, affording a sense of growth, personal gratifications, and enhanced self-esteem. A few examples will convey the tone of such positive responses.

I love mechanical work; I could eat and sleep with it; was always interested in it since I was a kid. [Rates himself "completely satisfied" with his job.] The work is highly skilled [but elsewhere he estimates that a new man can learn it in 3 months]; I can do it and they know my work; it's good, it's always good. If ever there was a man that's in love with his job, I'm that man.

[Also "completely satisfied" with job], I consider myself cut out for the job; I've always been interested in electrical things. At this job I have a good time even when I work hard. I like the idea of being leader in the electrical department and seeing that my ideas are carried out. Although I work hard, I am never under pressure. Approval of department head makes me feel happy and satisfied.

I've learned quite a bit in the job. It's always something new, especially when new models come out; you learn all new ways of workin' with the interior trim. It's kind of artistic work, you know, seeing how good you can make it fit and have a nice finish. You have to use your abilities; the more you use 'em, the better the job.

I like it; there's a chance for advancement; always a chance to learn something on that kind of a job; never a dull moment. The future looks better when you're learning a trade; you got something to look forward to. There's guys been in it 20 years and they're still learning.

It's fine; I enjoy the work, seeing that everything goes well. I have a chance to be a supervisor; I'd like that. All the workers work in harmony; there's good understanding on the job; the atmosphere is pleasant. They treat us like one big happy family. They give a man credit if he finds a better way; it's an open field; it awakens me a whole lot.

Useful type of work, making cars. Like the job very well; experienced at it. Tough job comes along, they want me to do it. Like the job and good at it. Good pay, good hours; a couple buddies I like to see.

In Chapter 8 we shall examine the evidence on job feelings more fully and try to arrive at a balanced evaluation of such diverse attitudes as the foregoing. Here we wish only to call attention to the intensity and variety of individual feelings invested in the job and the subjective importance that these feelings presumably possess, positively and negatively for the workers' self-regard and total life adjustment.

The causal relationship between job satisfaction and mental health, like other relationships between molar psychological variables, is forbiddingly complex. For purposes of our empirical analysis we find it necessary to adopt a grossly simplified working model that conceives of job feelings as produced by a man's total job situation and, in turn, as the cause of mental-health effects. Job feelings are construed as an intervening link between the job and its impact on mental health. Actually, of course, the state of mental health affects job attitudes at the same time as it is affected by them; and both the job feelings and the mental health have many common causes, for example lifelong personality attributes of cheerfulness or negativism and current environmental influences on and off the job. We are dealing with a constellation of *interdependent* variables in which each is both cause and effect of others. If this is understood and kept in mind, it still may be useful to center attention on the one particular linkage we have designated within the causal network.

Figure 1 presents this conceptual framework in schematic form. The main causal process is depicted as flowing from left to right, represented by the solid lines and heavy arrows. Other causal relationships are suggested by the lighter arrows indicating effects in a reverse direction and reciprocal interdependencies among the processes within the large rectangles. Our focus on occupational variables and their effects is shown in the dotted rectangles and connecting dotted lines. The central working hypothesis is that differences at a bring about differences at b which, in turn, have significant effects on c and d. Our empirical inquiry concentrates on these portions of the total picture.

In order to focus the analysis on the effects of *occupational differences*, we make the usual "other things being equal" type of assumption in regard to workers' personal backgrounds and present make-up. We assume, in this instance, that all these other determinants of satisfaction and mental health are sufficiently similar from one occupational group to another so that they do not exert serious differential effects that distort or obliterate the job-level effects. Our earlier analysis of the effects of prejob personal characteristics on mental health (Chapter 3) offers some justification for this assumption. Parallel comparisons with respect to job satisfaction yield similar results (the tables are not shown here). With this view, then, that job-level factors produce measurable differences of both job satisfaction and mental health, the question to be asked of our data is whether the two sets of effects are so correlated that

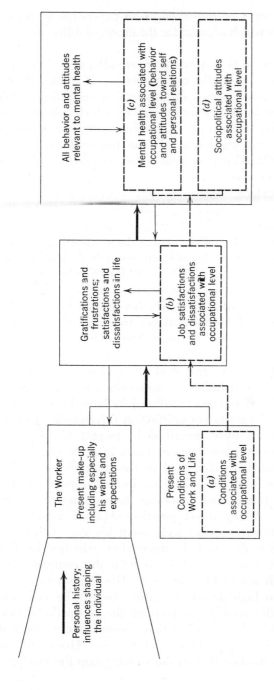

Figure 1   *A schematic representation of the place of job satisfaction and dissatisfaction as determinants of mental health.   (The present study deals with the relationships of a, b, c, and d represented by the dotted lines end boxes.)*

job satisfaction may be construed as an expression of gratifications and frustrations which account for the observed differences of mental health.

The first step is to test whether overall job satisfaction shows relationships that satisfy the requirements. If it does, we can then proceed to analyze degrees of satisfaction regarding *specific job factors* in order to obtain indications of which job characteristics appear especially influential in causing better or poorer mental health at different job levels. If the proposed interpretation in terms of job satisfaction is to be accepted, several statistical relationships should hold true.

In the first place, amount of job satisfaction should vary by occupational level in a manner paralleling the mental-health differences. Satisfaction should be more frequently reported as we ascend the occupational scale. This cannot be assumed as a matter of course since satisfaction depends on people's desires, expectations, and manner of perceiving their lot as well as on objective conditions. Wants may exceed means of gratification and cause dissatisfaction at all levels. The question is whether people in lower jobs *feel* their deprivations and disadvantages more or whether they contentedly "adapt" to their circumstances. Our results reveal that large differences of job satisfaction do occur between categories of factory occupations. A great deal of previous research uniformly supports the same conclusion.[1] More skilled jobs have higher proportions of satisfied workers; routine jobs have lowest proportions. The pattern in respect to job satisfaction corresponds to the occupational gradient we have described in respect to mental health. Summary figures from our data are shown in Table 5-1.

The job-satisfaction index used in the comparisons of this table combines eleven separate indicators, including responses to direct questions and volunteered favorable and unfavorable comments about the job. A key direct question obtained a five-point self-rating of how the respondent feels about his job. Other questions inquired whether the work is interesting, whether he thinks of leaving the job, how satisfied he is with the company, with his wages, and with use of his abilities.[2] The scores run from strong dissatisfaction to high degrees of satisfaction. The table makes it apparent that the relative positions of the occupational categories on the job satisfaction-dissatisfaction dimension are identical with their standing in respect to mental health. The correspondence extends even to the fact that in the young group the machine-paced

Table 5-1 Comparison of job satisfaction and mental health by occupational groups

Occupational Category	Young			Middle-aged		
	"High" on Job-Satisfaction Index	"High" on Mental-Health Index	Number of Workers*	"High" on Job-Satisfaction Index	"High" on Mental-Health Index	Number of Workers*
Detroit factories						
Skilled	67%	58%	33	78%	56%	45
High semiskilled				70	41	98
Ordinary semiskilled	54	35	46	66	38	82
Repetitive semiskilled	23	10	30	40	26	78
(Repetitive machine-paced only—*subdivision of preceding category*)	(27)	(7)	(15)	(28)	(16)	(32)
Small-town factories						
High and ordinary semiskilled	61	50	18	81	62	21
Repetitive semiskilled	22	33	18	36	46	22
Detroit nonfactory						
High semiskilled	82	68	28	...	...	3
Ordinary semiskilled	60	70	20	60	39	43
White-collar employees	68	75	40	75	54	28

* Totals on which the percentages are based.

workers do not differ appreciably from other repetitive workers in either satisfaction or mental health, and that among the middle-aged the two measures again agree inasmuch as both are lower for the machine-paced than for unpaced workers.

Data from small-town nonfactory and white-collar groups show roughly similar agreement. The only two exceptions are the groups of routine small-town workers whose job satisfaction is considerably lower relative to other groups than is their mental health. The nonjob activities and relationships of these men—on their farms and in small community settings—are presumably more satisfying and more conducive to mental health than are the nonjob activities of city workers. By the same token, they are likely to experience greater dissatisfaction with the contrasting impoverishment of life on the job.

In general, Table 5-1 shows that the first test question put to our data is satisfactorily answered. Amount of job satisfaction does vary by occupational levels in the manner required if it is to be of help as an explanation of the occupational variations of mental health.

The next question is whether the more satisfied workers are also the ones in better mental health. We already adduced evidence that this is true for the total group of factory workers. In Table 3-6, when men of high and low mental health are compared on the index of job satisfaction, it is seen that much greater proportions of those in good mental health are satisfied with their jobs. Stating the relationship conversely, we find that among the young men 56 per cent of those above average in job satisfaction have high mental health contrasted with only 13 per cent of those having below average job satisfaction. Among the middle-aged, the corresponding comparison shows 45 per cent to 28 per cent having high mental health (23 per cent to 54 per cent have *low* mental health).

Beyond these overall relationships, however, if the better and poorer mental health of occupational groups is tied to feelings toward the job, we should find the two measures associated for individuals within each occupational category as well as across categories. That is, the satisfied should tend to have higher mental health than their dissatisfied fellow workers doing similar work. This further test is needed since the correspondence of percentages shown in Table 5-1 could occur and yet there might be no causal connection between job satisfaction and mental health. To mention one such possibility, it might be that quite different aspects of jobs are responsible for satisfaction (say wages and agreeable treatment by the supervisor) and for mental health (say challenging opportunities for personal development and advancement), with no correlation between satisfaction and mental health except that provided by the linkage between the two sets of job characteristics when skilled and less skilled jobs are compared. In this event, for comparisons at each skill level where wages, supervision, and opportunities are relatively homogeneous, the indirect linkage of satisfaction and mental health would tend to disappear. If the correlation does not disappear, if the two variables still go together within each occupational category, the likelihood is increased that differences of job feeling have a direct bearing on mental health rather than their being separate and independent effects of job level.

The second test question, then, asks whether the association between job satisfaction and mental health does, in fact, persist among men at each skill level. The answer is again affirmative; the better satisfied do have higher mental-health scores on the average at each separate occupational level (Table 5-2). The one

Table 5-2   Proportion of workers having "high" mental health by occupational level for groups above and below average in job satisfaction

Occupational level	Job Satisfaction of Young			Job Satisfaction of Middle-aged		
	Above Average	Below Average	Total	Above Average	Below Average	Total
Skilled				60% (35)	40% (10)	56% (45)
} 68% (22)*	36% (11)	58% (33)				
High semiskilled				48 (69)	24 (29)	41 (98)
Ordinary semiskilled	52 (25)	14 (21)	35 (46)	35 (54)	43 (28)	38 (82)
Repetitive semiskilled	43 (7)	0 (11)	10 (00)	38 (23)	18 (44)	26 (73)

* Figures in parentheses show the number of cases in each cell on which the accompanying percentage is based.

exception that appears in the table (the middle aged ordinary semi-skilled) falls into line when we count the number of *low* mental health instead of the high only (30 per cent of the satisfied and 50 per cent of the dissatisfied have low mental health).   In this group as in all others, that is, men of below average job satisfaction have a substantially larger proportion of low mental health than do those above average in job satisfaction.   Even though some of the percentages in the table are based on extremely few cases (for example, there are only 7 young workers in repetitive jobs who are satisfied and only 11 in upper-level jobs who are dissatisfied), the results are consistently in the required direction.

We conclude that a genuine relationship exists between job satisfaction and mental health among workers in the separate job categories.   A further consequence of the results described here, in conjunction with those of Table 5-1, is that highest mental health occurs among the well-satisfied workers at top skill levels (60 and 68 per cent high mental health for middle-aged and young respectively) and lowest mental health is found among the dissatisfied at the most routine semiskilled level (18 and zero per cent respectively having high scores).

We come now to a third and final way in which we shall look at our data in order to decide whether job satisfaction helps to account for mental-health differences between occupations.   The analysis follows this reasoning: if job satisfaction is to be judged an explanatory factor, the groups above and below average satisfaction, considered separately, should show decreased mental-health differ-

ences between occupations. In other words, if job satisfaction is an
intervening variable that helps to explain the relation between occupational level and mental health, then the relation between these two
variables should be diminished when job satisfaction is held constant.
Specifically, since we are particularly interested in mental-health
effects at lowest job levels, let us ask whether men who are *satisfied*
in such work differ much from the satisfied in higher level work.
If job satisfaction is indeed a crucial variable, this difference should
be small compared to that for the entire occupational groups, satisfied and dissatisfied together.

In the extreme case, if occupational groups differed in mental
health solely because of differences in proportions of satisfied workers,
the occupational differences would tend to vanish within groups
homogeneous in respect to job satisfaction. Although our results
do not approach this extreme condition, they do demonstrate that
controlling job satisfaction produces an effect in the required direction (Table 5-2). Among the job satisfied in both age groups the
proportion in good mental health at the lowest job level approxi
mates the proportions at the next higher level more closely than
is true for the total group. Percentages of good mental health in
the lowest occupational group compared with all those above are,
for the young group as a whole, 10 per cent to 44 per cent; for the
job satisfied alone, the difference decreases to 43 per cent versus 60
per cent. Corresponding figures for the middle-aged are, in the total
group, 26 per cent to 43 per cent, and in the satisfied subgroup,
38 per cent to 46 per cent. If we consider only those having *poor*
mental health (not shown in the table), the results are more
extreme. Indeed, among the satisfied in routine jobs (middle-aged
group), there are actually *fewer* of low mental health than among
the satisfied in all higher level jobs combined (14 per cent versus
25 per cent).

By the same reasoning as the foregoing, *dissatisfied* workers in
more skilled jobs should not differ as greatly in mental health from
those in lower occupations as do relatively skilled workers taken
as a whole. This, too, is found to be true for the middle-aged group,
though not for the young where, as observed above, there are only
11 cases of dissatisfied in the top two groups which makes the
percentages highly unreliable. Within the middle-aged sample,
45 per cent of the total group of skilled and high semiskilled workers
have good mental health compared to 32 per cent of all less skilled.
Among the dissatisfied there is no difference at all in mental health,
only 28 per cent having high mental health in both the higher and

lower occupational groupings. The *dissatisfied* workers in the top two groups, in fact, have poorer mental health than the *satisfied* of the two low semiskilled categories.

Summary

The preceding analysis can be summarized as follows. Jobs in which workers are better satisfied are conducive to better mental health; jobs in which larger numbers are dissatisfied are correspondingly conducive to poorer average mental health. Moreover, in each occupational category the better satisfied individuals enjoy better mental health than those less satisfied. Finally, the satisfied in lowest-level jobs have mental-health scores similar to those of workers in higher jobs, and the dissatisfied among skilled and high semiskilled workers tend to resemble the lower-skill groups (this last for middle-aged only). The evidence as a whole accords with the hypothesis that gratifications and deprivations experienced in work and manifested in expressions of job satisfaction and dissatisfaction constitute an important determinant of workers' mental health. Our interpretation is that job conditions impinge on working people's wants and expectations to produce satisfactions and frustrations which in turn give rise to favorable or unfavorable perceptions of self-worth, opportunities for self-development, and prospective gratification of needs. These effects are reflected in the occupational mental-health differences revealed in our assessments.

While the results indicate that feelings of job satisfaction and dissatisfaction enter into the explanation of occupational mental-health differences, these feelings as measured by our index by no means fully account for the mental-health variations. Even within groups more extremely satisfied or dissatisfied, some differences of mental health persist between the higher and lower occupations. This signifies either that job satisfaction is not adequately measured by the index or that it is only one part of the explanation. Both are probably true. Other explanatory factors independent of job feelings might include, for example, differences of education, group values, and philosophy of life among occupational groups and differences of their circumstances, stresses and opportunities away from work. We shall have more to say concerning these other variables in later chapters. First, however, in the next chapter, we shall pursue the inquiry regarding sources of satisfaction and dissatisfaction on the job and the relation of these to mental health.

6.

Job-level characteristics that make
for better or poorer mental health

What makes jobs at higher skill levels more psychologically health-ful than lower-level jobs? What characteristics of work and employment relations are most responsible for the mental-health effects revealed in our assessments? The question lies at the heart of our study. It is crucial both for purposes of understanding the nature of occupational effects on mental health and for planning industrial changes in the interests of improved mental health. We tackle the question within the interpretative framework previously sketched. The working assumption is that the attributes of occupations have differing significance as sources of gratification or deprivation and correspondingly as determinants of mental health and that the differences are reflected in workers' expressions of satisfaction and dissatisfaction in regard to these job characteristics.

The analysis will parallel that employed in Chapter 5 dealing with the general job-satisfaction index. Once again it is necessary to keep in mind the complex patterns of causal interdependencies. Men's attitudes toward particular job conditions constantly inter-mesh with feelings about other aspects of the entire work situation, and these job-related attitudes not only affect mental health but are at the same time partially determined by it. Furthermore, each person's job feelings and mental health are joint effects of his personality and total life situation. To cut through the baffling intricacies of this reality we are forced to deal with abstracted and limited facets of the whole. Accordingly, we address ourselves to the simplified form of question suggested above: what are some principal characteristics of higher- and lower-level factory jobs that elicit favorable and unfavorable subjective reactions which help to

90

account for the observed differences in mental health among the occupations?

We have chosen nine key characteristics of jobs—or clusters of characteristics—for this analysis. They will be dealt with briefly in the order listed.

Job security
Physical conditions of job; work surroundings
Pay as such (as distinguished from last item on the list)
Use of abilities; interesting work
Repetitiveness and machine-pacing
Speed and intensity of work
Social conditions; supervision; coworkers; company
Job status and advancement opportunities; importance of the work
Income; pay as means of economic gratification

A good case can be argued for the causal potency of any or all of these as determinants of mental health. Indeed each has its advocates and its detractors. Witness the unending controversy over the alleged importance or unimportance of wages as a determinant of workers' morale. Or the readiness in some quarters to make "human relations" the panacea for ills of working life. Our own theoretical inclination is to emphasize the potential importance of all the job attributes, with recognition that the actual influence of some remains fairly constant while others shift considerably with time and circumstance. After reporting the empirical findings we shall return to further discussion of this concept.

The job levels referred to throughout this report obviously differ on several, if not all, of the job characteristics listed. Since many of the characteristics exert their influence simultaneously in any particular job, some procedure must be adopted for assessing their separate contributions. Ideally, the psychologist might like to manipulate the job factors, one at a time, in order to observe resulting changes of attitudes and mental health. The feasibility of such experiments that would compare the singular effects of the several influences is doubtful to say the least. In the absence of experimental controls, we shall attempt to weigh the separate influences by means of statistical crossrelations between mental health and workers' feelings or attitudes toward the different job attributes.

Each of the nine sets of factors is represented in our study by one or more indicators of attitude pertaining to the given cluster. We shall examine the relationships between these measures of job feeling and the assessments of mental health by applying the same three analytical tests used in the preceding chapter in reference to the general job-satisfaction index.   Restated, the tests are the following.

1. Is satisfaction in regard to the specified occupational character-istic more common at higher job levels than at lower levels?   If so, the correspondence with the occupational mental-health gradient carries a suggestion that this job attribute may contribute to the mental-health differences.   If there is no such correspondence, this creates a tentative presumption that the job characteristic does not help to account for the superior mental health in upper versus lower occupations.   This test alone is not decisive, however, since feeling toward the job attribute may not correlate with mental health, or may interact with other job-level factors either to augment or suppress the effect under study.

2. Do feelings concerning the job characteristic correlate with mental-health scores of individuals within single occupational cate-gories?   To the extent that this occurs, the probability is increased that this factor exerts a direct influence on mental health; insofar as the relationship is not found, the inference follows that such feelings do not directly influence mental health.

3. The decisive test, dependent on the preceding relationships, asks whether groups homogeneous in respect to the particular set of job feelings show diminished mental-health differences between occupations.   Taking subgroups that have relatively uniform feelings concerning the attribute in question should remove a major portion of whatever influence was exerted by variations of the attitude.   In short, by partially eliminating the influence of a presumed causal link between job level and mental health, we can determine whether this variable does in fact help to account for occupational differences in mental health.   If this procedure does not decrease the occupa-tional differences in mental health, the characteristic apparently does not play a significant part in producing the differences.[1]

We shall ask these analytical questions insofar as the pertinent data regarding each job characteristic permit.   Since in a number of instances the tests have to be applied rather loosely and incon-clusively, we shall supplement them by citing qualitative evidence as well.   The series of analyses will demonstrate that attitudes toward the several job characteristics are decidedly dissimilar in the degree to which they are related to the mental-health variations under study. Workers' feelings toward some of the job attributes show surprisingly little linkage either to occupational level or to mental health or both. In these instances it can therefore be considered improbable that the factor is responsible in any significant degree for job-level effects on mental health. This is true, in fact, of the first three of the nine characteristics listed earlier; they turn out to have almost no explanatory power in respect to occupational differences.

Feeling of job security

Concern regarding job security was expressed by equal proportions of men at all skill levels. The measure of concern consists of an index based on respondents' volunteered complaints in regard to unsteady work and layoffs, on reports of worry about losing their jobs, and on unsolicited mention of employment security as a national problem. Among the middle-aged men the percentages evidencing any feelings of job insecurity on the index, from high to low skill levels, were 44, 49, 51, and 47 per cent. Proportions who indicate more serious concern similarly show no trend by occupation; from high to low skill levels, the figures are 11, 16, 15, and 16 per cent. Among the young workers (with less seniority to protect them), the percentages of slight or serious concern are 58, 67, and 47 per cent; of serious concern alone, 15, 30, and 20 per cent. For both age groups it is apparent that there is no clear correspondence between job level and extent of insecurity feelings. Consequently, such feelings do not by themselves contribute in a direct way to the observed differences of mental health between occupations.

The results can be interpreted as the product of a strict seniority system of job tenure and perhaps a recognition that plant shutdowns or removals affect all employees. The less skilled feel no more threatened than those of higher skill. At least this appears to have been the feeling in 1953–1954. We do not know how the experiences of automation and unemployment during the past few years may have changed prevailing attitudes. At that time it is noteworthy that spontaneously expressed attitudes were preponderantly favorable in respect to job security at all skill levels among these men who had a minimum of three years seniority. Even at the two lower job levels, positive comments outnumbered the negative almost four to one in the middle-aged group and two and a half to one among young men.

The conclusion that fear of losing one's job is unrelated to *occupational group differences* of mental health says nothing about the mental health of *individuals* in relation to feelings of job security. As a matter of fact we find a definite tendency for persons concerned about unemployment to have lower mental-health scores or, conversely, for those of poorer mental health more often to evince anxiety on this matter. Over half of all workers who express considerable concern are in the low mental-health category as contrasted with only one-fourth of those who remain unconcerned about their job security. Moreover, the relationship is similarly positive, with minor inconsistencies, in the separate age and occupational categories (test 2 above).

When we apply the decisive third analytical test, however, it turns out that mental-health differences among occupations are only slightly affected by the variations of security feelings among individuals, and the effects that do appear run counter to an explanation of occupational differences as due to insecurity feelings. The occupational gradient persists almost unchanged in the young group and among middle-aged workers who feel secure about their jobs. Among the middle-aged who are more concerned about their job security, the ones in lowest semiskilled jobs have no poorer mental health than those in the two next higher job categories. Consequently, the relatively poor mental health observed at low occupational levels cannot be attributed at all to job insecurity feelings.

In sum, the entire detailed analysis indicates that under the conditions prevailing in the automobile industry at the time of our study, job security feelings, though related to the mental health of individuals, are not a factor in explaining occupational differences in mental health.

Attitudes toward physical conditions of work

Expressions of dissatisfaction regarding dust, dirt, heat, noise, and other features of the work environment are as common at upper-level jobs as at lower (proportions of men commenting negatively, from high- to low-skill categories, are: middle-aged, 31, 29, 22, and 30 per cent; young, 33, 11, and 30 per cent.) *Favorable* feelings are decidedly *less* frequent at the upper skill levels (middle-aged percentages: 9, 15, 26, and 29 per cent; young: 6, 30, and 30 per cent). This may occur because some of the favorable comments by lower-skilled workers are offered in a spirit of defensiveness, as if to say, "after all, there *are* some good things about the job." At higher-skill levels, on the contrary, agreeable surroundings tend to be taken for granted and not noted since there are more salient positive work characteristics to mention with pride. In any event it is clear that satisfied or dissatisfied feelings about work surroundings do not vary in agreement with occupational mental-health differences but, in fact, that they run slightly in the opposite direction. Moreover, in the case of this variable, there is no consistent or sizeable correlation with individual mental health within occupational categories (test 2) and no relationship at all of the kind specified in test 3 as evidence of a causal connection. The conclusion follows that physical working conditions do not elicit positive and negative attitudes that bear significantly on the higher or lower mental health of our occupational groups.

Wages

Feelings about wages present an interesting paradox. Satisfaction or dissatisfaction with pay does not differ among our occupational groups but this is decidedly not true of feelings in regard to the economic pinch associated with limited income. Resolution of the apparent inconsistency requires that a distinction be made between attitudes toward pay as such and pay as means for providing economic gratifications. As one worker, well satisfied with his wage, expressed it: "The pay is fair but you need a lot to live." At this point our focus is solely on feelings toward "wages as such"; later we shall deal with income problems or wages as economic means. Considered in the narrower sense, wages do not contribute to the differential mental-health effects of higher and lower occupations.

The most direct evidence comes from a question that inquired how well satisfied the men were with their wages. Responses reveal no tendency whatsoever for more skilled, better-paid workers to express greater satisfaction. The proportions of those well satisfied and dissatisfied are almost identical throughout the range of occupations studied, save that among the younger men the lowest skill group actually has the *highest* rate of satisfaction (percentages well satisfied, from high to low occupations: young, 36, 33, and 50 per cent; middle-aged 51, 48, 54, and 51 per cent).   These results are fully consistent with the well-established psychological generalization that people's perceptions and feelings are always determined by their varying subjective norms and frames of reference as well as by the objective reality.   Working people at more skilled levels receive higher wages to be sure but they also have higher expectations; they compare their pay with that of other workers of similar job status and training.   The same is true of men in low-skill positions; their standards of what is fair and proper compensation are such that as a group they experience no greater feeling of deprivation or disadvantage than do men in better-paying jobs.   In view of these facts, wages as such can not be considered a probable cause of the mental-health differences found to exist among occupational groups.

Comparison of *individuals* again reveals an extremely slight tendency for the dissatisfied persons in each ocupational category to have lower mental-health scores (test 2).   The relationship is less pronounced than that for total job satisfaction, for concern over job security, and for a number of other job feelings yet to be examined.   The comparisons called for in test 3 likewise fail to reveal any indication that feelings in regard to wages are responsible for occupational group differences of mental health.

Workers' volunteered comments also tend to support a negative conclusion in regard to feelings about wages as an explanation of mental-health variations by occupation.   In the early portion of the interview which dealt with the respondent's attitudes toward his life situation as a whole, without any indication of particular interest in the job area, fewer than one-fourth of the men mentioned wages. Approximately half of the references were favorable, half unfavorable.   A few more men in the lowest occupations express dissatisfaction than in better-paid jobs but the numbers are too small to demonstrate a trend.   Somewhat larger numbers speak of wages in the ensuing part of the interview when asked what they like and dislike about their jobs.   Even here, slightly less than half the men make any reference to wages, with two-thirds of the references favorable.   Although the proportion of favorable comments proves to be significantly greater at the upper occupational levels, the data fail to show any tendency for those expressing dissatisfaction to have lower mental health than their noncomplaining fellow workers. It follows that the volunteered feelings concerning wages, like the more formal ratings of wage satisfaction, do not help to account for the poorer mental health of people in lower factory occupations.

A warning is appropriate before we leave the foregoing conclusions. The results do not mean that pay is unimportant! Loose over-generalizations to this effect are all too common in the literature of industrial psychology, generalizations that do not stand up under critical scrutiny.[2] The findings here as in other studies are severely limited to the types of groups compared, the conditions, criteria of judgment, and methods of measurement. The conclusions stated above have to do with the effects of wage satisfaction on the mental health of factory workers; they say nothing about effects on contentment or on attitudes and morale in respect to company or union. Furthermore, we are dealing with auto workers whose wage scales are fairly uniform and stabilized by classes of work and are established and policed within a mature and accepted union-management relationship. What we find is that feelings about pay are not an important determinant of occupational mental health *under these circumstances*. But wages *can* loom very large indeed in working people's emotional reactions if their own pay appears unfair, sharply inadequate, or subject to arbitrary decisions according to their standards.

Extensive studies of working people under varied wage conditions will be required before conclusions can be drawn as to mental-health effects of exceptionally high or low pay and of situations where intense dissatisfaction prevails. It may be that concern over wages leads to vigorous effort for change rather than to anxiety, frustration, impaired self-esteem, or other symptoms of poor mental health. Our research unfortunately provides no evidence on such alternative effects since the varied conditions in regard to pay did not exist. On one important aspect of the matter, however, we shall have more to say later in this chapter when we come to consider wages in terms of the personal economic problems people experience. Conclusions concerning wages as *income* and *means to economic gratifications* may look very different from the indications confined to "wages as such."

Use of workers' abilities

In sharp contrast to the preceding three job characteristics which yield essentially negative conclusions, the next set of job variables proves to have strikingly positive bearing on mental-health differences among occupations. It is the cluster of characteristics pertaining to use of abilities and interest in the work performed. These attributes, of course, would be expected to relate closely to degrees of skill and variety of work operations represented by our four-level classification of jobs. The expectation is fully confirmed.

Responses to a question whether the job "gives you a chance to use your abilities" leave no doubt that men in higher and lower factory positions feel decidedly differently about this aspect of their work. Affirmative answers drop sharply from the skilled category to the routine semiskilled. Among middle-aged workers, percentages for the four occupational levels are 98, 73, 65, and 24 per cent (and for machine-paced, 19 per cent); in the young group, 79 (skilled and high semiskilled together), 62, and 17 per cent (machine-paced, 13 per cent). This is the steepest gradient exhibited on any question. Very similar results are obtained in response to an inquiry whether the job is interesting and enjoyable. Both questions indicate clearly that subjective feelings and perceptions correspond to the actual skill, variety, and responsibility of the jobs held. The extremely low proportions of favorable replies among the routine, repetitive workers is particularly noteworthy.

The next question is whether responses of this kind are related to mental health. They definitely are. For example, among middle-aged in the lowest-level jobs, three times as many of the men who feel that the work does not use their abilities have low mental-health scores as is true of those who feel that their abilities are used (53 per cent to 18 per cent). At the two upper skill levels, likewise, there are twice as many of low mental health among those who do not feel that the job uses their abilities (48 per cent to 25 per cent). In the case of the young workers, the number of negative replies at upper skill levels and of favorable replies at the lowest level is too small to permit useful comparisons within the separate job categories. However, if we combine the lowest two occupational groups as well as the top two, the relationship is found to be similar to that for the middle-aged. Here the contrast is sharper by percentages of higher mental health: for men in low-level jobs, those who feel that their abilities are used have 45 per cent high mental health to 10 per cent for others; at upper levels, it is 65 per cent to 28 per cent. In general, then, a strong positive association exists between workers' perceived use of their abilities and their mental health even within the same or similar types of work. Parallel

*Table 6-1   Proportions of high mental health by occupational
level and feeling regarding use of abilities*

| | Feel Abilities Are Used | | | | | |
| | Young | | | Middle-aged | | |
Occupational Level	Yes	No or Doubtful	Total*	Yes	No or Doubtful	Total*
Skilled				53% (43)	... (1)	55% (44)
} Skilled / High semiskilled	65% (26)†	28% (7)	58% (33)			
High semiskilled				48 (71)	23 (26)	41 (97)
Ordinary semiskilled				36 (53)	43 (28)	38 (81)
} Ordinary / Repetitive semiskilled	45 (31)	10 (40)	25 (71)			
Repetitive semiskilled				35 (17)	23 (53)	26 (70)

* The totals are slightly smaller than those in earlier tables because of missing or unclassifiable answers.
† Figures in parentheses show the number of cases in each cell on which the accompanying percentage is based.

results are found in respect to workers' reports of how interesting or dull their jobs are.

The third statistical test question is also answered affirmatively: occupational mental-health differences decrease, as required, when comparisons are made separately for workers who feel that their abilities are used and for those who feel the opposite (Table 6-1). The shrinkage is most pronounced among men who feel that their abilities are not used; indeed in the middle-aged group the occupational gradient of mental health disappears entirely. It is likewise considerably reduced among men who feel that their abilities are used (this becomes especially apparent when low mental-health scores are also compared[3]).

The statistical analysis as a whole leaves no doubt of the relationship: *workers' feeling regarding the use of their abilities is unmistakably associated with the superior mental health of the group in higher factory jobs and the poorer mental health at low job levels.* The evidence, as we interpret it, means that these job attitudes are a particularly important factor accounting for occupational mental-health differences.

Our interviews contain a number of volunteered comments that illustrate the subjective importance and poignant meaning of the job aspects under discussion. In the initial portion of the interview when the respondent was encouraged to talk about his life situation as a whole, with no hint that the interviewer had any particular interest in work-related attitudes, few ideas were expressed concerning as specific and ordinarily unverbalized a matter as the opportunities for self-expression and use of abilities afforded by the job. Nevertheless, the few comments of this kind that do appear are preponderantly positive in the upper occupational groups and negative in the lowest groups. When subsequent parts of the interview inquired more directly as to what was liked and disliked about the job, somewhat more frequent references to these job attributes occurred and again they are consistently related to occupational level. For young and middle-aged combined, only 2 per cent of the men in the two top occupational groups comment unfavorably concerning the dullness, lack of interest, and monotony of their work; in the ordinary semiskilled jobs the figure is 12 per cent and for routine work it rises to 28 per cent. Counting ideas expressed instead of the number of individuals, we find that of all volunteered references to job interest, 97 per cent are in a positive direction among skilled and high semiskilled, 72 per cent among ordinary semiskilled, and only 33 per cent among routine semiskilled.

The feeling tone of many such spontaneous remarks is conveyed by statements like the following.

I like the job; it's interesting, you see progress, new devices, new methods. Every job is a different one, not boring; get satisfaction from completing a satisfactory job, a *good* job.

It's a good job. You have an opportunity to use your own judgment, first to learn how to set up jobs and secondly to learn to improve on setups. Sometimes you run into problems that really need figuring and experimentation in order to lick them and I never feel better than after working on a job for 2 or 3 days and suddenly getting the desired results.

I enjoy the work; I've gone back to it gladly after being in business for myself. It's something new all the time, something different every day. You have to use ingenuity on it at times; you have to use your head all the time.

The job gives me a chance to learn something that may help me in the future. I enjoy doing it; it's precision work which makes you feel good about doing it; takes more know how than the previous job I had. I try to find out new or better ways of doing the work.

It's interesting because you put something together. Time goes fast. I can use my hands; I can find out what things will fit right; I can use tools. The job is a challenge to me; I like to find the best way things will go together. It gets very exciting at times; I am at the end of the line where the repairs have to be done.

By way of contrast, the darker side of the picture is represented by the following examples.

When you're there 23 years you get fed up with the monotonous routine. We've had some men crack up. No variety; same old thing all the time.

Monotonous, not too interesting, mostly same thing all the time; same routine every day, over and over. Nothing in particular I like about it; just a job.

It's a job; no better, no worse than most. At times it gets on your nerves, going to work and doing the same thing. I can get my production out fast and then sit around. I hate having to go to work every single day. I could train a man to do my job in a couple of hours.

Just a job. I can do it, that's about all I like about it. Just do the same thing over and over again and it is very dull. (What satisfaction?) Just getting my pay on the weekend.

It's OK; a little monotonous at times but it's fairly easy. It doesn't require any brains. I do the same darn thing 5 days a week and 40 hours a week; it gets very tiresome and time just drags along. I just operate a press and any dope can do what I do.

I dread the very fact of going in day after day; it's the same routine. You just stand in one place all day; it's like going around in circles; there's no end to it, it's so monotonous. Anyone can do it. You just keep making more and more pieces; it seems to be useless.

On the face of it, the conclusion that a mentally healthful job is one that is interesting and affords opportunity for self-actualizing use of one's abilities seems consonant with general experience and commonsense judgments as well as with a central theme of ego psychology. Although this does not make it true, of course, the agreement is reassuring. Results that revealed no such relationship would surely be suspect. We shall wait until other pertinent findings are presented before proposing more rounded interpretation of the kind suggested by this reference to ego motivations. At this point we emphasize simply that this particular set of job feelings appears to occupy a crucial place among the determinants of the mental health of industrial work groups.

Repetitiveness and machine-pacing of work

It would be easy to assume, as has often been done in the literature of industrial psychology, that feelings of boredom, lack of interest, frustration, and emotional maladjustment in low-skilled jobs are peculiarly the subjective accompaniments of the specialized, repetitive nature of the tasks. Caution is called for, however. Granting that the simplicity and repetitive character of such work may have important effects, this does not rule out the possibility that other attributes of the inferior jobs may be of equal or greater significance. Low-level jobs may at the same time impose greater physical strain and intensity, unsatisfactory interpersonal relations, lack of opportunity for promotion, and unacceptable economic and social status, for example. Accordingly, it is necessary to examine our data for further light on the influence exerted by all of these and other job attributes, insofar as pertinent material is available from the interview.

In this section we weigh the limited evidence at hand having to do with effects specifically dependent on simplicity, repetitiveness, and pacing of work operations. Are these the characteristics of work that rob jobs of interest and psychological healthfulness? Is it these that deprive production workers of a sense of personal significance, accomplishment, and self-fulfillment in work? The overall testimony of our data is that these factors do play a part but not an outstanding part. By themselves they are incapable of providing adequate explanation for the large subjective variations of work feelings and mental health in different occupations. Their influence is not negligible but neither is it great.

Illustrative evidence can best begin with a reminder of certain gross facts already reported. Men in routine, repetitive factory jobs are found to have lowest mental health as well as least job satisfaction, least interest in their work, and most feeling that their abilities are not being used. If these results are due to the simplified and repetitive character of low-level jobs, a further differentiation should occur among such jobs according to the *degree* to which these attributes are present. One convenient indicator of this degree is the duration of each cycle of work operations. Employing this measure, we find that there is only an extremely slight and statistically untrustworthy association with psychological effects in the predicted direction. Of all workers in repetitive jobs, 37 per cent were engaged in operations requiring less than one minute each. Men working on these most repetitive jobs had the same proportion of high mental health as all others, though a few more were of poor mental health (51 versus 42 per cent). No difference was found between those in work with cycles of 1 to 3 minutes versus periods longer than that. The results as a whole leave serious doubt that repetitiveness as such is a major cause of adverse job effects.

But perhaps *mechanical pacing* is the more significant factor, either acting alone or in combination with short cycles of repeated operations. Machine domination, typified by the assembly line, has long been a favorite target for critics concerned with protecting human values in industry. Contrary to these indictments, however, a number of observational studies and experiments have produced evidence that working people experience less strain and monotony, that they are psychologically *better* off, when their rate of work is externally governed and carries them along without the effort of voluntary decisions to maintain the pace. This type of conclusion skirts the crucial question of whether passive adjustment and relief from tension, contented functioning as a cog in the production machine, represent a desirable human condition. Since these questions are vital and still highly controversial, it becomes particularly important to review our evidence comparing workers on paced and unpaced operations.[4]

The general findings were set forth in Chapter 4. They revealed that among *middle-aged* workers those in mechanically paced production-line operations have lower mental health on the average than those on routine jobs where the pace is not governed by the machine. We now find that this apparent effect of pacing holds true independently of the degree of repetitiveness. Middle-aged men performing paced operations of short duration have poorer mental health on the average than those engaged in nonpaced operations of like duration, and a similar effect appears where the work cycle is longer. The relationship of machine pacing to mental health fails to hold true for the young men, and again this is the case regardless of length of work cycle. The two age groups exhibit corresponding contrasts when machine-paced and unpaced workers are compared in respect to job satisfaction, interest in work, and nonuse of the worker's abilities. In each instance differences of moderate size (15 to 30 percentage points) occur for middle-aged workers in favor of those on unpaced work while parallel comparisons reveal only negligible differences among young workers. The marked discrepancy between the age groups is of special importance here because it suggests that more complex factors are involved than a simple direct influence of constrained speed of work.

Accordingly, in the earlier discussion[5] we proposed a quite different kind of speculative interpretation, emphasizing the *meaning* of low-level production-line jobs in reference to men's feelings of success or failure, their status and "life chances," their sense of personal significance. The point to be stressed is that the observed differences between men on paced or nonpaced jobs (in the middle-aged group) are not necessarily due to this designated characteristic of mechanical pacing. The job is reacted to as a whole. Since the young group is no more unfavorably affected by paced than unpaced work, the suspicion arises that for the middle-aged, too, the effects may be accounted for in some considerable part by other negative job attributes associated with pacing rather than by the pacing itself. Examples of these other possible explanatory attributes are examined throughout this chapter; they include such characteristics as the use of abilities, relations with coworkers and supervisors, and opportunities for advancement. An attempt will be made at the close of the chapter to suggest the relative importance of these various interrelated job characteristics.[6]

Two supplementary notes are added here which bear on job aspects closely linked to pacing and repetitiveness.

(*a*) Our data offer no support for the contention that ordinary and routine semiskilled workers have better mental health if their work is so automatic that their minds are free to wander. Among middle-aged workers, those who "think of other things most of the time" while at work have slightly poorer mental health than others; in the young group there is no difference in either direction. The young men who think of other things express dissatisfaction a little more frequently than their fellows, but no similar tendency is manifested by the older group. In any event both the tendencies that do appear run counter to the view that daydreaming provides a psychologically successful or beneficial way of adjustment to routine jobs. Regardless of the amount of extraneous thinking, our data indicate that mental health remains poorest in these types of work. Finally, although the middle-aged group exhibits a large difference of mental health between those on paced and unpaced tasks, no corresponding difference occurs in respect to their reports of attention required by the job or their ability to think of other things.

(*b*) Opportunity to take voluntary breaks at work is presumed to offer relief from the grind of repetitive jobs and to carry some implication of at least a moderate amount of control over the work. This variable, therefore, might be expected to make for job satisfaction and mental health. In fact, no relationship of this kind is

found.   At the routine job level, mental health is actually a little
better for those who say they *cannot* take breaks.   Those who say
they do have such opportunity compare especially unfavorably with
workers in less routine occupations.   Apparently the availability of
short discretionary interruptions of work does not make for improved
mental health.

Speed and intensity of work

The next question is whether occupational differences in satisfaction and mental health are due to speed, intensity, physical strain,
and difficulty of work.   Evidence in answer to this question is
derived from comments volunteered by respondents when they were
asked a series of free-response, nondirective questions regarding their
lives and their jobs.   Negative references to physical strain and
fatigue occur infrequently at all job levels and not a whit more
among older than among younger workers.   There is no trend by
occupation and even on the lowest production jobs fewer than one
worker in ten complains on this score.   Comments classified along
the dimension of work being considered "hard" or "easy," where
there is no reference to physical difficulty, are overwhelmingly favorable at all job levels (33 positive to 7 negative comments even in
the lowest occupational category).   Once again there is no trend
by occupations.

Specifically in reference to speed and intensity of work, negative
statements, although infrequent, do occur most often among the
people on routine repetitive jobs (17 and 14 per cent for young
and middle-aged respectively as against only 5 and 4 per cent in
all occupations above the routine category).   Dissatisfied comments
come preponderantly from men on mechanically paced jobs but
even among these workers only one in five mentions speed-ups or
work pressure and only one in ten expresses strong feelings on this
point.   Older workers voice these complaints no more often than
the young men.   And most important for the present inquiry,
mental-health scores are no worse for the men who express concern
over the pace and intensity of work than for others.   It is observed,
too, that almost as many routine workers, chiefly ones on jobs not
mechanically paced, mention how *satisfactory* their required rate of
work is.   Altogether, volunteered responses concerning speed and
difficulty of work remain decidedly equivocal as to whether these

conditions are responsible, on balance, for any considerable part of the adverse effects of jobs at lower levels.

Congruent results are obtained in reply to a question concerning the effects factory work has had "on you." Men in routine production jobs refer to excessive fatigue and the physical and nervous strains of work a little more often than do those in nonroutine jobs. Even in this lowest and most disliked type of work, however, and even in response to the leading question that invited an allegation of ill effects, only one-fifth of the men mentioned any complaints of this kind. Again the older group does not differ from the young group. The mental-health scores of men who speak of such effects are slightly lower on the average than the scores of other men in the same job category, indicating that these complaints may account in some very mild degree for the poorer mental-health showing of the low occupational group as a whole. The number of cases and the size of the statistical differences are both too small to do more than suggest the possibility of this relationship. Moreover, the findings refer mainly to particular companies since over half the complaints considered here are concentrated in two of the thirteen establishments in this analysis.

These data, together with those previously reported, do not support a belief that work in the automobile plants imposes back-breaking toil, or is so speeded and intense as to be exhausting or productive of severe feelings of mental or physical strain for more than a small fraction of workers in a small number of plants. If such effects were being widely experienced, it seems certain that they would appear much more frequently and much more bitterly than is revealed in the content of our interview material. It would also be expected that if these aspects of work were important influences on mental health, they would exhibit much clearer statistical association with the mental-health assessments.

These observations are certainly not intended to extol assembly-line work or to celebrate the companies' enlightened protection of workers' welfare. Insofar as factory jobs are now relatively free of serious mental and physical strain, insofar as workers enjoy reasonably satisfactory human conditions of production, these results have come about in considerable part through vigorous and continued labor-union efforts. Moreover, a minority of workers in special factory situations continue to perform work operations that are unduly speeded and arduous. The fact remains, we believe, supported by evidence of the kind cited, that for the great majority of workers objective work-process factors like speed, repetition, work difficulty, and mechanical pacing are not now *major* causes of negative reactions and maladjustments. While they do play a part, in and of themselves they account in only small measure for the occupational mental-health effects we are seeking to explain.

This brings us once more to the reminder that unfavorable psychological effects associated with routine jobs versus more skilled and varied ones, and with mechanically paced versus unpaced operations, may be largely due to attributes of these jobs other than the repetitiveness, pacing, and speed as such. Perhaps the disturbing features are more subtle and complex; they may have to do primarily with absence of goals and challenge, feelings of low status and doubts of personal worth, lack of opportunity for recognition and advancement, and for accomplishment, growth, and self-expression. Work that is "uninteresting" may mean not so much boredom with repetitive tasks as a feeling of not going anywhere. Protests over speed-up and wages and robotlike performance may at the same time have roots in thwarted achievement, lack of significant participation, bleak prospects for improvement, despair of *ever* developing and using one's talents. Questions of this kind will continue at the center of attention in the following sections.

Human-relations aspects of the job

The last decades have witnessed an extraordinary growth of interest in "industrial human relations." Both in progressive management circles and among psychologists and sociologists concerned with the human side of industry, heavy emphasis is now placed on the immediate social conditions surrounding the worker. Efforts to improve morale and enhance the psychological well-being of the employee have brought greatly increased attention to the small work group, the personality and leadership methods of the foreman, relations of men with their fellow workers, and company policies and practices affecting the social climate of the work place. If these influences have the importance attributed to them, our interview data should exhibit significant correlations between them and measures of mental health. Accordingly, we now inquire whether these social features of the job help account for observed mental-health differences by occupational groups and among individuals within occupational categories.

Let us begin with supervision. In brief, our findings indicate that working people's attitude toward their boss is not an influence of any great importance in regard to their mental health. In the first place, since upper- and lower-level jobs differ extremely little in this respect, it appears that this factor does not contribute in a direct way to an explanation of mental-health variations among the occupations. In the young group, no difference at all is found by job categories; in the older group, differences occur only to the limited extent of 34 per cent rating their supervisor "very good" in the upper two occupations (5 per cent giving unfavorable or ambivalent evaluations) compared to 26 per cent in the lower occupations (12 per cent unfavorable or ambivalent).

Among individuals within each occupational category a moderate but irregular association is found between favorable feeling toward the boss and good mental health (statistical test 2). The association is not close enough to indicate that the influence of supervision is other than minor. When the third statistical test is applied, which compares the mental health of occupational groups separately among men who like their supervisor and among others who do not, the results reveal no consistent effect of attitude toward supervision. Differences of mental health between occupations show little change when the influence of feelings toward supervision is thus partially eliminated.

Another question tried to determine the effects of "closeness of supervision" by inquiring whether the man "directly in charge of your work comes around often to look things over or tell you what to do." Replies show no linkage at all with either occupational or individual variations of mental health. As far as these data go there is nothing to indicate that close supervision versus greater freedom and independence on the job leads to better personal morale and mental health.

Spontaneous qualitative comments concerning supervision agree with responses to direct questions in showing that the proportions of favorable and unfavorable attitudes are nearly the same in lower-level occupations as at upper levels. It is consequently improbable that these feelings in regard to supervision contribute to the lower job satisfaction or poorer mental health found in the less skilled jobs.

Next we examine the influence of workers' feelings toward their associates on the job. Under conditions of mass-production industry one of the few remaining sources of positive enjoyment for many workers in connection with work is found in their daily contacts with "buddies." The high value working people place on this aspect of life in the plant is frequently noted by knowledgeable observers and the same conclusion follows from a number of systematic inquiries.[7] Our own data agree with previous studies. Many workers speak of these personal relations as a principal source of pleasure. The special question for our present analysis, however, is whether this attachment to associates in the work group accounts for variations of mental health from one occupational level to another.

Measures of this variable do meet the first test: as we descend the occupational scale, successively smaller proportions of workers express regard and liking for their fellows. Routine repetitive workers are especially differentiated from others in this respect. An index of favorable feelings toward coworkers (described in Appendix B) yields the following percentages of positive attitudes, going from higher to lower occupations: for the young, 55, 48, and 20 per cent; for the middle-aged, 62, 49, 56, and 37 per cent. Surprisingly, however, further analysis reveals that within each occupational category only slight relationship exists between attachment to work-group companions and mental health. Among young workers, virtually no correlation is found in any occupational category. In the middle-aged group, men having definitely positive feelings toward their fellows average only a little higher mental health than others at each occupational level. In the lowest two occupational groups, for example, 35 per cent of those with positive feelings have high mental-health scores compared to 27 per cent of others; proportions in poor mental health are 36 and 47 per cent respectively. The association is not close enough to produce any clear reduction of occupational mental-health differences when the occupational groups are compared separately for above and below average feelings toward coworkers (statistical test 3). The results as a whole force us to conclude that feelings in regard to fellow workers contribute in only extremely moderate degree to mental-health differences, either within or across occupations.

We now ask the same questions in regard to workers' attitudes toward the company as a whole and its perceived treatment of employees as have been asked in respect to other job characteristics. It is entirely possible that lower-placed employees might have greater antipathies toward the company, with or without real basis, and that this might increase the amount of dissatisfaction, social alienation, and poor mental health among them. As the results turn out, these influences, too, appear to be minor though not entirely absent.

Attitude toward the employing organization tends to be less favorable among workers in the lowest jobs but the differences are small (in the younger group, 47 per cent of routine workers express positive feelings versus 55 per cent of the other occupational groups; among the middle-aged, 59 versus 70 per cent). No differences are present among the upper three occupational categories. Within separate occupational groups small but fairly consistent relationships occur showing somewhat poorer mental health associated with ambivalent and negative attitudes toward the company. The third statistical test likewise yields a very doubtful answer: when only those workers favorable to the company are compared by occupation, or only those less favorable, mental-health differences between occupations do not diminish in the young group, and in the middle-aged sample the decrease is so irregular that no clear conclusion can be drawn.

Analysis of workers' qualitative responses concerning their companies and the treatment of employees points to conclusions in agreement with the direct quantitative findings. The comments are predominantly favorable and are very similar both in content and feeling tone from one occupational level to another, though with unfavorable ideas appearing slightly more often among workers on routine-type jobs, especially in the younger group. Spontaneous references to the company or its human-relations practices occur very infrequently and with little intensity through the earlier nondirective portion of the interview, suggesting that these matters have no great saliency for employees. Again there are no significant differences by occupation. Altogether, the evidence supports the conclusion that, within the range of establishments studied, employees' attitudes regarding the company and its policies play a relatively small part in accounting for the better or poorer mental health of groups at different occupational levels.

Mental health in relation to characteristics of companies

The preceding conclusions are not to imply that mental health is constant from company to company. The results do not rule out the possibility that occupational mental-health differences may be determined in part by the organizational setting in which men are employed. Accordingly, we adpoted a new line of inquiry. The first question now addressed to our data was this: are mental-health variations by occupation similar in factories that differ in size, proportion of routine workers, and quality of industrial relations? This analysis produced one piece of unexpectedly suggestive information. In brief, *the inferior mental health of the lowest occupational group compared to the less routine "ordinary semiskilled" occurs only in very large plants.* For the four smaller establishments (really medium-sized, three of the four having 600 to 1100 hourly employees, the other somewhat larger) there is no difference of mental health between the two lower occupational groups though they do differ from the skilled and high semiskilled. Job satisfaction relationships are similar. We also checked to see whether the contrast of large and smaller plants might be due to differences of education of the employees, which would indicate a selection influence. No such differences are found.

We label the main relationship only "suggestive" since the numbers of cases by occupation within subsamples of plants are not large enough to yield highly reliable percentages. At the same time the results present a puzzling aspect inasmuch as they seem inconsistent with findings from small-town plants. The latter were establishments of even more moderate size, yet the low occupational groups differed from each other to the same extent as in the large Detroit plants. The apparently discordant results may be reconciled if one adopts a speculative reference-group hypothesis like the following: routine workers in small Detroit plants may consider themselves relatively well off in comparison with their opposite numbers in larger establishments since the latter are rather generally viewed as occupying most unenviable positions. Routine workers in small towns, having no such ready comparison groups who are worse off, may experience more severe feelings of deprivation relative to their acquaintances who hold somewhat better jobs than their own. Whatever the interpretation, the facts again call attention to the complexity of influences associated with contrasts of mental health between occupational groups. They thus add a further note of caution against conceiving the overall occupational results, particularly the poorer mental health in low-level jobs, as a direct, more or less automatic consequence of simplified repetitive tasks as such.

In respect to the Detroit sample we are left with strong indication that the specific job attributes responsible for lower job satisfaction and poorer mental health among repetitive workers, whatever these attributes may be, operate less influentially in smaller establishments. The alleged ill consequences of repetitive machine work have long been pictured in the literature as particularly serious in giant, impersonal industrial plants. Our Detroit data accord with this expectation. It appears that there is a combined effect of low-grade occupation and large-scale organization in a metropolitan setting which goes beyond the results of similar work under more favorable circumstances.

Several parallel analyses by establishments have similar implications. When plants are grouped not by size but by proportion of workers who are on routine repetitive jobs the comparatively poor mental health of the lowest occupational category tends to disappear in companies having fewest routine jobs. The relationship is less strong than by plant size, however, and exerts little additional influence when size is ruled out. We also compared companies more favorably and less favorably regarded by employees. It is in the latter that repetitive workers' mental health is poorest, both absolutely and relative to that of the next higher occupational group.

A final set of comparisons classified companies by the estimated quality of their personnel and industrial-relations performance. The estimates were obtained by means of a systematic quantitative rating procedure. Ratings were given by six highly competent "neutral" experts (arbitrators, mediators, and academic observers) who had intimate familiarity with industrial relations in Detroit firms during the period of the study.[8] On the basis of the ratings, companies were grouped into high, medium, and low in respect to industrial relations and personnel effectiveness. Here again, it is in the low-rated companies that repetitive workers have particularly poor mental health. Since nonrepetitive semiskilled are also considerably worse, the occupational difference does not change much. Similar relationships hold true even when allowance is made for size of plants. Nevertheless, through all these comparisons, size shows up as the strongest determinant. The favorableness of human relations in the company, either in the eyes of its employees or of detached experts, apparently exerts a small additional influence on mental health at lowest job levels. A few summary figures regarding the lowest occupational group under the several conditions referred to are shown in Table 6-2 to illustrate the relationships described.

The foregoing analysis of company influence has dealt solely with differences of mental health between occupational levels. But variations of mental health *between companies* are of sufficient

*Table 6-2   Variations of mental health of repetitive workers
in relation to characteristics of the organization*

Characteristics of Organization	Percentages of Repetitive Workers Having High, Medium, and Low Mental-Health Scores			Number of Workers*
	High	Medium	Low	
Smaller plants	29%	42%	29%	24
Large plants	18	32	50	78
Large plants with high proportion of repetitive jobs	16	26	58	43
All other large plants	20	40	40	35
Large plants with unfavorable employee attitude toward company	18	28	54	50
All other large plants	18	39	43	28
Large plants rated low in industrial relations by experts	12	31	57	49
All other large plants	28	34	38	29

* Totals on which the percentages are based. Each horizontal set of three percentages totals 100 except when rounding produces a total of 99 or 101 per cent.

importance to warrant a brief departure from the concentration on occupational differences alone.   Industrial organizations as well as job levels can be expected to have differential effects on the feelings and mental health of employees.   In fact, emphasis on improvement of workers' morale through organizational channels and management efforts has dominated thought and research in the field.   But evidence regarding differences of *mental health* between companies has been extremely scanty.

Our results amply demonstrate that some industrial organizations do enjoy a condition of mental health far superior to others, even when comparisons are confined to a single industry and locality. At the same time the evidence points to some of the characteristics that distinguish companies whose employees are above average or below average in mental health.   First, a few figures will indicate the extent of variation among companies.   In the company having best mental health, among 13 Detroit automotive plants, 50 per cent of the workers score high and 17 per cent low; in the poorest one, 28 per cent are high and 53 per cent low.   The other companies spread throughout the intervening range.   Since some companies have larger proportions of skilled or high semiskilled jobs, comparisons were also made using only men in the two lower-skill categories. The differences between companies remain equally great.

Next is the question what other characteristics of companies are associated with their high or low standing in respect to mental health.   Size of company shows a little relationship (equal proportions of high mental health in large and small companies, but 38 per cent low mental health on the average in large companies as against 27 per cent in smaller companies).   The difference is somewhat greater between companies having at least a moderately good reputation for personnel administration versus those rated poor by the experts (43 per cent high mental health versus 28 per cent). However, these factors of size and quality of personnel management are linked to the educational and economic attributes of the work force.   Companies with poorer mental health are those with large numbers of employees of below-average schooling and large numbers at low levels of skill and income.   These variables exhibit approximately the same relationship to company standing in mental health as do company size and quality of personnel relations.

The foregoing relationships indicate that mental health is best in establishments that are not too large, that employ fewer workers at low levels of skill, income, and education, and that have good personnel policies and practices.   Additional information is obviously desirable as to the specific features of personnel management that contribute most significantly.   Although no definitive causal connection can be established by our results, findings that bear suggestively on the answer are contained in the varying degrees of association between companies' mental-health standing and the feelings of their employees in regard to particular aspects of work conditions and relationships in the companies.   In brief, a sampling of such relationships reveals the following: mental health tends to be higher especially in companies where greater proportions of workers express favorable attitudes toward their work as being interesting and making use of their abilities, and where more of them have positive feelings toward chances for promotion and toward their fellow workers.   Company mental-health differences are considerably less closely associated with workers' feelings in regard to supervision, job security, and the company as a whole. Almost no relationship exists with attitude toward wages.

These intercompany comparisons are all affected by the substantial differences of education and skill levels in the companies. Consequently, they must be interpreted with great caution. The relationships *suggest* that intrinsic work satisfaction, congenial work-group relations, and promotion opportunities may be factors especially meriting further attention as conducive to improved mental health within an organization. In Chapter 8 we shall deal with company variations again but with the spotlight on differences of satisfactions and attitudes instead of on mental-health assessments. Meanwhile, we resume our primary inquiry into factors that help account for differences of mental health between factory *occupational* groups.

Job status and opportunities for advancement

The idea has become popular that what working people as well as members of the middle class want above all else is "social status" and advancement to higher status. Employment in low-status jobs is portrayed as inherently frustrating or threatening such desires and hence as conducive to poorer mental health. It would be foolish to deny that people in our society do develop "status needs," that these profoundly affect their feelings of self-esteem, and color their emotional adjustments to all aspects of their life situation. We begin this section with ready acceptance of the proposition that the status of occupations is important to their incumbents and that our overall occupational differences of satisfaction and mental health can be construed as reactions in part to status attributes associated with work of different kinds. But one cannot be too sure what the statement means. The popularity of status interpretations, one suspects, arises to some degree from a convenient ambiguity which permits each interpreter to read into the concept the meanings that suit his taste. It is made a catch-all which encompasses just about any conditions that have to do with a person's position in the social system.

Let us state the issue sharply in reference to our own data. There is no doubt that jobs as a whole, or factory jobs as a subdivision, do fall into a hierarchy of the kind used in this study. The disturbing unanswered question is whether this is a "social status" hierarchy—

or to what extent it is properly so regarded.   To minimize confusion we believe it wise to restrict *social-status* interpretations to the dimension signified by such terms as prestige, social standing, esteem, regard, respect.   Jobs at higher and lower levels do differ in respect to these values; but just as surely, and at the same time, they differ in regard to many other important values.   There is scant justification for leaping to the conclusion that, merely because jobs differ in social status, it is this attribute that determines given psychological effects.

When we ask working people to tell us how they feel about factory jobs compared to other types of work, the replies carry little in the way of "social status" implications.   All the factory groups agree in viewing factory work in a predominantly unfavorable light compared with other types of employment (two-thirds of the ideas are unfavorable), but the references are rarely to opportunities for promotion or success, social gratifications, getting ahead, or other goals that even indirectly suggest emphasis on social status.   Rather, the men stress the superiority of nonfactory occupations because of better earnings, more desirable physical conditions of work, health advantages, more pleasant and interesting work activities, greater personal freedom and independence.

In a word, social status, although important, is only part of the total picture.   An employee *may* be unhappy and suffer blows to his self-esteem on a low-level job by reason of status considerations; that is, because the job is held in low repute, is generally looked down upon.   But he, or others, may equally be frustrated and disheartened because the work is physically obnoxious, uninteresting and un-challenging, stultifying and unfulfilling.   He may seek promotion and increased pay to achieve "success" and prestige; but he may also do so in order to add to his and his family's comforts and en-joyments, to secure opportunities for self-expressive activities and self-respect (not by any means synonymous with efforts to win approval and respect from others).   What has to be recognized is the *variety* of motivations that are gratified or thwarted by conditions of working life.   Status conditions intertwine with other job characteristics in a fashion that prohibits singling them out as peculiarly salient.   Opportunity to use one's abilities on the job, for example, which proves to be decisively linked to mental health, may hold significant "status" meaning for one worker though for another it carries no such connotation but has to do with workmanship im-pulses and craving for "self-actualization."

These preliminary notes on social status are inserted not to play down its significance but to stress the necessity of specifying its meaning in order that inquiry may be conducted regarding status attributes of jobs in comparison with other attributes. If job status is stretched to include everything that distinguishes higher- from lower-skilled occupations, obviously it can no longer be employed analytically in attempts to answer the question of how large status factors loom relative to other job characteristics as causes of occupational differences of mental health.

As indicators of workers' feelings about job status we shall rely principally on responses to two questions, one pertaining to importance of the job, the other to prospects for advancement. The first inquired whether the worker feels that he is doing "something important" on his job or "just putting in time." Although relatively few choose the rather strongly worded negative alternative, the proportion of such responses increases considerably at lower skill levels. This is particularly true among the young workers (9 per cent of skilled and high semiskilled and 17 per cent of ordinary semiskilled versus 60 per cent of the lowest skill group). Only 3 per cent of the middle-aged answer negatively in the upper two skill categories, 9 and 18 per cent respectively at the two lower levels. This contrast by age again reflects the persistent inclination of the middle-aged to make the best of their lot by accenting the positive.

In both age groups, men who feel that their jobs are unimportant have definitely poorer mental health on the average compared with others. The difference is greatest in the case of those in routine low-level work. In this group approximately twice as many who see their job as lacking importance have low mental-health scores in comparison with those who feel that their jobs are important (61 per cent to 25 per cent among the young, 69 per cent to 38 per cent among the middle-aged). The third statistical test previously used cannot be applied due to the vanishingly small number who say their work is not important as we go up the occupational scale. Analysis of the limited data available, however, indicates that the low mental health of the least skilled occupational groups is disproportionately accounted for by workers who feel that their jobs are unimportant. In view of the small numbers we conclude merely that there is a strong hint that feelings of job importance contribute to differences of mental health between occupations.

Unfortunately for purposes of conclusive interpretation, there is the further difficulty that responses regarding job importance refer only in part to the social-status dimension. Most workers speak rather of the usefulness of the job process, the necessity for the work in the interests of production, and the amount of individual responsibility the job entails. These answers often contain indirect hints of status feelings and a number of the replies permit somewhat more confident inferences to this effect. A few quotations will illustrate the responses and the problem of judging the extent to which they carry social status implications.

It has to be important; we keep the wheels of industry rolling, we put up and maintain all the electrical equipment.

Doing something important. The engines are built for the Navy and I image the Navy is important.

I have to stay right on the ball to see that the car is in good shape before it leaves the plant.

The job is important because the output of the plant depends on materials. There is great responsibility in taking in materials and inspecting them.

The whole production line depends on my type of work.

It's important; you are the last word. If you make a mistake, the motor isn't any good.

If it wasn't for this job there would be a lot of people minus fenders, etc. I hold the only job in the classification and nobody can step in on it.

I have to know how to load [stock tractor]. They were happy when I got back from my vacation; they had a guy who was careless.

There aren't many men that know all the jobs like I do.

It seems every time I come in late the boss worries.

Doing something important; keeps factory running. When I was out, it took two men to replace me.

There's only two men in my classification for 5000 on production.

They can't do without us. I know we walked out one time and they had to shut the plant down; the whole operation can't go on if we don't do our job.

By way of contrast, phrases like the following express the low esteem of the job in the minds of other workers.

Just putting in time. No skill required. If I dropped dead, anybody could step right in.

I'm just working for the wages; someone else could do it.

Nothing important about it.

Important to the company but not to me.

Anyone can do this job.

Just making a living. It's nothing really important, making parts for automobiles; not like developing something to make people's lives better.

In the absence of more clear-cut evidence, we interpret the responses as containing at least a partial and doubtful indication of satisfaction or dissatisfaction with the standing and reputation of the job. On this assumption, the results mean that such feelings are more negative in jobs at the foot of the semiskilled ladder and that these unfavorable feelings are somewhat associated with poorer mental-health scores.

We turn now to the second question which bears some relevance to desire for status, a question pertaining to opportunities for advancement. One part of the question asks about the man's perceived chances for promotion; another part inquires what "getting ahead" means to him. After considering the data, we shall return to the question whether the job-advancement variable is properly interpretable as meaning opportunity for *social-status* enhancement. The usual assumption is that the lowest factory occupations offer least opportunity for upward mobility, that this condition thwarts men's ambition to progress (which in part represents their desire to achieve higher social status), and consequently produces frustration and maladjustment which will appear in the form of dissatisfaction and low mental-health scores. Our data conform to these expectations to some extent but primarily in a way that helps account for variations among individuals rather than serving to explain differences among occupational categories. We do find that lower jobs are perceived, especially by younger workers, as affording less chance for advancement. The middle-aged are pessimistic about advancement at upper skill levels as well as in lower-grade jobs. The proportions who believe they have little or no chance of getting ahead run as follows, from higher to lower skill: young, 31, 41, and 69 per cent; middle-aged, 64, 60, 54, and 69 per cent. But both age groups show a difference by job levels in the number who believe that they have a *good* chance for advancement: only 6 per cent of the middle-aged at the lowest job level say they have a good chance versus 22 per cent of all others; among the young men, 19 per cent versus 38 per cent. We also find that in every occupational group the men who feel that they have little or no chance for promotion are lower in mental health on the average than those believing the chances are better.

The crucial analytical test, which asks whether occupational mental-health differences are markedly decreased when the advancement variable is ruled out, produces results that indicate a very moderate influence by this factor. Only a slight and irregular

Table 6-3   *Proportions of high mental health by occupational level and perceived opportunity for advancement*

Occupational Level	Advancement Opportunity Perceived by Young			Advancement Opportunity Perceived by Middle-aged		
	Good or Fair	Little or None	Total*	Good or Fair	Little or None	Total*
Skilled				87% (15)	37% (27)	55% (42)
⎫	60% (20)†	56% (9)	59% (29)			
High semiskilled ⎭				58 (33)	28 (50)	40 (83)
Ordinary semiskilled	44 (23)	19 (16)	33 (39)	42 (33)	31 (39)	36 (72)
Repetitive semiskilled	13 (8)	0 (19)	4 (27)	41 (22)	18 (49)	25 (71)

* The totals are slightly smaller than those in earlier tables because of missing or unclassifiable answers.
† Figures in parentheses show the number of cases in each cell on which the accompanying percentage is based.

diminution of mental-health differences occurs among occupations when we consider separately the men who feel that they have promotion chances and those who feel the opposite (Table 6-3). In the young group the drop of mental-health scores from the two upper occupations to the "ordinary semiskilled" is much steeper among those who believe they have little chance for advancement (though the small number of cases makes the finding merely suggestive). As between the two lowest groups, on the other hand, even those young repetitive workers who say that they have good or fair chances still rate very low in mental health. Among the middle-aged, the clearest fact is the sharply higher mental health in all occupational categories for those who have positive feelings concerning advancement opportunities. Contrary to what is true of the young, those of the older repetitive-work group who see chances for promotion have relatively good mental health, equal in fact to that of the group immediately above them.[9]

In short, the relationships of the advancement variable are such that no simple generalization is justified to the effect that either presence or absence of perceived opportunity for upward mobility is a condition which accounts for differences of mental health among occupational groups as a whole. Nevertheless, there do appear to be real, though diverse, effects of the kind noted in the preceding paragraph. Lack of perceived chance for advancement does not help to account for the poor mental health of repetitive workers compared with "ordinary semiskilled" among young men but does among the middle-aged. In the young group, such feelings contribute to the explanation of low scores in the two lower occupational categories compared to the more skilled but this is not true for the older group. We conclude tentatively that feelings regarding advancement, with whatever expectation of enhanced social status this may imply, do have effects on the comparative mental health of occupational groups but that the influence is neither powerful nor uniform in the two age groups.

In order to interpret the bearing of these findings in regard to social status, it is necessary to inquire further into the *meaning* workers attach to job advancement. To what extent do they perceive job advancement as signifying status enhancement rather than in terms of other desired goals? The vast majority do want a chance to get ahead, however they define it. Relatively few say that they do not care at all about advancement (12 per cent of the young, 28 per cent of the middle-aged); most declare that such opportunities are important to them (65 per cent of young, 55 per cent of middle-aged). But what does "getting ahead" mean to them? We asked this question and attempted to classify the responses in order to see how frequently desires for improved social status could be inferred from the replies. Although the material gives no conclusive answers, it does cast considerable doubt on status-oriented interpretations.

Almost all the responses fall into three categories: getting ahead means earning more money; having supervisory duties, increased responsibility and authority; advancing to more skilled work, a "better job." The first category—better pay, steady income, keeping ahead of bills, and so on—is most common; approximately half the men at every skill level give this as at least one part of their answer. Among men in the two top occupational groups, the second category is almost as popular but it is less so in the lower levels, particularly among the routine repetitive workers. The third category, with more indefinite and miscellaneous content, shows no occupational trend in the young group but increases at lower skill levels among the middle-aged. Most important for present purposes is the rarity, either within these categories or apart from them, of responses that express status concerns in even a semiexplicit manner.

It is difficult to believe that if the status meaning of advancement were at all salient this would not reflect itself in many more of the answers to the question of what getting ahead means. That responses of this kind can readily appear if the worker has such feelings is demonstrated by the occasional replies which more or less clearly indicate that advancement is seen in terms of elevated social status.   A few examples follow.

Getting a better job, a better position; more respect from employees and employer and a raise in wages.

Holding a position where your ideas are respected by all; when your opinion cannot be pushed aside by anyone; when you tell people to do things they don't question you.

Being a foreman, being a supervisor.   Better pay, better bonus, and more standing.

To be top man in the department.

Getting better off financially and materially.   My life depends on it; we look forward to it . . . rising to a higher position and station in life.

Supervision, more pay, prestige, and self-satisfaction.

Higher classification like becoming foreman.   Or a different type of job altogether in which you start at lower salary but can work up higher —increase in title and salary.

Oh, having a position of authority, a respectable position I'd say.

To be a supervisor and still keep going; to hit the top.

If I'm fit for the job, becoming a foreman would be getting ahead. I'd be proud of it, too, because it would be a better position.

However, fewer than one in twenty workers respond in such ways. Typical replies of the vast majority are more like the following.

Higher classification; more money.

A better job; more interesting, easier on the nerves, and more pay. More responsibility and naturally more pay.

To me getting ahead is getting a more responsible job, more authority and more pay.

As long as I'm working I'm getting ahead.   With my wife working, I'm getting way ahead.

Getting a salary; when you get a salary, you have a steady income 52 weeks out of the year and pay sick days and vacations.

Better yourself in work; you could get transferred to more skilled job or to foreman; be more secure.

What I mean by getting ahead is more money.   With more money I can get the things I want.   The way things are now, I can just make ends meet.

A better job; an easier job and more money.

More or less reaching the goal you've got; getting in business for yourself, saving your money.

Getting a higher position with more money and more responsibilities and less friends.   I don't want to be a foreman; I've had it offered to me several times.

Buy a garage, own a repair shop, be my own boss. Even if I made less money for a while, that's what I consider getting ahead.

Some implicit considerations of social status are undoubtedly contained in these references to increased earnings, jobs with more authority, higher skill, and almost any other reference to "getting ahead." But to read status interpretations into the general run of such responses one has to resort to sheer guessing. Most of them have a quite different emphasis. Examination of spontaneous comments offered by the men through earlier portions of the interview yields similar findings. Their references to promotion and other ambitions reveal the same strong tendency to think in terms of more money to satisfy pressing material needs and provide a little enjoyment; better development and use of their skills, greater independence and increased responsibilities. There is seldom any slightest suggestion of interest in social status as the goal.

Taking all the evidence into account, we find little indication of concern with social-status enhancement on the part of most factory workers. When this conclusion is added to the earlier finding that the advancement variable in general bears only very moderate and irregular relationship to mental health, one's doubts are compounded as to whether opportunities for workers to improve their social status has much importance as a determinant of mental-health differences among occupations. Inasmuch as correspondingly weak indications resulted from the preceding analysis of workers' feelings about the importance of their jobs, our overall conclusion can assign only a decidedly secondary place to social-status characteristics of jobs as explanatory of the mental-health variations shown in the data. Admittedly, however, the measures of feelings in regard to the social-status characteristics of jobs are inadequate. We can say merely that insofar as our crude evidence gives clues, the relationship of job status concerns to mental health is unexpectedly limited.

Income

The earlier section on wages closed with a suggestion that even though workers' feelings concerning rates of pay showed little relation to occupational mental health and satisfaction, their *incomes* might well prove more important. What the money will buy and what problems the worker and his family encounter in making ends meet may be the significant factors.   To evaluate this possibility, we shall draw what inferences we can from the fragmentary evidence turned up in our study.   These straws in the wind do indicate that income differences help account for the poorer mental health of the lowest occupational groups.   The influence is limited, however, and must be seen as one element in a complex of multiple causes.

Our occupational classification, of course, is closely linked to income.   Consequently, gross comparisons of groups by income are much the same as those by occupation.   Identical conclusions can be drawn as to the association of mental health with economic level, whether the level is measured by income or by skill categories.   The principal measure of income that we shall employ is a four-degree classification which combines the worker's estimate of his earnings during the past year with his current hourly rate of pay.   The latter is added in order to refine and stabilize the coarse reports of income which were sometimes thrown off by misinterpretation of the question and by special conditions of prolonged illness, layoffs, or unusual overtime.   Employing the adjusted income classification,[10] percentages of high mental health from upper to lower incomes are as follows: young workers, 49 per cent (top two income groups together), 32 and 16 per cent; middle-aged, 53, 40, 33, and 27 per cent.   The figures are very similar to those by occupational levels (Table 4-1).   Income categories based directly on the men's reports of annual earnings show roughly corresponding differences in the proportions having high mental-health scores (young men, 63, 35, and 21 per cent; middle-aged, 48, 36, and 30 per cent).

When the relations of income and occupation to mental health are analyzed simultaneously, the comparisons leave no doubt that each contributes independently of the other, though the occupational influence is stronger, particularly in the young group.   The relationships are summarized in Table 6-4.   It appears that occupational differences persist without diminution at lower income levels in both age groups.   They likewise persist at higher incomes for young workers but are obliterated for middle-aged men except for the top skill group.   That is to say, below the topmost occupations, middle-aged men with relatively good incomes are about equal in mental health regardless of occupation.   But for those below average income, the occupational differences are substantial.   Conversely, the effects of income differences within separate occupational categories are moderate and somewhat irregular.   Nevertheless, in the two low occupational groups combined there is a pronounced gradient of

*Table 6-4   Proportions of high mental health
by occupational level and income*

Occupational Level	Income of Young			Income of Middle-aged		
	Above Average	Below Average	Total	Above Average	Below Average	Total
Skilled ⎫				57% (44)	... (1)	56% (45)
⎬	61% (23)*	50% (10)	58% (33)			
High semiskilled ⎭				40 (76)	45 (22)	41 (98)
Ordinary semiskilled	44 (9)	32 (37)	35 (46)	43 (21)	36 (61)	38 (82)
Repetitive semiskilled	0 (3)	12 (25)	10 (30)	44 (9)	23 (64)	26 (73)
Total	49 (37)	28 (72)		45 (150)	32 (148)	

* Figures in parentheses show the number of cases in each cell on which the accompanying percentage is based.

decreasing mental health from higher to lower incomes in both age groups.   This is particularly apparent when we use three income groupings in place of the two in the table; the percentages of high mental health by income in the two low-skill groups combined are as follows: young group, 29, 30, and 7 per cent; middle-aged, 43, 31, and 25 per cent.   The results suggest that income does play a part in producing occupational mental-health differences and that it has its greatest impact at the lower job levels.

The foregoing comparisons refer to the objective facts of income. But workers' subjective attitudes in regard to their earnings and their economic situation should tell us more.   Although we included no direct question tapping their feelings about the adequacy of their incomes or the severity of their financial strains, we did receive a considerable volume of volunteered comments on these matters. The problems obviously have high saliency as reflected in the intensity and repetition of thoughts on the subject.   The flavor of the negative statements is conveyed by quotations like these.

We meet the bills and that is about all.   Right now it is terrible; the kids need money for school, they need to go to the dentist, our furniture is falling apart.   We just live from pay to pay; we can't save a penny. Sickness in the family and for several years we only worked 3 or 4 days a week.

It's headache because of the cost of living; over our heads in debt. I haven't had a vacation in 6 years.   This house is too much for us, with the taxes and upkeep and the cost of living it's just too much. We can't afford to buy furniture. Income taxes are too high. Want to make a living—a fair living you might say; a good living is beyond most of us.

I'm working too many hours [60 to 80 hours a week] but I have to, to live decently. I have to depend on a second job to live as I'd like to and I don't like that. A man should be able to make it on one job.

I keep struggling along. I look for the worst; tomorrow is never rosy. . . . It's always been hard. I have to make an honest living; I go to the factory and I don't see any future in the factory. I worry about bringing up my family the way I want to. Want just enough so as I could get out of the rut of existence; that means having more money so as I could get more things like a house, a car, and things for family.

We got in a rut and don't know how to get out of it. Whenever we get on our feet, sickness and down we go. Can't get ahead; strikes or illness always set us back. Need housing now; paying 30 dollars a week for this basement apartment and it's no good. This is no place to live; no place for kids; drunks around; the wrong kind of neighborhood. Trying to get out of debt.

Wife working and I'm working two jobs; the workingman has to work very hard to have ends meet. . . . Rough going; I'd like to give my kids more; I have only one suit, yet I'm working 12 to 15 hours a day, Saturday too and Sunday sometimes. I can't even get the necessities of life now. Losing my health because of hard work.

I don't seem to get ahead; can't do what I want to; can't buy what I need. We need furniture and paint and lots of things. Bills! Want less financial worry and strain; so you can go out on a weekend and enjoy yourself once in a while.

High prices seem to keep you in debt all the time. I never seem to have enough money. I'd like to have a home of my own, I can't stand this dump and neither can my wife; be able to pay bills and do things I want to do like seeing movies, but I can't afford them.

The percentage of negative observations and complaints pertaining to personal economic problems rises as we go down the occupational scale. The proportions of workers offering negative comments, from upper to lower occupational groups, are, among the young, 24, 41, and 37 per cent; among the middle-aged, 18, 17, 29, and 37 per cent. These figures are in general accord with the expectation that concern over income would be more in evidence at lower job levels.

The key questions to be asked of the subjective response material are whether workers who express negative views regarding their economic condition are in poorer mental health than others, and whether occupational mental-health differences are diminished when only those who have no complaints are considered separately (statistical tests 2 and 3 of earlier sections). The answer to both questions is qualifiedly affirmative. With very minor exceptions, higher mental-health scores are found in the more satisfied or uncomplaining groups at each occupational level, for both age groups. The other question is the most critical one of all. In regard to it, we find that the required relationship is present among the middle-aged but not among the young. This means that in the young group feelings of concern over personal economic problems do not help account for the poorer mental health of workers in the lower occupational categories. Among the young men, occupational groups differ in mental health regardless of concern or lack of concern over personal income problems.

Among the middle-aged, mental health differences among occupations below the top skill group are pronounced for those with complaints about income (percentages of high mental health run 41, 33, and 15 per cent in the three lower occupations); the differences almost disappear for workers without such complaints (41, 40, and 33 per cent). It is only among those who feel the economic pinch, in other words, that mental health goes down substantially at lower occupational levels. The results support the hypothesis that income satisfaction is one of the factors accounting for differences in mental health among occupational groups. While the data do not indicate that this factor is overwhelmingly important, independently of occupation, and in fact suggest that it has decidedly minor influence as far as younger workers are concerned, the total evaluation gives it a place of considerable significance alongside the more narrowly job-related variables previously analyzed.

Summary

What answer can be given now to the ambitious questions posed at the beginning of this chapter? What do the results suggest regarding the characteristics that make skilled and varied factory jobs more mentally healthful than less skilled, routine jobs? The following paragraphs indicate tentative conclusions and interpretations derived from the analyses of this chapter.

Our overall working hypothesis has been that mental-health effects are provided by complex interactions of objective conditions and subjective dispositions. No single causes are likely to go far toward explaining intricate social phenomena such as occupational group differences of mental health. Accordingly, we have proposed a rather loose, broadly inclusive model which encourages open-ended quest for a multiplicity of job-related determinants. This is not to imply, of course, that all aspects of occupations have equally important effects. In fact, it is precisely these differences that our analysis seeks to discover and interpret.

In an effort to assess the significance of different aspects of jobs as determinants of mental health, we have focused on the *meaning* the job characteristics have for workers, the *feelings* men have about them. It turns out that attitudes toward a number of the job attributes exhibit only slight and ambiguous relationships to occupational level or to mental-health scores, or to both. Some of these results are surprising. For example, according to our data, feelings concerning wage rates, job security, and physical conditions of work have no explanatory value in accounting for mental-health variations between higher and lower factory occupations. It must be kept in mind that this and other conclusions refer to the range of variations within the plants studied and under circumstances then prevailing. How far the results are generalizable to other times and places remains for future research to discover. But the Detroit automotive industry of the mid-1950's cannot be dismissed as exceptional; in many ways it has become a symbol of large-scale modern manufacturing conditions.

Rational explanations for the negative finding in respect to the three job aspects just listed are not difficult to conceive. Although a substantial amount of dissatisfaction is expressed regarding each, this is no less true in more skilled than in less skilled and repetitive types of work. Concern over job security, though it has an appreciable relation to mental health of individuals, does not vary a great deal by occupation, presumably because layoffs typically affect all work groups more or less uniformly. At least this seems to have been the experience as perceived by automobile workers during the years preceding 1954. In the case of wages, the structure of going rates apparently had come to be about equally accepted at the several job levels so that the ratio of reward to expectation, and the resulting favorable or unfavorable feelings, are rather constant. Men in the least desirable jobs are as satisfied with their wage rates as are those in better jobs. The same seems to be true of physical work surroundings. In respect to all these conditions, it appears probable that any glaring sources of dissatisfaction have been corrected as a result of union pressures and management concern, thus tending to equalize workers' reactions at different job levels. Whatever the further interpretations, the conclusion from our data is that these three aspects of jobs play little or no part in bringing about the better and poorer mental health found in upper and lower occupations respectively.

Other job characteristics contribute in various degrees as determinants of the mental health of occupational groups. Decidedly the strongest influence is exerted by workers' feeling that the job does or does not give them a chance to *use their abilities*. This, and the closely linked perception of the job as *interesting* or not, exhibit stronger relationships to mental health than do any other of the variables analyzed. The simplest rationale for this finding would be one in terms of monotony or frustration engendered by performance of simplified, specialized tasks. But analysis of mental health in relation to reptitiveness, mechanical pacing, and similar work-process factors does not support this interpretation. Such variables account in only small measure for occupational differences of mental health. Everything considered, the most plausible interpretation, we believe, would view nonuse of abilities as causing lowered self-esteem, discouragement, futility, and feelings of failure and inferiority in contrast to a sense of personal growth and self-fulfillment resulting from more varied, responsible, challenging undertakings that afford opportunity to develop and use one's ideas and skills. We shall return to this line of interpretation and develop it further in the final chapter.

Speed and intensity of work on the production line have long been attacked as leading causes of nervous strain and fatigue that produce lasting ill effects, mental and physical. Under the conditions prevailing in Detroit automobile plants during the mid-1950's, we found little evidence of such differential negative effects of routine factory jobs. Only a very small proportion of men in these occupations (fewer than one in five) speak of excessive pressures, and these are largely concentrated in two of the thirteen plants. Moreover, the mental-health scores of workers who voice these complaints differ only slightly from those of others in similar work. As far as we can judge from our entire body of data, feelings directed against the speed, strains, and exhausting character of the job play a relatively minor part as contributors to the poorer mental health found at low occupational levels.

Although attitude toward wages as such proved to have no explanatory value, the analysis of *income*, or wages as purchasing power, produces more positive results. Among men in the two lower occupational categories, especially among those of middle-age, mental health is significantly associated with higher income and also with workers' more favorable feelings concerning their personal economic affairs. Among the middle-aged but not the young, occupational mental-health differences are pronounced for workers with economic complaints but are absent for those better satisfied. It is only among those who feel the financial pinch, that is, that mental health suffers substantially as one goes down the occupational scale.

Two other clusters of job attributes dealt with in our study have assumed special prominence in the contemporary literature on human aspects of work. They are social psychological factors included in what is popularly labeled "industrial human relations" and cognate factors bearing on the differential social status of occupations. We find that attitudes toward supervisors, closeness of supervision, feelings in regard to fellow workers, the company and its treatment of employees, all make extremely little difference as between upper- and lower-level jobs. They account in only very moderate degree for the better and poorer mental health that characterizes the several occupational groups in our study.

The larger organizational setting may be somewhat more significant since we find, in the Detroit sample, that the poor mental-health standing of lower occupations is confined to *large plants*. Relatively poor mental health of these groups is also more pronounced in plants rated unfavorably as to personnel and industrial-relations accomplishment. But none of the human-relations and organizational indicators, within the range of variation represented by these companies, appear to be of major consequence as influences on differential occupational mental health.

Since interpretations of occupational effects in terms of social status have been so greatly stressed in sociological inquiries, we were particularly interested in evaluating our data on the point, though with full awareness that we have only very inadequate indicators and that conclusions are therefore correspondingly tentative. With these reservations in mind, we note simply that workers' concern with the social-status aspects of jobs, in the sense of prestige and social standing, is little evidenced in our interviews though ample opportunity was afforded for such interest to manifest itself. Questions pertaining to the pros and cons of factory work, the importance of the man's own job, and his feelings about advancement and what getting ahead means to him elicit responses that only infrequently suggest status considerations. Other aspects of work loom much larger—earnings, agreeable and interesting work, pleasant surroundings, freedom and independence, for example. The several job meanings cannot be completely isolated, of course; unexpressed concern about esteem and social status may be present beneath the surface of other responses. But the assumption is at least open to question.

Statistical analysis does show that feelings of job importance make a difference. Men who say that their work is unimportant tend to have lower mental-health scores than their coworkers in similar jobs. Workers in the lowest occupational category who believe their work is important are equal in mental health to the next higher occupational group. Perceived opportunities for advancement likewise exhibit some relationship to mental health although it is a relatively weak and irregular effect. Since both these questions give only modest statistical evidence of association with mental health and since both leave serious doubts as to how commonly the responses reflect *status valuations*, we conclude tentatively that the social-status or prestige dimension of jobs compared in this study plays a quite limited role in accounting for mental-health differences between occupational groups.

Taken as a whole, the analyses of this chapter lead to the following conclusions: (1) A number of interrelated aspects of jobs contribute jointly to the mental-health condition of occupational groups. (2) One set of job characteristics is outstandingly influential: the chance the work offers a man to use his abilities, to perform a worthwhile function, to fulfill his role as a competent human being, and to find interest in his work and a sense of accomplishment and self-respect. (3) Subjective reaction to several other aspects of jobs have less bearing on the mental health of occupational groups but still contribute in some degree—most clearly in the case of feelings pertaining to income and personal economic problems; in slighter and more irregular manner in regard to the speed, intensity, and repetitiveness of work, supervision and other human relations aspects of jobs, and opportunities for advancement and improved social status. Wage rates, job security, and physical conditions of work have little or no explanatory value in accounting for poorer mental health at lower versus upper job levels.

Further relevant evidence will be examined in the next chapters, first in regard to the influence of personal and subjective factors affecting mental health and then with respect to additional attitudes and behavior associated with mental health at work and in life away from work.

7.

Personal characteristics

in relation to mental health

To this point we have been concerned with differences of mental health associated with occupational level. Other variables were introduced solely to ascertain whether job influences continue to be evident independently of personal and social characteristics of the men in the occupations. Although the occupational relationships were found to persist more or less regardless of personal characteristics, it was apparent that these other factors also have significant effects of their own. We now move these nonjob-connected variables to the center of the stage in order to inquire what they contribute to the explanation of mental-health differences within the factory population as a whole and in the occupational subgroups.

Two principal questions are to be asked: (1) How clearly are measures of workers' mental health associated with personal characteristics of individuals as compared with the relationship to occupational level? (2) To what extent are mental-health differences between occupational groups attributable not only to job influences examined in preceding chapters but at the same time to individual characteristics and to interaction between personal factors and occupational level?[1]

The complex interdependencies involved in answers to such questions are forbidding enough to demand a disclaimer at the outset. We cannot hope to go any great distance toward disentangling the network of personal, social, and industrial variables, past and present, which combine in intricate causal patterns to produce better or poorer mental health. Nevertheless, it appears useful to see what clues can be turned up which may shed some light on the processes and perhaps advance our understanding a short step or two. The analysis does not aim to discover single determinants of good mental health; it is almost certain that there are none. Rather the purpose is to portray some of the interrelationships that may serve as a basis for plausible speculation in regard to casual interconnections.

We begin with objective descriptive facts such as age, education, and childhood economic conditions. The second part of the chapter then proceeds to a consideration of prejob personality differences and subjective goals and values. A final section deals with some of the current values and desires of these working people.

Objective life-history variables

AGE

Our sample of factory workers consists of two age groups, men in their twenties and those in their forties. For the two groups as a whole, mental-health scores are nearly identical. When the age comparisons are made by occupational categories, however, it is discovered that the young have higher mental health than the middle-aged at upper skill levels (58 per cent high scores to 45 per cent; for high semiskilled alone, 61 per cent to 41 per cent); that they are equal in mental health at the ordinary semiskilled level (35 per cent to 38 per cent); and that they have lower mental health in low-level routine jobs (10 per cent high scores versus 26 per cent). The differences, although not large enough or based on enough cases to be taken as firmly established, are still decidedly suggestive. They indicate that age does affect the relationship between occupation and mental health.

A possible interpretation of this result was proposed in Chapter 4.[2] Briefly restated, it sees the young workers experiencing a sense of success and opportunity for further growth in the upper-semiskilled positions, whereas for middle-aged men these same jobs are more likely to be perceived as the end of the road. In lowest-level jobs, on the other hand, middle-aged workers have not had their aspirations aroused by any previous advancement and consequently they more readily accept their lowly position, provided it is not a machine-paced or production-line operation. Younger men, more of whom remain ambitious and unwilling to accept the implication of failure, and yet unable to see much hope of improvement, are more likely to feel frustrated, defeated, and hostile.

The interpretation receives support when we now compare age

groups on separate mental-health components.   In the better factory jobs the young score higher than the middle-aged on indexes of life satisfaction, self-esteem, personal morale, freedom from strong hostility, and purposive orientation toward work and career.   In low-level jobs the young are again more purposive than the middle-aged, but they are also more frustrated as evidenced by greater dissatisfaction with life, greater hostility, and lower personal morale and self-esteem.   The differences are not large but their direction clearly accords with the view that the middle-aged in lower jobs tend more than the young to achieve satisfactory adjustment by reconciling themselves more or less contentedly to the realities.   With only a touch of cynicism one may surmise that many of the young men destined to spend their years in routine jobs will also "adapt" and win better mental-health assessments by the time they reach middle-age.

If the question is raised, as indeed it insistently should be, whether this more contented acceptance signifies truly superior mental health, we must repeat that it is not here being compared with a condition of vigorous, purposive nonconformity, independence, or dissatisfied struggle for improvement but with low self-esteem, hostility, distrust, and feelings of defeat.   Even though mental health that depends on passive acceptance falls far short of the ideal of positive, self-reliant problem-solving orientation, it must still be evaluated as more satisfactory than a negative, embittered relation to life and self.   It is in this sense that the comparisons in favor of young workers at upper job levels and of middle-aged in lower-level jobs appear justified.

EDUCATION AND SCHOOL SUCCESS

The mental health of individuals in our sample is markedly affected by their educational level as well as by their occupation.   In fact the two exhibit a nearly equal degree of statistical association as may be seen in the percentages under "totals" in Table 4-4.   An index measuring "school success" has roughly the same substantial relationship to mental health for the total groups.

To understand the meaning of the relationships to mental health, it is necessary also to analyze the data for education and occupation simultaneously.   Our earlier analysis of the three variables concluded that amount of schooling does not account for differences in mental health between factory occupational categories.[3]   Mental-health scores tend to be better, on the average, the higher the job level regardless of amount of schooling.   We now ask the converse question whether mental health is better with increasing education and school success regardless of occupation.   On the whole the answer is definitely affirmative, though more clearly so among the middle-aged than the young.   In the young group, occupational effects are much larger and more consistent than educational effects. Among the middle-aged, mental health is higher for those of above-average schooling at each job level separately and similarly for those of above-average school success with the exception of the group in the lowest jobs.   In general, that is, effects of education do persist apart from occupation.

While occupation and education thus exhibit their separate influences on mental health, it is important to recognize that, at the same time, they have a degree of interdependence.   As a consequence the overall occupational mental-health differences do reflect the effects of more persons of better education being in higher jobs; and likewise the differences of mental health by education and school success are in part results of the better educated having disproportionate numbers in more skilled jobs which are favorable for mental health.   In both instances, however, the contribution of the other variable is secondary; the major portion of the effect is produced by each independently of the other.

The separate components of mental health all vary in a positive direction with education and with school success in both age groups. Among the young, closest relationship to education occurs on sub-indexes of self-esteem, personal morale, and sociability; closest relationship to school success is by self-esteem and freedom from anxiety. In the middle-aged group, personal morale and low hostility are the components most associated with both education and school success. For both age groups, but especially for the young, ratings of general purposive striving and purposiveness in work are markedly associated with education and school success.

The pronounced tendency for mental health and certain of its component indexes to be associated with schooling and school success is undoubtedly due to a complex combination of causes.   In part it may be that increased education directly improves mental health (for example, by cultivating more realistic perceptions and expectations, and a more informed, unemotional, rational approach to personal problems), but it is apparent that schooling also affects mental health through a variety of indirect linkages.   One possibility is that the individual's biological inheritance makes both for better or poorer mental health and a corresponding degree of school achievement. Favorable or unfavorable home background in early years may likewise serve as a common cause that produces the correlation between psychological health and school achievement. Or it may be that additional education leads to more appropriate job placement which in turn is conducive to better mental health. The data point clearly to the conclusion that the better educated tend to have higher mental health *both* by reason of being in better positions and because their education lifts their mental health above that of others in the same occupation. Similarly, education may favor or oppose nonvocational activities and relationships which foster mental health: for example, we find, as have other studies, that the better educated display more purposive behavior, engage more in organizational affairs, and tend more frequently to develop spare-time hobbies. It is not our purpose, or within our power, to judge the relative importance of these and other possible explanations of the interdependency of education and personal adjustment. The most reasonable conclusion is that there is no single key; and this conclusion dictates extreme caution in regard to any explanatory theory that stresses *one* casual process to the neglect of all the others.

The preceding observations have direct bearing on the hypothesis sometimes proposed which construes schooling as an indicator of individual's aspiration level, occupation as a measure of achieved success in life, and the disparity between the two as generating a sense of failure, frustration, and poor mental health.[4] According to this view men of limited education in low-level jobs should enjoy better mental health than those in the same low-level jobs who have more schooling. Our results do not confirm this expectation. Better-educated men in routine factory jobs do not exhibit poorer mental health than those of less education. The reason, we suspect, is that already suggested: that the effects predicted by this hypothesis are offset or overbalanced by *other* ways in which education relates to mental health.

But the matter is even more complicated, as can be illustrated by citing a few additional findings. In Chapter 4 we noted that comparisons of school success, unlike mere number of years of schooling, did show a little support for the foregoing status-incongruency hypothesis. The support is shaky, however, inasmuch as the group of above-average school success in low jobs, though having a relatively small proportion in good mental health as the hypothesis requires, also has slightly fewer of *low* mental health compared with the group below average in school success.   Further clues are now obtained when we analyze separate aspects of mental health in relation to schooling and occupation.   The overall relationship of mental health to education and job level together reflects an aggregate of contrary relationships among the component measures of mental health.   Better-educated workers in low-level jobs tend to have lower life satisfaction and self-esteem; on the other hand, they tend to have higher personal morale among the middle-aged and higher sociability among both the young and the middle-aged.   Table 7-1 illustrate these inverse relationships.

These counteracting tendencies cancel out the effects of education occupation incongruity on total mental-health assessments, leading to the absence of relationship previously noted.   Nevertheless, the two particular mental-health dimensions that do manifest the hypothesized relationship are precisely the ones that might be most expected to do so.   Self-esteem and satisfaction with life can be presumed to depend to greater degree on vocational achievement in relation to aspirations than would feelings of social distrust (personal morale), social withdrawal, and other elements of mental health which are more likely to derive from lifelong influences apart from the job.   These latter components might be expected to reflect the direct contribution of education in helping a person at any economic level more effectively come to terms with his world.

Table 7-1   Proportions of educational groups at two lowest occupational levels who have high scores on selected mental-health components

	Young		Middle-aged		
Mental-Health Components	Some High School or Less	High School Graduates	Eighth Grade or Less	Some High School	High School Graduates
Life satisfaction	25%	11%	38%	33%	18%
Self-esteem	18	11	22	14	12
Personal morale	25	21	19	32	59
Sociability	32	47	21	44	59
Number of workers*	57	19	81	57	17

* Totals on which the percentages are based.

The foregoing analysis underscores the multiform nature of mental health as well as the complexity of its determinants. Some aspects of personal adjustment may benefit from given antecedent or current conditions while other aspects simultaneously suffer impairment. In regard to education and school success, the conclusion is that they do contribute to the mental health of factory workers, partly in a direct manner and partly in more intricate interaction with position in the occupational hierarchy. Educational effects transcend any one causal explanation such as aspiration-achievement disparity and, in fact, this particular causal factor may be submerged, as it is in our overall mental-health results, by other effects of schooling.

CHILDHOOD INCOME LEVEL

Mental-health linkages to amount of schooling are roughly paralleled by relationships to several other indicators of prejob socio-economic status. All the childhood socioeconomic variables agree in showing that *persons economically disadvantaged as children tend to be below average in mental health as adults.* The gradients of average mental-health scores are comparable in steepness to those by occupational levels. Moreover, the differences by early background factors show up regardless of later job level; they reveal themselves in comparisons within each occupational category separately. As previously emphasized, however, these relationships do not account for the variations among occupational groups; they are additional or complementary determinants. The two sets of factors, those representing early background circumstances and those associated with later employment, are *both* important, in the main independently of each other.

The most direct measure of childhood economic condition obtained in this study is a five-point rating by each respondent estimating whether his family was "well above average financially, a little above average, about average, a little below average, or very poor." These reports of family income prove to be strongly related to mental health in the young group (high mental health by 42 per cent of those with family income average or above versus 18 per cent among those below average) and moderately related in the middle-aged group (44 to 31 per cent). Crosstabulations of mental health by family income and education reveal that although schooling has somewhat larger effects than family income, the latter contributes additionally. Their combined effect increases the mental-health differences so that, for the young, those high in both education and income contrasted with those low in both have 56 and 14 per cent high mental-health scores respectively; correspondingly for the middle-aged, the proportions are 60 and 22 per cent.

By separate occupational categories, the mental-health differences associated with boyhood economic conditions are still evident: workers coming from poorer homes are of lower average mental health than others in each occupational group (figures in Table 4-5). Consequently, the effects of childhood economic conditions cannot be written off as due to the later influence of the kinds of jobs the boys go into. Moreover, there is extremely little difference in early income by present occupation, unlike the case of education and school success both of which contribute prominently to later job level.

Combinations of childhood income and schooling also continue, within separate occupational groups, to relate more closely to mental health than either does by itself. The proportions classified as mentally healthy are strikingly great among men of high or medium childhood income and high education presently occupying skilled positions (among middle-aged, 12 of 15 have high mental health; among young, 9 of 11). As was the case for education alone, neither early family income nor a combination of it with education exhibits an interaction effect of a kind to cause men with more favorable background to have poorer mental health in low-level jobs than do those with unfavorable backgrounds. The influence of childhood socioeconomic conditions and of later occupation appears to be additive or compensatory so that better than average early advantages are associated with better mental health even in low occupations.

OTHER SOCIAL CONDITIONS IN CHILDHOOD

Many other specific indicators of childhood conditions have been examined in relation to the mental-health assessments of individuals. Two or three of these exhibit clear, meaningful correlations with mental health but most display doubtful and highly variable relations. A combination of twelve items in regard to early life deprivations shows somewhat greater stability. Findings from these analyses will be briefly summarized here not because the results offer any comprehensive explanations of mental-health differences but in order to illustrate that early life-history circumstances are influential along with later conditions and that the influences operate in complex interrelationships that preclude simple conclusions based on statistical crossrelations of two or three variables. Indeed, the more we have analyzed the available data and reflected on the indirectness and intricacy of the dynamic processes involved, the more surprising it has seemed that even a few major factors like education and family income level shows up as clearly as they do.

Other specific items that yield meaningful results pertain mainly to social and economic advantages and disadvantages which can be interpreted as having direct impact on the psychological development of the child. Such influences are exemplified, first, by a comparison of individuals from broken versus intact homes. The data accord with the reasonable expectation that parental separation represents an adverse condition for the growth of emotional security, ego strength, and other elements of mental health. In both age groups, the men who spent their boyhood with both parents alive and together have slightly better mental health on the average than do others (in the young group, 39 per cent have high mental health compared to 20 per cent of others; in the middle-aged, 40 per cent to 34 per cent). Similarly, only 25 per cent of the young workers who report that their parents were not very happy together have high mental-health scores versus 40 per cent of others; corresponding figures for the middle-aged are 18 versus 43 per cent.

Since no clear differences occur between occupational groups on these variables, they do not help account for observed differences of mental health between occupations. But they do apparently contribute to *individual* health regardless of occupation.

Another question inquired whether the respondent's mother worked outside the home. In these lower-income groups this would in part indicate economic need but perhaps it also reflects some neglect of children in the home. In any event, mental health is somewhat better where the answer is in the negative (37 per cent high mental health to 27 per cent among the young; 42 per cent to 25 per cent among the middle-aged). Here again there are no substantial differences of response between occupational categories.

Relations of mental health to father's occupation present a good illustration both of influence in the expected direction and, at the same time, of puzzling discrepancies. In the young group, mental health is especially high among sons of skilled workers (63 per cent high versus 23 per cent of all others). This holds true even for sons now in ordinary semiskilled jobs, workers who are downwardly mobile from the father's occupation. In the middle-aged sample, however, sons of skilled fathers have no better mental health than others and those in lower-level jobs (downwardly mobile) are in poorer mental health than others in the same occupations (22 per cent high mental health versus 35 per cent). This contrast between the age groups is possibly accounted for by the interpretation previously suggested to the effect that by the time semiskilled workers are in their forties they are likely to feel at the end of the road as far as personal progress is concerned and, in the present connection, to sense the permanence of their failure to equal their fathers' skill level. The *young* men still entertain vague hopes of rising. But immediately we are confronted with other discordant results: the relationships in regard to white-collar fathers do not conform to this pattern. Sons of white-collar fathers are below average mental health in the young group but slightly above average in the middle-aged sample.[5] Our conclusion is simply that we do not have the detailed data that would be necessary to account for such discrepancies. We do not know enough, for example, regarding the nature of the white-collar jobs held, the father-son relations, reasons for the son's going into blue-collar employment, what kinds of friends and associates he had (his "reference groups"), and so on. All that we can safely say, on the basis of a statistical search that goes considerably beyond that reported here, is that our gross findings in respect to intergenerational job mobility fail to reveal any consistent effects on mental health.[6]

Equally baffling examples are presented by contrasts between the two age groups in respect to correlations of mental health with foreign versus native parentage and with parents' religion. In the middle-aged group mental health is a little higher among sons of native-born fathers; in the young group this relationship is sharply reversed (27 per cent of those with American-born fathers have high mental-health scores versus 48 per cent of those with foreign-born fathers). A parallel reversal of proportions occurs by religion. More Protestant than Catholic workers have high mental health among the middle-aged (45 per cent to 36 per cent), while the opposite is found in the young group (42 per cent of Catholics have high scores versus 28 per cent of Protestants). The reversal still holds if we take separately the men who now attend church regularly and those who do not. It seems probable that the reversed relationship for religious affiliation mirrors the same constellation of influences as are present in regard to parents' birthplace, the foreign being more largely Catholic. One possible clue is that the comparatively poor mental health of the boys of American stock in the young group occurs predominantly among those in the two lower job categories. This difference in low-level jobs disappears among the middle-aged. Once again the interpretation may be that the young Americans who are second generation or more entertain higher expectations and correspondingly greater frustration than those from immigrant families, but that by middle-age these unattainable ambitions are abandoned with resultant psychological improvement.

A number of other life-history items show little or no relation to mental health or they manifest such irregularities as to make them meaningless. For example, mental health bears almost no relation to parents' education though we had anticipated that it would. Likewise, extremely small and inconsistent effects are associated with region of the United States in which the respondent spent his boyhood and the size of the community where he grew up. Results of this kind together with the preceding ones sufficiently demonstrate the variations and irregularities of relationship of the specific variables. Efforts to uncover significant uniformities by crosstabulations that introduce additional variables encounter insurmountable obstacles due to the limited size of the sample and other deficiencies of the data.

More fundamentally, however, we must question whether it is reasonable to expect stable, lawful connections between adult mental health and specific background conditions. Even if we assume that each exerts some influence, this may occur in such diverse contexts and in such variable ways, dependent on complex interacting conditions and personal make-up, that it would indeed be remarkable if many significant statistical regularities were to emerge. The more reasonable quest is one that seeks specific items that can be construed as potential indicators of broad influences advantageous or disadvantageous for personal development and mental health. We were fortunate in choosing a few such indicators—socioeconomic variables like education and family economic level—that do have clear bearing on subsequent psychological adjustment. This means, we infer, that these represent pervasive powerful influences that are not readily submerged or counteracted by other conditions, and are not likely to be perceived favorably instead of unfavorably in certain settings (as, for example, foreign parentage might be).

This line of thought implies that the separate socioeconomic indicators that do show clear relations to mental health probably reflect common underlying influences of economic and cultural advantage or disadvantage, or relative deprivation. Accordingly, we decided to construct an aggregate index of "deprivation" composed of twelve sets of responses including economic position of the family, limited schooling, broken home, and the other items listed at an earlier point.[7] Childhood deprivation, measured by this index, correlates with adult mental health to just about the same extent as do its principal components, education and childhood income level. In the young group, 23 per cent of the more severely deprived have high mental health versus 34 per cent of those moderately deprived and 50 per cent of the least deprived; among middle-aged, parallel proportions are 24, 44, and 63 per cent. In both age groups the association holds for each separate occupational category with the one exception of young repetitive workers, for whom no difference occurs between more and less deprived.

In sum, childhood advantages as measured by this most general index do bear substantially on later mental-health differences *among individuals*. Using this measure, however, we again find that the prejob factors account in extremely slight degree for mental health differences *among occupational groups*. The occupational gradient persists almost unchanged, in both age groups, for men above and those below average in childhood deprivations. Among the middle-aged there is a moderate additive effect; those least deprived *and* in skilled work show 73 per cent of high mental health while those most deprived and in repetitive jobs have only 15 per cent of high mental health (in contrast to 56 versus 26 per cent for *all* skilled and *all* repetitive respectively). In the young group this cumulative effect is absent. However, in neither age group is there any significant evidence of an incongruency effect whereby those most favored (least deprived) in childhood might react especially negatively in low-level jobs.

We conclude this sketch of findings in regard to objective life-history variables with the following summary statements.

1. Factory workers differ in mental health not only by reason of their present occupation (as demonstrated in preceding chapters) but their mental health is also related to their age, education, and other prejob personal and social conditions. Childhood socioeconomic advantages or disadvantages along with education appear especially influential.

2. Relationship of individuals' mental health to these personal factors is of approximately the same order of magnitude as was found for the correlation with occupational level. This statement

applies to the larger middle-aged sample; among the young workers, occupation produces considerably greater effects than do these personal influences.

3. On the whole, the influences from early life and from present occupation relate to mental health independently of each other. Neither accounts for the effects of the other in any large degree, though there are complex and varied causal interactions which result predominantly in moderate additive effects, so that a combination of favorable childhood conditions and skilled occupation yields the best mental health; poor background and low job placement result in fewest satisfactory mental-health scores. No consistent evidence points to "status incongruity" effects whereby lowest mental health would occur rather among workers with *favorable* background who are now in the most routine jobs.

4. Though the statistical findings on these points do not dictate any particular theoretical interpretation, they fit readily into the framework sketched in Chapter 1. The results appear particularly consonant with explanations in terms of childhood social and economic influences broadly advantageous (or the opposite) for the development of good mental health. Although the influences operate through diverse and complex causal interconnections, the evidence suggests that it is predominantly a matter of direct continuance into later life of favorable or unfavorable childhood psychological effects, rather than a process primarily involving congruity or incongruity between early expectations and subsequent realizations. We shall later examine these two explanatory conceptions more fully, drawing on all of our findings to assess their implications for overall conclusions.

Childhood subjective characteristics

The next general question is whether adult mental health is forecast by childhood personality qualities and dispositions. The question has many facets and evidence from a study like the present one is meager since inquiry into these matters was a quite secondary objective. Even so, the available findings are well worth summarizing in order to see what additional light they may cast on explanations of mental-health differences.

In Chapter 4 it was noted that prejob differences in personal traits, ambitions, and values failed to account for the superior mental health of men in upper factory occupations and the less satisfactory psychological condition of those in routine lower-skilled jobs. Our conclusion was that differences of mental health between occupations are not due primarily to *selection* processes which might differentially sort those of high mental health potential into better jobs and those of limited potential into lower jobs. Without discarding this conclusion, we propose now to look in greater detail at these subjective variables in order to answer the same questions we have dealt with in the immediately preceding pages with respect to objective background facts about individuals. How closely, that is, do the measures of childhood traits and values correlate with adult mental health, and to what extent do these childhood characteristics contribute, along with later occupational conditions, to the explanation of group differences in mental health?

INDEXES OF CHILDHOOD ANXIETY, HAPPINESS, AND SELF-CONFIDENCE

The content of these indexes is summarized on page 73 and specified more fully in Appendix B. The reader must again be reminded of the caution noted earlier in regard to these indexes. They are based on the working people's own *reports* of their childhood experiences. Consequently, the data are colored to an unknown extent by the present needs and biases of the men, particularly by each person's powerful inclination to protect and enhance his current ego feelings. Since these motivations may distort the picture of his boyhood in varied and unpredictable manner, there is no method for "correcting" the reports. Conclusions simply have to be weighed with the nature of the evidence kept in mind.

Inasmuch as the index of anxiety and maladjustment is itself designed as a measure of essential aspects of mental health during earlier years, it is not surprising that it proves to be closely related to adult mental health. The men whose responses indicate high childhood anxiety tend to have lower mental-health scores as adults (of the high-anxiety group only 15 per cent of the young and 20 per cent of the middle-aged have high mental health contrasted with 46 and 47 per cent of all others). The correlation is of roughly the same size as was found for education and other objective indicators of personal characteristics—and also for occupational group comparisons.

Here again the question arises whether the relationship is due to persons with better childhood adjustment being in higher-level jobs. Little difference of this kind is evidenced between occupations though a slight tendency occurs for men now in routine semiskilled jobs to have had poorer prejob adjustment than did others. The important fact, however, is that the correlation of childhood adjustment with adult mental health holds for each occupation separately in both age groups, with the sole exception of young workers in the lowest jobs. In this last case, *better* childhood adjustment is associated with *poorer* mental health at present (of 11 individuals well adjusted as children, 9 now have low mental-health scores in contrast to only 5 of 19 who were less well adjusted in childhood). Apart from this one subgroup, the measures of adjustment in boyhood and in later life do correlate consistently in a manner not dependent on their association with occupational level.

Indexes of childhood happiness and self-confidence yield results essentially similar to the foregoing.[8] All three indexes exhibit moderately good correlations with adult mental health both for factory workers as a whole and by separate occupations, save for the exception noted in the preceding paragraph which reappears less strikingly for the other indexes. Since the number of cases involved in this young group of routine workers is very small and the internal relations are not entirely consistent, perhaps we should merely attribute the results to "chance" and let it go at that. However, the findings are sufficiently suggestive to call for interpretation, especially since they appear congruent with explanations already proposed in earlier pages.

The subgroup that manifests the inverse relationship consists of young workers who were well adjusted, self-confident, personally secure during their boyhood. It is not difficult to suppose that these are persons who would particularly experience a keen and painful contrast on finding themselves in routine, impersonal, unchallenging jobs. For the middle-aged, time has blunted the sharp edges of the contrast; among the younger men the disagreeable realization is still dominant. They exhibit notably poor scores on self-esteem, life satisfaction, and personal morale. The interpretation, in a word, is akin to the idea of incongruity between aspiration and achievement but we would extend this to include contrast between earlier confident and contented self-acceptance and the later bitter experience of a drop to relative uselessness, impersonality, and lack of self-expression. Perhaps it is not so much failure to make anticipated gains as experience of actual loss. In either case, feelings of personal frustration and lowered self-esteem are central.

The *general* conclusion from this analysis of childhood indexes is that reports of prejob feelings and behavior are predictive of later mental health. Assuming the reports to be reasonably authentic, one can infer that individual differences in mental health are determined by the persistence of childhood behavior patterns and attitudes toward self as well as by such later life conditions as are represented by position in the factory occupational hierarchy. Finally, the data indicate that differences in prejob personal adjustment do contribute, though in a decidedly minor way, to bringing about the poorer average mental health in lower-level occupations.

CHILDHOOD GOALS AND VALUES

Childhood differences may be looked at not only in terms of personality qualities but also with attention focused on the boys' ambitions and value systems. We would expect differing aspirations and underlying desires to play a part in determining the psychological consequences of later occupation and associated life conditions. To check on possible relationships of this kind we obtained responses indicative of boyhood goals and orientations and attempted to answer the following questions: how do more career-minded boys who go into the factory compare with others in their subsequent adjustments to life? Do boys who manifested interest in workmanship and self-expressive activities suffer ill effects of routine jobs more than do others?

The measures available are again crude indicators based on workers' own testimony regarding their prejob attitudes and behavior. Some 40 different categories of boyhood hopes, aspirations, and values were derived from answers to a series of questions concerning feelings, attitudes, activities, and personal relations in childhood. The general nature of the measures is described in Chapter 4 (p. 73). We have prepared extensive tabulations of these indexes in relation to mental health, from which we shall report selected illustrative results.[9]

In general, what we find is that boyhood values and hopes correlate only very slightly with later mental health when the entire factory population is considered, but that significant relations do appear when occupational groups are looked at separately. The variation of the relationship by occupation is particularly apparent in the contrast between men in the lower job categories and those at higher levels. This is fully meaningful and in accord with theory. Given aspirations and values naturally should lead to dissimilar psychological results depending on the degree to which later position affords opportunity for fulfillment of the desires. On the whole, our data conform to these expectations though the statistical associations are of only moderate strength.

For the workers as a whole, undifferentiated by occupation, a few illustrations will suffice to show the kinds of association between childhood orientation and adult mental health. In the middle-aged group, there is a moderate tendency toward low mental health among those with boyhood emphasis on values of emotional security and personal adjustment, need for affection and friendship; toward high mental health by those who value self-worth and respect. Among the young, again a slight tendency appears for lower mental health to be associated with high valuation of adjustment and emotional security in childhood. This is the only linkage manifested in both age groups; it is understandable in a commonsense frame of reference that views the emphasis on these values as elicited by early experiences of insecurity and inadequacy which persist through later years. In the young group, high mental health occurs a little more often than average among those who valued influence and leadership, appreciation and affection (opposite to the tendency among middle-aged), and who expressed hopes for success, career, and status (this, too, contrary to the tendency among the middle-aged). In all instances, these relationships for the total sample are much weaker than ones we have previously reported in respect to objective conditions of childhood and childhood personality qualities.

Results by occupational categories are of greater interest here. As noted earlier, our theoretical guidelines which conceive mental health as dependent on gratification of ego motivations, or progress toward such gratification, would predict that the personal desires of early life must produce different consequences for persons now situated at upper or at lower job levels. We come to a more direct test, that is, of the frustration or incongruity hypothesis discussed earlier which argues that boys with higher aspirations confined to routine work will have poorer mental health than will less ambitious boys. Although our evidence is not unequivocal, in the main it tends to lend support to the hypothesis.

The strongest supporting evidence comes from indexes representing career and success ambitions. For example, in the middle-aged group, only 16 per cent of those who manifested such ambitions in boyhood and are now in repetitive low-skill jobs have high mental health in contrast to 43 per cent of others in the same job. No difference at all appears in occupational categories above the lowest. Among young workers, similar results are obtained on parallel indexes though not on this particular one. The most significant differences for the young group occur when we compare boys who reported personal success goals as a major hope with those who expressed no such aspirations. In routine jobs, the former have 64 per cent in poor mental health, the latter 31 per cent. Here again, no difference of this kind appears in any of the other occupational groups. Much the same results are obtained, though less strongly, when the comparison is based on whether the boys' ideas of future work specified white-collar and skilled positions or not. However, high valuation of social approval and prestige in boyhood does not produce similar effects. Interest in workmanship and use of abilities does. In fact, most of the relevant measures of boyhood orientation do exhibit a slight inverse relationship between high boyhood goals and present mental health at low job levels, in line with the theory. This last statement is more clearly applicable to the young group; the results are irregular among the middle-aged.

The moderate support found here for the interpretation that attributes poor mental health to a discrepancy between aspiration and achievement is quite compatible with our previous inferences. The conception, we suggested earlier, is valid but partial. It represents one significant aspect of a vast network of diverse motivations and expectations in relation to the conditions that provide gratifications or impose deprivations. Consequently, this particular contrast is sometimes powerful enough to show itself in the statistical data and at other times is submerged by more dominant influences, depending on circumstances. It should be recalled, for example, that among young workers childhood emotional adjustment exhibits a stronger "incongruency effect" than do any of the measures of boyhood aspirations. At a minimum, it would seem necessary to greatly extend the ideas of aspiration and achievement, so that aspiration would include *all* ego-involving dispositions and achievement would cover satisfactions of *every* sort of need and desire.

The final matter to be added before leaving the indexes of prejob value orientations is the question repeatedly asked concerning other variables: to what extent do they account for differences in mental health between occupational categories? In a word, the answer is that they contribute extremely little to the occupational differences. For all the relationships examined, either the occupational groups exhibited only the most limited selection effects based on prejob aspirations and values, or the correlations of mental health with these prejob attributes were too small, too erratic from one occupational level to another, or actually in the wrong direction, to help explain the poorer mental health of low occupational groups.

In brief, then, we conclude that evidence in regard to boyhood goals and values reveals unexpectedly small and irregular relationships to later mental health. Nevertheless, one distinctly suggestive finding is the further support for the interpretation in terms of aspiration-achievement discrepancy. Young workers in the lowest occupational category whose boyhood attitudes and activities indicated higher vocational aspirations tend now to have poorer mental health. The evidence is somewhat spotty, to be sure, and taken in conjunction with results for other variables and for both age groups leads again to only qualified acceptance of the interpretation. We believe that it is rather to be construed as one aspect of a more general explanatory theory of the kind proposed in the introductory chapter, which we shall review at a later point in the light of our results as a whole.

Adult goals and values

In the preceding section we have asked to what extent personality attributes and value systems discernible in reports concerning childhood are determinants of individual and occupational differences of mental health. We wish now to consider the same question with respect to *present* differences of values and goals of the auto workers studied. Do the men differ in their current basic desires; do occupational groups differ; and are the variations significant for mental health? In view of results already reported, it may be anticipated that we shall discover no very close relationships and particularly that *occupational differences* of mental health will continue to be accounted for largely by unequal opportunities for gratification which the different job situations afford rather than by dissimilar wants to be gratified.

We have two bodies of data relevant to the present phase of the inquiry. One consists of volunteered responses to the question:

"What would you say you really want most out of life?" The other utilizes check responses to nine items representing "things people say they want in their lives" (for list of choices, see Appendix A, A8). Both questions were asked in the first part of the interview before any hint had been given of special interest in job-related matters. Here again we shall report only the major results revealed by the analysis together with a few illustrative examples.

The problem of causal interpretation of relationships is even more formidable in this connection than it was with respect to childhood variables. There we could at least somewhat plausibly assume separation along a time dimension; here we cannot. Any statistical association of goal values with either occupation or mental health may reflect diverse causal possibilities: the wants can as well be effects as causes, or still more likely they may be indirectly related as components of a complex network of interrelated personality and situational variables. With acute awareness of these limitations, we shall nevertheless try, at this point, to consider the wants *as if* they were an independent variable. In this way we may be able to estimate the outer limits of their contribution to the mental-health variations of interest to us. In a later chapter we shall treat the goal values as themselves aspects of personality and mental health rather than as possible causes.

To test the relations of differing goals to mental health we chose two clusters of wants, one expressing ambitions (job advancement, self-improvement, use of abilities), the other referring to goals of ease, adjustment, and enjoyment (work less, easier life, freedom to do what you want to, comforts, happiness, friends, peace of mind). For the entire group of young workers neither of these indexes shows any association with mental health. Among the middle-aged, those who still hold to their ambitions tend not to be in as good mental health as the unambitious (23 per cent high mental health versus 41 per cent of all others). This finding nicely fits the frustration interpretation. The effect is most pronounced, however, not at the lowest occupational level but among the ordinary and upper semi-skilled (middle-aged). Similarly, in the young group a hint of the same relationship occurs only among the ordinary semiskilled, not among those on most routine jobs. Ambitious workers still on the lowest rung of the ladder apparently experience less damaging frustrations than those part way toward their goals.

At all occupational levels, a relatively small proportion of workers expresses aspirations for personal growth and success and, more surprisingly, the percentage remains fairly constant from one skill level to another, with a range only from 22 per cent to 30 per cent among the young and from 9 per cent to 18 per cent among the middle-aged. These small variations, moreover, do not follow a pattern that would at all help to account for observed differences in mental health between occupational groups. Nevertheless, differences in success motivations may markedly affect the mental health of *individuals*, particularly at intermediate skill levels, as pointed out in the preceding paragraph.

The other index, signifying goals of ease and enjoyment, bears no relation to mental health in either age group. Neither does it reveal substantial differences of frequency from occupation to occupation nor consistent associations with mental health at separate job levels. Equally negative results are obtained from another index, derived from the check list of wants, representing desires for self-expression in work and leisure.

Other results from the check list are somewhat more positive; certain value choices do tend to indicate better or poorer mental health. The comparisons give some indication that mental health benefits from forward-reaching values that seem attainable and that it is less favorable where values are held which are likely to remain unrealized. For example, 60 per cent of the young men who include "getting ahead" as one of the "three or four things [they] want most" receive high mental-health scores versus only 25 per cent of all others. At the lowest job level, however, where there is least prospect of satisfying the desire, the positive relationship disappears. Among the middle-aged, furthermore, for many of whom getting ahead has become a forlorn wish, the relationship reverses, with 30 per cent high mental-health scores among those still entertaining the goal versus 42 per cent for all others.

The following comparisons point toward a similar conclusion. Middle-aged workers who prize leisure as a goal ("spare time to do the things you enjoy"), have especially high mental health at upper occupational levels and especially poor mental health at low occupational levels. In routine jobs where the wish is more likely to be an "escapist" desire, only 13 per cent of those expressing this want enjoy good mental health compared to 33 per cent of those not naming leisure as a goal. Only four young workers in routine jobs choose this goal but all four have low mental-health scores (as against 10 of 26 who do not name this goal). Consistently, in terms of a frustration interpretation, mental health is decidedly below average for both younger and older men who select personal independence as a goal ("not to be pushed around and made to do things")—a desire that is almost sure to be thwarted for most factory workers. Clearly contrasting findings, in full accord with theoretical expectations, occur when we turn to persons who select "a lot of good friends" as one of their wishes since this is patently an attainable goal not dependent on limitations imposed by their economic situation. We find that in both age groups and in both upper and lower occupations mental health is better than average for the men who place good friends high on their list of values.

Our general conclusion from the evidence on personal value differences is that although they do not appear to be powerful determinants of mental-health variations they do enter into the total causal network in an eminently meaningful way. Stated most simply, the results suggest that workers who want what they cannot realistically hope to achieve tend to be in poorer mental health, those whose wants are ones they can more reasonably move toward satisfying tend to enjoy better mental health. The findings, in a word, are compatible with a frustration interpretation. Both the personal and the occupational variables possess explanatory power; the quality of workers' adjustments varies with their differing personal attributes and needs, but it turns quite as fully on the differing opportunities for gratification afforded by the positions they occupy.

Summary

The results sketched in this chapter are tangential to the central concern of the study. The principal purpose of the research was to ascertain the psychological effects of factory work, particularly lower grades of semiskilled work, on working people. This has been the preoccupation of preceding chapters. Since prominent occupational effects were evident, the companion question naturally arises whether personal characteristics of individuals are also important determinants of mental health, and how they compare in importance with current situational factors typified by occupational differences.

Four classes of personal and social characteristics have been sampled, facts of social background and personal history, childhood personality, childhood goals and values, and adult goals and values. All show some relation to adult mental health, most of them quite clearly in respect to *individual differences* but only slightly and inconsistently in respect to occupational group differences. On the whole, the personal characteristics are associated with mental-health variations among individuals to roughly the same degree as are the occupational influences. This is substantially less true of the "goals and values" measures than of prejob personality and socio-economic indicators.

In the main, the personal variables and the current situational variables represented by occupation exert their influence in relative independence of one another. Personal variables play only a small part in accounting for differences of mental health associated with job level; and conversely occupational effects do not account for the correlation of individual characteristics with mental health. Since all psychological effects are obviously a joint product resulting from the personal make-up of the individual, as determined by his entire past, and the opportunities and stresses of his present life situation, the two sets of influences, of course, cannot be really independent. What our results mean is that, within the range of variations represented in the sample and using the measures adopted in the study, interaction effects are relatively minor. Favorable and unfavorable occupational positions produce effects not drastically changed by differences of personal attributes and background and, likewise, favorable and unfavorable background characteristics tend for the most part to be associated with corresponding mental-health effects more or less regardless of occupational level.

Interaction effects are by no means absent, however. There is evidence of moderate combined effects in a number of the relationships that have been reported. The joint effects are of two contrasting types: sometimes the two sets of factors (personality and occupational level) exert additive influence tending to produce effects according to their combined favorableness; in other instances they exhibit an effect of contrast or incongruity such that, for example, certain favorable childhood conditions (creating high expectations) combine with low present job to produce especially *poor* mental health instead of raising it above that of persons with inferior background as well as inferior jobs. Our evidence as a whole indicates that this disparity principle is only weakly supported; that effects in this direction are inconsistent and of limited size.

Two broad conceptions have seemed helpful in our attempt to interpret the findings: (1) Generally advantageous or disadvantageous social and economic influences in childhood exert effects on personal development and self-feelings that carry over directly as determinants of subsequent mental health. (2) Later conditions of work and life provide gratification and impose frustrations in relation to established wants and expectations in a manner that fosters or impairs self-esteem and overall mental health. Disparity between aspiration and achievement, with resultant sense of failure, is one important aspect of this total process. But the general picture is that of an extensive network of individual motivations, expectations, and personality characteristics (far broader than aspirations for achievement and success alone) which interact with an equally wide range of favorable and unfavorable environmental conditions to elicit attitudes, feelings, and behavior that are "successful" and "healthy," or less so, depending on the entire constellation.

Under special circumstances either the personal or the situational influences may have clearly predominant effects. And one or the other of the causal processes noted in the two preceding paragraphs may appear ascendant. To the extent that the persons studied are homogeneous and the present circumstances are diverse, it will obviously be the latter that "make a difference," that "account for" mental-health variations. If the persons are of varied personalities, abilities, and backgrounds, then these individuating factors will naturally tend to loom large as explanations. In this perspective, what our empirical research indicates is that under the "typical" mid-century American conditions of the study—as to types of workers, industry and jobs studied, economic and social setting at the time, and so on—neither the personal nor the situational (occupational) influences assume a position of decisive priority over the other. Both are clearly significant and they make contributions of the same order of magnitude. The major emphasis on *occupational* effects throughout the book is dictated not by evidence that these are of *superior* importance but solely by the nature of our interests and purpose in conducting the study.

8.

The worker's orientation to his world—

1. Relation to the job

The range of behavior to be considered in assessments of mental health has no circumscribed limits. The quality of working people's adjustments is indicated by *all* their activities, attitudes, and feelings. Previous chapters have utilized an index of mental health based on a selection of such indicators. This chapter and the following ones take a wider view; they provide a more rounded description of the psychological condition of industrial workers and their relationship to their world, building on the mental-health components of earlier sections but adding many other attitudes and behavioral characteristics which also reveal better or poorer mental health. Each attribute of behavior is treated here as important in its own right, each as a meaningful aspect of the worker's relation to his world. We shall not only describe the attitudes and activities but also venture some evaluative judgments in the belief that the implications in respect to mental health are of a nature that commands some degree of valuational consensus in our society.

The underlying nonscientific question of these chapters asks simply: how *satisfactory* is the total picture of workers' attitudes and adjustments in each major sector of their lives—in their work and in nonwork spheres? This evaluative judgment obviously cannot be derived directly from empirical research evidence. However, our aim is to supply a little better factual basis for such judgments and for the resulting social and industrial policies that constantly have to be hammered out by all persons and groups concerned.

Working people's orientations, feelings, and activities will be examined under four headings: the job; free-time or nonjob-related activities and attitudes; social and political attitudes and outlook; feelings toward self and personal goals. The analysis focuses on

156

Detroit factory workers with particular attention to those on simple
semiskilled production jobs.   The first of the four areas is considered
in this chapter; the remaining three in the following chapters.

In Chapter 1 we asserted on the basis of our own and other
studies that the worker's job is a highly important sector of his
life.   It looms large as part of his total self-image.   It may constitute either a central, positive, satisfying aspect of life or a serious
source of discontent and negative sentiments toward himself.   This
being so, his gratifications and frustrations in work would be expected to play an essential part in his happiness and mental health.
Consequently, we directed much of the current study to these job-
related feelings and attitudes.

The voluminous literature on industrial workers presents sharply
discordant answers to the question of how satisfying their jobs are.[1]
Generalizations commonly polarize toward one extreme or the other,
tending to create a bright picture of happy, well-motivated workers
or a bleak, negative view of men alienated from work, grimly
enduring it, or bent on escaping from it.   Neither view, we believe,
is valid as applied to the contemporary American scene.   Evidence
has accumulated from enough careful studies to demonstrate that the
typical condition is distant from both extremes.   Most men in
factory jobs are neither acutely discontented with their work nor
do they find it stimulating and enjoyable.   There is little bitterness
and likewise little enthusiasm.

Extent of job satisfaction

Results from our own research help to depict more clearly this
less simple in-between orientation.   The two salient conclusions,
foreshadowed by preceding chapters, are that: (1) overall job
feelings of automobile workers are predominantly favorable though
at the same time there is enough dissatisfaction to suggest need for
substantial improvement; and (2) large and important differences
exist between occupational skill levels with pronouncedly more
negative reactions among men on routine production jobs.

The most general and direct interview question on this matter
asked the worker to choose one of five phrases telling how he feels
about his job.   A large majority of the total factory sample say
they are "completely satisfied" or "well satisfied" (58 per cent of
young; 73 per cent of middle-aged).   In addition, 25 per cent of the

young and 16 per cent of the middle-aged say "neither satisfied nor dissatisfied." This leaves only 17 per cent of the young and 11 per cent of the middle-aged responding negatively with "a little dissatisfied" or "very dissatisfied" (this last extreme response is given by only 7 and 1 per cent respectively of young and older). If accepted at face value, these replies suggest a very high level of general contentment, particularly on the part of middle-aged workers. However, it is necessary to go back of these first results and beyond them in order to reach balanced conclusions.

In the first place, one must ask what it means when workers declare that they are satisfied or have neutral feelings. Most of the men see little likelihood of moving out of their present type of work. This is especially true of the middle-aged. Consequently, they have a strong need to believe, to convince themselves, that the job is at least reasonably satisfying. To admit the opposite, even to themselves, is tantamount to recognizing that in the vitally important sphere of work their lives are irremediable failures. That admission is too painful for most men to face. It follows that there is a built-in bias toward accenting the positive, toward expressing job satisfaction. One may reasonably conjecture, then, that many of the men who reply "neither satisfied nor dissatisfied" are merely avoiding open acknowledgment of underlying dissatisfaction. Likewise a number of those who declare themselves "well satisfied" may be stretching in a favorable, self-reassuring direction.

Parallel speculations regarding the subjective meaning of dissatisfied responses are equally interesting. Two types of workers might be expected to voice discontentment: (1) those of high personal morale who are hopeful of changing to more satisfactory jobs and hence find nothing painful in condemning their present employment, and (2) those whose alienation, negative self-feelings, and low morale (poor general mental health) make job-defeatist attitudes a natural component of the unhappy "syndrome." Analysis of our data reveals few of the first type, many of the second. Men who express job dissatisfaction are usually not those high in mental health or those expecting promotion or making genuine efforts to change jobs. On the contrary, the job dissatisfied tend to have low mental-health scores (11 per cent of the young dissatisfied have high mental-health scores versus 48 per cent of the satisfied; among the middle-aged, it is 24 versus 43 per cent); only one in ten perceives good chances for promotion and only one-fourth are doing anything to seek or prepare for other work. In a word, although a healthy, constructive discontent that prompts efforts for change is surely possible, we find that the actual job discontent is rarely of this kind. Rather it is symptomatic of frustration and personal defeat.

When answers of workers in different occupations are compared on the job-satisfaction question, we find the most unfavorable feelings expressed by those in routine semiskilled jobs. Table 8-1 summarizes the results. Men on repetitive production jobs are consistently most dissatisfied as a group, among both young and middle-aged, in Detroit and in small towns—with the single exception of middle-aged white collar employees who express dissatisfaction equal to that of routine production workers. It should be remembered that this white-collar group consists of male office employees who in their forties remain in subordinate positions at salary levels similar to the upper manual groups; they are white-collarites who have been left behind. Among factory workers, we find the upper and ordinary semiskilled approximately as satisfied as the skilled and as the nonfactory and young white-collar groups. Only the routine, repetitive workers, particularly the young men, are strik-

Table 8-1   Comparison of occupational groups on a direct question regarding job satisfaction*

Occupational Category	Young				Middle-aged			
	Satis-fied	Neither	Dis-satisfied	N†	Satis-fied	Neither	Dis-satisfied	N†
Detroit factories								
Skilled }	67%	27%	6%	33	80%	11%	9%	45
High semiskilled					78	13	9	98
Ordinary semiskilled	65	22	13	46	74	15	11	82
Repetitive semiskilled	37	27	37	30	60	23	16	73
Small-town factories								
High and ordinary semiskilled	72	17	11	18	82	14	5	22
Repetitive semiskilled	33	33	33	18	60	10	30	20
Detroit nonfactory								
High semiskilled	79	10	11	28	...	...	...	3
Ordinary semiskilled	65	0	35	20	70	21	9	43
Detroit white collar	70	15	15	40	61	25	14	28

* Would you look at this card and say which of these statements tells how you feel about your job?   Would you say you are:

____completely satisfied
____well satisfied
____neither satisfied nor dissatisfied
____a little dissatisfied
____very dissatisfied

† Totals on which the percentages are based.   Each horizontal set of three percentages totals 100 except when rounding produces a total of 99 or 101 per cent.

*Table 8-2   Comparison of occupational groups as to their preference for a different type of work**

Occupational Category	Young Per cent Choosing *Different* Work	N†	Middle-aged Per cent Choosing *Different* Work	N†
Detroit factories				
Skilled	52%	29	50%	42
High semiskilled			79	95
Ordinary semiskilled	80	46	76	80
Repetitive semiskilled	86	29	84	73
Small-town factories				
High and ordinary semiskilled	60	15	40	20
Repetitive semiskilled	81	16	75	16
Detroit nonfactory				
High semiskilled	48	25	. . .	3
Ordinary semiskilled	65	20	81	42
Detroit white collar	39	39	56	27

* If you could go back to the age of 15 and start all over again, would you choose the same type of work you are in now or a different type of work?
† Totals on which percentages are based. Some N's are slightly smaller than those in earlier tables because of missing or unclassifiable answers.

ingly more discontented. The nature and extent of the dissatisfaction may be more fully assessed by reference to additional questions.

A question that serves as a useful corrective to the unduly favorable impression conveyed by the preceding figures was worded as shown at the foot of Table 8-2. The proportions of workers who reply that they would choose a different type of work are given in the table. Three of every four Detroit factory workers, young and middle-aged alike, would not wish to go into the same kind of work again. Regardless of whether in reality they would do so, the replies nonetheless reveal present attitudes far short of contentment with what they are now doing. Among men on repetitive jobs the vote is more than five to one in favor of a change. Routine production workers again prove to be the most dissatisfied group.

In a way the results are even more telling when men were asked, earlier in the interview, whether they are now thinking of leaving the work they are in. Well over half the young men say that they are, with strikingly higher proportions at lower-level jobs—35 per cent of skilled and high semiskilled, 57 per cent of ordinary semiskilled, and 83 per cent of repetitive semiskilled. No corresponding gradient occurs among middle-aged; approximately 40 per cent in each occupational category say they are thinking of changing. It appears that a majority of middle-aged men in the lowest jobs accept their job status as settled; many who doubtless thought about leaving in their twenties have abandoned the idea—and hope—by the time they reach their forties. In fact, 66 per cent of all young workers and 57 per cent of the middle-aged say that there have been times, recently or in the past, when they thought of leaving the kind of work they are doing. This wish for different work cannot be interpreted as predominantly healthy ambition since the mental health of the men desiring change is much poorer on the average than that of workers who do not want a change (26 per cent of young men wishing for change have high mental health versus 55 per cent of all others; corresponding figures for the middle-aged are 33 per cent to 49 per cent).

Short of leaving the job, which is not a readily feasible alternative for most men, they can stay away from work now and then. Absenteeism depends only in part on job attitudes, of course, since it is affected by health, economic need, and numerous other influences. Nevertheless, to see what it might reveal, we asked each man how many days he had been absent in the past year. The results are in the expected direction. Young workers have a little higher rate of absences than the middle-aged which corresponds to their higher rate of dissatisfaction. There is also a slight tendency for the lowest skill group to be absent more than those in better jobs. And, consistently in both age groups, mildly greater absenteeism occurs among the job dissatisfied. In all these comparisons, the median absenteeism is approximately 4 days a year for the group having poorer attendance versus 3 days a year for the others. Of the men who express satisfaction with their jobs, 15 per cent were absent more than 6 days; of all others, 28 per cent were absent this much. An analysis of company records of absences yields essentially the same results. We conclude that this tangible, economically significant manifestation of job feelings agrees with other lines of evidence that reveal less satisfactory orientation to work in routine jobs.

Prevalent opinions of factory workers in regard to production jobs and factory employment as a whole also indicate extensive work dissatisfaction. We need only recall and supplement the evidence along this line noted in Chapters 1 and 5. In brief the findings are the following. Replies to the question "How do you feel about factory work in general compared with other kinds of work?" were coded into five categories from strongly favorable to strongly un-favorable. Among young factory workers those giving predomi-nantly unfavorable evaluations outnumber the favorable three to one. Among the middle-aged it is one and a half to one. Young workers on repetitive jobs are unfavorable eleven to one! A classification of ideas expressed rather than of individuals shows the responses approximately two to one in the unfavorable direction for both age groups. With such low opinions of their "calling," workers as a whole can hardly be considered highly satisfied.

A follow-up question inquired: "What effects do you think pro-duction jobs have on men—does it do anything to them?" The wording of this question naturally elicited references to adverse job effects. Nevertheless, one-third of the answers avoid the nega-tive, saying: no effect, it depends, or some similar expression. The more significant fact, however, is the readiness and intensity with which many of the men specify the ill effects: "makes you go nuts"; "hard on nerves"; "morbid and depressing"; "they get in a rut, don't have anything to look forward to"; "kills your ambition"; "makes you old before your time"; "like a battery, all the juice is gone"; "makes a man crabby, always tensed, can't relax"; "get nervous, jumpy, I've seen some where their hands just shake"; "makes them a nervous wreck, after 20 years he's all shot"; "they stagnate on the job, don't develop themselves, like a robot"; "become dull dummies like me, made me an old man fast, a tired old fool, that's the factory for you"; "they push until every drop of blood is out of you"; "pretty damned disgusted, made me a hard guy to live with"; "they do the thinking for you, you just work"; "every year I hate it more, nervousness gets worse every year"; "you've a feeling of tiredness even though the work isn't hard, you get depressed, feel all worn out"; "awful monotonous, you actually hate it"; "makes me irritable, feel like blowing my top"; "a man can't hardly take that kind of work." The largest number of complaints refer to bad health and fatigue, nervous tension, being in a rut with no chance for growth, and the dull, monotonous, joyless nature of the work.

When we inquired further what effects working in a factory has had on *you*, there is an interesting decrease of negative replies on the part of semiskilled production workers. The 68 per cent of responses naming bad effects in the preceding question now drops to 47 per cent. The latter figure may be an understatement produced by self-protective denial of damaging effects to one personally; or it may be a more authentic firsthand report unbiased by hearsay and the conventional derogatory image of production jobs. In any event, either figure is large enough to weigh heavily on the negative side and thus further to reduce the impression of a large balance of job satisfaction over dissatisfaction that was reported earlier in responses to the direct general question.

A rich supply of further evidence was obtained from workers' volunteered comments pertaining to their jobs and from a number of questions concerning specific job attributes. A first set of data comes from the initial section of the interview in which respondents were encouraged to talk about any aspects of their lives they wished. A large number of comments referred to their jobs even though no previous hint had been given that we were particularly interested in the work sector of their lives. All these ideas were subsequently classified as positive or negative in regard to the job. The proportions, by occupational categories, are summarized in Table 8-3.

Table 8-3   Proportions of positive and negative comments pertaining to the job by different occupational groups (Part A of the interview)

Occupational Category	Young				Middle-aged			
	+	+ and −	−	Number of Com- ments*	+	+ and −	−	Number of Com- ments*
Detroit factories								
Skilled }	65%	10%	25%	92	58%	15%	27%	111
High semiskilled }					48	21	31	230
Ordinary semiskilled]	57	10	33	105	41	21	38	177
Repetitive semiskilled	33	12	55	73	38	21	41	169
Small-town factories								
High and ordinary semiskilled	65	12	24	34	74	0	26	46
Repetitive semiskilled	35	8	57	37	47	15	38	45
Detroit nonfactory								
High semiskilled	60	21	19	79	...	...	...	5
Ordinary semiskilled	54	17	30	54	50	20	30	111
Detroit white collar	52	16	32	100	50	20	30	66

* The totals on which percentages are based. Each horizontal set of three percentages totals 100 except when rounding produces a total of 99 or 101 per cent.

For factory workers as a whole the findings again show a preponderance of favorable over unfavorable comments, roughly to the same degree as is true for nonfactory groups. Here again, too, we encounter increasing dissatisfaction as we descend the skill hierarchy. At the lowest job level the negative expressions outnumber the positive, especially strongly among young workers. Further analysis reveals that a considerable portion of the favorable comments at the time (1953–1954) consisted of remarks like "I've got a steady job," "good seniority," "no layoffs." If we subtract all references to job security or the salient fact of having a job, the remaining figures show just about equal percentages positive and negative for the total Detroit factory sample. In the lowest occupational category the proportion becomes overwhelmingly negative, 69 per cent negative to 27 per cent positive among young workers and 53 per cent to 36 per cent among middle-aged.

A parallel tabulation was made of all positive and negative ideas expressed in the next section of the interview where workers were asked in several different ways what they think of their job and what they like and dislike about it. Although the occupational differences are less pronounced (Table 8-4), they consistently ex-

Table 8-4   Proportions of likes and dislikes about the job by different occupational groups (Part B of the interview)

| Occupational Category | Young | | | | Middle-aged | | | |
	Likes	+ and −	Dis-likes	Number of Ideas Coded*	Likes	+ and −	Dis-likes	Number of Ideas Coded*
Detroit factories								
Skilled	61%	7%	32%	230	65%	5%	30%	262
High semiskilled					68	5	27	538
Ordinary semiskilled	62	7	31	264	64	4	32	439
Repetitive semiskilled	50	4	46	163	57	5	38	383
Small-town factories								
High and ordinary semiskilled	66	7	27	100	71	8	21	111
Repetitive semiskilled	52	5	43	99	56	3	41	102
Detroit nonfactory								
High semiskilled	66	7	27	191	65	5	30	20
Ordinary semiskilled	58	7	35	127	63	7	30	246
Detroit white collar	63	10	26	261	74	4	22	167

* The totals on which percentages are based. Each horizontal set of three percentages totals 100 except when rounding produces a total of 99 or 101 per cent.

hibit the same preponderance of favorable ideas over unfavorable for factory workers as a whole and the same diminution of the favorable ratio for men in the repetitive semiskilled category. Both here and earlier, moreover, comparisons of occupational groups in small-town factories reveal similar tendencies to a like extent.

But it is not enough to arrive at the conclusion that men in the auto plants are neither ideally happy nor miserable and bitter; nor even that there is much more indication of satisfaction than of dissatisfaction though with enough of the latter to suggest vast possibilities for improvement; nor that men in routine production work are the most dissatisfied. It is important further to inquire about the *directions* of job satisfaction and dissatisfaction. What are workers' positive and negative attitudes in respect to the several main characteristics of the job? What aspects motivate and satisfy them? What features thwart and alienate them?

Intrinsic satisfactions and dissatisfactions of work

Both the research and the popular literature concerning industrial work are replete with statements asserting that factory work itself is typically goalless, dull, without appeal; that it is made tolerable, and even pleasant, only by the agreeable social side of the work-group relationships. A variation of the theme contends that jobs are truly satisfying only insofar as they gratify needs for personal achievement and visible success in work performance. It is sometimes alleged that all other aspects of the job, such as wages, job environment, security, supervisory treatment, and the like, have negative significance only; their deficiencies cause *dissatisfaction* but their favorable presence is not a source of positive satisfactions. They can be "dissatisfiers" but never "satisfiers." Simple semiskilled jobs, consequently, can afford no genuine satisfaction. Since these propositions have gained considerable currency, it is of special interest to examine our evidence bearing on the issue.[2]

We begin by considering what the worker's attitude is toward the intrinsic character of the work itself. Does it give him any feeling of self-expression, growth, joy of accomplishment? In these respects more than any other, men on routine production-line jobs differ from their fellow workers employed in more varied and skilled operations. An overwhelming majority of the factory workers interviewed do find positive satisfaction in the work itself; for most of them it is by no means the unmitigated dreariness so frequently assumed to be the case. In the group on routine repetitive operations, on the other hand, even though expressions of satisfaction are not completely lacking, many more of the workers report the job dull and stultifying.

In addition to evidence reported in Chapter 6 (pp. 97–101) revealing the special significance of work that is interesting and challenging, further pertinent facts on this point follow. Of all volunteered comments referring to job interest, self-expression, and feelings toward the work itself (including pride of performance, quality of product and operations, etc.), 78 per cent are positive as against 13 per cent negative among factory workers who are not on routine repetitive jobs (9 per cent were not classifiable as positive or negative); among repetitive workers, the percentages are 48 per cent positive and 44 per cent negative. The figures for *young* repetitive workers, not yet inured or resigned, are only 36 per cent positive to 59 per cent negative. Factory workers in small towns show the same sharp difference between workers on the simplest jobs contrasted with others. White-collar and nonfactory manual groups are much like the nonroutine factory people in proportions of favorable and unfavorable attitudes toward the nature of their work operations.

There is scant support here for generalizations that are either glowingly favorable or dismally bleak in regard to factory workers as a whole. But the unfavorable position of routine production-line workers cannot be missed. The positive and negative feelings on different jobs are vividly illustrated by statements like those that follow.

By men on repetitive jobs:

I hate the job. It is like playing a record over and over again. I go in Monday and wait for Friday.

I've been doing that job for 20 years and they can hire a man off the street and he will be able to do the job as well as I can.

Just putting in time; there's nothing to look forward to.

Everything is automatic; practically everything is done for you by the machine. You don't even have to know how to set up the job; someone does it for you.

I've been working on motors for 26 years and in all that time I've done about five different operations; don't know anything about motors yet. Little chance to show that you can do better work.

It's just routine work and that's it. Can't use your noggin; no head work at all.

Steady grind, same thing over and over. You don't need brains for it; there's no variety at all.

Positive sentiments are also occasionally expressed by men on simple routine jobs. For example:

They say I do good work; I've always tried to. I like to know that I had a part in making a good product.
I get satisfaction in doing my work and doing it right.
It's the best job I ever had. I just like it, no kicks at all. I know I do it as good or better than the next guy. It's not too simple and not too hard, just right for me.

By men on more skilled or varied jobs:

I like to solve problems; my job gives me a chance to take responsibility and make something of it. I do the best I can all the time because I enjoy it.
You'll never know enough about it; you always have a chance to learn more. You have to set up your own work; you have to figure things out for yourself. The blueprints only tell you what they want; it's up to you to get it.
Boring at times until a tough job comes up; then you have to think a lot and figure out the trouble; it's a test to see who will win out, the motor or me. [But] you're restricted to one part and can't do every job completely even if you know how to do it.
Satisfaction in doing it the way it should be done. If it's like it should be, and I try to do it that way, then I'm satisfied. I take pride in my work.
Job is interesting and enjoyable in every way. It uses my abilities to every advantage; it's complicated.
I feel that each car is a little better because I worked on it.

Most of the foregoing material consists of answers elicited by very general nondirective questions in regard to the worker's job feelings. We did not rely solely on spontaneous comments evoked by such questions, however, to learn how men react to their work, but proceeded to ask more directed questions in order to secure responses on several essential job attributes from all the workers. Data from these questions reveal still more clearly the preponderant negative feelings, or at best passive acceptance, by repetitive work groups contrasted with the preponderantly positive orientation of all other groups. This may be seen in the figures of Tables 8-5 and 8-6. The proportion of workers who consider their jobs "really interesting" declines precipitately from the nonrepetitive factory

*Table 8-5   Comparison of occupational groups on a direct question regarding interest in work**

	Young				Middle-aged			
Occupational Category	Inter- esting	Not Very Inter- esting	Dull and Monoto- nous	N†	Inter- esting	Not Very Inter- esting	Dull and Monoto- nous	N†
Detroit factories								
Skilled					89%	11%	0%	45
High semiskilled }	79%	21%	0%	33	83	17	0	97
Ordinary semiskilled	62	36	2	45	73	26	1	82
Repetitive semiskilled	17	47	37	30	32	50	18	72
Small-town factories								
High and ordinary semiskilled	72	28	0	18	91	5	5	22
Repetitive semiskilled	29	47	24	17	24	29	48	21
Detroit nonfactory								
High semiskilled	92	8	0	26	...	...	...	3
Ordinary semiskilled	63	32	5	19	60	33	7	42
Detroit white collar	79	21	0	38	78	15	7	27

* On the whole would you say that your job is (show card):

(1) really interesting and enjoyable

(2) or would you say that it is all right but not very interesting

(3) or would you say that it is dull and monotonous

† Totals on which percentages are based. Some N's are slightly smaller than those in earlier tables because of missing or unclassifiable answers. Each horizontal set of three percentages totals 100 except when rounding produces a total of 99 or 101 per cent.

groups to the simple repetitive category. Nearly four-fifths of factory workers on nonrepetitive operations say the jobs are "really interesting," roughly the same proportion as occurs for white-collar and nonfactory manual workers. Once more it is to be recalled that these positions above the most simple, repetitious ones consti- tute the vast majority of hourly paid jobs—about three-fourths of all automobile-plant manual employees. Sharply contrasting with this majority group, only one in four of the repetitive workers ex- presses similar interest in work.

Closely related results appear in answer to a question whether the job affords opportunity to make use of one's abilities (Table 8-6). Most workers, apart from those on repetitive operations, are satisfied that they can use their abilities. The opposite is strikingly true of the repetitive work group. From two-thirds to four-fifths of them complain that the work is oversimple; that they have no chance to live up to their possibilities, to do what they are capable of doing.   Of the still smaller group on the *most* repetitious paced operations (work cycle of less than one minute), only 1 of 20 is satisfied in this respect; 17 of 20 say definitely that the work is too simple.   As expressed by the sardonic comment of one worker: "It don't take no Einstein."

A significant minority of "ordinary semiskilled," engaged in somewhat more varied work, feels the same way; more than one-fourth of them say they have no chance to use their abilities.   It is also observed that the "ordinary semiskilled" in nonfactory employment complain even more frequently on this score than their opposite numbers in factories, though the sizable proportion still falls well below the number of repetitive factory workers with similar negative feelings.

Feelings of factory workers toward the inherent interest and challenge of their work are intimately linked to their general satisfaction with the job.   For example, 82 per cent of the men who find the work interesting have high job satisfaction while only 44 per cent of all others express a similar degree of satisfaction.   The relationship exists at each occupational level for both young and middle-aged workers.   These relationships, together with similar ones for

Table 8-6   Use of abilities on the job— comparison of occupational groups*

Occupational Category	Young				Middle-aged			
	Yes, Use Abilities	?	No, Too Simple	N†	Yes, Use Abilities	?	No, Too Simple	N†
Detroit factories								
Skilled }	79%	6%	15%	33	98%	0%	2%	44
High semiskilled }					73	18	9	97
Ordinary semiskilled	62	7	31	42	65	9	26	81
Repetitive semiskilled	17	17	66	29	24	9	67	70
Small-town factories								
High and ordinary semiskilled	47	12	41	17	76	5	19	21
Repetitive semiskilled	17	0	83	18	19	5	76	21
Detroit nonfactory								
High semiskilled	84	8	8	25	...	...	...	3
Ordinary semiskilled	47	5	47	19	56	5	40	43
Detroit white collar	77	8	15	40	75	14	11	28

* Would you say your job gives you a chance to use your abilities or is the job too simple to let you use your abilities?   (How is that?   How do you mean?)
† Totals on which percentages are based.   Some N's are slightly smaller than those in earlier tables because of missing or unclassifiable answers.   Each horizontal set of three percentages totals 100 except when rounding produces a total of 99 or 101 per cent.

use of abilities, indicate that the intrinsic appeals of work are more closely interrelated with total job feelings than are any other of the job characteristics studied.

Several other interview questions contribute interesting sidelights on workers' orientation toward the work itself. One is the question whether they feel that their job is important. Although most workers reply affirmatively, again this is less true of those in the most routine types of employment. If we limit our count to answers that refer to the work itself (not, for example, "important because making good money"), only one-third of young workers on repetitive jobs say it is important, contrasted with 82 per cent of those more skilled. In the middle-aged group, a like comparison shows 64 per cent to 89 per cent. Factory workers as a whole have very nearly as high a proportion positive as have nonfactory workers. For the vast majority, work is not regarded merely as putting in time, not simply a burden to be endured for the sake of extraneous rewards. It possesses some importance for all except the young men in routine jobs

At the same time, the work leaves much to be desired in the way of enthusiasm or positive motivational appeal. For example, when we asked "Are there any things you particularly look forward to at work each day?," over half the men said there was nothing (in the lowest skill group, 63 per cent answered in this way). Only one in five of all factory workers mentioned looking forward to anything about the work itself and this shrinks to one in eight for "ordinary semiskilled" and one in fourteen for "repetitive semiskilled." As another fragment of evidence indicating something less than ideal motivation in work, we note that 55 per cent of Detroit auto workers say that the men in their shop could turn out more work or better work if they wanted to; and decidedly the most common reasons given for not doing so are laziness, lack of interest, preferring to take it easy, and similar attitudes.

But speed, stress, and intensity of work are likewise intrinsic features of many factory jobs. These characteristics are angrily denounced by a small but significant minority of workers, particularly when their attention is specifically directed to the human effects of production jobs. Through earlier portions of the interview, however, in discussion of their own work, relatively few voice complaints on this score. As we noted in Chapter 6, even among workers engaged in most repetitive machine-paced operations, fewer than one in five speak of speed-ups or undue work pressures. Only one man in ten of those on production-line jobs (one in fifty of all semiskilled workers) expresses strong feelings such as the following in regard to his own job: "you're working at top speed all the time, you have to drive yourself all the time"; "you have to work too fast, it makes you nervous and tense"; "they always want more than they can get out of a man; after a man passes 45 he just can't work at that top speed and keep his health"; "they go like a house on fire, always in a big hurry; you've got to be moving every single second." Perhaps complaints of this kind are not more frequent because speed tends to be merged with other objectionable attributes of the work to create a total undifferentiated aversion to the drudgery, the steady wearing grind of dull routine labor. Whatever the reason, workers' negative reactions to work emphasize tiredness, monotony, and futility much more than speed.

Everything considered, despite the occasional denunciations, it appears that the great majority of our factory workers find considerable satisfaction in their work, to almost the same degree as do comparable nonfactory groups. But there is a less favorable side as well, reflected in their low esteem of factory jobs, their desire to leave this type of work, the fairly numerous complaints of health effects and fatigue, and the relatively passive, unenthusiastic attitudes toward the intrinsic characteristics of the work. The positive appeal of work is at a decidedly lower level among men engaged in routine semiskilled operations, though even there a sizable minority finds some degree of satisfaction in the work itself. These statements refer, of course, to factory work under conditions obtaining in Detroit auto plants in the 1950's. Very different conclusions might be drawn where wages, personnel policies, work speed and intensity, and surrounding conditions are below average and where workers have no effective means of protest and change. In most present-day American industry, however, with organized workers and managements jointly controlling working conditions and labor relations, we would expect the foregoing findings to be typical.

Satisfactions and dissatisfactions in regard to extrinsic characteristics of work

The next question is how workers feel toward major aspects of the job aside from the inherent character of the work itself. Do the *extrinsic* attributes also function as positive motivations, as "satisfiers" when they are in accord with desires, or only as "dissatisfiers" when they are inadequate? Earlier we mentioned the two contrary views: (*a*) that factory work in and of itself is unrewarding and is made tolerable only by the agreeableness of social relationships ("human relations") and other conditions of employment, or (*b*) that the extrinsic attributes cannot compensate for intrinsic lacks, that nothing but intrinsic opportunities for workmanship and achievement can bring real satisfaction, whereas the other aspects of jobs are important only in that they produce, or do not produce, negative attitudes. Our evidence, we believe, points rather to the conclusion that both the intrinsic and the extrinsic job features operate as both satisfiers and dissatisfiers. In fact, the division seems to us artificial and untenable on theoretical grounds as well.

The extrinsic aspects of jobs to be dealt with here are those we introduced in Chapter 6. For the most part they prove to be matters toward which favorable attitudes predominate. This is especially true in regard to job security (this was during the years 1953–1954) and the social conditions of work including both interpersonal and organizational relationships. Somewhat less favorable attitudes are expressed in respect to physical conditions of work, wages, and promotion opportunities. In the following pages we shall say a little more about these separate job factors. But the immediate point to be stressed is that significant *positive* attitudes exist, along with larger or smaller numbers of negative reactions, toward every category of job conditions. This strongly suggests that they may all function in some measure as "satisfiers"; that attitudes toward the job are a product of the total situation and may be clearly favorable or unfavorable for many reasons, not solely because of inherent enjoyment of work process and whatever sense of achievement it affords. Indeed, almost half the men for whom the job is not very interesting and who do not find use for their abilities nevertheless feel well satisfied with the job. Apparently, the positive job feelings of these men are accounted for by satisfactions derived from extrinsic aspects of work even in the absence of intrinsic satisfiers.

Let us begin with feelings about physical working conditions— dust, dirt, heat, noise, and so on, and their real or imagined injurious effects on health. When working people were asked how factory work compares with other types of jobs, the most common replies were those referring to objectionable work environment. Also in earlier parts of the interview when men specified what they liked and disliked about their own jobs, the physical context of work again received frequent and predominantly unfavorable comment.

Three points of special interest appear here: one is that although a majority of spontaneous references to work surroundings are negative, some 40 per cent are favorable.   These job attributes are seen by many as a source of gratification, not merely as "dissatisfiers." For example, when workers are asked how they feel about their jobs, in a number of instances the answer is "nice clean place," "good clean work," "good surroundings," "can't beat the working conditions," "excellent ventilation," "air-conditioned plant makes job very enjoyable."   These replies are sometimes the first ones given and ones accorded major emphasis as positive appeals of the job.   The second observation is that the proportion of *positive* comments is much greater in the two *lower* skill categories than at higher skill levels (49 per cent positive at lower levels versus 24 per cent at upper).   Job environment is apparently more likely to be perceived as a "satisfier" in lower-level jobs.   Finally, it is in the lower jobs that attitudes toward physical working conditions are most clearly associated with general job satisfaction.   In the repetitive semiskilled group, among the job satisfied 64 per cent of the comments are favorable versus only 21 per cent among the dissatisfied.   For all higher occupational groups the difference is only 41 per cent favorable by the job satisfied versus 28 per cent by the dissatisfied.   This suggests that satisfaction with physical work surroundings is not particularly consequential for overall job feelings in the more skilled and varied occupations which possess other more significant advantages, but that in routine jobs these external factors assume an important place.   Workers in the least-skilled occupations presumably reach for whatever positive satisfactions are available.   In the absence of intrinsic rewards of workmanship and achievement, many workmen tend to find gratification in favorable external circumstances.

The same interpretation in part would seem to apply to wages though in this instance people at every occupational level appear equally to derive satisfaction from the "extrinsic factor."   At the same time, of course, many are dissatisfied that their pay is not higher.   In our study, pay does not loom as one of the most salient job conditions; fewer than half of the men interviewed include it in their volunteered remarks about things liked and disliked in the job.   The positive comments slightly outnumber the negative.   More representatively, in response to a direct question which secured replies from everyone, 48 per cent declare themselves well satisfied with their wages, 29 per cent are dissatisfied, and 23 per cent say they feel neither satisfied nor dissatisfied. No large differences occur between occupational levels; men in less-skilled positions are neither more contented nor more discontented with their pay than are the more skilled.

The job dissatisfied, as would be expected, are likewise more dissatisfied in regard to wages at each occupational level. Attitudes in regard to wages, however, are by no means a decisive influence on job feelings since we find a majority (57 per cent) of the men dissatisfied with their pay are nevertheless well satisfied with the job as a whole. At the same time it is to be noted that the proportion jumps to 80 per cent among men well satisfied with wages, clearly indicating the positive correlation between feelings about wages and feelings about the job. The relationship is somewhat weaker in the low-skill group, suggesting that feelings in regard to wages are less important in accounting for differences of overall job orientation among men in this group than is true for men in better jobs. It suggests, too, that other job attributes may be more significant elements accounting for differences of job satisfaction at the routine work level. These interpretations receive further support when we examine the volunteered comments. Spontaneously expressed feelings about wages show a moderate association with job satisfaction in occupations above the lowest skill group, but in the repetitive work group there is no association at all. Moreover, among workers on routine jobs complaints concerning bad working conditions are much more closely related to job dissatisfaction than are negative feelings about wages.[3]

Altogether, then, wages do not stand out as a matter on which the workers in our study feel deeply or as a factor which accounts in any large degree for their differing amounts of job dissatisfaction. Nevertheless, pay is spontaneously referred to fairly often both as a positive and a negative job influence; it appears to be as much a source of satisfaction as of dissatisfaction.

We must repeat the warning of Chapter 6 against unwarranted generalization of what is said here in regard either to the relative unimportance of wage rates or the amount of favorable feeling. Under other circumstances wages can become a dominant emotional concern, overwhelmingly potent as a source of discontent and frustration. But among auto workers at the time of this study there is no evidence of such saliency or dissatisfaction.

Opportunities for promotion are mentioned much less often by the men interviewed than are wages or working conditions. The comments are slightly more favorable than unfavorable in the younger group (56 per cent favorable); a majority (62 per cent) are unfavorable among the older workers. The contents of the volunteered responses indicate that we are again dealing with a job feature that operates both as satisfier and dissatisfier, though without marked intensity of feeling in either direction for most workers. Scattered protests do occur in regard to the play of politics and favoritism—"too many brothers-in-law," "too much politics," "you have to belong to a clique," "if you don't know the bosses personally you will never get ahead," "I haven't learned how to polish apples," and "I'm not a Mason so promotion is out, I guess."

Men in the lowest semiskilled jobs are most pessimistic about advancement; volunteered negative ideas outnumber the favorable three to one as contrasted with equal numbers positive and negative for all more skilled workers. A direct question obtained similar evidence based on the total sample rather than on the minority who contributed spontaneous ideas. The question asked: "How do you feel about your chances for getting ahead?" The context left no doubt that this referred to getting ahead occupationally. Fifty-five per cent of the young and 39 per cent of the middle-aged believe that they have either a good chance or some chance for advancement. Both proportions drop to 30 per cent in the low occupational category, leaving 70 per cent who feel that they have little or no chance. In this repetitive semiskilled group only one in five of the young and one in eighteen of the middle-aged think the chances are actually good. Even in the skilled and high semiskilled groups there are only two to five young and one of five middle-aged who view the chances as good.

Responses to the direct question on opportunities for advancement correlate moderately with general job satisfaction in all groups except the middle-aged at the two lowest skill levels. Despite the tendency for perceived lack of opportunity to be accompanied by diminished job satisfaction, however, it is still found that most workers who see little or no chance of advancement (62 per cent of them in fact) express high satisfaction with their jobs. This is not greatly different from the 76 per cent figure among those who feel that they do have opportunities for promotion. The difference is much larger for young workers, as we would expect since they are naturally more concerned about their vocational prospects. Among young men, 71 per cent of those who feel that they have chances for promotion are well satisfied with their jobs versus only

42 per cent of those who perceive little or no chance; among middle-aged the same comparison is 78 per cent to 67 per cent.

A cognate question asked workers how much they *care* about chances for advancement in their work. Over half the men say it is important to them (65 per cent of the young; 55 per cent of middle-aged), but most of these replies fail to convey any sense of strong conviction. Answers range from flat assertions that "I don't care nothing about it" or "I don't care much; what I do now is worry-free; they run a foreman crazy" to positive declarations like "I would give *anything* to get into supervision." But most typical are such replies as "I'd like to get ahead, I guess most men do," "I'd like a promotion if it didn't mean too many headaches and gripes," "sure I care," "I suppose I still care," "it would be nice but I don't think it's possible," "I guess I care."

In contrast to the preceding percentages, more than 90 per cent of men in white-collar positions declare that advancement is important to them. In our factory population no large differences are found between occupations though in the young group those at the lowest skill level are inclined to care less than young men in better jobs (23 per cent of the low group say advancement is not at all important to them compared with 8 per cent of all other young workers). A strong tendency is observed, especially among young workers, for those who care most about getting ahead also to feel that they have opportunities; or, conversely, those who see opportunities tend to feel that promotion is important.

Both perceived opportunity for promotion and feeling that promotion is important are associated with greater job satisfaction. However, the former is much the more closely and independently linked to job satisfaction. In fact when its influence is removed, by taking separately those who believe opportunity exists and those who do not, we find that *caring* about advancement bears no relationship to satisfaction in the young group while among middle-aged men the relationship is inverse. Among these older men, that is, satisfaction is consistently greater for those who have lower aspirations, who have come to feel that promotion is *unimportant* to them.

All in all, feelings in regard to job advancement are somewhat more negative than positive. This is decidedly the case among routine production workers. At every job level, however, considerable numbers voice optimism regarding their chances and since these tend to be men with above-average job attitudes, it would appear that promotion opportunities function as a source of positive motivation while at the same time lack of opportunity, especially at lower job levels, constitutes a continuing source of discontent. For a significant minority of both age groups, hope—or despair—of promotion persists as a vital aspect of their overall orientation toward the job.

The remaining extrinsic attributes of work to be considered here are ones toward which working people express especially favorable attitudes. These include feelings in regard to job security, as of the time of the interviews and for our sample of men having a minimum of three years seniority. Spontaneous references to steady work, layoffs, seniority protection, and job security generally are fairly frequent (mentioned by one man in four) and run more than three times as many favorable as unfavorable. The readiness and emphasis with which a number of these men refer to the security of their job offers evidence of its importance to them as a positive gratification, not a mere absence of dissatisfaction. Among their first comments about the job are ones like "it's steady," "no layoffs," "it's a good secure job," "most of all it's steady and dependable," "I'm very secure there, I've got top seniority," "I have always had a job, I've been lucky enough to work everyday," "I work steady and have hospitalization and don't have to worry about anything."

For some workers, of course, job security is also a matter of negative concern: "the main thing is the work is not steady the year around"; "you never know when you are going to be laid off"; "about all I worry about is getting laid off"; "if demand slackens I'll not be so good, frankly I'm concerned about it"; "layoffs really get me down, thats about the only thing worth mentioning." When we asked explicitly whether the worker ever worries about his work and if so what he worries about, one in seven stresses his fear of layoff, for example: "I worry about being laid off," "I just worry sometimes that it won't last," "sometimes worry that I could be out of a job."

Job-security feelings exhibit no significant differences from one occupational level to another. Likewise they reveal only very slight relationship to degree of job satisfaction; the job dissatisfied speak favorably of their security of employment almost as often as do the job satisfied.

Since we must assume that the impact of this variable changes radically with changing conditions of industry and the labor market, we conclude simply that under conditions existing at that time (Detroit employment rates were neither good nor especially bad in

1953), job security was a matter of marked importance to workers as indicated by the frequency and repetition with which they referred to it, and that their feelings were predominantly positive. For most workers in our sample there were no serious fears or complaints even among the routine semiskilled.

A last set of attitudes pertaining to the job has to do with the social environment of work, industrial "human relations." Volunteered comments on these matters fall into three groups: relationships with fellow workers, supervision and treatment on the job, and feelings about the company, its policies and employee services. Judged by frequency of mention, relationship to first-line supervision is most important of these while references to the company are least frequent. Favorable ideas far outnumber unfavorable in all these categories, about five to one in regard to coworkers and better than two to one in the other relationships. Occupational differences are extremely slight; the sole instance in which a majority of comments are negative occurs in the attitudes toward supervision by young workers at the lowest occupational level, where there are nine negative to five positive references.

Here again workers' spontaneous replies reflect both positive satisfactions and disagreeable irritations. Expressions of satisfaction, for example, include: "work is congenial; nice to work with a group that has teamwork, companionship among the boys"; "a friendly family-type bunch, been together years"; "like the people I work with, particularly the inspector that works with me is one of the greatest guys I know"; "a cheery bunch of fellows, it's not too often there are dull moments during the day"; "hard work but it is like a vacation; [want to get there] to shoot the breeze; I like to see my friends." In regard to supervision and the company, "I like the people I work for; they're courteous and considerate"; "an exceptionally good foreman, very good man to work for"; "the greatest satisfaction comes from being appreciated"; "awful nice bosses to work for"; "a good company to work for and shows a lot of interest in workers"; "I have a job with the best company in the world, they treat us swell"; "a splendid firm, it's a perfect setup for me." A few examples on the negative side are: "sometimes the people you work with get on your nerves"; "I don't like the people I work with"; "we don't get along with each other"; "the guy I work with is bossy"; "men in the group are not well matched temperamentally"; "so many bosses telling me what to do, they try to load more jobs on me"; "job isn't too bad but foreman riding me makes it tough"; "foreman can make things miserable every day; whole department thinks so"; "you do the best you can and they keep at you; it burns me up"; "most mismanaged place I've ever seen"; "they [company] don't care about you"; "want to get as much out of you as they can."

Although each of the foregoing volunteered sets of attitudes shows some association with differences of overall job satisfaction, the relationship is especially strong and clear in respect to negative feelings toward the boss and his treatment of workers. The last-named linkage to job satisfaction exists at upper as well as lower skill levels and in both age groups. This is unlike what we found in the case of attitudes toward physical work conditions where the relationship was close for workers on repetitive jobs but slight for more skilled workers.[4] Although the causal connections are by no means unambiguous, the evidence points to the tentative conclusion that supervisor-employee relations bear importantly on the job satisfaction of significant minorities of blue-collar workers at all occupational levels whereas physical work environment is important principally at low levels.

The foregoing results in respect to human relations are based on comments volunteered by those workers who felt strongly enough about the particular job aspect to prompt positive or negative statements. When we asked separate questions on these matters of all workers, the responses exhibit the same overall favorableness and the same tendency to correlate at least moderately with general job satisfaction. Replies to the direct question on supervision, however, as compared with the volunteered opinions, do not relate nearly as closely to overall job feelings. Apparently, the conclusion just stated in respect to the importance of attitude toward the boss is largely confined to workers who have articulate complaints or particularly intense feelings about their supervisors. For the great majority of men, attitude toward supervision carries no implication of job satisfaction or dissatisfaction.

More generally, the results from separate questions are as follows: questions on supervision, fellow workers, and the company each revealed only a small minority of approximately 10 per cent of all factory workers who expressed negative feelings and a somewhat larger number, in the range of one-fourth to one-third, who were strongly favorable. Differences by occupational level are negligible save that coworkers are more highly esteemed by upper skill groups and least highly regarded at the routine job level, particularly among young workers. Attitude toward the company is clearly associated with general job feeling, both at the favorable and unfavorable ends of the scale. In respect to supervision, those extremely favorable have no higher job satisfaction than the moderately favorable, but men who rate their boss bad or "not so good" are much less likely to be well satisfied with their jobs. Liking or disliking fellow workers is linked with degree of job satisfaction in the young group but not among the middle-aged. It is also of interest that men who work alone do not differ in job satisfaction from those who work with others.[5]

Differences of workers' orientations from company to company

A brief section is added at this point to call attention to the important variations of workers' attitudes that occur from one company to another. The purpose here is parallel to that in Chapter 6 where we temporarily shifted our focus from *occupational* differences to a comparison of *organizations*. Just as the findings there revealed large variations of mental health between companies, we now note similar significant contrasts of workers' job-related feelings and attitudes. The results again serve both to underscore the importance of organizational and management factors and to offer suggestive indications as to company attributes that help to account for the differences of morale and satisfaction.

The range of variations among companies is illustrated by figures like the following: the most favorably regarded of the thirteen Detroit automotive establishments studied is rated excellent or good by 100 per cent of its employees who were interviewed; the company receiving least favorable ratings had only 42 per cent who considered it excellent or good. One nonmanufacturing organization in our sample was so rated by a mere 14 per cent of its employees. The general question on satisfaction with the job found 92 per cent of the men well satisfied in one automotive company as compared to 50 per cent in another. Other more specific attitudes—toward wages, opportunity to use one's abilities, chances for promotion, job security, and many more—showed similar large variations among companies. The *average* difference between the best and poorest company on these various measures is 42 percentage points (which happens to correspond to the difference above in respect to job satisfaction). We also tested to see whether the attitude differences are due to differences of skill level between companies by making comparisons that used only the two lower semiskilled occupational groups. The attitude differences between companies remain equally large. It is thus clear that orientations of employees differ greatly by organizations independently of skill level.

Comparisons between larger and smaller companies in respect to the various attitudes reveal consistent tendencies for workers in the smaller (really medium-sized) plants to have more favorable orientations. For example, definitely positive feelings toward the company are expressed by 82 per cent of workers on the average in the smaller establishments as against 54 per cent in the large. In the smaller plants, 84 per cent are well satisfied with their jobs; in the larger plants, 66 per cent. Other job-related feelings exhibit corresponding differences. When, instead of size of company, the criterion is the experts' rating of personnel policies and practices,[6] we find that companies considered least satisfactory also have somewhat less favorable employee attitudes than the companies rated higher though the differences are smaller than those by company size.

It is of particular interest to see which specific sets of job feelings are most closely associated with the standing of companies on overall job satisfaction and attitude toward the company. These relationships should offer clues regarding possible significant determinants of favorable and unfavorable orientation to the job and to the company. In respect to job satisfaction, the findings are these: companies that rank high are those in which men more commonly feel that the jobs are interesting and use their abilities and where their attitudes are favorable toward the speed and intensity of work, physical conditions, wages, supervision, opportunities for promotion, and toward the company as a whole. Relationships are considerably more tenuous with regard to feelings about job security, ease of work, fellow workers, and employee services. Supervision is closely related on the negative side especially; that is, organizations in which job satisfaction is high differ notably in having extremely few workers with *unfavorable* reactions toward their boss. In sum, the results indicate that organizations may develop positive job feelings partly by making work itself agreeable and attractive and partly by management efforts with respect to compensation, supervision, promotion, and related personnel practices. When we analyze attitudes toward the company rather than toward the job, similar findings emerge but with specific work factors, wages, and promotion much less prominent. Along with generally favorable job orientation, the more salient, closely related factors become security of employment, good supervision, and organizational characteristics having to do with personnel and labor-relations policies, company product, and employee benefits and services.

The principal conclusions to be drawn from the comparisons of companies are (*a*) that the organizations do differ very substantially in the extent of employees' positive orientation to work and to the company, and (*b*) that these intercompany variations are accompanied by clusters of associated attributes that point to organizational factors which may account for the better or poorer company accomplishments. Favorable company characteristics include the objective factors of moderate-sized versus very large establishments and good personnel management (as judged by experts[6]) and such attitudinal factors as positive feelings toward the intrinsic interest and challenge of the work and toward pay, supervision, job security, and other features of approved labor and personnel-relations policy. These organizational characteristics are all intercorrelated, with intricate interdependencies that preclude clear causal interpretations centering on separate factors. We observe simply that the relationships are consistent with an impressive accumulation of research evidence over the years that indicates the vital bearing of these same characteristics of work operations, organization, and human-relations management on the creation of satisfactory employee morale. Although the present study was designed to make *occupational*, not company, comparisons, and although occupational differences have steadily been our central concern, the results do underscore the importance of organizational differences as well.

Orientation to the job—a summary

Through the foregoing pages we have been concerned with the question: how "satisfactory" are workers' feelings and attitudes toward their jobs? It should be kept in mind that our data refer to men who have been regularly employed over a period of years, who are sufficiently successful and well enough adjusted to have kept their jobs. Our interest centers not on their objective success in meeting performance standards, however, but on evidence regarding their subjective orientation to work. Taken as a whole the evidence supports neither the extremely optimistic nor the extremely pessimistic conclusions frequently advanced. Our factory workers are not completely happy, strongly motivated, unequivocally pleased with their work life; nor are they alienated, defeated, and depressed. They neither love the job nor hate it. Most characteristically they accept it in good spirit though with serious reservations and little enthusiasm, but not dejectedly, resignedly, or with "quiet desperation." They express numerous dislikes, criticisms, and complaints but still larger numbers of favorable evaluations. Many more of the total group are well satisfied with their jobs, everything considered, than are dissatisfied. This is especially true of middle-aged men, even when we make allowance for self-protective, ego-enhancing tendencies to accent the positive. At the same time, however, relatively few would choose to go into the same work again and most do not speak well of factory employment, particularly of production jobs, compared to other types of work. In a word, the predominant feelings of job satisfaction connote only a moderately contented adjustment to the job in the absence of realistic alternatives that would be better liked. Reasonably happy acceptance, yes, but with large unrealized possibilities for more positive motivation and increased satisfaction.

The preceding statements refer to the total factory group. Attitudes of the 25 to 30 per cent on routine, repetitive production operations are decidedly more negative. A large majority of their spontaneous comments about their work are unfavorable. A small but significant minority bitterly denounce the speed, strain, and unending weariness of the work. Responses to direct questions reveal that few of the workers on repetitive jobs find their work interesting or feel that it affords a chance to use their abilities. It is this feeling of lack of challenge in the job, the absence of opportunity to make worthwhile use of their capabilities, that stands out as the most striking contrast between men in the simplest semiskilled jobs and those in even slightly more skilled and varied types of work. In the main, men in occupations above the most routine find that work is interesting and offers a chance to use their abilities; the opposite is the case in routine repetitive jobs.

Despite these inherent frustrations of routine jobs stemming from the nature of the work itself, a substantial majority of the middle-aged repetitive workers declare themselves well satisfied and even the young men divide equally between those maintaining that they are well satisfied and those dissatisfied. We interpret this to mean that since the routine specialized occupations fail to offer intrinsic satisfactions of effective workmanship, accomplishment, and personal growth so vitally important in more skilled tasks, most workers in the lower jobs adaptively tend to emphasize extrinsic features of work which provide substitute sources of satisfaction and self-esteem. Many expressions of pleasure and gratification in respect to these extrinsic attributes support the view that there are multiple "satisfiers" as well as "dissatisfiers" in work and that both may be found in the "context" of the job as well as in intrinsic job "content."[7]

We do not mean to minimize the deprivations and dissatisfactions of low-level jobs. We point out merely that many working people do not experience such work as intolerable, a curse to be endured, "an endless frustration and bitterness." One can recognize the serious lacks and disagreeable characteristics of the jobs, as in some measure almost all the workers do, and yet see that the job also contains sources of enhanced positive self-feelings and coveted satisfactions. Perhaps most important of all on the positive side is the sheer fact of having a job in contrast to not having a job. Deep personal satisfaction and sense of worth derive from "belonging," being a useful, functioning member of the industrial society. Beyond this there are many gratifications, arising, for example, from superior job security, from comfortable working conditions, friendly social relationships at work, and from the infinite variety of desired goods and services for self and family that comparatively high wages make possible. Even in the absence of intrinsic work interest and appeal of challenging tasks, these other potential rewards of the job surely cannot be denied or ignored. Our findings indicate that for most workers they do indeed produce a favorable balance of feelings toward the job as a whole.

In sum, we would say that the working people we studied maintain reasonably satisfying and satisfactory relations to their work but at a level far removed from ideal. Even those in routine types of work have learned to live with their jobs, if not joyfully at least with moderate contentment. For more thoughtful and idealistic students of society this certainly does not suggest that all is well. In the perspective of a "good society" it might be wished that dissatisfaction and protest were more in evidence. We shall return to these larger speculations and evaluations in the final chapter.

Here we conclude simply by underscoring the "in-between" position dictated by our data. The predominant overall orientation to the job is positive, not negative.   Most workers are satisfied but not too well satisfied.   Especially in simple routine jobs they are acutely aware of the lacks, irritations, and debilitating grind.   In the more skilled and varied jobs, intrinsic rewards of the work itself supply a strong additional element of attraction and opportunity for healthy growth and self-actualization.   Despite the absence of such opportunities in low-level positions, most workers find substitute and compensating extrinsic rewards that enable them to accept their work life without bitterness and even in most cases with a kind of mild, passive, somewhat fatalistic satisfaction.

9.

The worker's orientation to his world—

2. Life away from the job

In this chapter we summarize certain findings concerning attitudes and adjustments of workers in the nonjob sectors of their lives. Our basic question remains the same: how "satisfactory" are their feelings and behavior and how different from one occupational level to another? Are men more satisfied or less satisfied in their life outside the plant than at work? Is life fuller and richer, more self-expressive and rewarding off the job? Do the limitations and deprivations at work carry over to create a correspondingly narrow and passive leisure? And do the men who find stimulation and joy in their work also participate with enthusiasm elsewhere? That is, do activities and feelings away from work represent spillovers from the job, congruent with in-plant orientations, or are the two spheres alternative and compensatory, so that men experience gratifications primarily in one or the other? These questions suggest the frame of reference for the ensuing analysis.[1]

Satisfaction with life: responses to direct questions

We begin by considering responses to a direct question asking how satisfied the worker is with his life in general. The question was asked at the start of the interview before attention had been directed to any particular sector of his life. Approximately two-thirds of all factory workers declare themselves well satisfied; one in six says he is dissatisfied (Table 9-1). Men in the factory differ little from nonfactory employees. The proportions satisfied and dissatisfied with life are roughly similar, moreover, to the proportions satisfied and dissatisfied with the job (Table 8-1). However, middle-aged

*Table 9-1 Comparison of occupational groups on a
direct question regarding satisfaction with life**

Occupational Category	Young				Middle-aged			
	Satisfied	Neither	Dissatisfied	N†	Satisfied	Neither	Dissatisfied	N†
Detroit factories								
Skilled					68%	16%	16%	44
High semiskilled }	76%	12%	12%	33	70	20	10	97
Ordinary semiskilled	65	13	22	46	71	15	14	80
Repetitive semiskilled	57	30	13	30	62	12	26	73
Small-town factories								
High and ordinary semiskilled	89	0	11	18	77	14	9	22
Repetitive semiskilled	67	22	11	18	65	25	10	20
Detroit nonfactory								
High semiskilled	79	14	7	28	...	...	...	3
Ordinary semiskilled	68	16	16	19	74	24	2	42
Detroit white collar	79	8	13	38	71	14	14	28

* Which of the statements on this card comes nearest to saying how you feel about your life in general? Would you say you are:

___completely satisfied
___well satisfied
___neither satisfied nor dissatisfied
___a little dissatisfied
___very dissatisfied

† Totals on which percentages are based. Some N's are slightly smaller than those in earlier tables because of missing or unclassifiable answers. Each horizontal set of three percentages totals 100 except when rounding produces a total of 99 or 101 per cent.

factory workers tend to be slightly better satisfied with the job than with life, and young routine semiskilled workers are much *less* satisfied with the job than with life. The latter are decidedly more like higher skill groups in respect to life satisfaction than in job satisfaction. In the small-town sample this last relationship holds also for the middle-aged, perhaps because many of them have chosen to live away from the city in order to enjoy their small farms and convenient opportunities for fishing, hunting, and boating. Except for the low-skill groups, life as a whole is not rated more satisfying than the job sector alone.

Results from other sections of the interview give further meaning to these responses, partly supporting and partly modifying the foregoing indications. Here, as in the case of job satisfaction, there is little doubt that most persons feel impelled to think of themselves as reasonably well satisfied and consequently to bias their self-ratings in a favorable direction. Moreover, it may be surmised that many negative feelings exist even when the net balance is considered favorable. Evidence of this diversity is plentiful in responses to different questions.

When working people were asked whether they have as much chance to enjoy life as they should have, from 70 per cent to 80 per cent of each occupational subgroup replied affirmatively. Differences by occupation are small, though white-collar employees and young nonfactory workers have slightly higher proportions satisfied and the routine factory group is a trifle less positively inclined than are other factory workers. Less favorable results appear in men's feelings about their future. Optimistic or contented answers to the question "How do you expect things to turn out for you in the future?" drop sharply among young workers, from 69 per cent at the skilled and high semiskilled level to 49 per cent among the ordinary semiskilled and 37 per cent among repetitive semiskilled. A similar gradient is not present among semiskilled workers in the middle-aged group; approximately half the men at each occupational level view the future optimistically. White-collar workers and young nonfactory workers again express a slightly more favorable outlook than the factory group.

Several other questions inquired about particular aspects of life—for example, how the worker feels about living in (or around) Detroit. Again the replies are preponderantly favorable though few are enthusiastic. Occupational groups differ only slightly, with white-collar employees and small-town factory men more commonly well satisfied. Other questions deal with home and family life and with spare-time activities. It comes as no surprise that overwhelming majorities are well satisfied in these areas; fewer than 10 per cent of the factory workers declare themselves definitely dissatisfied. Variations by occupation are slight, though it is worth noting that among middle-aged routine workers 14 per cent are explicitly dissatisfied with their family and home life compared to only 6 per cent of factory workers above that level. This *could* reflect the domestic consequences of continued job tension and dissatisfaction over the years.

Another direct question asked: "Do you feel that you are accomplishing the sorts of things you would like to in your life? (If yes) What things aren't you accomplishing?" Replies are again preponderantly positive (70 per cent). Once more, too, occupational differences are very small. Nonfactory workers appear a trifle more frequently contented (79 per cent) and the same is true of young white-collar workers (80 per cent) but not of the middle-aged. Factory workers on repetitive jobs are indistinguishable from "ordinary" semiskilled but both are slightly less satisfied than the high semiskilled. Money and material possessions are much more often mentioned by all groups, both on the positive and negative side, than are any other accomplishments. Successful marriage, family, and home come next. Routine factory workers show no clear or consistent differences from other semiskilled groups in the kinds of accomplishments they mention.

Taken as a whole, results from direct questioning like the foregoing indicate the following. (1) The vast majority of factory workers in our sample have a quite positive rather than negative orientation to life conditions. Moreover, their attitudes are no less favorable than those of nonfactory blue-collar workers and even in comparison with white-collar employees the differences are small and indeed could be caused by chance variations of sampling. (2) On these general satisfaction questions differences are likewise not great between factory workers at higher and lower skill levels, though the routine semiskilled are a little less satisfied. The decidedly greater job dissatisfaction of this group appears to carry over in only mild degree to feelings of dissatisfaction about life. The life-satisfaction component of mental health, that is, fails to reflect substantial and consistent adverse effects commensurate with the discontented job feelings of the low-skilled production workers.

Satisfaction with life: volunteered responses

Extensive further evidence on these issues is contributed by several indirect, free-response questions. Our interviews began with a series of these broad questions inquiring how the respondent feels about the way his life is working out, whether he has had good breaks or bad breaks, what things give him satisfaction, what things run counter to his wishes or cause him worry or unhappiness. The general picture derived from these questions for the entire Detroit factory sample may be seen in Table 9-2. Most notable is the overwhelmingly favorable feeling in regard to leisure activities, and to a lesser extent toward family matters, in contrast to the prominence of negative comments concerning other life conditions, both

Table 9-2   Proportions of positive and negative comments by factory workers regarding several aspects of life

Classification of Comments	+	±	−	Number of Comments*
Leisure and social activities	98%	1%	1%	590
The job	48	17	35	957
Family relations; wife and children	45	30	25	676
Own health, age, competence, etc.	44	16	40	477
Life experiences and relationships (other than current economic)	41	15	44	269
Personal economic condition	21	48	31	371
Social conditions, war, politics, people, etc. (with no clear personal reference)	13	7	80	364
Total	48%	19%	33%	3704

* The totals on which percentages are based. Each horizontal set of percentages totals 100.

economic and noneconomic.   It is of interest to note, too, that for the total of all comments the proportions favorable and unfavorable are nearly identical with the percentages pertaining to the job.   This would mildly suggest that life on and off the job may not differ greatly in the balance of satisfactions and dissatisfactions they afford.   In both spheres, positive points outnumber negative but fall short of a clear majority, surely not indicative of any pervasive *joie de vivre*.   A few further details, with particular attention to occupational comparisons, are spelled out in the following paragraphs.

Comments in regard to spare-time activities occur principally in response to a question asking the worker about his current sources of satisfaction.   Consequently, only enjoyable pursuits are mentioned. But parallel questions inquiring about matters he is not well satisfied with, or things that depress or worry him, virtually never elicit reference to leisure activities. This is true in all occupational groups. Apparently negative feelings are directed against interfering life circumstances rather than against the leisure pursuits themselves. For example, complaints about lack of spare time are classified elsewhere, under either economic or noneconomic unfavorable circumstances. The findings certainly cannot be taken to mean that men are completely content in their spare time, as later sections of the chapter will show.

Turning to response dealing with the workers' family relationships, we note that, although favorable expressions far outnumber the unfavorable, fewer than half of the total are clearly on the positive side. The typical positive comment refers to the excellent qualities of the wife, happy marriage, pride in children, and so on; the unfavorable most often stress family illness, quarrels and strains, regret that he is divorced or unmarried or childless. There are no strikingly large differences by occupation, but semiskilled factory workers in Detroit do show less satisfaction with family relationships than appears in the other groups. This is notably true in comparison with the middle-aged white-collar group (67 per cent positive comments to 13 per cent negative) and the young workers in small towns (65 per cent to 15 per cent); but it holds only a little less strongly for most of the other groups as well. This result adds a further hint of the same kind noted previously to the effect that family problems may be increased by semiskilled factory employment in an industrial metropolis.

In the category of health, age, and competence taken as a whole, positive and negative comments are almost equal in number and there is surprisingly little variation between factory occupational groups or between older and younger factory workers. When we divide the category into its two main parts this is no longer the case: for health and age, ideas run 54 per cent positive to 31 per cent negative; in contrast to this, expressions of competence or adequacy are only 29 per cent positive and 54 per cent negative. Significantly, middle-aged men on repetitive production jobs express more negative feelings than any other group concerning age and health. Group differences also appear in respect to personal competence. Ideas in this category refer above all to deficient education and consequent lack of vocational and financial success. Such comments occur decidedly least, and opposite expressions of personal satisfaction and self-confidence decidedly most, among skilled, white collar, and nonfactory upper semiskilled in the younger age group (ratio of two to one positive). Among factory semiskilled of both age groups, the ratio is two to one in the negative direction. Two other occupational groups show still more negative ratios: the middle-aged white collared and the nonfactory lower semiskilled. The former, it will be recalled, are employees who in their forties remain stuck in relatively low salaried positions.

The fourth set of comments in Table 9-2 includes a variety of ideas pertaining to past and present personal experiences, problems, social relationships, and philosophy (apart from respondents' current economic situation which constitutes a separate category). The feeling tone of the comments is more negative among young factory workers and it grows more negative in both age groups as one descends the skill hierarchy.

In respect to their personal economic situations workers express preponderantly negative feelings. The strong feelings and personal significance attaching to these economic concerns is suggested in the list of negative comments quoted in Chapter 6 (p. 125). Yet the men frequently bracket some relatively favorable comment with the complaint, so that our classification actually shows the largest number of economic references falling in the ambivalent, positive-and-negative category. For all factory workers together, the tabulation shows only 21 per cent favorable comments to 31 per cent unfavorable, with 48 per cent between. Young workers are especially negative compared to the middle-aged group. By occupational level, the lower groups not unnaturally express much more dissatisfaction in this area of personal finances and economic problems. The proportion negative in the two low-skill groups combined is 38 per cent (there is little difference between them, quite reasonably, since their incomes are the same); above the occupational level the proportion falls to 23 per cent (these upper skill groups enjoy a sizable income advantage). Detroit factory workers do not differ substantially from men in comparable nonfactory occupations in their feelings regarding their economic situation.

The final category in Table 9-2 comprises observations and opinions about the world, from local garbage collection and the weather to the threat of nuclear war. It includes thoughts about the races and classes of men and the conditions of their lives; the things enjoyed and the things disliked about the neighborhood and the city; reactions to policies and to social, economic, and international affairs—to all the things men talk about, in fact, that do not find a place in other parts of the classification. Taken together, this conglomerate of ideas is reacted to with overwhelmingly negative feelings, more negative than the personal economic category, the job, or any other aspect of the life situation. Apparently this means simply that people are prone to enumerate their gripes, sorrows, and concerns rather than their blessings. In the Detroit factory sample, there is virtually no variation between higher and lower occupational levels. Nor do nonfactory groups exhibit tendencies significantly different. To whatever extent sundry dissatisfactions of the kind represented here are indicative of poorer adjustment, we must conclude that this aspect of mental health is unaffected by relatively low occupation and income within the range of the factory jobs studied.

To recapitulate, we have seen that factory workers at all levels respond to general questions in regard to their lives away from the job with expressions of predominant satisfaction and positive outlook differing little in tone from that of comparable nonfactory groups. Although their volunteered comments contain many complaints concerning both their economic circumstances and a variety of personal and social problems, other important areas of life are seen in a highly favorable light which more than balances the disagreeable features. For most workers the resultant is a definitely positive orientation. Routine production workers, as well as men holding better jobs, give evidence of accepting their world in good spirit. Despite their complaints and frustrations, all but a very few appear to find compensating satisfactions, partly in their work and more universally in family relationships and leisure activities.

Satisfaction in different sectors of life

Toward the end of the interview we asked the respondent to make a direct comparative evaluation of several essential sectors of his life. The question took this form.

In which one of these general parts of your life would you most like to have things different than they are? (Subsequently: Which are you *best satisfied* with in your life?)

Your spare-time activities
Your friendships
Your home and family
Your job
Your religious life

As to *dissatisfaction*, indicated by desire to have things different, the job is most often named and spare-time activities are next. Altogether, 39 per cent of Detroit factory workers say the job; 27 per cent say spare-time activities; 13 per cent refuse to choose, a number of them declaring that they wish none of these parts of their lives different than they are now. The remaining choices are scattered. The only large variation by occupation appears in the high proportion of routine semiskilled who express dissatisfaction with the job sector (58 versus 33 per cent of all others) and the correspondingly smaller number mentioning spare-time activities.

The relatively extensive dissatisfaction with spare-time pursuits in the total sample is striking in view of the extremely favorable opinions of these activities by men who mentioned them in their spontaneous comments. This suggests that persons not too fully satisfied in this regard failed to mention their negative feelings. On the other hand it must be observed that since the question presents a forced choice, dissatisfaction with one's spare time may be quite mild and yet greater than that toward any of the alternatives.

Choices of the life area considered most *satisfying* show a substantial majority in all occupations saying home and family (57 per cent of young men and 66 per cent of the middle-aged). Friends rank next, with a count of 20 per cent among the young and 7 per cent of the older. The other answers each receive from 5 to 10 per cent of the total. Occupational variations are again small though it is of interest that the job is chosen as the most satisfying part of life by only 2 per cent of routine production workers compared with 9 per cent of other factory men. On all the choices, Detroit factory workers as a whole are just about the same as the nonfactory and non-Detroit groups.

A number of other indexes and questions provide information relevant to the points under consideration. First, in respect to family relationships, we have an index of satisfaction based on six sets of coded responses, some previously referred to and some additional.[2] This index shows Detroit factory workers, both older and younger, less satisfied than those in small towns and slightly less so than white-collar employees. Among young workers, but not the middle-aged, men in nonfactory positions are also better satisfied than the factory group. Middle-aged repetitive workers again score lower in family satisfaction than do men in jobs above that level (27 per cent have high scores and 18 per cent low compared to 39 per cent high and 12 per cent low in the nonrepetitive jobs). We also obtained a coder's rating of each worker's adjustment to home and family. The five-degree rating is a global estimate arrived at by reading responses to all relevant interview questions.[3] Essentially, it yields a count of persons whose family adjustment is judged to be doubtful or unsatisfactory in terms of friction, disharmony, and tensions. In the Detroit factory group, 21 per cent are classified in the doubtful or poor adjustment categories. This compares with 10 per cent of nonfactory, 14 per cent of white-collar, and 13 per cent of small-town workers. The proportion rises to 28 per cent of the middle-aged in the two lower occupational groups. In sum, both the index of family satisfaction and the adjustment ratings indicate that urban factory workers tend to have family difficulties more than do comparable occupational groups and that in the middle years of life this is especially the case in low-skill groups.

Parallel analyses were made with respect to nonfamily social adjustments and organizational activities. We begin with a coder's rating similar to the one in regard to family adjustment.[4] In this instance the rating represents the effectiveness and satisfying-ness of the person's relations to people, groups, and associations outside the family. The figures point in the same direction as those in regard to family but less strongly and consistently. Men at upper occupational levels rate higher on the average. Among the young, 15 per cent of the skilled and high semiskilled receive low ratings compared to 25 per cent of the two least-skilled groups; among the middle-aged the large difference is between the skilled, with 16 per cent rated low, and all others, with 30 per cent low. In neither age group are routine repetitive workers any worse than the ordinary semiskilled immediately above them. White-collar employees of both age groups and young nonfactory workers rate much better than factory men (only 10 and 6 per cent respectively receive low ratings).

Measures of social adjustment

Our most general measure of social adjustment is derived directly from workers' responses, independently of the foregoing ratings. It is an index of sociability, or inversely of social withdrawal, which we described earlier and used as one of the six components in the mental-health assessment employed through preceding chapters.[5] At this point we wish to compare the occupational groups by means of this index (Table 9-3).

Repetitive production workers tend to have higher percentages of socially withdrawn than do other groups. The more skilled groups,

*Table 9-3　Comparison of occupational groups on an index of sociability (freedom from social withdrawal)**

| | Young | | | | Middle-aged | | | |
Occupational Category	Socia-ble	Neither	With-drawn	N†	Socia-ble	Neither	With-drawn	N†
Detroit factories								
Skilled ⎫					56%	22%	22%	45
High semiskilled ⎭	67%	15%	18%	33	43	25	32	98
Ordinary semiskilled	41	35	24	46	41	23	36	82
Repetitive semiskilled	27	37	37	30	25	37	38	73
Small-town factories								
High and ordinary semiskilled	67	11	22	18	57	24	19	21
Repetitive semiskilled	50	17	33	18	32	27	41	22
Detroit nonfactory								
High semiskilled	72	21	7	28	...	...	...	3
Ordinary semiskilled	80	10	10	20	33	26	42	43
Detroit white collar	60	25	15	40	50	29	21	28

* The index is described in Appendix B.
† Totals on which percentages are based Each horizontal set of three percentages totals 100 except when rounding produces a total of 99 or 101 per cent.

along with white-collar employees and young nonfactory workers, are considerably more sociable.

What the index signifies in more concrete terms is conveyed by its separate component items (listed in Table 3-5). Table 4-3 reports factory workers' responses to a number of these questions. The figures there, plus supplementary comparisons with men in other occupations, tell us, for example, that routine factory workers tend to have fewest friends (47 per cent report three or more good friends whom they see often, compared to 55 per cent in the two upper skill categories, 64 per cent of nonfactory workers, and 69 per cent of white-collar men). In reply to the question "How important is it to you to have friends?", 23 per cent of the routine production group say it is not important compared with 17 per cent of the more skilled, 12 per cent of the nonfactory, and 12 per cent of the white collared. Other questions, with a few exceptions, show similar small differences indicating that urban low-skilled factory workers tend to be less socially integrated and participative than other occupational groups. For example, the proportion of men who belong to more than two organizations (labor union and church are far the most common) is lowest for Detroit semiskilled workers, both factory and nonfactory in this instance (24 and 22 per cent respectively, as against 49 per cent "joiners" in small towns, 40 per cent of Detroit skilled, and 35 per cent of white-collar employees).

Reports of church attendance (not included in the foregoing index) reveal that in the younger Detroit factory group the rate of regular or frequent attendance is much lower than that of other occupations. Among the middle-aged a similar but less pronounced tendency is present in comparison with white-collar and non-Detroit groups, but in comparison with Detroit nonfactory workers the difference is slightly in the reverse direction. Young factory workers, especially those at lower skill levels, are also much less likely to vote than nonfactory and white-collar workers (38 per cent of the young workers—48 per cent of those in routine jobs—never or seldom vote, compared to 21 per cent of young nonfactory and 15 per cent of white collared). The middle-aged show this contrast only in comparison with white-collar employees and even there in much reduced degree.

Further evidence of the relatively unsatisfactory social adjustment of production workers comes from their answers to several checklist items. For example, "These days a person doesn't really know who he can count on." The spirit of social isolation and distrust revealed by agreement with this proposition exists to a strikingly great extent in the repetitive production group. Percentages signifying distrust run as follows (two age groups combined): 57 per cent of repetitive semiskilled, 40 per cent of other factory, 31 per cent of nonfactory, 24 per cent of small-town, and 21 per cent of white-collared workers. Another indicator of poor social adjustment is the item: "On the whole, do you usually like to be by yourself rather than with other people?" Affirmative replies are given by 33 per cent of routine workers in Detroit plants (34 per cent in small-town plants), 25 per cent of other Detroit factory workers, 24 per cent of nonfactory, 18 per cent of white-collar, and 15 per cent of small-town workers in nonrepetitive factory jobs.

The foregoing findings do not justify any sweeping generalization, either favorable or unfavorable, in regard to the social adjustment of factory workers. On the one hand, we detect a preponderant tendency, particularly on the part of routine production workers, to have less satisfactory family and social relationships than are observed in other groups; on the other hand, it is also true that most of the occupational differences are small and not uniformly evidenced on all indicators. Perhaps the soundest conclusion is that the auto workers as a whole have moderately satisfactory family and social relationships, not greatly different from other middle- to lower-range occupational groups, but that at the same time a sizable minority, particularly among routine production workers, exhibits attitudes and activities that compare quite unfavorably with other groups and with generally accepted ideas of desirable social adjustment.

Spare-time activities

As a final part of our inquiry into nonjob aspects of the worker's life, we asked a series of questions to determine how he spends his time at home and away from home and what hobbies and interests he has. The information secured on these matters reinforces one's doubts as to whether the spare-time activities of most working men represent, even in mild degree, a full, rich, self-expressive use of leisure as contrasted with narrow, impoverished ways of "killing time."

The most commonly mentioned activities are the following, in descending order of frequency: visiting and talking with relatives, friends, and neighbors, including parties, dances, playing cards, and so on; watching television; outings, walks, drives, picnics, going to parks or lakes; work around the house, garden, and garage; hunting, fishing, camping; participation in sports like swimming, boating, skating, and baseball; attending sports events as a spectator; and reading. The proportionate number of references to these several types of activity remains fairly uniform across occupations. The only exception of note is that white-collar employees mention reading much more commonly than the blue-collar workers, and the young white-collar workers also emphasize intellectual and artistic interests and activities like music, painting, photography, and theater (two-thirds of this young group refer to such pursuits compared to only a fifth of the young factory workers). White-collar workers also indicate more participation in social life, both in formal organizations and in informal gatherings and visits. Apart from these exceptions, factory workers do not differ markedly from other groups nor do low-skill workers differ substantially and consistently from upper-skill groups. Examination of the tabulations impresses one with the similarities rather than contrasts between production workers and others.

On several specific activities we also asked for estimates of amount of time spent. Television viewing of course overshadows reading and other intellectual or self-expressive pursuits. More than three-fourths of the men interviewed listed television as one of their spare-time activities while fewer than one-fourth mentioned anything in the broad range of serious reading, music, art work, theater, or hobbies. Television is slightly less popular among skilled and white-collar workers, but men on repetitive jobs spend no more time watching than do other semiskilled men (approximately 40 per cent of the skilled and white collared report over 10 hours a week devoted to television compared with 56 per cent of all semiskilled and 53 per cent of those on routine jobs). Contrasting with these figures are the percentages who spend over *six* hours a week reading books and magazines of all kinds; skilled and white collar, 18 per cent; all semiskilled, 10 per cent; repetitive semiskilled, 13 per cent. Furthermore, this reading most commonly consists of fiction, sports, and popular magazines. Serious editorial and technical reading is less frequent among all semiskilled, factory and nonfactory, than in skilled and white-collar groups, but once again the low-skilled production workers differ extremely little from other semiskilled men. Forty per cent of all semiskilled admit that they spend *no* time reading either magazines or books (for the routine semiskilled the figure becomes 46 per cent). Although virtually all the men interviewed report that they read newspapers regularly, interesting differences appear when they are asked what parts of the paper they read. In the low-skilled group, 30 per cent of the young and 19 per cent of the middle-aged read nothing beyond headlines, sports, and comics; this is the practice of 13 per cent of higher semiskilled (age groups combined) and 9 per cent of both skilled and white collar.

When we later inquired directly whether the individual has any hobbies or special interests, all occupational groups, including routine workers, report such activities about equally often. Nearly half the men declare bluntly that they have no hobby or special interest of any kind to occupy their spare time. Most of them have previously stated that their time at home, aside from resting and television, is largely absorbed in household chores and work on the car, in the garden, and similar duties. Many others, reluctant to acknowledge a lack of interests, obviously strain to name something even though it is apparent that very little time is devoted to the activity and that it possesses little depth or meaning in the man's life. This stretching is revealed in responses such as the following where the man names a hobby but, upon being asked how much he does along that line, confesses that it amounts to almost nothing. For example, "fooling around with motors—I used to fix cars but I don't do it any more"; "pigeons, I used to raise them—we don't raise them any more, only a few left," "collecting arrowheads—sometimes years go by [without doing anything]," "woodwork and gardening— I have a jigsaw and tools for the garden but I can't do that sort of stuff"; "drawing—I had a set of supplies but they're all used up now"; "I like to re-do furniture—I ain't done none in years now"; "shuffleboard—at the bar about once a week"; "save things like stamps and now mostly receipts and paychecks to compare with budget." In these and numerous other instances the worker has not so much as mentioned the alleged hobby when answering a preceding series of questions about how he spends his time when not working.

In addition to many such doubtful replies, another 20 per cent speak solely of their interest in hunting, fishing, bowling, baseball, golf, or other sports. Although it is difficult, of course, to draw a line between leisure pursuits that are really significant for the person and those that are not, it would appear that in most instances these activities occur rather infrequently and have questionable importance as means of self-expression and enduring personal satisfaction.

In any event, if we omit sports activities as well as alleged hobbies that are patently incidental or fictitious, there remain about one-fourth of the factory workers who describe avocational interests which they take seriously. For perhaps half of these men, that is for 10 to 15 per cent of all workers, the activities are of genuine current significance in their lives as sources of pride and enjoyment. The proportion is noticeably greater among the skilled than the semi-skilled, but there is no clear difference between upper and lower semiskilled groups. The hobbies lie predominantly in the area of mechanical and woodworking craftsmanship, but a wide variety of other interests are represented, including, for example, photography, music, sketching and painting, writing for publication (one person), serious study (also one person), and active work in organizations. This last category, covering all types of organizations, might be expected to include a substantial number of men. Actually, however, only 17 of the 407 Detroit factory workers refer to any active organizational participation away from work, anything that goes beyond attending church services or occasional meetings and social events. Only four workers mention spending any time on labor-union affairs or labor political action;⁶ six men are active in church work, five in political or civic organizations (with no union connections), three in lodges, and two in Boy Scout work (three individuals appear twice in these figures).

The following quotations offer examples of strong personally significant special interests and hobbies, beginning with instances of work in organizations.

My hobby is the labor movement and union participation. I am on the executive board of my local. I take an active part in union problems at meetings and extra sessions. I'm very much interested in the labor movement of today.

I've got a *lot* of hobbies and interests [names 7 or 8, including very active participation in community and political affairs]; I'm in 22 organizations altogether; campaign manager, district Democratic Party; on Political Action Committee of local union; on board of a community teen-age center, etc.

I'm president of [ethnic-group citizens club]; there are 700 members. I like to work in organizations; we give a lot to charity.

I like to get involved in local politics; chairman of civic association; vice-president of political party club; on township planning board and secretary of area development council.

Work at the church; chairman and secretary at meetings. It's my life's work; I enjoy it very much; my number one project.

I'm a Scout Master; I've been in it for 30 years now. I work with a troop of boys; take them out on field trips, out in the woods; I plan different things for the scouts; I get a lot of satisfaction out of working with boys. . . . [When asked what he reads] just the Scout material.

Stamp collecting for years and years; I attend the annual exhibits; I correspond with stamp collectors all over the world. I've got two rooms upstairs for my stamps [insisted on showing these to the interviewer who notes "a very elaborate layout of maps, collection books, first-day covers, etc."]

I'm always busy in my basement workshop, inventing, repairing; also draw, sketch mechanical things. [Has 3 patents on household devices; has already sold several hundred of one that he built a machine to produce.]

I do a lot of carpenter work and building; I built this home and just completed the annex. Now I'm laying a sidewalk around the house. I modernized the place and do a lot of handiwork—cabinets, shelves, etc.

Put this down in your book: I have only one spare-time interest which I hope to turn into a full-time profession— the art of physical therapy. I have patients come to me for treatment; I'm working for a degree; don't have time for much else.

My hobbies: carpenter, painter, violin-maker, clock-maker—all creative hobbies. I'd like to have more spare time for painting, carving, violin-making. [Interviewer saw two of his paintings; also played a violin he had made and found it "remarkably good" also saw a large grandfather clock "with intricate scroll work . . . very fine work."]

Literary hobbies; I write short stories and articles. I have sold a few stories to New York publishers; also edited a small local newspaper. [Studied journalism for 2 years at night school.] I read a great deal, mostly articles about medicine; research results of new drugs are very fascinating to me . . .

I like to fool around with antique furniture; I like to buy old broken down furniture and refinish it; make a stain that will match the rest of the furniture. A painter in Grosse Pointe refers all his work of that kind to me; then I get paid for it.

Building boats and sailing crafts; at present am building a 26-foot motor cruiser. I have one big hobby—photography. I have a lot of cameras, some foreign ones. I have entered contests for unusual shots and pictures. I am good at photography but never good enough to win first prize.

Gardening—raising beautiful roses. I have spent my life on roses and know a lot about them. Whenever I have the chance, I visit public rose gardens and pick up new ideas about special kinds and sizes. Sometimes I visit the greenhouses where I used to work.

Other respondents describe diverse interests such as watch repairing, learning to fly, making sketches from photographs, umpiring and coaching (25 hours a week in summer), putting out the church paper, completing rooms on second floor of house, archery (making bows and arrows and shooting at archery club), making cigarette lighters, repairing musical instruments, working on model planes and ships, taxidermy (birds and small animals since 12 years old), collecting records of light classical music, working on used cars (buying, repairing, selling them).

It is necessary to remind ourselves that these active and meaningful uses of leisure are reported by less than 15 per cent of all workers. This means that one can stress either the positive or the negative nature of the observations. The minority of workers represented by the quotations exemplifies the favorable side; the contrasting unfavorable side is seen in the large majority of workers who have found no such creative outlets or means of personal growth and satisfaction. Yet, even for the latter, the picture is by no means completely negative. It is true that much of their nonwork life, aside from television and "just resting," is taken up with shallow routine pastimes and home duties; that over and over their reports sound the same refrain: "work around the house," "take care of the garden," "putter around the yard (or basement, or garage)," "take care of the car," "cleaning, painting, fixing things up," "helping the wife," and so on. But to some limited extent these activities, too, afford opportunity for expression of workmanship impulses, use of abilities, and a sense of accomplishment. In the absence of more adequate self-fulfillment, they occupy a meaningful place in men's lives, as is indicated by the pride and positive valuation with which a number of respondents speak of them. For example: "bought the home semifinished and finished it up; I did a nice job on it"; "I work in the garden a lot; I like to grow things—flowers and vegetables"; "I get a great deal of pleasure and satisfaction out of working around the house and making it comfortable to live in"; "satisfaction from my home; I enjoy working in the yard; my hobby is gardening . . . ; I really enjoy working around the house; I like to keep busy"; "we [wife and I] get pleasure from building up our home and doing things around the home together; I don't know what other things can satisfy a person except working around the house; that suits *me* fine."

All in all, we must conclude that only a small proportion of factory workers enjoy genuine self-expressive hobbies but that a considerably greater number find partial substitutes in the form of social and athletic activities, household and garden duties, repairs and odd jobs on their homes, cars, electrical and mechanical appliances, and the like. Much of what they report lends itself to the interpretation that they are groping for meaningful ways to fill their spare time. By and large, they do what lies at hand since they are uneducated for more imaginative uses of leisure and appear to have almost no conception of the limitless possibilities and intrinsic satisfactions of becoming absorbed, for example, in challenging quests for knowledge, in creative arts and handiwork, or in community services and social or political movements. It is the dearth of such endeavors, we believe, that most deserves emphasis. Whatever the reason, it is clear that few indeed of these urban industrial workers are stimulated or aroused by their union, their church, or any other community influences or leadership. The rare individuals who do find some measure of fulfillment, personal worth and self-justification through their nonwork activities stand as an important demonstration of what *could* be true for many more.

Finally, since it is so often asserted that workers engaged in dull, repetitive jobs are prone to spend their spare time escaping into alcohol and gambling, we tabulated responses bearing on this issue. When describing their spare-time activities about one-fourth of the manual workers mention drinking. The proportion of skilled and white collar run slightly lower. Routine semiskilled do not differ from higher-level semiskilled. At a later point we asked each worker directly how much time he spends in bars and taverns and whether he ever does some pretty heavy drinking. On both questions occupational group differences are too slight to be meaningful except for manual workers in general versus the white collared (numbers spending considerable time in bars are 30 per cent for repetitive workers, 26 per cent of other Detroit factory men, 25 per cent of nonfactory, 16 per cent of the white-collar group). Taking these groups in the same order, proportions acknowledging heavy drinking are 21, 22, 20, and 13 per cent. Our data lend no support to the contention that assembly-line workers find it necessary more than others to dissolve their tensions in alcohol. The above percentages of heavy drinking include numerous cases who said "once in a while," "perhaps once a month," "not often," and so on; only 3 per cent of factory workers spoke of frequent excessive drinking (only 2 of 103 production-line workers). Replies in regard to betting, playing cards for money, dice and numbers games, and other gambling yield similar results. Less than 5 per cent of all factory workers say they gamble in any of these ways oftener than once a week. No significant occupational differences are manifested. Percentages who engage in these activities *at all* run 28 per cent of repetitive semiskilled, 27 per cent of other Detroit factory workers, 21 per cent of nonfactory, 23 per cent of white collared.

To the extent that drinking and gambling can be considered signs of unsatisfactory mental health, the foregoing findings diverge from earlier results indicating that low-skill groups have poorer mental health. This lack of complete consistency underscores the diversity of variables comprehended within the concept of mental health. As the results in Chapter 4 demonstrate, certain putative indicators of mental health are more closely and others less closely associated with occupational levels. Not only in the matter of drinking and gambling but in respect to a number of other specific attitudes and behaviors we are forced to conclude either that these are facets of adjustment not affected by job level in the same manner as are most of the mental-health indicators or that the potential relationship is hidden by counteracting influences. The complex lifelong constellations of personal and situational variables responsible for adjustive and maladjustive behaviors cannot be expected to produce neat, uniform patterns of effects associated with individuals' present occupation. It is remarkable enough that the observed average differences emerge, based as they are on tendencies among a number of disparate indicators of mental health. It is doubtful whether we can ever hope to disentangle specific determinants of particular consequences such as those illustrated by drinking and gambling.

Relationship between satisfactions at work and away from work

One of the key questions at the beginning of this chapter asked whether satisfaction and dissatisfaction on the job carry over into nonwork life. Do men with negative work feelings tend also to have negative attitudes toward activities and relationships off the job or are they the more likely to seek compensatory enjoyments, to find their satisfactions outside the plant *instead of* at work? The most general and direct evidence on this issue consists of the interrelationships among the several questions and indexes pertaining to degrees of satisfaction in different sectors of life.

Before we note the intercorrelations, let us bring together figures that compare proportions of workers who say that they are completely satisfied or well satisfied versus those less satisfied in the principal areas of their lives (Table 9-4). Home and family and leisure activities outrank other sources of satisfaction. Work is definitely a less satisfying aspect of life in the younger group and notably so for young men in repetitive work. As previously discussed, both life satisfaction and job satisfaction are less prevalent among workers in routine production as compared to those in better jobs.

Our primary question now is how these dimensions of satisfaction are related to one another. Tetrachoric correlation coefficients indicating degrees of interrelationship are shown in Table 9-5.[7] The first fact to observe is that the correlations are all positive; men satisfied with one aspect of their lives *tend* to be satisfied with other aspects. The relationships are not extremely strong, however, and some are near the vanishing point. If we focus on feelings of satisfaction with life as a whole we see that it is closely related to both family-and-home satisfaction and job satisfaction and substantially, though considerably less, to leisure-time satisfactions. The only other correlations approaching those with general life satisfaction are the ones between family-and-home and leisure satisfaction and, for the young group only, between job satisfaction and satisfaction with living in Detroit (coefficient of .52). The correlations un-

Table 9-4   Proportions of Detroit factory workers well satisfied in different sectors of their lives

	Percentages Who Answer "Completely" or "Well Satisfied"			
	All Occupations		Repetitive Jobs	
Area of Life*	Young	Middle-Aged	Young	Middle-Aged
Family and home life (F24)	84%	87%	82%	80%
Leisure time activities (F6a)	78	76	77	71
Life in general (A3)	66	68	57	62
The job (B4)	58	73	37	60
Number of individuals†	109	298	30	73

* The four questions pertaining to different areas of life were in parallel form but were widely separated in the interview. The wording of questions may be found in the interview schedule, Appendix A. Numerals in parentheses identify the location of the items in the interview schedule.
† Totals on which percentages are based.

Table 9-5   Intercorrelations of responses to questions regarding satisfaction in different sectors of life

	Tetrachoric Correlation Coefficients*				
	Life Satisfaction	Job Satisfaction	Family-Home Satisfaction	Leisure Satisfaction	Community Satisfaction
Life satisfaction	. . .	.58	.67	.40	.23
Job satisfaction		. . .	.34	.26	.32
Family and home satisfaction			. . .	.48	.12
Leisure-time satisfaction				. . .	.20
Community satisfaction					. . .

* Entries in the table are medians of the separate coefficients for young and middle-aged groups of Detroit factory workers. Coefficients are based on 109 cases in the young group and 298 in the middle-aged group.

doubtedly result from a very intricate network of direct and indirect causal connections.

Job satisfaction is part of this system of interdependent feelings; it is positively linked, though to a moderate degree, with each of the other measures of satisfaction. The relationships are thus consistent with an interpretation that conceives favorable or unfavorable job feelings as carrying over to produce corresponding feelings in other sectors of life. But caution is called for since by the same logic one can argue that each life area has its influence on each other area. In addition, common causes, either personality factors or background environment, may affect feeling reactions in all spheres. Effects of the job constitute only one limited part of the explanation. Nevertheless, once this is recognized, it still remains significant that the correlational evidence is congruent with a "spillover" interpretation as opposed to a "compensatory" interpretation of job feelings in relation to nonwork aspects of life. Certainly, and this is the point of vital importance, there is no indication of *inverse* relationship which would support the idea that men who are more dissatisfied in work find extra enjoyment away from work or, conversely, that those dissatisfied at home and in leisure manage especially to find satisfaction in work.

The foregoing inferences all pertain to general trends, of course, to probabilities about workers in large numbers. Particular individuals do sometimes exhibit the inverse linkage of job satisfaction with outside dissatisfactions or of job dissatisfaction with compensating enjoyment of home and leisure. But they are the exceptions, not the rule.

Finally, it should be noted that the observed relationships argue against an interpretation that would attribute degrees of satisfaction exclusively to individual personality differences regardless of varying situations. According to such a view some people will be well satisfied, others dissatisfied, across the board, in respect to all the different aspects of life. In that case, equal proportions should express satisfaction in the different areas and uniformly high correlations should exist between the various satisfaction responses. The fact that we find substantial differences of percentages satisfied and that low correlations occur, with large and rationally interpretable variations among the correlations, implies that different circumstances produce different feelings, that to an important degree satisfactions are *situationally* determined rather than depending solely on individual differences of personality.

10.

The worker's orientation to his world—

3. Sociopolitical attitudes

In the two preceding chapters we have considered possible mental-health implications of working people's relations to their jobs and to their personal lives away from work.   We now inquire similarly in regard to their orientation toward the larger social, economic, and political aspects of their world.   Interest still focuses on the question of how "satisfactory" or "healthy" or "desirable" the observed attitudes are.   Even though knowledge of men's social attitudes does not lead to unequivocal answers regarding the condition of their mental health, the evidence does help provide a basis for evaluative judgments.   Although each evaluator will make assessments within the framework of his own social values and philosophy, we suspect that the judgments may reveal a high degree of consensus (though this surely does not imply a guarantee of their validity).   In any event, it is useful to see what the broad social orientations of working people may add to the total picture of their adjustment to life.[1]
     Naturally we are forced to deal with only a very limited sample of sociopolitical attitudes.   Principal attention will be given to the following: general acceptance of the values and norms of society versus feelings of social alienation, distrust, and low morale; democratic outlook versus authoritarian, antidemocratic attitudes; labor-oriented economic and political views versus views opposed to those of organized labor; liberal versus illiberal orientation in respect to free speech, race relations, and international relations.   How do attitudes on these matters differ within the industrial working population?   How are they related to mental health, to job satisfaction, and to other personal variables?   And beyond the empirical findings lie the value-laden issues of whether positive mental health, in the interests of both individuals and society, is more satisfactory or less

so if working people are contented with the status quo or if they strive for change; if they seek individual solutions to their problems or if they support organized collective action; if they favor or oppose liberal humanistic social policies in areas of civil liberties, human rights, and foreign affairs.

The dividing line between sociopolitical attitudes and elements of more personal outlook is unclear and necessarily somewhat arbitrary. Indeed it is this very intermeshing that makes an excursion into political and social orientations relevant to the purposes of this inquiry. Accordingly, we shall begin by references to certain indicators of personal feelings that occupy a borderline position between workers' personal and social dispositions.

Social alienation (personal morale)

First, let us recall the set of responses that manifests feelings of social distrust, futility, cynicism, alienation. These attitudes were earlier brought together, on their positive side, in our index of personal morale, one of the components of the mental-health assessment. At the same time, they provide an important measure of sociopolitical orientation. What they show is that negative attitudes, lumped together as "anomie" or "social alienation," occur much more commonly in our urban factory population than in other groups and more among men in lower-skilled occupations than among those of higher skill. Scores on the index of personal morale reveal these large occupational differences (Table 10-1). It is apparent that Detroit factory workers as a whole, and particularly production-line workers, are prone to give anomic, socially alienated responses.

Supplementary comparisons on specific questions lend added concreteness. For example, on the check-list item "Most people are out for themselves and don't care what happens to others," 53 per cent of all Detroit factory men agree; 62 per cent of the repetitive work group agree. Quite apart from comparisons with other groups, figures like these, in and of themselves, signal the presence of a serious problem of social morale. That the concern properly centers more on urban factory workers than on other employed groups of the kind studied here is attested by a comparison of the preceding percentages with those that follow: 37 per cent of small-town workers agree with the quoted statement; 40 per cent of Detroit nonfactory

Table 10-1   Comparison of occupational groups on an index of
personal morale (freedom from "anomie")*

	Young				Middle-aged			
Occupational Category	High Personal Morale	Neither	Low Morale (Anomie)	N†	High Personal Morale	Neither	Low Morale (Anomie)	N†
Detroit factories								
Skilled } High semiskilled }	42%	30%	27%	33	49% 30	38% 38	13% 33	45 98
Ordinary semiskilled	30	22	48	46	34	27	39	82
Repetitive semiskilled	13	27	60	30	21	27	52	73
Small-town factories								
High and ordinary semiskilled	28	50	22	18	52	33	14	21
Repetitive semiskilled	22	56	22	18	36	32	32	22
Detroit nonfactory								
High semiskilled	64	18	18	28	...	...	...	3
Ordinary semiskilled	50	35	15	20	37	37	26	43
Detroit white collar	75	20	5	40	64	18	18	28

* The index is described in Appendix B.
† The totals on which percentages are based. Each horizontal set of three percentages totals 100 except when rounding produces a total of 99 or 101 per cent.

workers do, and 29 per cent of white-collar workers. Similar comparisons show 50 per cent of routine production men agreeing that "Getting ahead in this world is mostly a matter of luck and pull" as against 36 per cent of other factory workers, 32 per cent of those in small towns, 26 per cent of nonfactory, and 13 per cent of white collar. Likewise, 26 per cent of the routine factory group believe that "In spite of what some people say, the lot of the average man is getting worse, not better," while other groups range from 9 per cent to 16 per cent replying in this way. Again, 57 per cent of the routine group feel that "These days a person doesn't really know who he can count on"; the proportions in other groups run from 21 per cent to 40 per cent. One-third of the factory workers agree that "Nowadays a person has to live pretty much for today and let tomorrow take care of itself." And one factory worker in six goes so far as to say that "It's hardly fair to bring children into the world with the way things look for the future" (only one in eighteen of all other men answer this way).

The distrustful, pessimistic outlook reflected in these responses is part of the poorer mental health of factory groups discussed in earlier chapters. Whether the attitude differences are directly attributable to job influences or not, they represent significant facts about the adequacy of men's adjustments and social orientation at higher and lower skill levels.   Nor can the occupational differences be explained away as due to the more limited education of lower-level factory workers.   Although anomic responses do show clear inverse correlations with amount of schooling, we find that the occupational differences persist even among men of approximately equal schooling. Comparing only cases of "some high school," for example, we discover that 51 per cent of the routine semiskilled have high anomie scores versus only 30 per cent of other factory workers and 14 per cent of all other men in the study.   The differences are of nearly the same size as those for the total sample in which educational variations are permitted to add their influence.   At the same time it is true that within each occupational category men having only elementary-school education are most frequently anomic.   In a word, factors associated with occupation and with education are independently influential.   This parallels the conclusion of Chapter 4 in regard to mental-health scores.

Finally, it is to be noted, too, that personal morale or anomie scores correlate moderately with job satisfaction, life satisfaction, and other components of the mental-health index (most strongly with the "hostility" component).   We are dealing, that is, with a web of interrelated feelings and behaviors.   Attitudes of social alienation like those reported here are of particular interest at this point insofar as they carry implications in regard to sociopolitical orientation.   We suggest that men who adhere to beliefs—and especially disbeliefs—of the kind illustrated in this section would seem most unlikely to function as effective citizens or members of a healthy society.

Authoritarian attitudes

We proceed now to a second important cluster of attitudes that also belong both in the domain of personality and that of social attitudes, namely authoritarian or antidemocratic tendencies.   Attitudinal measures of authoritarianism have been widely used in social research of recent years and at the same time have been widely and severely criticized.[2]   Without entering into the controversial theoretical issues, we shall comment briefly on responses to a few typical items taken from authoritarian scales.   The remarkable fact, duplicated in numerous previous studies, is the extensive agreement expressed by "good Americans" with statements sharply at variance with democratic ideals of individual freedom and equality. For example:

The *most important* thing to teach children is absolute obedience to their parents.   (56 per cent of Detroit autoworkers agree.)
There are two kinds of people in the world: the weak and the strong. (55 per cent agree with this.)
Any good leader should be strict with people under him in order to gain their respect.   (38 per cent agree.)
A few strong leaders could do more for this country than all the laws and talk.   (34 per cent agree.)

On the last two items, but not on the first two, repetitive production workers answer somewhat more than other factory workers in the undemocratic direction (45 versus 35 per cent on strict leadership and 41 versus 31 per cent on leaders instead of laws and talk). On all the items, white-collar employees have a much lower rate of agreement (average of 24 per cent on the four items compared to 46 per cent for the factory workers).   Nonfactory manual workers and those in small-town factories also show less agreement than Detroit auto workers (average of 32 and 37 per cent as against 46 per cent). Analyses employing an index based on six items leads to essentially the same conclusions.

Middle-aged auto workers manifest more authoritarian attitudes than the young group but this difference as well as the above-noted difference between skill levels is accounted for in large part by the strong tendency of persons with less education to give authoritarian responses.   Authoritarian attitudes also correlate substantially with our measures of mental health, particularly with the component indexes of hostility and personal morale.   We shall later point out the significant association of these authoritarian tendencies with attitudes regarding race relations, foreign policy, and free speech.

Aside from evidence of relationships, however, responses like those reported here demand serious attention.   The views subscribed to make it difficult to avoid the conclusion that large segments of the industrial working class are oriented in a highly unsatisfactory way judged by the accepted standards of our democratic society.   Workers ready to agree that strong leaders are to be preferred to "laws and talk," that children should be taught absolute obedience, that the world is polarized between the weak and the strong, can hardly be staunch defenders of self-government by free, independent, self-reliant men.   Whether one thinks of these beliefs as *elements* of inadequate mental health or as attitudes loosely associated with limited education, low socioeconomic position, and poor mental health is relatively unimportant. In either case they form significant and disturbing parts of the picture that portrays ordinary men's orientation to their world.

Working-class versus middle-class views

Next we shall note working people's attitudes toward a sample of more explicitly sociopolitical relationships and issues. Although opinions on these matters do not directly demonstrate superior or inferior mental health, they can contribute valuable insights in regard to such aspects of adjustment as the men's social consciousness and class identification, the quality of their social outlook, and their reality orientation.

A first set of attitudes has to do with "working-class views" as contrasted with middle-class views. Each respondent was assigned a rating on a five-point scale running from strongly working-class to strongly middle-class oriented. The estimate is based on his answers to a block of six questions, chiefly of a free-response type, asking how he feels about the way things are going in this country and what changes he would like to see made; what people or groups feel the same as he does and what ones feel differently; what working people can do to change things; what keeps people from getting ahead and what helps them to get ahead; how he feels regarding government aid for people in need and about government control over business. Several of these questions will later be dealt with separately but in order to obtain a general index the individual's responses are first weighed as a whole, according to criteria like the following.[3]

Working-Class Views		*Middle-Class Views*
Favor greater equality of income and gains for common people	vs.	Things are pretty satisfactory as they are; no change needed
Favor governmental-welfare and social-security measures and greater control of business	vs.	Cut government spending; hold down welfare measures; reduce "interferences" with business
Causes of people's getting ahead or not: emphasis on social conditions, institutions, etc., rather than personal responsibility	vs.	Opposite emphasis
Solutions to problems through social, political, organizational means	vs.	Solutions through personal initiative, etc.

The use of an index of "working class" views need not suggest a Marxist theory of class consciousness and class struggle. Students of American labor are virtually unanimous in their conclusion that class feelings in a European sense are rare and unimportant in the United States. What we are studying here is rather a feeling of identification with economic group interests but, since a designation like "working-group views" inadequately conveys the idea, we adopt the term "class" for convenience.

Scores on this rating classify 81 per cent of Detroit factory workers as predominantly working-class oriented, 72 per cent of small-town factory workers, 76 per cent of nonfactory manual employees, and 27 per cent of the white-collar group. Proportions rated *strongly* working class among these same groups run 37, 24, 28, and 9 per cent. There are no clear trends by factory skill levels or by education and income (routine workers are only a trifle more strongly working class than higher skill groups, 41 versus 35 per cent). The relationship to job satisfaction is somewhat closer, the dissatisfied tending to be more working-class oriented (45 per cent of job dissatisfied are strongly working class compared to 32 per cent of the satisfied).

The vast majority of these Detroit-area workers express attitudes that belie popular generalizations to the effect that Americans are one homogenized middle class with an essentially common sociopolitical outlook. The present results do not indicate that industrial workers are "going middle class," even those at skilled and upper semiskilled levels.

A few details will inject further meaning into the working-class designation. Working men desire social and economic changes; few are content with things as they are. Only one worker in ten is so accepting or inert that he wants things "to go along pretty much the way they are" rather than feeling that there are "some important changes" to be made. The advocated changes are virtually never radical ones, however, and not unnaturally, they most commonly refer to cost of living, wages, taxes, steady employment, and other economic improvements to benefit working people. Ideas referring to peace and desires for governmental policies to preserve peace are next most numerous. Other responses scatter over needed political reforms, moves against domestic Communism, better schools and recreational facilities, return to religion, and many more suggestions each by a relatively small number of persons.

Of special significance here are the answers to a follow-up question asking what people or groups are likely to feel the same as the respondent and what ones are likely to feel differently. We derive substantial justification from the replies for the conception of working-class versus middle-class views. Over half the responses of our factory population spontaneously name working people, labor class, unions, and the like, as agreeing and the wealthy, big business, management, and so on, as thinking differently. Replies of this kind are particularly frequent among middle-aged workers in low-level jobs. Other group differentiations—in terms of religion, political party, education, ethnicity, and so on—are mentioned with only trifling frequency. The sole exception comes in the large number naming Communists and similar anti-American groups as differently oriented. The outstanding fact is that attitudes toward social change are seen by workers as views shared by people situated like themselves versus opposed views held by business and upper-income groups.

When we next inquired whether the ordinary working man "can do anything to make things more the way he wants them," approximately one-fourth answer "no," or "hardly," or "it's almost hopeless," or some equivalent expression of powerlessness. Such declarations of futility are especially frequent among factory workers, most of all in the middle-aged low-skill group (36 per cent of the latter versus 20 per cent of other factory workers and only 14 per cent of nonfactory and 13 per cent of white collar). Comments like the following exemplify these views: "I wouldn't know what he could do"; "no, he hasn't got the power"; "no, he ain't got no chance; they won't stick together"; "no, the money runs this country and if you don't have it you can't do nothing"; "no, he's just a speck; he doesn't amount to a thing"; "no, because he just doesn't have connections; if a working man gets into politics he forgets about other working men so working man never gets a break"; "no, hell no—the s.o.b. that he elects will do what the politicians pay him to do so what difference does it make"; "no, the big businessmen and the government control things."

The majority is more positive. When it comes to *what* they can do to make things more the way they desire, their replies divide into three principal categories: voting and political action (much the largest number); action by labor unions or other organizations; and efforts by individuals through self-improvement, personal initiative, hard work, and moral qualities. The sharp contrast is between those who stress collective solutions and those who rely on

individualistic means. This contrast enters prominently into our
rating of working-class orientation. The middle-aged low-skill
group stands out as especially weak in its support of political action, a finding congruent with the comparatively high proportion
in this group who feel impotent to effect desired changes. Another
suggestive finding is that among young routine workers only one in
eight speaks of *individual* action while above that job level the ratio
is one in three.

A few quotations will illustrate the foregoing threefold classification: (1) "He can elect men to office who will do what he wants and
needs done"; "all stick together in unions and vote regularly; they
could change things by voting right"; "a man should get out and
vote or he has no say-so at all; he can't do much but at least he can
do that"; "sure—put pressure on his Congressmen and labor leaders";
"yes, vote—but they usually give you two crooks to choose from";
"the only thing you can do is when the election comes, form a peti-
tion to get a third party started." (2) "One man can't do much;
his only hope is through an organization like a union"; "I think if he
becomes more conscious of his labor representation, takes more
interest in the union, attends meetings and voices his opinion, he
can improve conditions"; "he can organize so that they can submit
what he wants to the proper people; do better as a group than by
themselves"; "take an active part in organizations that are for the
things he is for"; "by demanding what they want via collective bargaining." (3) "Through education you could do more; teach people
to better themselves"; "he can work harder and prepare himself for
a better future through education and training"; "have more ambition and try to get ahead"; "he can start a business or go to night
school"; "yes, by going to school and getting an education and going
up himself; better himself by learning a trade"; "he can learn to be
more alert and to raise his voice in protest against injustice"; "he
can go to church and pray to God."

Another block of questions has to do specifically with beliefs about
the common man's opportunities for getting ahead. The point of
special interest to us is whether getting ahead is perceived as dependent on the individual's own qualities and efforts or on situational
factors that presumably require correction through social action.
When the issue is raised in this personal success frame of reference,
the responses heavily emphasize individual qualifications and deficiencies. What keeps men from getting ahead is, above all else,
their limited education and ability—but also their lack of ambition,

industry, and other necessary personality attributes. These are obvious explanations to offer and four out of five respondents do so. More interesting is the fact that nearly half the men also stress economic conditions, poverty, absence of opportunity and influence, bad home background, and other environmental obstacles. Moreover, many men who speak only of poor education and personal weaknesses undoubtedly mean to attribute these to unfavorable early environment without stopping to say so.

When a following interview question explicitly called attention to the possibility that external influences may be important by asking "who or what is to blame" for people's not getting ahead, answers divided about equally between blame of the person himself and blame of circumstances, the business system, politics, early home life, and other environmental conditions. A final question which asked what *helps* people to get ahead elicited replies consonant with the preceding ones; emphasis is again very strongly on *individual* abilities and virtues, with education and training in the forefront. Nevertheless, more than one-third of the workers also suggest either that *opportunities* (for jobs, training, promotion) are likewise important or, still more frequently, they point to pull, influence, "knowing the right people" as the prescription for getting ahead.

Typical answers that stress personal qualities as obstacles are: "lack of education, that is the only thing"; "well, education is the most important thing"; "not having a trade or an education" [such responses occur over and over again]; "lack of ambition"; "laziness, that's all"; "not having good judgment; we all have opportunities, only some people don't know how to take advantage of it"; "not really trying to get ahead, not being sure what they want in life"; "self-pity; when they get into that habit they stop trying to improve themselves." Conversely, personal qualities that *help* to get ahead are: "Having education, working hard"; "the first thing would be education; if you have a good education that would take care of it"; "ambition, education, pull"; "some people can mix and meet people and this is a help in getting ahead"; "being a hard worker, keeping his nose to the grindstone"; "being thrifty"; "not living beyond their means"; "a good line; you have to learn how to bluff your way"; "will power is about the only thing; I believe you can achieve just about anything you want if you think hard enough about it and make up your mind to do it."

The contrasting focus on external determinants appears in statements that what helps is "steady employment"; "a prosperous period"; "most important, maybe, is getting the right breaks"; "if you have pull, you are all set"; "to get the breaks in getting ahead it's who you know that counts." The things that interfere are: "Our economic system; it's impossible for everybody to be successful; there isn't enough to go around"; "some have not had opportunity for education"; "selfish politicians and selfish businessmen"; "money, politics, breaks in life"; "not knowing the right people"; "not having the right friends to push you up; you got to have pull."

Attitudes concerning government help

Two questions concerning the part that government should play in social and economic affairs also contribute to the composite rating of working-class views. The first of these inquires about government help to meet human needs—for housing, medical care, and income for aged and unemployed. Each man was asked how he feels regarding these matters and whether the government should do more or is already doing too much. Three-fifths of the factory workers unqualifiedly favor increased government help and five out of six favor at least as much as is now being done. Only 10 per cent express general disapproval; the remaining 7 per cent are doubtful or ambivalent. Improved social-security payments receive especially strong endorsement while opposition is most often expressed in respect to "socialized medicine." Several check-list items on these issues yield similar results. Very large majorities, over 80 per cent, vote for increased aid for low-cost housing and improved unemployment compensation; a smaller majority of 58 per cent approves governmentally supported medical and hospital care.

Several of the points respondents emphasize, pro and con, may be seen in the following examples.

I feel that the government should use their money to do everything it can along that way—everything; should do more especially for old folks. The government is the people and why shouldn't they use the money where it will do the most good.

It should help them with every facility in its power; it can't do too much for the citizens in good standing of the U.S.; that's what it's for, to meet the needs of its people.

If government spent money here instead of overseas we would have better houses, care of old people, etc.; always helping other countries, forgetting about us; they should do more—they tax enough.

I believe the government should help those who are unable to help themselves except when it comes to medical care; I don't believe in socialized medicine.

I think it's coming more of a government responsibility; maybe it's socialism—whatever you call it, it's here to stay.

The government should take care of the old people and lower the age of pensions to 55; there should be more hospitals supplied by the government; they should be run by the government so that they would cost less for the patient. They should do something about housing, but better than they did before.

No, I don't think it is the government's business to do any of those things in a democracy such as ours. The results prove it; people want the government to take care of them but that would be socialism of the worst kind.

Well, I figure the government should stay out . . . ; man should be more self-reliant, not a ward of the state.

No, I don't believe in that; that is socialism Americans must take care of themselves. People, so many people, get accustomed to handouts and charity.

Government is doing enough; more the government does, the more we are going to have taxes up.

I'm against all government aid except for those unemployed through no fault of their own; government is doing too much except in the case of the unemployed. It is costing too much in the way of taxes; also it makes people lazy if you baby them too much.

An index of favorableness to government help was derived from the preceding questions[4] and will become part of the general labor-orientation index to be dealt with shortly. On the government help index, young factory workers are the most liberal occupational group. Middle-aged factory men are likewise much more commonly for government aid than white-collar or small-town workers, but they are about the same as Detroit nonfactory men of the same age bracket. Those of lower skill and income are especially for government help. On this index, unlike that for working-class views, the job dissatisfied do not differ from the better satisfied.

Attitudes toward control of industry

The other question pertaining to government action asks what amount of control should be exercised over business and industry. Does the government now have too much to say about business operations, about the right amount, or should it have more to say? One-third of Detroit factory workers believe that government should exert increased control; four-fifths think that controls should be either as they are now or greater. Occupational-group comparisons reveal no clear differences among Detroit factory workers, but white-collar workers are strikingly more in favor of decreased controls (43 versus 18 per cent of factory men) and less in favor of increased controls (8 versus 31 per cent).

Comments by factory men who favor more control and less control, respectively, well illustrate one aspect of the contrast between what we have labeled a working-class versus a middle-class orientation. For example, typical statements by workers who want the government to have more say are: "past history has shown that control is necessary"; "big business is getting too big; it should be restricted"; "shouldn't let companies get away with tax evasion and huge profits"; "government should regulate monopoly"; "business makes more money than it should and the government ought to control profits that are too high"; "keep the prices down; I mean really down"; "companies are producing too fast and then there will be a big layoff; government should control production." A "middle-class" orientation of other workers is illustrated in the following: "the country was built up without government interference and it shouldn't interfere except when business goes too far"; "no, I believe in free enterprise; go back to letting industry be American again by not interfering"; "companies should be able to run their own business; the government's got enough to do without messing around in business"; "government interference in business and industry can lead to socialism and unrest"; "if I had a factory I wouldn't want someone to come and tell me how to run it—would you?"

Three check-list items also bear directly on the issue of business freedom and control. The items, which call for agree-disagree responses, are these.

In general, the profits of business and industry are higher than they should be:
Working people should have more to say about how things are run in factories than they have now.
Wealthy businessmen have too much influence in running things in this country.

On the first question, 70 per cent of all factory employees agree. There are no differences by skill level. On the second item, 60 per cent agree, with the two lowest factory groups slightly more heavily in favor (65 per cent compared with 53 per cent). The last item is more solidly subscribed to at all skill levels; 79 per cent agree with the charge. White-collar workers are much more favorable to business, though surprisingly large proportions express "working-class" views (41, 37, and 54 per cent agree with the three statements in the order listed).

An index of attitude toward business, using the three items together with the general question regarding government controls, shows even more clearly the contrast between manual and white-collar attitudes and the especially critical feelings toward business in the lower income and lower skill groups. Men dissatisfied with their jobs also have more unfavorable attitudes toward business than the satisfied.

Attitudes toward labor unions

A final component in our assessment of working people's prolabor orientation focuses on their attitudes toward unions. Virtually all the Detroit factory workers were members of the auto workers' union (the UAW-CIO since this was before the AFL-CIO merger); less than 2 per cent of our sample were not members. Likewise, the small-town sample had only one nonunion man and, of the others, 82 per cent belonged to UAW, 18 per cent to other unions. The nonfactory workers in Detroit distributed as follows: 3 per cent UAW; 30 per cent in other CIO unions; 45 per cent in AFL unions; 22 per cent nonunion. Of the white-collar sample 19 per cent were union members, all UAW. In view of these union affiliations it is not unexpected that opinions run strongly favorable to unionism.

We began the questioning on this topic with a wide-open inquiry: "Now I'd like your opinion about labor unions. Taking the unions as a whole, how do you feel about them and the things they do?" Many pages would be required to do justice to the replies but the following excerpts will suggest the range and intensity of attitudes.

I think it's the best thing that has ever happened. The worker is beginning to live like a human being for the first time in the world's history.

A wonderful thing for the poor man; he can defend his rights better through collective bargaining; he's not just a number any more.

I'd say they're the finest thing that ever happened to the working man; it helps him make a decent living, gives him more security, keeps him from being pushed around.

I think the unions are 100 per cent. Without the unions the working man wouldn't have a chance. It used to be class rule. Today everyone in the shops is equal no matter if you're an Elk, K. of C., or nothing.

I feel that they're doing a good job in many ways—in keeping a balance of power between the owners of industry and people who work for them. Gives a man a chance to do something about a situation that was obviously unfair, whereas before there was nothing he could do about it.

They're good but like everything else they got bad guys in them. They do a lot of good for us but there is plenty room for improvement.

Some of their principles is all right and others I don't believe in. They help the working man all right but sometimes they get too big; nothing should be too big because then you get corruption.

Well, they could do a lot more for the average worker; it's gettin' so you gotta have a connection even in the union in order to get 'em to do something for you.

They do some good but not as much as they used to; they have become too friendly with management.

The unions are getting too much in politics and trying to run the factories and things.

The union is big business now—just like the owners.

They started off pretty good but getting too much power now and too much politics.

I can't honestly see where they have done much good; I think the changes they secured would have come anyway.

Well, they started out all right but they went to hell. Those guys— all they want is an easy buck.

It's a racket; they collect the dues and don't do anything. They just organized the union to give themselves a good job.

Unions have their place but they are getting too big for their britches. There is so much racketeering going on among union heads; to me the greatest abuse in the United States is the freedom of unions and union heads. [Earlier in the interview:] Unions are just as greedy as management. Too much power is dangerous; whoever is in power has the tendency to abuse it.

A classification of the answers reveals that 70 per cent of the Detroit factory workers are clearly pro-union without qualification or with minor qualifications; 22 per cent are pro-union but with serious criticisms and reservations; only 8 per cent express predominantly anti-union attitudes even if we include those somewhat on the fence. Small-town factory men are still more heavily pro-union; Detroit nonfactory workers are a little less so (57 per cent clearly pro-union, 32 per cent pro but with serious reservations, and 11 per cent opposed); and white-collar employees are still less favorable (39 per cent pro, 35 per cent heavily qualified, and 26 per cent opposed). No clear differences exist among the four factory job levels.

Other questions yield similar results. For example, when asked whether they usually side with the company or the union in disputes, factory men divide 60 per cent for the union, 35 per cent who say "sometimes one and sometimes the other" or "it depends," and less than 5 per cent choose the company. Likewise, when we inquired why companies and unions disagree or have trouble, 34 per cent refer solely to faults of the companies whereas only 6 per cent blame the union; 60 per cent say it is a matter of "opposed aims," "conflicting interests," "faults on both sides," "misunderstanding," and so on. To probe further, we inserted the question: "Some people say neither the union nor management cares much about the common worker—he gets squeezed in between. What do you think about this statement?" Approximately two-thirds of the factory workers definitely reject the idea; one-third agree though more than half of these qualify their agreement by saying that it is true of the union "to some extent," "at times," "in certain cases," or equivalent expressions. A striking finding here is that routine production workers agree more often than do men in better factory jobs (46 per cent agreement versus 29 per cent). These workers in low-level jobs apparently tend to feel that they are the forgotten men, neglected by both union and management. Yet they do not turn away from the union; despite their complaints they remain almost unanimously pro-union.

Here are a few illustrations of ideas expressed in reply to these last several questions, beginning with reasons assigned for siding with the union and feeling that it does care about the workers, then continuing with some statements in an opposite vein.

[Side with the union] because they are dedicated to the working people. The company wants money and has no regard whatsoever for the workers.

They [the unions] have the working man's interest at heart.

I *am* the union; the union is fighting for me.

The company looks out for the company; the union looks out for the men.

The union is fighting to improve the working man's conditions. It's the common worker that makes the union; if the men didn't want the union there wouldn't be one. The union is for the good of the worker.

The company sure as hell don't care much about the common worker; if a man dies right out there it wouldn't hurt them a bit in the world. The union'll take care of a man as best they can.

It's true [that neither union nor management cares much]—the common worker is only a tool for the union politician. [Doesn't side with either] because the unions are unreasonable too often.

I agree—there are too many big shots in the union; most of them only care about themselves.

It's true—they're both out to make all they can off the worker.

Union could have done a hell of a lot more; could have gotten more money if we had honest leadership.

The unions have to do something with the dues they collect so they have to make a little trouble so the working man will think they're doing something for them. . . . The worker really doesn't matter to the company—and on the union side, they just want the dues.

A coder's rating of feelings toward unions, based on the entire block of questions, shows results that conform closely to what has been reported on separate questions. We now find 87 per cent of the factory workers classified as pro-union (67 per cent with no reservations), 8 per cent doubtful or balanced between favorable and unfavorable feelings, and 5 per cent preponderantly unfavorable. A still more general index, combining check-response items with the rating,[5] was used to make further comparisons. On this general index, factory workers remain clearly more pro-union than other groups and again no significant differences occur between higher- and lower-skill groups, income groups, or groups with different amounts of education. It is worth underscoring the point that workers who are better off than others support the union as strongly as those who are less successful. Contrary to popular belief, moreover, there is no tendency for workers most dissatisfied with their jobs or with life in general to be more pro-union than others. Nor are those most favorable toward their company either more or less pro-union than average.[6]

A general index of prolabor orientation

Rather than dwelling longer on the separate sets of attitudes, we turn now to analyses that deal with a total labor-orientation index which combines the foregoing subindexes of working-class views, attitude toward government help, toward business and its control, and toward labor unions.[7] Scores on this general index serve as a rough measure of "liberal" socioeconomic attitudes in the sense of the "New Deal," "Fair Deal," "Presidential Democrats"[8] which accords in the main with the position of the major labor unions of the country.

Variations of labor orientation by occupation are summarized in Table 10-2. Detroit factory workers are clearly more labor oriented

*Table 10-2   Comparison of occupational groups on index of labor orientation**

Occupational Category	Young				Middle-aged			
	High	Medium	Low	N†	High	Medium	Low	N†
Detroit factories								
Skilled }					40%	27%	33%	45
High semiskilled }	39%	48%	12%	33	40	33	28	98
Ordinary semiskilled	59	37	4	46	44	43	13	82
Repetitive semiskilled	53	33	13	30	49	37	14	73
Small-town factories								
High and ordinary semiskilled	33	44	22	18	29	29	43	21
Repetitive semiskilled	28	56	17	18	36	36	27	22
Detroit nonfactory								
High semiskilled	18	57	25	28	...	...	...	3
Ordinary semiskilled	45	35	20	20	28	51	21	43
Detroit white collar	10	20	70	40	11	43	46	28

* The index is described in the text and in Appendix B.
† The totals on which percentages are based. Each horizontal set of three percentages totals 100 except when rounding produces a total of 99 or 101 per cent.

than other groups, the young to a greater extent than the middle-aged. The contrast with white-collar employees is particularly striking, but differences are apparent also in comparison with small-town workers and Detroit men in nonfactory employment. Within the factory population, the two lower-skill groups are a little more labor oriented in line with what their more disadvantaged position would lead one to expect, and a significantly large minority of middle-aged factory men in the more skilled jobs have a low degree of prolabor orientation. Relationship to income is similar, the top group manifesting less prolabor attitudes. By educational categories those with less schooling have higher proportions labor oriented. This is markedly true for the middle-aged and a hint of the same relationship holds for younger workers. Even for men with equal amounts of schooling, however, differences of labor orientation among occupational groups persist, though with some irregularities. In short, the moderately greater prolabor feelings of lower-level workers is not explained away or accounted for by their more limited education.

We next ask to what extent labor orientation reflects dissatisfaction. Are the more dissatisfied men the more labor oriented? The answer is definitely affirmative in both age groups: the less satisfied factory workers are more inclined to embrace prolabor views. This is equally true whether we refer to job satisfaction or to satisfaction with life in general.[9] But one would expect this relationship to vary by job level and this proves to be the case. The hypothesis is that dissatisfaction and frustrations operate more strongly in lower-grade jobs, causing men so situated to be especially in favor of government and union programs which they perceive as correcting inequities and advancing their interests. Consequently, the most labor oriented should be the dissatisfied at low job levels. The evidence supports this interpretation. Among routine production workers, 60 per cent of the job dissatisfied have high labor-orientation scores compared with only 31 per cent of the satisfied. The relationship disappears in the two upper skill categories; the satisfied and the dissatisfied have identical proportions strongly labor oriented (40 per cent each).

Just as our earlier analysis interpreted job dissatisfaction as an intervening process accounting in part for poorer mental health at lower occupational levels, in corresponding manner it now helps account for labor-oriented sociopolitical attitudes. It appears that *strong labor orientation is generated by the combination of disadvantageous economic position and overt feelings of dissatisfaction.* To complete the picture it is necessary, of course, to be aware of the complex influences that determine differences of personal dissatisfaction and the directions in which the dissatisfaction expresses itself —whether, for example, in support of the labor-oriented reforms represented in our index. The influences are partly those of the men's present subculture and social milieu, including their labor union, and partly their individual life experiences. The contrasting labor-orientation scores of white-collar and blue-collar workers illustrate the former influences; differences associated with amount of schooling, poverty in childhood, and similar elements of life history exemplify the latter. As one specific example, illustrating the joint effect of present occupation and background social influences on labor-oriented attitudes, we shall summarize data regarding childhood economic circumstances (family income level) along with current job level. The figures in Table 10-3 indicate the cumulative effects of skill level and childhood background on present socioeconomic attitudes among middle-aged workers. At each occupational level, the more unfavorable the early economic circumstances the more likely men are to be strongly labor oriented; and

Table 10-3   Percentages of high labor-orientation scores by middle-aged groups of specified occupational level and childhood income level

Childhood Economic Circumstances

Occupational Groups	Above Average	Average	Below Average	Total
Skilled and high semiskilled	19% (26)*	41% (69)	50% (46)	40% (141)
Ordinary semiskilled	33 (9)	44 (43)	47 (30)	44 (82)
Repetitive semiskilled	38 (13)	48 (27)	56 (32)	50 (72)
Total	27% (48)	43% (139)	51% (108)	

* Figures in parentheses show the number of cases in each cell on which the accompanying percentage is based.

for each childhood income level, the lower the present job the more frequent are labor-oriented attitudes (with one minor exception). The trends are similar for younger workers but with irregularities due to small numbers. The relationships resemble the ones described earlier showing how mental health varies with these same two conditions (pp. 70–74 and 139).

We have interpreted both sets of findings, those pertaining to mental health and those referring to labor orientation, in the same fashion, as manifestations in part of dissatisfactions which in turn result from relatively disadvantageous work and life conditions in the presence of desires and expectations that remain unfulfilled. In other words our theoretical guidelines suggest that the same deprivations that lead to personal frustrations, lowered personal morale and self-esteem, and poor mental health also lead to disapproval of current social arrangements and encourage desires for reform. According to this reasoning, individuals and groups characterized by less satisfactory personal adjustment might be expected also to be more favorable to labor-oriented social change. But this is not a *necessary* tendency; the degree to which it exists requires empirical testing. At the same time it calls for penetrating reflection on the intricacies of the relationship. We shall first note the empirical results and then return to the perplexities of interpretation.

The hypothesized inverse correlation between mental health and labor-oriented attitudes does appear in our data. In both age groups those having high mental health are less labor oriented, those of poorer mental health are more labor oriented. The high mental-health group (ages combined) has exactly equal numbers of strong and weak labor orientation (40 per cent of each) as contrasted with the low mental-health group where those of strong labor orientation outnumber the weakly labor oriented three to one (56 per cent to 18 per cent). Furthermore, the relationship holds true consistently for each separate skill level and, with trifling exceptions, for separate groupings by amount of schooling. These last facts are important since they mean that the association of labor-oriented attitudes with lower mental health is not accounted for by their respective linkages with job level or education.

Another finding of interest is the close statistical association of labor orientation with the "anomie" component of mental health. Feelings of anomie or low personal morale, reflecting discouragement, pessimism, alienation, and distrust in regard to social relationships may be viewed as a bridge between personal frustrations and the socioeconomic attitudes represented in the labor orientation index. Indeed, the anomic feelings and the labor-oriented attitudes may constitute a single loose constellation of reactions to disappointed hopes in regard to one's self and one's world. Of the low personal morale group, 59 per cent are strongly labor oriented as against 28 per cent of those with high morale; only 16 per cent of the low-morale workers are weakly labor oriented compared to 51 per cent of the high-morale workers. These relationships persist for different educational levels separately; they cannot be explained away as due to amount of schooling. Conversely, the linkage of labor orientation with education tends to disappear when we take high and low personal morale groups separately. This fact fits the suggestion that labor-oriented attitudes and anomic feelings are interwoven as parts of a total attitude complex or orientation to life. What is said here in reference to the personal morale component holds true, though in reduced degree, of other aspects of mental health.

The foregoing relationships do not imply that workers are more prolabor in outlook *because* they are maladjusted. More plausibly, as suggested earlier, the correlation can be considered a result of common causes which produce both the sociopolitical attitudes and the personal disturbances. A crucial question is whether the dual effects are *necessarily* associated. Is there any inevitability about the relationship or does it depend on particular social circumstances that may change, or be changed?   Concretely, is there any reason why a worker cannot be strongly in favor of labor-oriented reforms and working-class views and yet be personally happy, self-confident, relatively free of anxieties, hostilities, and despair—in *good* mental health?   An obvious answer is that there are many such persons. In our own data, large numbers of workers are exceptions to the general tendency; they are of high mental health and at the same time strongly and actively labor oriented.   The question becomes why there are not more.   Why is the predominant trend the other way?

Even though no confident answer can be given, the question does bring us face to face with a fundamental dilemma.   To put the issue sharply, the liberal sociopolitical attitudes themselves may be construed as intrinsic elements of the total anomic, mentally unhealthy outlook; or, alternatively, they may be considered a realistic, eminently healthy reaction of working people to their life situation but a reaction that, in our society, has become fortuitously associated with feelings of alienation, anxiety, failure, and self-derogation. "Fortuitously" here would refer above all else to the effects of our cultural emphasis on middle-class themes of individual success, competitiveness, personal responsibility, and associated values which tend to undermine the self-esteem of disadvantaged, "unsuccessful" workers and consequently to direct their dissatisfactions inward upon themselves as well as outward upon needed changes of socioeconomic conditions.   The question is whether the dissatisfactions now largely privatized (that is, focused largely on self and interpersonal relations) can be reduced without diminishing dissatisfaction that is directed toward effectuation of change in the broader sociopolitical sphere. To whatever extent cultural values of individual competitive success may be deemphasized and replaced by high valuation of cooperative participation in collective social improvement, we might expect personal frustrations to be alleviated.   With different aspirations and self-expectations, working people might more commonly be devoted to working-class goals while enjoying first-rate mental health.

It appears that even our labor-oriented workers only halfway accept working-class views while still adhering to individualistic beliefs about getting ahead.   It should be recalled that we found somewhat poorer mental health among middle-aged workers who are personally ambitious than among those who do not care about advancement.   Perhaps this is the "American dilemma" of production workers—to eschew career aspirations, to be more fully, self-acceptingly working class, or to suffer continuing tensions and sense of failure and futility because of internalized middle-class "success" goals that are not consonant with their situation. We shall return to these fundamental questions in the final chapter.

Attitudes toward freedom of speech

In order to sample working people's attitudes toward a quite different range of social issues, we selected a few questions pertaining to free speech, Negro-white relations, and American foreign policy. As in previous sections, our interest centers on the question of how "satisfactory" the orientation of workers is in regard to these important noneconomic issues. Again there are no objective criteria of "mentally healthy" answers; we can merely assert, as before, that descriptive facts are useful as a starting point for evaluative judgments. In this instance, moreover, the democratic humanistic values of our society provide a wide consensus as to what attitudes are healthy and desirable.

Opinions on free speech were tapped in a series of four questions.

Should a person be allowed to speak in public for things that most people believe are completely wrong and definitely bad?

Should people be allowed to speak in public against our democratic form of government?

Should people be allowed to speak in public against all religion?

What about colleges and universities—do you think that it is a good thing to have colleges where people study all kinds of ideas even if many of these are ideas that most of us believe are untrue and harmful? Why do you feel that way?

Responses to the first two questions divide almost equally between approval and disapproval of freedom to speak (49 per cent in favor to 44 per cent opposed on the first question; 42 per cent favorable and 48 per cent opposed on the second question). Opposition to free speech against religion mounts to more than two to one (30 per cent in favor, 69 per cent against). Opinion regarding free circulation of ideas in universities goes the other way (61 per cent for, 34 per cent against). These results, we think, indicate disturbingly weak adherence to principles of civil liberties presumed to be basic features of the American political system. The illiberal replies reflect a fear of bold thinking, open discussion, and a problem-solving approach to the world that can hardly be thought compatible with really good mental health.

Differences among groups are relatively small. Factory workers oppose free speech a trifle more often than white-collar employees (on the four questions above, median percentages against are 45 per cent for factory men and 38 per cent for white collar) and the two lower factory groups tend to be less tolerant (50 per cent would deny free speech on the average versus 40 per cent in the upper skill categories). Education plays a somewhat larger part among factory workers and contributes to the skill differences just noted (median percentages opposed to free speech on the four questions run 55 per cent for eighth-grade schooling or less, 46 per cent for some high school, and 38 per cent for high-school graduates). This correlation with education agrees with previous studies concerning attitudes toward civil liberties.

In our population of factory workers, attitudes toward freedom of speech are not significantly correlated with personal satisfaction, in work or in life generally, or with measures of mental health. However, there is a mild tendency for middle-aged men of low personal morale—that is, the anomic, distrustful, pessimistic—to be more intolerant of free speech (51 per cent against free speech versus 42 per cent by the men of higher morale). This relationship does not occur among young workers. But in both age groups we find a closer relationship of responses regarding free speech with the authoritarian attitudes described earlier. This linkage would be expected on logical grounds since the authoritarian items also express disrespect for rule of law and ideals of equality. For young and middle-aged together, 62 per cent of men having high authoritarian scores are opposed to free speech as compared with 42 per cent opposition by all others.

The results as a whole lead us to reject the hypothesis that intolerance in respect to free speech occurs in any marked degree as a manifestation of above-average frustration or of poor mental health. At the same time, the intolerance is associated with a cluster of authoritarian attitudes which do relate to poor mental health. This emphasizes once more the complex interdependencies of the feelings and behaviors that go to make up good or poor adjustment. We conclude that the feelings expressed in regard to civil liberties, although they pose extremely grave problems for a society concerned with maintaining basic democratic ideals, have only very limited dependence on personality factors and correspondingly limited significance in reference to individual differences of mental health among working people.   In the larger frame of reference proposed at the beginning of this chapter, nevertheless, the lack of more general adherence to principles of political freedom must be considered an unsatisfactory condition of the society as a whole, whether or not one cares to call it a condition of poor mental health.

Attitudes regarding race relations

The two remaining sets of social attitudes, toward Negro-white relations and American foreign policy, raise these same questions in more acute form and with evidence of closer ties to variations of personal adjustment.   We relied on the following comprehensive free-response question to tap the men's attitudes toward race relations.

What do you think ought to be done about race relations in this country—that is, between whites and Negroes?   (How do you mean? Would you make that a little clearer to me?)

Answers were classified on a five-point scale.   The scale categories are specified in Table 10-4 which shows the proportion of Detroit factory workers giving each type of answer.   In case of doubt a response was placed higher rather than lower on the scale; hence whatever constant error is present tends toward *underestimation* of the actual extent of race prejudice.

Table 10-4   Attitudes of Detroit factory workers toward Negro-white relations

Attitudes	Young	Middle-aged
For full equality and against segregation	14%	22%
Equality and nonsegregation with reservations	6	6
Ambivalent; pro and con; noncommital	20	15
Mildly anti-Negro and/or prosegregation	20	19
Strongly anti-Negro and/or unqualifiedly prosegregation	40	38
	100%	100%
Number of individuals	(109)	(285)

The meaning of the categories is illustrated by the following quotations from the interviews.

1. Treat them all alike; they are as good as we are.
Things should be equal between all people; each man has to be accepted on his own merits.
If we are a Christian nation we must act as Christians and realize that white and black are brothers.   That's the test!
2. I think this country is big enough for both to live in peace.   I associate with colored every day and I get along with them.   They should have equal rights.   I'm against intermarriage of course.
I don't have anything against them; I work with them every day; I know a lot of them that are very good people.   I just don't believe in mixed marriages.
3. They can't help it that they're here and I guess they have to stay. Most of them are decent and I guess in time the thing will work itself out on its own merits if we just leave things alone.
I think they're mixing too much.   But they're human; they fought for this country—I guess you gotta treat them equal.
4. Keep them by themselves.   I like them; they're good people—but I don't like to live next door to them, my kids raised with them.   The colored should have a village for themselves; they don't want to bother us and we don't want to bother them.
Just the way it is; the present ideas are all right.   They've got to live too.   As long as everyone stays on their own side of the fence things work out OK.
5. They say they're equal but they're not; they still got that blood in 'em.   Only 1 in 500 are as good as the white man.   They should be segregated, have their own territory.
If I had my way I would stick them in one state and not let them all over the country and not try to live like a white man.

Nearly 60 per cent of Detroit factory workers expressed segregationist views in stronger or milder terms.   Only one in five declared himself fully for racial equality and integration.   These negative attitudes among auto workers are especially disconcerting in view of the vigorous educational efforts of their union during the entire postwar period.   We are unable to say how much opinions of Detroit workers have changed during the decade of intensified struggle for racial equality since the study was carried on.

It is noteworthy and disturbing that our data show young workers fully as prejudiced as the middle-aged.   Moreover, men born in the Northern states are as unfavorable to equal treatment as those from the South.   Differences by occupation are small and irregular. Nonfactory blue-collar workers are indistinguishable from the auto workers. Only the young white-collar group is markedly more liberal and even among these men just under one-half are in the two most equalitarian categories. Workers who completed high school have more favorable attitudes than others, both among young and middle-aged (for the combined age groups, 43 per cent of high-school graduates are prosegregation compared to 64 per cent of those with eighth-grade schooling or less and 62 per cent of the "some high school" group).

A number of additional social and personal characteristics relate to racial attitudes but none very closely. By religion, for example, Catholics were a little more frequently equalitarian than Protestants among nonfactory workers and young factory workers but not in the large middle-aged factory group. Workers who are most liberal on socioeconomic questions are not more liberal in regard to race; in fact they tend to be a little more segregationist. Factory men who belong to more than two organizations tend to have somewhat better attitudes on race than do their fellow workers. A last illustrative finding is that downwardly mobile factory workers, that is those whose present job is of lower economic status than jobs they held earlier, show no greater proportion prejudiced than do others. This is directly contrary to one form of the scapegoat theory that sees downward mobility as generating bias.

Our principal interest here lies not so much in relationships like the foregoing as in the question whether race prejudice is associated with feelings of personal dissatisfaction, low morale, authoritarian attitudes, and poor mental health. Relationships to these personality variables do exist but not at all strongly. To begin with the least related, both job satisfaction and life satisfaction appear to have almost no bearing on attitudes toward Negroes. This again argues against a conception of race prejudice as a matter of personal frustrations displaced on a convenient target. The general index of mental health relates somewhat more closely to responses regarding Negroes (67 per cent of the men having low mental-health scores are for segregation compared with 57 per cent of the intermediate category and 52 per cent of those with high mental health). The anomie or personal morale component of mental health shows percentages almost identical with those for the total mental-health index. The clearest relationship of all is that with authoritarian attitudes; the proportions of prosegregationists by high, medium, and low authoritarian scores run 71, 62, and 38 per cent. This result conforms to other studies which find a definite association of minority-group prejudice with antidemocratic, authoritarian attitudes.

The evidence as a whole here leads to the same central conclusion as that in regard to freedom of speech, namely that the attitudes revealed are so sharply at variance with fundamental values of our democratic society that they bespeak a seriously unsatisfactory psychological condition. The fact remains that a majority of the workers hold such views, and that large numbers of these men have high mental-health ratings. We take this to mean that when such beliefs, basically contradictory of professed values though they are, receive social support and ready-made rationalization, they become nearly as acceptable to the mentally healthy as to the unhealthy. Personal determinants of prejudice are then largely submerged in the tidal wave of reference-group influence that affects all. But to the extent that the contradictions are exposed and made more inescapable, through education, agitation, and public discussion, we may expect the blanket influence to diminish and differentiation according to individual dispositions to increase. Consequently, we would conjecture that the inverse correlation of race prejudice with mental health may be growing larger. But speculation aside, the stark facts of Table 10-4 speak for themselves.

Orientation in regard to American foreign policy

Finally, we asked two questions to secure an indication of workers' orientation with respect to America's place in world affairs.

What do you think should be America's position in world affairs— what should this country do about the way things are going in the rest of the world?

What do you think the United States should do about working with the United Nations? (How do you mean? In what way?)

Answers to the first question were classified into two broad categories of "internationalist" versus "isolationist." Any response favoring effective American leadership, foreign aid, and positive action abroad, either alone or in collaboration, was assigned to the former; other answers advocating noninvolvement, taking care of domestic problems first, relying on our defenses, and so on, composed the second category. Of all classifiable answers by factory workers, 55 per cent are internationalist, 45 per cent isolationist. Factory workers are not clearly different from our other occupational groups (save that small-town workers are more isolationist, 58 per cent being so classified), nor do the auto workers differ much by skill levels (though middle-aged skilled tend to be more isolationist, 61 versus 43 per cent of the semiskilled).

The most pronounced relationships of these orientations in respect to international policy among factory workers are with education, anomie, and authoritarian attitudes. In the young group, amount of schooling has a substantial effect; proportions internationalist are 36 per cent of those with eighth grade or less, 57 per cent of those with some high school, 74 per cent of the high-school graduates. In the middle-aged group there is no relationship to education. But both age groups show a strong tendency for persons of low morale and those with authoritarian attitudes to be more isolationist (for the young and middle-aged together, 57 per cent of the anomic or low-morale workers are isolationist versus 34 per cent of those having high morale; correspondingly for high and low authoritarian scores the figures are 55 versus 26 per cent). Degree of life satisfaction is unrelated to foreign-policy views. The general assessment of mental health shows a slight tendency for those who rate low, particularly among the middle aged, to be more isolationist.

Replies to the second question, pertaining to the United Nations, were coded as follows—with percentage figures shown for the two age groups combined.

Should work with UN—unqualified answer	60%
Should work with UN—mild qualifications but still clearly favorable	13%
Should work with UN—but serious qualifications; doubtfully favorable	18%
Critical of UN and no indication that US should work with it	9%

Here, too, factory workers do not differ greatly from men in other occupational categories though they are a trifle more negative than nonfactory and white-collar groups. No significant differences occur between skill levels. Responses to this question likewise show little relationship to personal variables.

If one assumes that a broad world view and acceptance of international responsibilities are more in accord with superior mental health than are their opposites, then the foregoing findings point in the same direction as those in regard to free speech and race relations. The cluster of "satisfactory" personal orientations represented by high personal morale, nonauthoritarian attitudes, and to a lesser degree the attributes of good mental health generally, tend to extend also to approval of free speech, racial equalitarianism, and positive participation in world affairs.

The samples of social, political, and economic attitudes reported in this chapter may well carry more significant implications in respect to sociopsychological problems of our entire society than of the particular segment composed of industrial working people. Nevertheless, differences do exist among the groups studied, and with some uniformity the evidence indicates that factory workers, particularly those on lower-level semiskilled jobs, have orientations that reflect greater dissatisfaction and alienation. This appears most directly in measures of anomic and authoritarian attitudes and hostility, including related negative opinions toward free speech, race relations, and liberal foreign policies. But it is manifested also in the opinions and feelings having to do with what we have labeled labor orientation. This cluster of working-class and prolabor views is probably not so much a direct result of individual frustrations and social alienation, however, as it is a relatively independent product of the same economic and social disadvantages that tend under existing cultural conditions to generate both the negative feelings and the motivation to social reform in line with economic self-interests. It is quite possible that our repeated question, "how satisfactory" are workers' orientations from a mental-health standpoint, should receive unlike answers as between the prolabor attitudes on the one hand and the feelings of social distrust, hostility, and antidemocratic inclinations on the other hand. The former represent realistic, positive, more or less effective and cooperative problem-solving efforts; the latter show the attitudes of factory workers to be even less satisfactory than those of comparable groups, judged either by the norms of a free, democratic society or by the standards of good mental health. The disparity points up the challenging question whether people at middle and lower economic levels can be dissatisfied enough to maintain a vigorous spirit of social protest and improvement, including but reaching beyond immediate material self-interests, and yet avoid feelings of personal frustration and dissatisfaction directed toward themselves with resulting low morale and unsatisfactory mental health.

11.

The worker's orientation to his world—

4. Attitudes toward self

and personal goals

In any assessment of people's mental health and total life orientation, the feelings and attitudes they hold toward themselves, their aspirations, expectations, accomplishments, and interpersonal relationships are of paramount importance. We have referred to such feelings, directly and indirectly, at many preceding points. We shall now consider elements of the evidence insofar as they contribute a little better basis for judging how "satisfactory" workers' feelings are in regard to themselves and their life goals.[1]

Purposive orientation versus passive adjustment

A first set of questions has to do with workers' purposiveness. To what extent do they manifest an active striving orientation to life rather than an inert acceptance? Do they direct their efforts vigorously toward goals? In an attempt to deal with these questions we earlier described a rating of purposive striving and concluded that this quality is an indispensable aspect of good mental health in contrast to mere passive contented adjustment. Although cautious interpretation is required inasmuch as intense purposiveness also occurs as a neurotic expression of inner conflict and frustration, the empirical results reveal a decided predominance of the *positive* association of purpose with good mental health (pp. 35, 48–49). We also found that measures of purposefulness parallel other mental-health indicators in showing that factory workers at upper levels of skill stand considerably higher on the average than men in lower-grade jobs (pp. 62–64).

238

It is important to add, now, that factory men as a whole show less striving toward the attainment of goals than do our other occupational groups. In fact, clearly purposeful orientations are rather uncommon among industrial workers. Systematic estimates of a "purposive life style" based on all relevant parts of the interview indicate that only 30 per cent of the young and 20 per cent of the middle-aged could be classified as exhibiting strong, healthy, purposeful attitudes and activities.[2] This contrasts most strikingly with the young white-collar group of whom 69 per cent are so classified. Although young men in nonfactory manual work have approximately the same proportion strongly purposeful as do those in the factory, many fewer of them are extremely *lacking* in this quality (23 per cent of the young factory men are very weakly purposeful in regard to work—37 per cent of those on repetitive jobs —versus only 13 per cent of the nonfactory group; in respect to *non-work* purposefulness the proportions rated very weak are 51 per cent of the factory group versus 19 per cent of the nonfactory). These figures support the view that factory work tends to stifle ambition and initiative in young men, not only in respect to work career but in ways that affect life away from work as well.

Fewer middle-aged men than young manifest strong purpose in respect to work and career, in all the occupational groups, with only small differences between the factory men and others. However, the routine production workers number many more who have given up, who manifest little or no purposeful spirit in respect to work (48 per cent receive the lowest rating versus 15 per cent of all other middle-aged factory workers, 14 per cent of white collar, and 26 per cent of nonfactory men). This lowest factory group thus exhibits the same disproportionate deadening of initiative that appears among younger workers. No corresponding differences appear in respect to nonwork purposiveness; the middle-aged groups are all much alike.

The early discussion of purposiveness referred also to an index of "active life and career orientation."[3] This measure combines responses indicative of initiative, ambition, self-reliance, desire for success. As would be expected, young men score higher than the middle-aged (among factory workers 59 per cent of the young and 39 per cent of the older obtain medium or high scores). There is also a strong tendency for the more skilled to stand higher than the less skilled in both age groups (percentages are given on p. 64). Among young men, both white-collar employees and nonfactory blue-collar workers manifest this active life and career orientation somewhat more frequently than factory workers (75 per cent of white collar and 73 per cent of nonfactory have high scores compared to 59 per cent of the factory group). In the middle-aged group the same tendency occurs in comparison with white-collar men (50 per cent of white collar versus 39 per cent of factory workers have high scores) but blue-collar workers outside the factory are about the same as those in the factory.

Specific responses that enter into the index tell a more directly meaningful story. A first example is the question:

Some people push hard to change things and make their lives more like what they want; other people are content to take life as it comes. What about you—do you push hard to change things in your life, or are you content to take life as it comes? Why do you feel that way?

Only 31 per cent of the young auto workers and 25 per cent of the middle-aged say that they push hard; 49 and 64 per cent respectively are content to take life as it comes or are so vague and doubtful as to indicate dubious purposiveness at best. Slightly larger proportions of white-collar and nonfactory workers reply with expressions of positive, active orientation. Comments of the factory men are illuminating both on the positive and negative side. For example:

Worthwhile things, in fact everything in life that counts, must be worked for and pushed for.

My ambition is to better myself; a person must have something to strive for.

It [pushing hard] gives you something to work for and look forward to; be able to get enjoyment out of life.

I feel nobody will give me anything; I got to do things for myself.

Work, work, work—that's the only way to get things you want.

I always try to get ahead and not give up; once you stay in one spot you are licked. We are all living to get ahead so that when we are 50 to 60 we can see what we have done.

I push hard as I can; life is a continual trap—so you gotta watch and plan all the time.

I hope I'm pushing hard; man was born to push and push. Life must be earned; one must work hard for happiness and security.

Oh God, I have been pushing and slaving all my life and where have I got!

The preceding comments are by men who say that they push hard; the following are by those "content to take life as it comes."

You've just got to take things as they come, what else can you do?

Why push when you can't accomplish it; why try to be something you can't?

I've been around long enough to know you can't fight it.

I don't have to kill myself for something; life is too short.

I'm happy-go-lucky; I never felt like worrying about anything; life is what it is, there isn't too much you can do about it.

I'm the contented kind; it makes life less complicated and less worry.

I quit pushing, I guess. There's a time when I did but the last 8 or 10 years I sorta slowed down [now 42]; I guess I just got tired of trying to get somewhere and you don't.

There's such a thing as beating your brains against the wall. Some things you just can't change; might as well accept them and adjust yourself to them.

I feel it's past my time to do any pushing.

I'd rather work steady and take it as it comes; if you push too hard you don't enjoy life.

I don't push hard; it's no good—because I never know what will happen no matter how I try.

What is going to happen is going to happen; you can't better it by pushing.

Nothing else we can do; that's life. You have to take things as they come; nature determines your life.

I don't think we can change things; whatever our life turns out is what it is. Things are set for people; life is planned for us; not much we can do.

No use going out to try to change things; I'm content.

Both the numerical results and the quotations call attention to the very limited self-expectations, the degree of passivity, fatalism, and resignation that characterize many of the workers. Nor is there much exhiliration manifested in the replies of the strivers; most of their answers reflect a spirit of grim submission to the unpleasant necessity of continuing struggle. The tone of the statements as a whole suggests an outlook on life that is a far cry from a sturdy, vibrant, and self-reliant condition of positive mental health.

Another item used in the career-orientation index has to do with the strength of desire for job advancement. Our typical worker declares that it is important to him (58 per cent say so, though only 24 per cent are classified as saying "extremely important"); but in almost all cases he is doing nothing about it. Furthermore, the nature of his ambitions, as indicated by his ideas of what "getting ahead" means, reinforces doubts as to the satisfactoriness of the vocational goals that are most prominent. The aims refer principally to increased income, authority and responsibility, and vague qualities of "a better job." We pointed out in the earlier analysis of these ideas the absence of any emphasis on status enhancement; we now wish to stress the equal scarcity of goals that suggest self-development, self-expression, improved opportunities for performing interesting, useful, important work, for feeling one's worth and realizing one's potentialities. There is scarcely a hint of such objectives. This may not be surprising but it is nonetheless a significant commentary, we believe, on the limited self-image and sense of personal possibilities of industrial workers in contemporary America.

Personal goals—volunteered responses

The most directly pertinent material in respect to workers' goal values is secured from questions near the beginning of the interview which first encouraged the respondent to tell in his own words what kinds of things he wants out of life and then presented him a list of nine "things people say they want" with the request that he designate those *he* wants most. Some results bearing on individual differences of mental health are reported in Chapter 7 (pp. 150 153). In the present connection our attention centers rather on the content and significance of the responses insofar as they help depict the conception men have of themselves and where they are heading.

A classification of workers' answers to the free-response question about what they want most in life is given in Table 11-1. Heaviest emphasis is on material gratifications and economic security, followed by desires for welfare of family, greater leisure and happiness, good health (especially by the middle-aged), and more satisfactory work (especially by young men). Probably no one would quarrel with any of these aims or contend that they are incompatible with good mental health. They reflect approved values of our culture; all are commendable in and of themselves. But most notable is what the workers do *not* say. Desires are extremely infrequent that point either to personal growth and self-actualization or to more effective social participation, helping others, and contributing to making a better world. Spiritual and religious values are equally rare. In fact, the percentages in the last five lines of Table 11-1 attest to the extreme rarity of all the intangible and idealistic goals. In only a fraction of these cases, moreover, does the interview as a whole suggest that religion or a spirit of altruism and idealism plays any deep or pervasive part in the worker's life.

*Table 11-1   Factory workers' volunteered responses
to a question regarding their life goals* *

Classification of Responses	Percentage of Workers Mentioning Goals within the Specified Categories	
	Young	Middle-aged
More money; good home and good living; material comforts; ability to pay bills	73 %†	63 %†
Welfare and happiness of family; ambitions for children	59	39
Security of job and income—now and for retirement	43	85
Leisure and enjoyment; easier, happier, more independent life; friends, travel, etc.	33	42
Health of family and self	20	35
Goals of personal advancement, accomplishment, success		
(a) Emphasis on material advancement; a good (better) job or own business; keep busy, etc.	22	11
(b) Emphasis on personal growth, self-expression, satisfying achievement	3	3
Altruistic goals		
(a) Social reform or service; own action to help people	1	2
(b) Other reference to welfare and happiness of people, world peace, etc.	1	4
Spiritual and religious goals		
(a) Specific reference to church, God, Christian life, etc.	1	3
(b) Other: moral life, peace of mind, etc.	2	1

* The question reads as follows: What would you say you really want most out of life?   (Will you tell me a little more about what you want?   How do you mean?)   What other kinds of things do you really want in life?

† Percentages are based on 109 young and 298 middle-aged men.   The percentages total more than 100 per cent, since each man could name several goals; we coded and tabulated a maximum of five ideas for a respondent.

One young factory worker of the entire 109 interviewed mentions a place for religion among his life goals ("be a good church member") and only one other indicates a significant religious commitment at other points in the interview. Among the middle-aged a few more, but only 3 per cent in all, include goals having a religious connotation (only 4 per cent even when we add those evidencing such sentiments elsewhere in the interview). The following quotations illustrate the few replies that do reveal religious or spiritual goals.

Do God's work and lead a good Christian life. [Earlier] I've got my work at the church——it's my life's work.
I want to serve the Lord the most; go to church and be with Christian people and work for the Lord.
To always have my religion; my main goal is to save my soul; life is just short, eternity is forever.
More than anything else I'd like to have peace of mind—not to have any worries and enjoy life, even if I don't have all the money I really would like to have.
Well, a nice home and a good Christian life is about as good a thing as a man could wish for.
What a person really needs most is being spiritually and morally right; that's most important, rest of it don't matter.
I would like to see people more tolerant and more spiritually minded rather than materially minded. I feel people are too cash conscious. I would like to live in an environment where people think more and view things more like myself.

Another small group of responses is classified under the heading of altruistic or welfare goals. Some of these merely express wishes for a better world, like the following three.

I would like to see peace in the world instead of war—peace, everybody workin' and satisfied.
I wish there was more honesty in the world; too many crooks. I wish people wouldn't fight so much. There's too much bickering; wish there was more harmony in the world.
I want my children to be successful and turn out well—to be of service to mankind instead of only self. Want the country to be strong, but just; don't think they are just now.

A few other workers manifest much more active motivation and personal effort toward helping others (category *a* under "altruistic goals" in Table 11-1). There are also several respondents who do not mention such aims when asked about their life goals but who nevertheless exhibit this orientation in their activities. If they are included in the category, the percentage for the middle-aged group rises from 2 per cent to 4 per cent. The following are examples of the most service-oriented cases.

I want to feel that I can contribute to society in general, bettering other people's lives and seeing that they get a fair deal. . . . I hope to get a political appointment. [He is very active in his union and political party]. In politics I feel I can accomplish all that I want in life.

I don't want more than I've got—an active life, a fine growing family, the finest friends in the world. [Extremely active in civic and political affairs; "try to be a force for good in my community"; "get a lot of satisfaction whenever I see a good bill passed in Congress or in the Legislature, or a good man get into office."] I'd like to see my children become healthy, happy men and women—good citizens who make a contribution to the world they live in and never forget that their welfare is dependent on the welfare of those around them.

[Want most] An active life, able to take part of being a good American and seeing that I can do my part to see that good people get into high office. [Vice-president of a lodge and secretary of a political club.] I go up to Lansing and help the Governor with the Democratic cause.

[No mention of social goals but active in a number of civic and political organizations.] All the organizations I belong to keep me pretty busy. I like to get involved in local politics. [Chairman of a civic association, vice-president of a political club, secretary of an area development council, etc.]

[Sources of satisfaction] The fact that I've always been able to help someone else. I get a kick out of making someone happy who is unhappy. I like to be a champion for someone who cannot speak their piece or is in some other way at a disadvantage. [Active in local union and holds several offices. Would like to change jobs to do] public relations work, sociological work, or rehabilitation work. I think I could do something that would be beneficial to more people.

The remaining category of goals that carry a touch of idealism consists of wishes for satisfying personal achievement and self-actualization. Here, too, the number of workers so classified is very small. Illustrative of their responses are these.

[Want in life] To be able to learn all I can about the welfare of mankind and the betterment of civilization; to have time to get around, meet people, learn their ideas, increase my knowledge.

Want more time for hobbies—flying, stamp collection, repairing old motors and putting them to new uses.

I think everybody likes achievement; I didn't want to set the world on fire but I did want some recognition. [Satisfactions in life] Oh, just the fact that you are able to master something. I like to master anything; I am a little more than mildly interested in radio and TV, scientific things like electronics.

Want to devote myself entirely to physical therapy; that's about all that matters. [Satisfactions] Spending time helping people with their physical ailments by treating them.

To have a small house down at the beach, do some writing—a library nearby. There's only one thing I'd like to do—I'd write again. I started a novel at one time, four or five short stories, and some poetry.

To understand—ability to know and see things as they really are; to enjoy what you understand, appreciate life itself. [Satisfactions] Ability to learn as you go along; it's nice to be able to learn things in everything—work and living itself.

In sum, Table 11-1 and the quotations reveal that only a very small minority of factory workers give voice to life aims that reach beyond the usual goals of enjoyment, health, and economic improvement and opportunities for self and family. The goals in general remain starkly mundane and commonplace. One searches the answers in vain for more than an occasional trace of active reform spirit or devotion to larger purposes or ideals that transcend the individual himself and his family. With only a few possible exceptions, there is no sign that the men entertain dreams of social change or that they have any thought of working for "social causes." There is scarcely a hint of wanting to be caught up in a social movement or of becoming involved in collective efforts worthy of a man's dedication. In this heartland of progressive, idealistic labor unionism, not a single worker of the more than four hundred interviewed, in discussing his life aims, so much as *mentions* union activities or desire to help achieve union goals (though in other parts of the interview, four men do describe vigorous participation in union work). What is impressive in the men's reports of their life aims is the absence of larger horizons, the poverty of their aspirations and self-expectations; the pedestrian, unaroused, unstimulated conception of their potentialities, whether for the enrichment of their private lives or for effective action toward social ends.

A list of typical quotations will exemplify the somber, earthbound quality of the general run of life aims categorized in Table 11-1.

A good living; to not have to want things; a new car, a vacation now and then, a good home.

Well, I'd like to have a home; it don't have to be fancy or nothin'. I'd like a car good enough to get around in; it don't have to be new.

Money! If you have that you can get anything you want; I'd buy a house in a better neighborhood, better clothes and furniture, and stuff like that.

Plenty to eat and wear, a good car, and a nice home. What else is there? When you've got that, you've got everything.

Clean decent living, plenty of food for the kids, well-clothed kids and healthy; a better home to live in.

Security—meaning that my children get a chance at education and become good citizens.

Want to sell this house and buy a farm where the kids can grow up like they should.

I'd like my family to have things I didn't have, like a college education which would help them get a good job.

A complete feeling of security would make me more than satisfied and settled.

A good job I guess, where I can more or less depend on myself and not be out of work and have money when I need it.

I'd like to be able to retire early with security; I don't want to work like a dog for the rest of my life.

Enough leisure time to enjoy life, with enough financial security to take the strain out of everyday problems of just existing.

Oh, a chance to relax, more time to enjoy life in my old age; a chance to get up in the hills and be out in the country more.

I'd like to be able to travel if I could afford it.

The only thing I want is my health and health of my family; I don't care too much about money.

Good health is the main thing.

Settle down on a nice little piece of land and raise chickens or minks; to have enough money so I don't have to want nothin' awful bad.

A better job that pays more money and less work.

A little place of business; get out of the shop. I don't care about a lot of money.

I'd like to go up north and rent cabins or have a gas station.

I'd like to have a position, not a job—a really good job.

I would like a better job with more pay and responsibility.

To be able to do what I want to do—to take time off when I feel like it, to be my own boss.

I want to be free from doing the same thing day after day.

All of the foregoing is seriously misleading if it leaves the impression that the narrowness of personal goals is distinctively characteristic of *factory workers*. Men in nonfactory manual employment and even white-collar employees express life aims that differ little from those of factory workers. One significant exception is that young workers in the other occupational groups, including small-town factory workers, are more than twice as likely as young Detroit auto workers to voice desires for more satisfactory jobs and personal achievement. In this vital area of aims, young urban factory workers, and to a more limited extent the middle-aged also, do appear more purposeless than comparable groups though the number expressing such wants remains small in all groups. As to wants indicative of social consciousness and idealism or spiritual goals, there is no evidence that these exist in the nonfactory population appreciably more than among factory men.

We also find that substantially the same life aims are stated by factory workers at higher and lower skill levels. Among young men, however, the two top skill groups are a little more likely than the two lower semiskilled groups to give answers that refer to better jobs and personal development. Among the middle-aged this trend does not appear. If low-level production jobs are destructive of hopes, ambitions, and ennobling self-expectations, the evidence at hand argues that these effects are almost equally present in more skilled and varied types of work. Broad cultural influences and the temper of the times are probably much more important determinants than the job—and these would tend to produce similar effects among men throughout the range of working-class and lower middle-class occupations. Our data accord with such an interpretation.

Results of a very similar character were obtained when we inquired, at a later stage of the interview, what the respondent thinks "most people want out of life." Replies to this more projective-type question place the same heavy emphasis on material goals above all others, followed by references to happiness and enjoyment of life. Next in order of frequency come objectives of economic security, welfare of family, and good health. Remaining responses scatter widely, again with extremely few suggesting wants for personal growth and self-expression, greater freedom and independence, or creative activities and achievement. Virtually none mention that people may want to help others, to work for social improvement, or to devote themselves to humanitarian ends. In short, the motives attributed to others duplicate the earthy, unimaginative, self-centered conceptions of life purposes that we observed in the workers' statements of their own wants.

Personal goals—check-list responses

Complementary findings from a check-list question regarding personal goals are now to be placed alongside the preceding evidence.

The list of goal values is reproduced in Table 11-2 with the percentages choosing each. The constrained choices represented in this table are not directly comparable with the free answers summarized in Table 11-1. The greatest difference arises from the fact that the listed goals omit altogether the simple want for money and consumer

Table 11-2   Factory workers' choices of goals most wanted in life*

		Percentage Choosing Each Goal			
		(a) As the One Most Important		(b) As Among the 3 or 4 Most Wanted	
Goal Values		Young	Middle-aged	Young	Middle-aged
To have a satisfying home life	(5)†	39%‡	38%‡	68%‡	72%‡
To have things settled and secure in your life, and not have to worry about the future	(2)	19	27	55	62
To enjoy the work you are doing and be able to do a good job of it	(4)	7	6	53	47
To have a lot of good friends	(3)	7	7	39	35
To help people—to do things for other people	(8)	3	5	31	30
To have people think highly of you and appreciate what you do	(1)	5	3	28	32
To be treated as an independent human being, and not be pushed around and made to do things	(9)	7	4	30	24
To get ahead in the world and rise to a higher position and be better off	(6)	9	6	38	25
To have a lot of spare time to do the things you enjoy the most	(7)	0	3	14	27

* The question was worded as follows: Here is a list of some things people say they want in their lives. Which *three* or *four* of these things would you say you personally want most? Please look at all of them before you decide. (Show card containing list.)
    Which one of these things you just picked is *most* important to you?
    Which one of these nine things is *least* important to you?
† The parenthetic numeral designates the order in which the item appeared in the list of 9 goals presented to the respondents.
‡ Percentages show the proportion of workers who selected the goal, based on totals of 109 young and 298 middle-aged. Percentages in the first two columns total slightly less than 100 per cent since a few respondents failed to answer; percentages in the last two columns cumulate to more than 100 per cent because each man named 3 or 4 goals.

gratifications. We take for granted the overwhelming popularity of such a category and consequently felt that it was not needed in the list. Of the nine goal values that were presented for choice, two stand out among first choices—a satisfying home life and a life of security, stability, and freedom from worry. Other choices of a single most important goal spread widely through the list.[4] Both age groups particularly shun spare time for enjoyment as a leading aim. Young men also take an especially dim view of the goal of helping people, whereas the middle-aged turn away especially from seeking social approval and appreciation.

When the choice was broadened to include several life aims, the same two goals remain most popular but enjoyment of the job rises to a strong third position and all the other goals receive numerous votes, too, so that a quarter or more of the men name even the least preferred ones—save for the single exception that only 14 per cent of the young men include enjoyable leisure among their choices. When asked to designate the *least* important value, both older and younger men name the goal of spare time for enjoyment by a wide margin.

In the main, the check-list responses support the same inferences and give rise to the same disturbing questions as the volunteered statements of aim. There is a similar emphasis on passive goals of security and home life and the same relative weakness of appeal of active self-realization whether through creative leisure, personal independence, advancement, and social approval or through altruistic service and devotion to helping others. One marked contrast does appear in the sharply higher popularity of work satisfaction as a goal when it is explicitly brought to attention. What this may mean, we suggest, is that workmanship impulses, desires for enjoyable achievement and use of one's abilities on the job, are deep and strong but are so commonly thwarted and suppressed, so seldom even talked about as aims (for example, in union speeches or bargaining demands) that few workers spontaneously think of them. And not to think of them is likely to mean abandoning them. If this is a correct interpretation, important implications follow, implications caught up in the observation that "men capable of doing so much are asked to do so little." We would add: capable *and latently desirous* of doing so much.

Detailed comparisons of occupational groups on the check-list responses reveal a number of sizable and meaningful variations beyond those shown in the free responses. This is particularly true

among the young workers. For example, the goal of independence
(not to be pushed around) is stressed much more by young men
in ordinary and routine semiskilled jobs than by any other group
(37 per cent of them include it, compared to only 15 per cent of the
more skilled, 10 per cent of nonfactory, 15 per cent of white collar,
and 11 per cent of small-town workers). Young factory workers
at all skill levels place less emphasis on getting ahead in the world
than other young groups do (28 per cent of the factory group versus
38 per cent of nonfactory, 45 per cent of white collar, and 44 per
cent of small-town groups). Young men in routine factory jobs are
also less inclined toward goals of workmanship (47 versus 61 per
cent of skilled and high semiskilled, 68 per cent white collar, and 67
per cent of small-town semiskilled). In this case, similar but less
pronounced differences exist also among the middle-aged. Insofar
as these two last-mentioned goals represent ambition and self-expression, the results agree with the free responses in indicating that
factory workers in production jobs have lower self-expectations than
their counterparts in other work.

Middle-aged groups differ much less than the young, on the whole,
and with greater irregularities. Passive goals of security and satisfying family life are chosen fully as often by white-collar and nonfactory blue-collar men as by those in the factory. Goals of leisure
and helpfulness likewise prove no more attractive to other occupational groups than to the older factory workers. In fact, desire
for enjoyable leisure is even less popular among middle-aged white-
collar men than in other groups (it is included in choices of 11 per
cent of white collar, 27 per cent of factory workers). White-collar
people also choose the goal of being highly thought of more frequently than others (46 versus 32 per cent of factory middle-aged—
and only 26 per cent of those in routine production).

Our conclusions are as follows: (*a*) The aims and goal values
of factory workers at both upper and lower skill levels are similar in
the main to those of comparable occupational groups. Variations
produced by occupational circumstances appear to be relatively
minor compared to the effects of common cultural influences that
lead all groups to focus their desires overwhelmingly on security
and material gratifications, on passive, comfortable satisfactions of
family life and pleasures of consumption, with little emphasis on
intangible goals of personal achievement and self-expression and
almost total neglect of altruistic devotion to social causes and participation in collective efforts for human betterment. Few men

respond in a manner that points to any larger meaning in their lives, any touch of idealism or imaginative purpose beyond simple security, happiness, and well-being of self and family. (*b*) Insofar as there are dissimilarities, they indicate reduced ambition and less desire for personal achievement and for satisfactions of workmanship on the part of factory workers, particularly those in lower-level production jobs. The lower-level semiskilled, compared to other groups, also express more frequent desires for independence, escape from regimentation and being pushed around.

From earlier sections of the chapter, two other conclusions may be added. (*c*) The general level of purposive striving and active orientation to life is relatively low among factory men and lower in the routine production groups than among those doing more skilled and varied work. The greater proportion manifesting *weak* purposefulness is particularly observed. Factory employment, especially in routine production tasks, does give evidence of extinguishing workers' ambition, initiative, and purposeful direction toward life goals. (*d*) There is a clear positive correlation of overall purposefulness with mental health. The association is not simple and uniform, however. Relationships of life goals to mental health appear rather to be of the kind described in Chapter 7 (pp. 151–153), summarized in the proposition that workers who want what they cannot realistically expect to achieve tend to be in poorer mental health, while those whose wants are ones they can move toward satisfying tend to have better mental health.

Attitudes toward self

We have been asking what men expect of themselves, what aspirations and life purposes they have. A closely related question to which we now address our inquiry is whether they have positive feelings about themselves. Do they like what they are and what they see themselves striving for—or are many of them inwardly insecure, anxious, uncomfortable, bitter, and hostile? These feelings are essential components of our overall assessments of mental health, of course, and much of the evidence concerning them was summarized in Chapters 3 and 4. We now examine parts of the data further in order to focus more sharply on what is characteristic of our factory workers in respect to their orientations toward self.

Central to this portion of the inquiry are the responses indicative of self-esteem. The index based on these responses provides a measure of positive versus negative self-feelings, the degree of satisfaction, confidence, and sense of worth or adequacy that men feel in respect to themselves. On the whole the attitudes and orientations are disappointing for anyone who hopes for a bright-colored picture of rugged, self-confident American working men. Although the factory workers are only moderately worse off on this dimension than other occupational groups of similar economic level, considerable numbers reveal weak and unfavorable attitudes in regard to themselves.

Young workers on routine jobs are particularly lacking in strong positive self-feelings. On the general index of self-esteem, only 27 per cent of them (and 43 per cent of all young factory workers) have high scores compared with 54 per cent of the nonfactory men and 60 per cent of the white-collar workers. In the middle-aged bracket the lowest skill group also averages lower self-esteem than the more skilled and the white-collar groups (36 per cent have high self-esteem scores compared with 45 per cent of the manual workers at the three higher levels and 50 per cent of white-collar workers); but they score about the same as the nonfactory blue-collar workers.

To appreciate more fully what this relative lack of self-esteem means, it is necessary to look at replies to separate questions such as the following examples.

Do you feel that you can do much to make your future what you want it to be?
> 40 per cent of all factory workers and 50 per cent of repetitive production workers give a negative answer or one that is doubtful or ambivalent. Replies by white-collar and nonfactory groups reveal greater confidence, percentages dropping to 25 and 17 per cent respectively (age groups are combined for these percentages and those that follow).

Do you feel that you are accomplishing the sorts of things you would like to in life?
> 30 per cent of factory workers reply negatively compared to 25 per cent of white collar and 22 per cent of nonfactory workers.

Do you often blame yourself and feel bad over things you have done?
> 52 per cent of factory men answer affirmatively, 38 per cent of white collar, and 64 per cent of nonfactory workers.

Do you ever get so blue and discouraged that you wonder whether anything is worthwhile?

27 per cent of the factory group say "yes," 34 per cent of those on routine jobs, versus 16 per cent of white collar and 21 per cent of nonfactory workers.

The first two of the preceding items also included follow-up questions that solicited more detailed answers. These qualitative responses contain many interesting illustrations of workers' positive and negative feelings about themselves. The contrast may be seen in the following two sets of comments.

Indicative of positive self-regard:

Yes, by hard work and paying strict attention to doing a good job I will be promoted to a better, more responsible job. I've been promoted and expect to go a lot higher in the future.

Oh, definitely; you only accomplish what you set out to do. My belief is that you can achieve anything you really want to.

Yes, right now I figure on becoming a foreman pretty soon.

Yes, I'm a good mechanic and I'll be in demand. I can handle almost any kind of machine; make machines work. [Accomplishing?] Yes, I believe I have; I've never failed.

I think a man can do anything if he wants to and has got the know how. I wanted a house, a home, and got that—I built it myself.

If I can't do it [make his future] who can? It's a matter of will power. If I want something I can get it; nothing can stand in my way.

Yes [accomplishing things he wants] establishing a respectable home, trying to raise my children in a way that would make good citizens; trying in my own life to live it so I believe it is right, keeping my conscience clear.

Yes, indeed, I can feel myself getting there; I have one more year of study, then I can hang out my shingle and open an office [as physical therapist].

I'm making a living and have most of the things I want and need; I'm enjoying myself and my family is happy.

I don't let things bog me down; I never leave a job undone; I like to go into new fields.

Indicative of negative self-regard:

No [cannot do much about future], I don't have no education.

No, I don't see what I can do about it; I don't know the right people to get ahead any.

Not me, I'm too dumb.

No, I don't think I can; for one thing, I haven't got the ability.

I could if I'd do it; it's never too late if you've got the ambition. Guess I just haven't got it. [Accomplishing?] No, I ain't getting no place. [Earlier] My conditions are my own fault.

Not a great deal any more; it all comes back to not being able to put yourself across. Sure as anything, somebody is going to ask me the wrong question at the wrong time and I'll get tongue-tied and that will end it.

No [not accomplishing]; I'm not working to get ahead like I should.

No, I can't give my family a decent home and I can't keep up with doctor and hospital bills.

I'm not satisfied with myself; I think I could do better if I applied myself in a different vocation.

I know I'm capable of doing better but I'm afraid to go ahead; almost get sick at my stomach when I go apply for a job.

I don't know but there's something in me makes me feel I'm not doing much of what I really feel good about.

No, things I plan never turn out.

The findings leave little doubt that a substantial minority of industrial workers lack the pride, self-confidence, belief in themselves, and tranquility which go with high self-esteem. This conclusion receives further support from the answers men give to questions tapping their feelings of nervous tension and symptoms of anxiety. Several examples follow.

Are you often worried and upset?
"Yes" by 26 per cent of factory men, 30 per cent of those on routine jobs, versus 10 per cent of white collar and 14 per cent of nonfactory workers (age groups are again combined for these and the following percentages).

Are you ever bothered by nervousness?
"Yes" by 35 per cent of factory men, 26 and 27 per cent of white collar and nonfactory workers respectively.

Are you ever bothered with headaches, indigestion, or any of the common ailments you see on this card? Please look at all of them and tell me which ones ever bother you. (List of 14 shown)
56 per cent of factory workers report two or more ailments compared with 45 per cent of white collar and 44 per cent of nonfactory workers; 34 per cent of the factory men report three or more ailments, versus 27 and 23 per cent of the other two groups.

A general index of anxiety gathers these and similar indicators into a single score. On this index 35 per cent of young factory workers have high anxiety scores as against only 8 per cent of white-collar and 8 per cent of nonfactory workers. No differences of this kind are exhibited by the middle-aged groups, but among these older men there is a slight trend by skill level (high anxiety by 20 per cent of the skilled, 33 per cent of ordinary and high semiskilled, 37 per cent of the repetitive semiskilled). As a whole, that is, the tendency is for evidences of anxiety to occur more fre- quently than average among semiskilled factory workers.

Responses grouped under our index of personal hostility show a similar tendency toward less healthy reactions by sizable numbers of factory men. Replies like those in the following items illustrate the point.

> Do you think most people can be trusted?
>> 29 per cent of all factory workers say "no" compared with only 7 per cent of white collar and 18 per cent of nonfactory workers.

Over the years there are a lot of things a man comes to learn about people. What are some of the main things you have learned about people?
>> 34 per cent of factory men reply by mentioning bad qualities or warnings and cautions concerning people; the other groups are less antagonistic, 24 and 22 per cent answering in the negative vein.

Do people often get on your nerves so that you want to do just the opposite of what they want you to do?
>> "Yes" by 26 per cent of factory men (31 per cent of the young) versus 12 and 17 per cent of white collar and nonfactory respectively.

Do you sometimes boil inside yourself without letting people know about it?
>> 63 per cent of factory men (74 per cent of those on machine-paced operations) answer affirmatively versus 56 and 57 per cent of the white-collar and nonfactory workers.

Do you ever feel like smashing things for no good reason?
>> 15 per cent of factory workers and only 3 per cent of white collar and 10 per cent of nonfactory signify that they have such feelings.

The index of hostility based on replies like the foregoing finds high hostility scores by 27 per cent of the young factory workers compared to 5 and 6 per cent in the two comparison groups; either medium or high scores by 73 per cent versus 30 and 31 per cent in the comparison groups. Among the middle-aged, the contrast of factory and white-collar men is similar (21 per cent to 4 per cent strong hostility; 63 per cent to 39 per cent medium or strong), but in this age bracket the nonfactory group scores approximately the same as those in factory employment. Within the factory population, men in lower-level jobs are a little more hostile on the average than the more skilled.

Workers' orientation to their life situation—an overall rating

A final set of comparisons to be reported makes use of a classification of respondents according to their predominant orientation to their life situation. Respondents are assigned to one of four categories by a rater's estimate based on reading of the entire interview record. The broad categories of orientation or "life style" are:[5]

A. Active, strong, purposeful attitudes and conduct. Believes in himself and seeks self-expressive activities; lively interests and zestful striving toward realistic goals.

B. Passive contentment with his lot in life. Moderately to well satisfied with all aspects of his life; little or no pushing toward new goals but a positive friendly adjustment to things as they are.

C. Resigned acceptance, neither happy nor unhappy, neither contented nor in revolt. Weak, passive, drifting, apathetic.

D. Frustrated, more or less unhappy about life situation and prospects without realistic efforts to change them. Ineffectual, emotional, and defensive reactions; anxious or hostile or depressed, etc.

We dealt earlier with the first of these categories, the purposeful group, versus all others.[6] A more complete description of proportions in the four categories, by occupational groups, is presented in Table 11-3. The principal finding is the larger proportion of resignation and frustration among lower-level factory workers and their smaller amount of purposive striving compared to other occupational groups. The contrast with white-collar employees is particularly notable, but comparisons with upper skill levels in the factory and with nonfactory tend irregularly in the same direction. Combining percentages of the resigned and frustrated, only 12 per cent of the upper two skill groups are so classified among the young versus 38 per cent of the two lowest groups; among the middle-aged, corresponding figures are 27 versus 45 per cent. For the two age groups together, just over half of the repetitive production workers fall into these two least satisfactory life-style categories. No other occupational group, save the similarly situated middle-aged workers in small towns, has nearly so large a proportion with these unfavorable orientations to life.

Table 11-3 Comparison of occupational groups on overall orientation to life*

Occupational Category	Young A Active, Purposeful	Young B Passive, Satisfied	Young C Resigned Acceptance	Young D Frustrated, Unhappy, Maladjusted	Young N†	Middle-aged A Active, Purposeful	Middle-aged B Passive, Satisfied	Middle-aged C Resigned Acceptance	Middle-aged D Frustrated, Unhappy, Maladjusted	Middle-aged N†
Detroit factories										
Skilled }	49%	39%	9%	3%	33	22%	58%	13%	7%	45
High semiskilled						19	50	27	4	98
Ordinary semiskilled	15	48	28	9	46	26	39	27	9	82
Repetitive semiskilled	33	27	30	10	30	14	32	38	16	73
Small-town factories										
High and ordinary semiskilled	33	33	33	...	18	33	48	24	...	21
Repetitive semiskilled	22	50	22	6	18	14	36	32	18	22
Detroit nonfactory										
High semiskilled	30	63	7	...	27	...	...	...	...	3
Ordinary semiskilled	35	40	25	...	20	21	42	35	2	43
Detroit white collar	69	21	8	3	39	26	44	26	4	27

* The classification into four categories is described in the text and in Appendix B.
† The totals on which percentages are based. Each horizontal set of four percentages totals 100 except when rounding produces a total of 99 or 101 per cent.

In short, the further consideration of men's feelings toward themselves in these last pages, and the ratings of their overall "life style," add to our earlier indications that large numbers of industrial workers are troubled by negative self-feelings, personal anxieties, inner tensions, and defensive emotional reactions. In other workers, deficient self-esteem and lack of confidence take the form of resigned acceptance of life, neither happy nor unhappy but passive, inert, disengaged from the concerns of the world. Factory workers, especially those at low skill levels, are somewhat worse than our other groups in these respects. But quite apart from statistical comparisons, we believe that the responses in and of themselves provide a basis for evaluation. Here, as at many previous points, the interview content is directly meaningful (it possesses "face validity") in its implications regarding the questionable quality of mental health displayed by the men studied.

12.

Conclusions

The aim of this study was to obtain evidence regarding the mental condition of workers in modern mass-production industry. Specifically, the study focused on Detroit automobile workers in the mid-1950's. Small samples from other occupations were studied for purposes of comparison. It was hoped that the research not only would contribute a somewhat clearer assessment than previously available of the quality of factory workers' life adjustments at different occupational levels, but also that it would provide useful indications of factors responsible for better or poorer mental health in the occupational groups. We come now to a summing up of what has been accomplished toward achieving these objectives and to a consideration of implications the findings may have in regard to industrial organization and social policy.

Summary of results

We shall begin with a brief recapitulation of our principal results and then proceed to questions and interpretations that extend beyond the empirical findings.

1. Large numbers of the automobile workers manifest feelings, attitudes, and behavior that signify none too satisfactory life adjustments or mental health. This is illustrated by such specific facts as these: from one-fourth to one-half of the men studied say that they are "often worried and upset," are "bothered by nervousness," that "most people cannot be trusted," that they sometimes "get so blue and discouraged that [they] wonder whether anything is worthwhile," that they "often feel restless, wanting to be on the move doing something but not knowing what," that they feel either

260

dissatisfied with life or "neither satisfied nor dissatisfied," that they are not accomplishing the things they would like to in life, and they do not feel that they can do much to make their future what they want it to be. These and many other responses reveal extensive enough feelings of inadequacy, low self-esteem, anxiety, hostility, dissatisfaction with life, and low personal morale to raise serious questions concerning the general condition of psychological and social health of industrial workers.

2. *The outstanding finding is that mental health varies consistently with the level of jobs the men hold.* When we compare the factory workers by occupational categories, the higher the occupation (in respect to skill and associated attributes of variety, responsibility, and pay), the better the average mental health. Those in skilled jobs have highest mental health scores, followed by the upper semi skilled, the ordinary semiskilled, and lowest of all, the men in routine, repetitive types of work. Data from comparable groups of small-town factory workers, Detroit blue-collar workers in nonfactory employment, and white-collar workers support the conclusion that mental health is least satisfactory among men in low-level production jobs.

The preceding comparisons are based on a quantitative index of mental health which utilizes responses to some fifty interview questions. Justification for the use of the index is demonstrated by its close correspondence with global estimates of mental health given by several highly qualified psychiatrists and clinical psychologists who systematically read and rated a subsample of the interview protocols. The agreement of the index with the independent judgments gives assurance that our results have to do with better and poorer mental health in fundamentally the same sense that the concept is used by professional clinicians. It is to be remembered that here and throughout the study we refer solely to degrees of *positive* mental health, not at all to mental *illness*.

3. A crucial question arises whether the occupational differences in mental health are effects of the job and its associated conditions or are due to *differential selection* of the kinds of persons who enter and remain in the several types of work. Analysis of our data strongly indicates that the observed differences of mental health are not accounted for by the amount of education or other prejob characteristics of the men in different job categories. The dependence of mental health on occupational level is genuine; the relationship cannot be explained away as due to extraneous factors. This does

not mean, of course, that personal characteristics are not also important; mental health has many independent roots, but here our interest centers on the influence of occupation. And regarding this, the evidence underscores the existence of significant occupational effects apart from other determinants.

In more general terms, the results emphasize the importance of *situational factors*. Persons differently situated in the economic system tend to enjoy better mental health or to suffer poorer mental health according to their position. This finding becomes the more striking since it occurs within the limited range represented by the comparatively secure, well-paid auto workers of this study. We are not making comparisons of successful working men with submerged, underprivileged, poverty-stricken groups but with other successful members of the labor force. The evidence of substantial differences of mental health by job strata within this population leads us to reject both the idea that problems of emotional adjustment are to be charged to the "human condition," equally affecting all persons in a distressingly imperfect world, and also the too commonly held view that observed variations of mental health are attributable solely to individual differences of personality make up. In addition to differences by skill level within Detroit factories, our evidence also indicates that white-collar workers, small-town workers, and young nonfactory workers have better mental health than the Detroit factory group.

4. The relationship of mental health to job satisfaction is central to our interpretation of both the foregoing results and the subsequent more specific findings. We conceive of job feelings as constituting a link between the gratifications and deprivations of the total job situation and the mental-health effects of these conditions. Poorer mental health occurs in lower-level jobs as a consequence of the more severe deprivations and frustrations in such jobs compared to higher-level occupations. Workers' expressions of job satisfaction or dissatisfaction are the overt manifestations of these occupational experiences. Actually, of course, the relationship is more complex; job feelings and the components of mental health are parts of a constellation of interdependent variables in which each is both cause and effect of others. For our analysis, however, attention is focused on one aspect of the interrelationships; job feelings are construed as an intervening link between the job and its impact on mental health.

The empirical evidence is congruent with this view of the relationship: (*a*) Large differences in the prevalence of job satisfaction do occur between higher and lower occupational groups. Dissatisfaction is notably great among workers in routine, repetitive production jobs. (*b*) Jobs in which workers tend to be most satisfied are likewise the ones conducive to better mental health; those in which larger proportions are dissatisfied are ones with poorer mental health. (*c*) In each occupational category, the better-satisfied individuals enjoy better mental health on the average than do those less satisfied. (*d*) When we partially eliminate the influence of job satisfaction by taking separately the men having above-average satisfaction and those below average, the mental-health differences between occupations diminish. *Satisfied* workers in low-level jobs differ little in mental health from the upper groups; the *dissatisfied* in higher occupations tend to be similar to men at lower levels. All these relationships accord with the hypothesis that gratifications and deprivations experienced at different occupational levels and manifested in expressions of job satisfaction and dissatisfaction constitute an important determinant of workers' mental health. Job satisfaction is the link between objective conditions prevailing at different occupational levels and the observed occupational variations in mental health.

5. Job satisfactions and dissatisfactions arise from the varied liked and disliked attributes of the work situation. Examination of the way these feelings and attitudes toward various job characteristics relate to mental health enables us to discover which attributes appear to be especially responsible for better mental health in more skilled and varied occupations and for poorer mental health in less-skilled routine jobs.

The analysis suggests that many interrelated characteristics of jobs contribute jointly to the comparatively high or low average mental health of occupational groups. The following specific conclusions emerge: (*a*) By far the most influential attribute is the opportunity the work offers—or fails to offer—for use of the worker's abilities and for associated feelings of interest, sense of accomplishment, personal growth, and self-respect. (*b*) Next most clearly important are feelings in regard to income and financial stress at upper and lower skill levels. (*c*) Feelings toward several other aspects of jobs show more limited and irregular relationship to mental health, including the pace, intensity, and repetitiveness of work operations; supervision and other human relations on the job; and opportunities for advancement and improved social status. (*d*)

Attitudes toward wage rates (as distinguished from problems of income mentioned under *b*), job security, and physical conditions of work appear to have little or no explanatory value in accounting for poorer mental health at lower versus upper job levels. The relatively small part played by a number of these job attributes presents some surprising departures from traditional beliefs; their meaning is discussed later, in the section of the chapter devoted to interpretations.

6. Comparisons of industrial establishments also reveal large differences in employees' mental health, job satisfaction, and job-related attitudes. The substantial variations from company to company, even within a single industry and locality, underscore the importance of organizational and management influences which, by the nature of the case, play a small part in the preceding comparisons of *occupational groups* within identical organizational settings. The variations between companies are associated with a number of company attributes that provide suggestive clues as to some of the explanatory factors accounting for the differences. In part we see the same underlying factors at work in the company differences as in the occupational comparisons, but other explanatory variables also appear. Company ranking on mental health is clearly related to size of plant, for example. Mental health is poorer in large establishments and, in Detroit companies, men on repetitive jobs have particularly poor mental health only in the very large establishments, not in the medium-sized ones. Companies also rank lower in mental health if they have a large proportion of employees at low levels of education and skill, if the quality of personnel policies and services is below average, and if workers' attitudes are unfavorable toward use of their abilities and opportunities for promotion. When companies are compared in respect to job satisfaction, other company characteristics also become significant—for example, employees' feelings about speed and intensity of work, working conditions, wages, and supervision.

7. Although the present research is concerned primarily with the way in which *occupation* affects mental health, it is recognized that the characteristics of *individuals* are also important determinants. Under the conditions of this study, the two broad sets of factors, those associated with occupational level and those pertaining to personal and social characteristics of workers, account in roughly equal degree for observed differences of mental health *among individuals*. As previously stated, however, mental-health differences

between *occupational groups* are attributable in only very slight degree to the personal variables.

Results here are based on personal factors of four kinds: samples of objective descriptive facts like age, education, and childhood economic level; prejob personality attributes; childhood goals and values; and current life goals. Mental health of individuals is most clearly associated with differences of education, childhood socioeconomic advantages, and childhood personality traits. Further analysis of these and the other personal variables brings to light complex interrelationships which, though not unequivocal, nevertheless provide useful insights regarding the varying subjective effects of occupational position.

In the main, the personal attributes and the current situational variables represented by occupation exert their influence relatively independently of one another. The effects tend to be additive so that a combination of good childhood conditions and skilled occupation yields the best mental health whereas poor background and low job placement result in fewest satisfactory mental-health scores. In other words, favorable or unfavorable prejob influences generally continue to be evidenced in later life adjustments. However, there are also more complex causal interactions that produce incongruency effects which result in especially *poor* mental health for persons of good background and correspondingly high expectations who are presently in low-level jobs. One form of this disparity is that between high aspirations and low achievement. Our results offer some support for explanations in terms of such disparities, though the observed effects are not of impressive size or consistency.

8. In Chapters 8 to 11 we no longer confined our analysis to the measure of mental health but considered a wider sampling of behavior and attitudes having to do with working men's outlook on life and their orientation to their world. The primary aim of these chapters is to bring together evidence on the basis of which readers, each according to his own standards, can better arrive at evaluative judgments of how satisfactory the attitudes and adjustments of industrial workers are, as represented by our sample from the Detroit automobile plants. Closely associated with this aim is the effort to specify problem areas and points of unsatisfactory adjustment which particularly call for remedial action and improvement. These implications for social action are discussed in the final part of the present chapter.

Analyses of workers' orientations, treated under the four broad headings of these last chapters, are very briefly summarized in the following paragraphs.

(*a*) In regard to work and the job, the predominant orientation is moderately positive. Most workers are satisfied but not too well satisfied; most are neither acutely discontented with their work nor do they find it stimulating and enjoyable. There is little bitterness and likewise little enthusiasm. Relatively few would choose to go into the same work again and most do not speak well of factory employment, particularly production jobs. Especially in simple routine jobs they are keenly aware of the lacks, irritations, and debilitating grind. In more skilled and varied jobs, intrinsic rewards of the work itself supply a strong additional element of attraction along with opportunities for growth and self-actualization. Despite the absence of such satisfactions in low-level positions, most workers find substitute and compensating extrinsic rewards that enable them to accept their work life without distress and even in most cases with a kind of mild, passive, somewhat fatalistic contentment.

(*b*) In regard to their lives away from the job, factory workers express predominant satisfaction and positive outlook differing only a little either from one job level to another or in comparison with nonfactory groups. Although the men's volunteered comments contain many complaints concerning both their economic circumstances and a variety of personal and social problems, other important areas of life are seen in a sufficiently favorable light to more than balance the disagreeable features. For most workers the result is a definitely positive orientation. Even routine production workers have overall feelings of life satisfaction only slightly lower than other groups and not at all commensurate with their relatively great *job* discontent. In general, however, feelings toward different sectors of life tend to be in agreement; the tendency is not, as often alleged, for individuals dissatisfied with their jobs to find extra, compensatory enjoyment in their leisure, nor for those least contented away from the job to be especially satisfied at work.

Factory workers as a whole have moderately satisfactory family and social relationships, not greatly different from comparable occupational groups. The routine semiskilled men, however, compare unfavorably with other groups and with generally accepted ideas of desirable social adjustment. Spare-time activities of most workers tend to be narrow and routine, with little indication of self-development and self-expression or devotion to larger social purposes.

Many appear to be groping for meaningful ways to fill their spare time but with little conception of the possibilities and with inadequate preparation or stimulation.

(*c*) Our inquiry into the sociopolitical orientation of working people takes two directions, one concerned with their working-class and prolabor views, the other with their attitudes toward basic tenets of democracy and their own relationships to the larger society. The former, as would be expected, shows factory workers heavily favorable to labor unionism, to government aid for the needy, public regulation of business, and other collective actions they perceive as protecting and benefiting the common man. On these matters, they do not appear to be going "middle class." In regard to broad questions of democratic values and personal identification with the society, we find enough evidence of authoritarian attitudes and alienation from social norms and democratic principles (including substantial opposition to racial equality and free speech) to present seriously disturbing problems. Though such problems are by no means confined to industrial workers, the factory men do show up worse than our comparison groups—and this is particularly true of those on low-level production jobs.

It thus appears that the same occupational and social disadvantages that tend to produce low personal morale and other features of poor mental health also lead to certain antidemocratic feelings as well as to greater motivation toward prolabor economic and political changes. The conjunction poses the challenging question whether the sociopolitical reform orientation is *necessarily* associated with the unhealthy mental conditions or, alternatively, whether the connection is fortuitous, occurring only under certain existing cultural conditions. Under other conditions, one suspects, the predominant tendency might be for workers' dissatisfaction to express itself in vigorous social protest and reform without at the same time turning into personal frustration and negative self-feelings.

(*d*) Finally, a further look at the men's attitudes toward themselves and their life goal discloses a picture that bears little resemblance to the idealized image of sturdy, self-confident, enterprising American working men. Fewer than one-fourth of the factory workers could be classified as exhibiting strong, healthy, purposeful orientations. Men engaged in routine production show notably weak ambition and initiative in regard to work compared to other occupational groups; among young workers this deadening of purposive striving is likewise evident in regard to the nonwork sector of life.

When the working men were questioned about what they really want most in life, their answers overwhelmingly specify financial and material goals and wishes for security, family welfare, health, and happiness. There are strikingly few expressions of interest in personal achievement, self-development, and self-expressive activities; even fewer references to altruistic aims or desires to participate in collective efforts to help others or to work for the improvement of society. In the main, the same emphasis on earthy, self-centered goals characterizes all the occupational groups, suggesting that the effects arise from common cultural influences rather than from circumstances peculiar to parts of the industrial population. There are enough exceptions, however, among factory workers as well as others, to brightly illustrate the humanly rewarding possibilities of more imaginative and idealistic life purposes.

Working people's feelings toward themselves also reveal many negative features. On a general index of self-esteem, for example, factory workers have more low scores than do comparable groups—and again the less-skilled factory groups are worst off. The attitudes include feelings of ineffectualness, inadequacy, lack of accomplishment, self-blame, and discouragement. Related evidence comes from interview items and indexes that show greater anxiety and hostility in the factory groups. Larger numbers are also rated as exhibiting overall reactions to life that reflect either frustration and emotional defensive tendencies or resigned, weak, and passive acceptance devoid of confidence and enthusiasm.

Meaning of the results

Our findings dictate conclusions that are neither extremely bright nor extremely somber in respect to the mental health of industrial workers. The great majority of the men studied are living simple, normal family lives, rather circumscribed and routine but moderately happy and active, without serious emotional problems or personal maladjustments. Not a few, however, manifest low self-esteem, social alienation, anxiety, and related symptoms that add up to decidedly less than satisfactory mental health. A meliorative interest naturally focuses attention primarily on this darker part of the picture in order to inquire why the psychological condition of many workers falls short of what appears possible and desirable.

How are we to understand the inadequacies, their nature and their causes? Why do working people, particularly those in low-skilled production jobs, not enjoy better mental health than they do?

The general answer, we believe, is given in the psychological guidelines proposed in Chapter 1. Like any other complex social behavior, the indicators of mental health have *many* determinants, partly in the background and present make-up of the persons involved and partly in the total range of circumstances now affecting them. Our major interpretation is that poorer mental health occurs whenever conditions of work and life lead to continuing frustration by failing to offer means for perceived progress toward attainment of strongly desired goals which have become indispensable elements of the individual's self-identity as a worthwhile person. Persistent failure and frustration bring lowered self-esteem and dissatisfaction with life, often accompanied by anxieties, social alienation and withdrawal, a narrowing of goals and curtailing of aspirations—in short, tendencies toward the varied feelings, attitudes, and behaviors we have assessed as constituting poor mental health.

What our comparisons of occupational groups signify is that conditions of work and accompanying mode of life at lower skill levels do, in fact, impose more severe deprivations, frustrations, and feelings of hopelessness, with consequences of the kind described. Workers in better positions experience a greater degree of fulfillment of their wants and enjoy correspondingly greater feelings of satisfaction, adequacy, and self-regard.

The foregoing interpretation needs to be extended in several directions. First, consideration must be given to the fact that there are significant variations of wants and expectations as well as underlying constancies. Our basic explanation emphasizes the common goals, the fact that workers at different occupational levels share fundamentally similar wants but are confronted by decidedly dissimilar opportunities for satisfying these wants. The proposition that our egalitarian American culture develops such common desires—for material well-being, success, freedom, equality, respect, to name a few—scarcely requires defense. But adequate interpretation of our mental-health findings must go beyond this general relationship to take into account, also, the development of aims that differ from one person to another, from group to group, and from situation to situation.

A most important example is seen in the tendency of men to accommodate their aspirations to their appraisal of the opportunities open to them—hence the frequently commented on "wantlessness" of the poor. Our own results present repeated illustrations; the unsatisfactory mental health of working people consists in no small measure of their dwarfed desires and deadened initiative, reduction of their goals and restriction of their efforts to a point where life is relatively empty and only half meaningful. Industrial workers, like all the rest of us, are caught on the horns of a dilemma: if they want *too much* relative to what they are prepared to strive for with some degree of success, the result is defeat and frustration; if they want *too little,* the consequence is a drab existence devoid of color, exhiliration, and self-esteem. Good mental health demands a middle course. Men in lower-level occupations, where means for want satisfaction are more limited, least often find the happy middle ground. Their poorer mental health reflects a loss of motivation and initiative as well as greater dissatisfaction and frustration in respect to the reduced aims that remain.

No blanket indictment is warranted, however, to the effect that curtailment of desires and contented acceptance of whatever life offers necessarily signifies poor mental health. It depends on how extreme the abandonment of active striving and what alternative possibilities exist for reasonably successful purposive behavior. There can be little doubt that in our culture passive contentment is deemed less psychologically healthy than a vigorous, self-reliant, problem-solving orientation aimed at satisfying persistent wants. On the other hand, when the alternative to quiescent acceptance is a continued sense of frustration and defeat, with embittered feelings toward self and others, then a realistic reduction of expectations is judged preferable by comparison. Thus reduction of striving is at one and the same time an aspect of poor mental health and a safeguard against even worse mental health.

This explanation in terms of wants that are too great or too small is clearly an oversimplification; it entirely omits vital questions concerning the *direction* of the wants. Instead of merely suppressing or abandoning goals, men may *redefine* their aims; they may develop alternative, more appropriate goals toward which they can strive with a sense of worthwhile accomplishment and genuine satisfaction. Our research reveals many instances of this process—for example, when workers in jobs devoid of intrinsic interest focus instead on extrinsic rewards like wages and security; or when they turn to self-actualizing, creative hobbies away from the job to take the place of what is unattainable at work. To some extent, that is, industrial workers maintain their mental health by adapting their wants to available opportunities for gratification.

Our results indicate, however, that most workers are not too successful in this regard; we have repeatedly had to note not only deficiencies of motivation and enjoyment in work but also the relative barrenness of leisure-time interests and the restricted character of life aims. Given the structure of wants and expectations that our culture typically instills into workers, there is little tendency for them to develop other aims that might better fit their situation and better contribute to mental health. Insofar as industrial workers set their sights on material possessions, individual success, and employment in interesting, independent, self-expressive work, most of them are headed for disappointment—often with feelings of failure, self-blame, and accompanying symptoms of unsatisfactory mental health. The basic question raised here is whether the prevailing value system of our society interferes with good mental health for large sections of the population. It sometimes seems almost as if the pervasive emphasis on money, competitive success, and pleasures of consumption had been designed to produce frustration and undermine self-esteem among the disadvantaged and less successful. One can feel sure that the consequences would be very different if societal influences operated more strongly to develop and reinforce goals of personal growth, self-expressive use of leisure, participation in collective efforts for social improvement, and other opportunities for self-actualization not dependent on the very things that are largely denied the general run of industrial workers. But perhaps the cultural values are too firmly rooted to permit of such change. We shall deal further with this difficult and challenging problem in the last part of the present chapter when we reflect on possible social policy implications of our results.

The preceding discussion refers primarily to gross findings pertaining to broad categories of people. We wish now to add that the same explanatory motivational concepts apply to our more detailed results as well. Such interpretations have been suggested at many points, in respect both to personal determinants of mental health (individual differences) and to specific job characteristics (occupational differences).

In regard to *individual variations,* we interpret mental-health effects as reflecting the degree to which each person's wants, expectations, and self-conception meet with gratifying or frustrating conditions. His mental health is less satisfactory to the extent that his world proves irreconcilable with his conception of the person he is and the person he is striving to become. Workers who want what they cannot realistically hope to achieve tend to be in poorer mental health; those who can move toward satisfying their wants tend to enjoy better mental health. Our results as a whole indicate that both the personal and the occupational aspects of want gratification possess explanatory power: the quality of workers' adjustment varies with their differing personal goals and needs but it turns quite as fully on the differing opportunities for gratification afforded by the positions they occupy, even within the limited range of occupations dealt with in this study.

The foregoing interpretation might be called a "general theory of incongruence" in contrast to "special theories" of aspiration-achievement discrepancy and status incongruence. The *general* theory is identical with the explanatory guidelines we have employed: variations in mental health reflect the degree of discrepancy between what people want and the opportunities available to them for gratifying those wants. When formulated more narrowly, however, as a *special* theory which specifies discrepancy between level of aspiration for success and level of achievement, indicated by present occupation, we find it has only limited validity within the factory population studied. The reason, we believe, is that motivations are so diverse and interact with other determinants of adjustment in so intricate a manner that this *particular* influence, though an important element of the total process, may or may not be powerful enough to show itself, depending on the entire context. Desires for status and success are parts of a complex motivational structure in which other unsatisfied wants may loom larger as sources of incongruence, disturbing frustrations, and unsatisfactory mental health.

Finally, a few further notes are needed in regard to our analysis of *occupational characteristics* that make for better or poorer mental health. In the framework of our explanatory concepts, what the results mean is that various job attributes are more important or less important as determinants of mental health depending on how they relate to the total structure of workers' wants and expectations at the time. Most significant for mental health is *whatever* the working men perceive as especially satisfying and ego enhancing or especially thwarting and frustrating. These perceptions, in turn, depend on the entire network of influences, subjective and objective, temporary and enduring, that shape men's desires, self-images, and beliefs about their situation.

In this perspective, a crucial question arises whether the influences are so varied and shifting, from time to time and situation to situation, that no stable conclusions can be drawn concerning separate factors. For example, when wages are good and steady employment seems assured, these aspects of jobs are likely to be of small concern; but let earnings deteriorate or unemployment threaten and the same characteristics take on vital importance for workers' life adjustments. So it is with many other changing conditions of working life. Moreover, not only the absolute amount of change counts but also the *relative* favorableness or unfavorableness—relative, that is, to what has been customary; relative to other groups, near and far; relative to basic living standards, to the profits of industry, and so on; and above all, perhaps, relative to what is currently believed possible, reasonable, and just. These comparative judgments obviously involve not only the objective conditions but likewise the expectations that have been created by the worker's past and present experiences, including the social and political forces operating to arouse and intensify particular demands. In the aggregate, these considerations carry an impressive warning against acceptance of specific empirical findings as supplying stable, dependable conclusions to the effect that this job characteristic is important and that one is unimportant as a determinant of mental health.

Shall we then conclude that there is no stability or generality at all to such results as we have reported concerning job attributes? We believe that this extreme position is unwarranted since, despite the forces of change, there is a considerable degree of constancy to men's deep-seated wants and likewise to the availability of means for gratifying the wants. It can be safely predicted, for example, that working people in our culture will continue to crave more of the material goods and comforts of life and that many of the less fortunate will inevitably experience strains of relative deprivation. Similarly, a vague desire to engage in more interesting, self-actualizing activities appears to be sufficiently widespread and deep-rooted, and commonly enough unrealized, to constitute an enduring source of discontent and unsatisfactory adjustment for considerable numbers of men in low-skilled occupations. Since analysis of our data accords with these expectations, it seems plausible to interpret the findings on these variables as having probable significance beyond the particular conditions of the study. On the other hand, when we find that feelings concerning job security and wage rates do not account for mental-health differences among occupational groups, we may well question whether this result possesses stability or general validity. It appears more reasonable to suppose that in respect to such variables severe differential strains are likely to occur with changing industrial situations and economic conditions. Reflections like the foregoing lead us to adopt a middle position on the issue of whether *general* conclusions can be drawn in regard to the relative contribution of separate job factors to group differences of mental health.

Reviewing the meaning of our findings in regard to occupational differences in this perspective, we arrive at the following summary statements.

(*a*) Only future research can discover how much such results change from one situation to another. Meanwhile it may be noted that the Detroit automobile plants of the 1950's cannot be dismissed as exceptional; in many ways they have become a symbol of modern manufacturing conditions.

(*b*) Under these conditions, poorer mental health in lower-level occupations was accounted for in only the slightest degree by workers' reactions to wages, job security, and working conditions, factors ordinarily given major emphasis as causes of adverse effects. We interpret our findings to mean that glaring and remediable sources of frustration and discontent have been moderately well corrected as a result of union and management efforts, thus tending to equalize workers' reactions at different job levels. Nevertheless, enough effects are evidenced, both favorable and adverse, to suggest that these job attributes *could* readily exert salient influence on mental health under changed circumstances.

(*c*) Several aspects of jobs that have been greatly stressed in the human-relations literature as key factors determining employee morale turn out to have quite limited relationship to our observed differences of mental health. These results serve, at very least, to underscore the need for skepticism and caution about assigning a dominant role to supervision, status, and other social attributes of the job.

(*d*) The largest effects we find arise from intrinsic rewards and constraints of the work itself, particularly the chance the job affords men to use their abilities, with all that this signifies. This influence and that of income differences were commented on earlier. Our interpretation is that, at higher- and lower-level jobs respectively, these factors are subject to the most satisfying gratifications or the most severe and persistent incongruence between what workers want and what the jobs provide.

(e) The motivation theory employed in this interpretation of job effects is to be distinguished from several other psychological views that have been prominently used for such purposes.

In the first place we have explicitly avoided the idea that the job must satisfy certain immutable needs; also the view that wants are structured in a fixed hierarchical order of potency, such that lower, more compelling motives have to be satisfied in set sequence before higher ones exert their influence. Rather, we believe, many different motives may become dominant, depending on the cultural and subcultural influences, the changing conditions and degree of thwarting experienced, and the perceived opportunities to implement the desires.

We likewise seriously question attempts to classify wants into ego motives and nonego motives, with the latter (including economic goals, security, etc.) relegated to a position of secondary importance. We find more theoretically tenable and empirically valid a conception that recognizes some degree of ego involvement in *all* socially meaningful motives. Economic goals, for example, are of intense *personal* concern to working men and profoundly affect their adjustments to life.

Finally, and not unrelated, there is a third view that conceives of job attributes as divided into "motivators," the positive "satisfiers," versus "hygiene factors" which pertain to maintenance or security and which have importance only in a negative sense, as "dissatisfiers" when they are deficient. All through our analysis of occupational characteristics, we encountered evidence that points to an opposite conclusion. Both theory and data appear to us to make the distinction unacceptable. Workers find satisfaction and positive motivation not only in workmanship and achievement but likewise in income, job conditions, and the various other so-called hygiene factors.

Lest the core meaning of the study be lost in the consideration of these subordinate issues, we shall close this section by restating the major conclusion—that men's position in the occupational hierarchy substantially affects their mental health, that low-level jobs have especially adverse effects on the average, and that this result occurs largely by reason of the incongruity between personality needs and the nature of job characteristics, opportunities, and demands. The balance of our inquiry has sought to discover workers' characteristics, job attitudes, and orientations to life that are associated with the occupational effects on mental health.

The problem for industry and society

In the remaining pages we want to consider some possible implications of the study for the guidance of social aims and policies. This means that while we shall continue to keep one eye on the relevant results, our speculations will range far beyond conclusions based on the data. Furthermore, we shall assume in this discussion that the key conclusions we have reported will be confirmed and extended by subsequent studies.

Let there be no ambiguity regarding our conception of the psychologist's role here. The questions to be dealt with involve basic value issues to be decided by the whole of society. On such matters the psychologist must not presumptuously attempt to play God; his function is not to prescribe but modestly to offer what facts he possesses and to suggest alternative directions and perspectives for consideration and debate by all concerned. There is great merit, we believe, in the mere posing of critical questions that are commonly avoided. Hopefully the questions may possess some distinctive quality by reason of the special knowledge and insights that a psychologist brings to bear. But the psychologist also has values; his own orientation is bound to influence the selection of questions he asks and the possible answers he emphasizes. With this caveat, we proceed to state our own considered judgments and queries.

The first and most important requirement is a more general recognition of the problem. Only as people become convinced that a seriously unsatisfactory condition exists, and only as the condition is defined and clarified by descriptive facts, can it be expected that remedial action will ensue. Three principal elements enter into an appreciation of the problem: (a) understanding of the meaning of "positive mental health" as a salient goal of a good society and recognition of the enormous possibilities of fuller and richer psychological development for most individuals; (b) knowledge of the large differences of mental health among population groups in higher and lower socioeconomic positions and in different organizational settings; specifically, in terms of our results, the relatively poor mental health of semiskilled workers, particularly of those employed in routine production jobs; (c) recognition that routine jobs are not about to vanish as a result of automation, that the problem is not about to be solved through the complete replacement of men by machines, but that many millions of American workers will continue to be employed in low-level semiskilled occupations and will continue to make their life adjustments as best they can. As knowledge of these matters becomes more widespread, one may anticipate intensified efforts by the lower-placed groups, their leaders, and agencies concerned with their welfare to bring about social and industrial changes aiming to ameliorate the condition.

The grand purpose of such efforts will be nothing less than the creation of a better society in which men can more fully realize their best potentialities. The goal is an industrial and social system that functions with consistent regard for the psychological well-being of people. Along lines of our earlier discussion, this must include increased attention both to the adequate gratification of "worthy" existing wants and to the development of new, more "appropriate" goals. These statements, if they do nothing else, serve to make vividly clear the difficult value questions which are unavoidable in proposals for improving mental health.

For example, how much weight should be given to considerations of individual freedom and self-development compared to such powerful contending objectives as increased productivity and the growth, military defense, and competitive strength of the nation? What proportionate resources should be devoted to upgrading the mental health of "the masses" as against the cultivation of special excellence (artistic, intellectual, administrative) among those endowed with natural talent and leadership potential? Perhaps most acutely difficult of all, what is "adequate" gratification or self-realization; what are "worthy" desires and "appropriate" goals—and who decides? These questions must be answered—but not by the psychologist or, in our view, by any other elite group. The answers, usually accepted on faith with a minimum of critical thought, need to be hammered out, we believe, through processes of endless discussion, group pressures, social experimentation, and working compromises, involving all sectors of society.

Some of the questions become less baffling once they are defined and placed in a psychological frame of reference, though in large part the answers will still depend on people's basic value positions and social philosophy. To begin with, it helps to recognize that the shorthand expressions "adequate gratification of existing wants," "self-actualization," and "realization of men's full potential" are not used in any definitive or absolute sense. One critic, for example, complains that he has "difficulty in seeing concretely the self-actualized man." This misses the whole point that what is sought for *all* men is a greater *degree* of gratification, self-development, and self-expression than that previously attained. There is no "right" amount; only "more," in keeping with rising desires and expectations of the persons under consideration.

A further, less obvious point of clarification appears necessary to deal with the troublesome problem of destructive, petty, and anti-social impulses. Is the gratification of these motives also to be encouraged? The approach to an answer lies, we think, in conceiving of good mental health as limited to the actualization of motives and abilities that have become integral parts of the person's *approved self*. In general, this positive self-conception incorporates the prevalent value norms of the culture, internalized by the individual in the course of his personal development. Hence, for most people, self-actualization consists of attitudes and behaviors that express, in higher or lower degree, the motives and human potentialities positively valued in civilized society. To the extent that individuals remain "unsocialized," that is, with self systems that have failed to internalize basic cultural values, improvement of their mental health demands not actualization of their present wants but emotional and motivational reeducation to bring them into accord with fundamental human values.

Application of this criterion of acceptable versus unacceptable self-actualization is fraught with difficulties and dangers. Contrary to our intent, it could easily be turned into a defense of conformity. Nevertheless, some such distinction appears indispensable. But it surely must not be construed in a manner that would rule out honest dissent or even rebellion as esteemed forms of self-actualization. Under certain conditions the most highly "socialized" persons may well be the most revolutionary.

We indicated earlier that social efforts to improve mental health can be divided into measures for providing better satisfaction of present personality needs, discussed in the preceding paragraphs, and, second, programs for the development of more appropriate wants. In respect to efforts of the latter type, two underlying assumptions that have been implicit throughout our discussion should be stated explicitly. The first is the proposition that men can grow; that human personality is malleable; that it is largely a product of social learning and undergoes continuing modification by changing social conditions and influences. To be sure there are limits imposed by the biological nature of man and the particular characteristics of individuals. But we believe that, in the present state of knowledge on these matters, the most defensible working conception is one which stresses the vast possibilities of new and varied goals that men at all economic levels can set for themselves. This contrasts with the contention that "human nature" is fixed; that men's current goals and predilections can be taken as unchanging; that working people are passive, dependent, intent only on immediate bread-and-butter objectives and this is the way they always will be.

The second guiding thought in regard to men's acquirement of new goals is concerned with the issue of what alteration of wants is desirable and who decides. Again our answer is that people must decide for themselves; it is not for the "experts" to prescribe what men *should* want. To a great extent, of course, the decisions are made impersonally, by social-historical forces which have shaped the traditional values of the society that are now passed on, without deliberate choice, from generation to generation. The deep-cutting query here is whether these conventional goals call for much more critical assessment and reevaluation than is accorded them. A society like ours, in a world of revolutionary change, a world increasingly aware of psychological needs and potentialities, must debate not only its "national goals" but the personal goals of the individual as well.

In the interests of good mental health for the ordinary run of working people, for example, it could be that our society might decide to reduce the tremendous emphasis on goals of personal achievement and competitive individual success and to cultivate stronger interests in cooperative group activities, altruistic social service, participation in political and economic reform movements, creative leisure-time pursuits, and other presently neglected life purposes. Such shifts might go far to enrich life, to diminish painful experience of failure, to let men move toward satisfying, attainable goals with attendant positive feelings of self-esteem. Whether deemphasis of individualistic achievement motives would retard "progress," as is often alleged, and how it might change the definition and direction of progress for good or ill, no one can say with assurance. It is precisely these basic questions that call for continuing debate and collective decision in the light of all the wisdom that can be mustered.

Obviously persons in positions of leadership, at all levels and in all kinds of organizations, bear a grave responsibility in this connection. So, too, do social scientists and intellectuals generally. Although they cannot give answers, they have an obligation to raise questions, to point out alternatives, and to indicate comparative gains and losses likely to result from given changes—and from failure to change. The present study finds its place here; it produces small bits of evidence relevant for society's evaluative judgments. More important, perhaps, it evokes questions of the kind already suggested.

With the foregoing as background, we shall now ask more pointedly what industry can and should do about mental health and then, similarly, what can be expected and hoped for in the larger society.

INDUSTRIAL MANAGEMENT AND THE
MENTAL HEALTH OF WORKERS[1]

Our purpose here is to indicate directions for further inquiry and debate. The following propositions and questions aim to give a realistic perspective on management's role in respect to the mental health of industrial workers and to stimulate critical examination of the part management plays.

1. The essential function of the industrial organization is effective production; it is not industry's responsibility to improve mental health. This is true, that is, save as (*a*) such improvement is a means for the better achievement of management's ends, the building of a successful, growing, profitable organization; or (*b*) management is induced by laws, contracts, and informal pressures from inside and outside the organization to make changes in the interests of mental health. This is simply to assert that productivity, costs, and related economic criteria are paramount in management's policy decisions. The business firm is not a welfare agency. An enterprise operating in a competitive economy cannot sacrifice any part of its productive efficiency without suffering a relative disadvantage and to that extent jeopardizing its survival. It follows that any single firm can work for the fulfillment of noneconomic values, including the psychological well-being of its employees, only to the extent that such objectives are compatible with maintenance

or increase of overall efficiency. Hence enlightened personnel policies that create favorable attitudes and contribute to mental health must be justified by evidence or argument showing that they pay off in long-run productivity and profits. Socially conscious industrial executives of high moral purpose will be unable, generally speaking, to implement humane feelings that cannot be *economically* justified.

Even within the restrictions imposed by adherence to efficiency principles, management's actions may contribute substantially to better or poorer mental health. It is this impact that is referred to in the preceding exception *a*. The effect is evident in the large differences that occur among companies. More fully stated, the point is that better mental health of workers comes as a by-product of the organization's self interested, enlightened efforts in regard to personnel and labor relations. Although few companies set themselves the explicit objective of improving mental health, it has become commonplace for most companies to try to increase job satisfaction, motivation in work, and general "morale," with emphasis on favorable feeling and loyalty toward the company. The varied human-relations activities directed to these ends, if carried on with reasonable honesty and intelligence, are likely at the same time to produce better mental health. This benign side effect cannot be taken for granted, however; mental health is surely not synonymous with heightened company morale though the two tend to be associated. Demands for production and profits often negate the favorable influence of well-intentioned human relations performance.

We shall comment further on the possibilities and limitations of management efforts in their relation to mental health under section 2. Even though it is our judgment that management's human-relations activities, taken as a whole, make a significant positive contribution to mental health in industry, we must add this strong reservation: if improved mental health of workers is really a vital social objective in and of itself, then it is much too important to be left chiefly to the indirect and sometimes contradictory effects produced by the voluntary actions of management oriented toward a different set of goals.

These last statements bring us to the second significant exception *b* noted at the beginning of these remarks on management's role. Insofar as the industrial organization is oriented (properly) to its own economic ends, it seems obvious that other important human values will tend to be neglected unless they are forcefully pressed by groups concerned with these other, often conflicting, goals. This, of course, is what has happened throughout the industrial revolution, both in respect to economic interests opposed to those of the business firm and in regard to varied human values divergent from the productivity-efficiency-profit objective. It is no accident, for example, that factory laws and labor-union pressures were required to secure adequate protection of workers' physical health and safety. The patent fact is that employees have diverse needs that are not going to be met by voluntary action of managements operating within a system of single-minded devotion to economic goals. The interests of efficiency have to be balanced against other human interests; compromises have to be reached that are acceptable to employees (and their unions) and to society as a whole. After all, industrial organizations are instruments of a changing society, subject to its control.

Social controls and pressures directed toward improved mental health of workers will depend primarily on influences and agencies independent of management. It is for these reasons that we specially stress the possibilities of and need for programs concerned with positive mental health by workers' own organizations, by the community as a whole (including participation by business leaders in their role as socially minded citizens), and by agencies of government. The initiative for significant change cannot be expected from management functioning as management; it must come from elsewhere. But if substantial changes affecting industry are brought about by pressures from below and from outside, management will learn to accept them—even perhaps welcome them—insofar as the changes are imposed on competitors as well as themselves and consequently do not place them at a disadvantage compared to others. The final section of this chapter focuses on these possibilities in the society at large. But first we take a closer look at what management contributes and fails to contribute.

2. Management thinking has been undergoing extensive alteration during the past few decades. There has been a striking increase in the attention paid to "human relations." It is now recognized by almost all industrialists that the health, perhaps the very survival, of the organization depends on achieving and maintaining human conditions that are satisfying and productive. In part, the rising expectations of working people and the growth of labor unions pushed industry into action; in part, executives independently become aware of the enormous possibilities and constructive advantages of more fully developing and motivating their employees.

The core of the change is a shift from strict, hierarchical, authoritarian leadership to looser controls and leadership by persuasion. This signifies more than first meets the eye. To persuade, it is necessary to *understand* people's attitudes and feelings, to deal with the worker as a complete person rather than as a "hired hand." If the manager is to be successful, moreover, it is unlikely that he can "get away with" clever techniques and manipulative skills as a substitute for genuine respect and good will toward his subordinates. This requirement applies from top to bottom of the organization. Our choice of the phrase "management by persuasion" means something more; it expresses our deep suspicion of slogans and preachments that falsely imply more radical moves by management toward "industrial democracy" or voluntary yielding of power over the determination of significant goals and policies of the enterprise. Whether by gentle persuasion or otherwise, management still manages. But if it does so with greater appreciation and consideration for the people managed, this can scarcely fail to have favorable effects on the self-feelings and mental health of men so treated.

To fill in these sketchy statements, we shall mention a few characteristic trends of enlightened human-relations programs and then proceed to the critical question of how much these newer management developments may be expected to do for the mental health of workers. The three descriptive points of emphasis we have chosen are these: (1) The need for managerial understanding and acceptance of men's varied *noneconomic* motives and complex personality needs as well as the economic ones, and apppreciation of individual *potentialities;* efforts to adjust conditions, rewards, opportunities, and appeals accordingly, including both substantive job changes (advancement and job enlargement, for example) and personnel practices, supervisory treatment, and so on, geared to workers' pride, workmanship impulses, personal insecurity, and other diverse wishes and expectations. (2) Appreciation of the vital place occupied by group processes and influences; the opportunity and need for management to foster healthy, cohesive, loyal work groups (for example, by limiting their size and keeping them intact, by best arrangement of work stations, favorable conditions for social interaction at work and during rest periods, and many other such procedures); encouragement, within the limits of feasibility and considered policy, of group decision making and shared responsibility on specified matters; supervisory relationship to the group that, above all else, is forthright, honest, and expressive of genuine sentiments (no gimmicks and charm-school artificiality). (3) Careful evaluation of the total organization, its philosophy and structure, from a human-relations standpoint and adoption of modifications that can be agreed on—even drastic ones affecting top-level personnel, decentralization of authority, elimination of entire echelons from the chain of command, and so on; in general, recognition that improved human relations at lower levels depend on the reality of support received from higher levels.

It is highly probable that management changes of the kind indicated will continue and will expand. They represent a necessary corrective to the human deficiencies of the bureaucratic organization with its tight hierarchical authority system and "scientific management" principles. The newer style management will flourish because it contributes to the overall effectiveness of the enterprise. But our question here is whether it also contributes to the personal happiness and mental health of working people. The general answer, though with later qualifications, seems clearly affirmative, even with reference to workers employed in semiskilled production jobs upon whom our interest centers. More pronounced benefits probably accrue to professional, technical, and managerial employees.

Focusing on semiskilled only, and assuming that human-relations procedures are conducted with integrity and competence, we would anticipate gains such as the following: Work and employment relations are presumably made somewhat more agreeable and less frustrating as a result of increased respect and consideration by bosses and the removal of unnecessary irritations; by a generally improved climate of friendliness and support; by assurance of fair treatment (on this and many other points the credit due the union must not be overlooked); by increased pride and satisfaction through identification with a company "that cares," having a job at "a good place to work," and, where such possibilities exist, having opportunities for training and advancement, counseling services, and a wide variety of other employee services. In addition, employees *may* derive gratification from increased individual or group participation and responsibility, though managerial efforts in this direction can easily backfire if they lack real substance, appear manipulative, or arouse false expectations with subsequent disillusionment. Significant gains, little realized as yet, may also be provided by job-enlargement procedures which permit the worker to perform more challenging tasks that combine previously fragmented operations.

Without in any sense belittling constructive contributions such as those listed, it is necessary to view the other side of the coin as well, to consider what is left undone with regard to mental health even when management performs beyond reproach. Managerial activities that have positive value for workers naturally lie in areas where the needs and aims of the individual and those of the organization are compatible. But there are likewise important areas of incompatibility. Too often the tendency has been to assume complete identity, or at least basic harmony, between management's objectives and those of workers, ignoring opposed interests and conflicts inherent in the contrast between goals of *economic efficiency* and the intangible goals of peaceful unpressured living, free self-actualizing activities, and the entire gamut of nonutilitarian human purposes. With few exceptions, experts in the field of industrial human relations shy away from these problems of continuing conflict, or dismiss them with glib suggestions of how employees can be shown that they can best satisfy their own needs by working for organizational objectives.

By the nature of its functions, management is not in a position to initiate actions for better satisfying all the important intangible needs of working people. It cannot introduce changes that either run counter to the economic interests of the enterprise or that lie outside its legitimate sphere of concern. An example of such limitations is seen in unwillingness to abandon productive but distasteful methods of work. A great deal of evidence, in the present study and others, shows that workers on repetitive jobs feel deprived and stultified by the endless dull routine, that many of them poignantly wish for more interesting and challenging work in which they could use their abilities and derive a sense of worth and self-respect. But it is this brute fact of specialized, simplified tasks that is basic to efficiency in numerous mass-production processes. With the most considerate supervision imaginable and with the entire repertoire of enlightened management methods, such jobs will still be what they are; they will still produce their adverse effects on mental health.

Even if a little job enlargement is introduced and a little leeway is granted for the worker to do the job his own way, it still falls far short of really using his abilities or challenging his resources. Similarly, typical plans that permit participation in trivial decisions are at best a pleasant, appreciated gesture; at worst a deeply resented sham. It seems most doubtful, too, that administrative skills or salesmanship to make workers *want* to do what they *have* to do contributes to their self-fulfillment. Yet a highly regarded psychologist can refer to this sort of manipulative control and engineered consent as a way "to maximize the satisfactions" of the workers— implying a startling curtailment, indeed, of working people's range of satisfactions.

Other illustrations of necessary limitations on management's contributions to mental health may be briefly noted. Many workers are oppressed by feelings of futility and powerlessness; they yearn for an effective voice in the control of their own work, a genuine sharing in decisions and responsibility. But industry, even where the management is most progressive, is a long way from really meaningful dispersion of decision-making authority at low job levels. *Significant* involvement of semiskilled and unskilled workers (as in plans of "workers' management") can be expected only if pressures *outside of management* were to mount to a point that would mean fundamental changes of the enterprise system, an outcome certainly not visible in America at present. With more immediate relevance, workers' desires to exercise effective, independent influence in industry cause them to turn to organizations and leadership of their own choosing. Labor unions are in a position to satisfy important psychological needs that management cannot, precisely because the union (assuming that it is democratically run) offers opportunity for achievement in which the individual fully shares. Wage increases, job security, improved working conditions are vastly more satisfying and ego enhancing if won by the men's own organization than if graciously bestowed by management.

A final most significant limitation on management's actual and potential accomplishments in respect to mental health has to do with the need for expansion of working people's horizons and the creation of new goals. The business organization, in its own self-interests, can scarcely engage in the stimulation of heightened self-expectations among workers at low job levels when industry is unable to provide opportunities for gratifying the aroused wants. Passivity, "want-lessness," lack of purpose as aspects of unsatisfactory mental health, whether or not they are *caused* by industrial influences, certainly are not being widely *remedied* by industry. Nor is the redirecting of life aims into paths more promising of self-fulfillment in leisure an undertaking to be left primarily to industry.

None of the foregoing is intended to blame or condemn industry. It is simply not the function of the industrial organization to do nearly everything that may be socially desirable for the sake of mental health. Fortunately, much of what progressive business management has learned to do in its own interests does contribute at the same time to the psychological health of its employees. This positive role of industry will doubtless expand over the years in response to increasing pressures and demands of workers and the community. Yet much of life is lived away from the job; industry is one of many institutions. Our final comments will be concerned with these other influences on mental health in the larger society, particularly the possibilities they present for general improvement of working people's "positive mental health."

CONTEMPORARY SOCIETY AND THE
MENTAL HEALTH OF WORKERS[2]

Let us begin this final section with the reminder that our study does not indicate especially *poor* mental health among Detroit industrial workers. We have no reason to conclude that they are worse off psychologically than other major groups of comparable income and education who constitute the "working class" and "lower middle class." By ordinary standards the attitudes and life adjustments, particularly of the men in skilled and upper-level semiskilled jobs, are reasonably satisfactory. Our concentration on what can be done to *improve* mental health does not imply that it is now notably bad but expresses rather our conviction that it can be made much better. The desirability of improvement is especially clear in the case of men employed in routine, repetitive production jobs.

In line with our previous analysis, we see efforts to improve the general level of psychological well-being as requiring attack on two broad fronts. One has to do with more satisfactory gratification of existing wants that have become significant to the individuals' self-identity; the other deals with the creation and arousal of new wants and expectations that may bring about richer satisfactions and self-development.

The first is most familiar and can be dismissed with a few words. Outside of industry as well as inside, innumerable specific changes can be made to reduce frustrations and increase the joys of living. Most obvious and pervasive are increases of the material goods of life, all the things that money can buy. "War on poverty" is at the same time war for better mental health. Workers' steadily rising planes of living, including greater economic security, more leisure time, improved housing and wholesome environment for children, medical care, and everyday comforts, although they do not in themselves assure good mental health, do furnish invaluable assistance. Beyond these, and to some extent built upon them as a foundation, loom endless possibilities of intangible gratifications suggested by a mere listing of categories such as readily available opportunities for appropriate continuing education and training; better recreational and entertainment facilities (for music, drama, art; libraries, museums, parks and playing fields in greater numbers and more conveniently located, and so on); more inviting, realistic opportunities for individual and group participation in all manner of social, political, religious, labor, and community activities. Nothing new here; but still enormously important that the linkage to positive mental health be recognized—along with the dismal fact that vast and damaging inequalities persist between socioeconomic groups in all these matters.

It is apparent, however, that progress toward superior mental health requires inner changes of *men*, not merely improved external conditions. What is most importantly called for, we would argue, is nothing less than a drastically modified system of values, a new philosophy of life. People of the kind we studied, and to a considerable extent the same is true of other groups, are living humdrum existences. Though most are moderately happy, few are enthusiastic; almost none are fully, intensely alive.

What is missing is a purposeful spirit of trying to live up to their true potentialities, to guide their activities in terms of future-oriented self-conceptions. As far as we can judge, only a tiny fraction holds any firm faith or energizing belief in worthy ends beyond the immediate and personal. The trouble is that without worthwhile goals life is empty and, beneath the surface, deeply unsatisfying. Moreover, those workers who are most purposive predominantly set their sights on personal success. It would be strange if it were otherwise in a culture so permeated with worship of this goal. For great numbers of manual workers the result is disappointment and frustration.

We have referred to these matters at previous points and have mentioned directions in which society may move toward solutions. The problem in its full dimensions amounts to that of remaking man and society, a somewhat too formidable project to be outlined here. Instead, we are content merely to add a bit of concreteness to our earlier suggestions. In essence, what we have proposed is that vigorous continuing public discussion and further extensive research be carried on to make people vividly aware of the problem and the

feasibility of changes in the interests of better mental health. We
would hope that as many agents of opinion formation as possible,
certainly not neglecting grass-roots influencers among working people
themselves, will see the importance of fostering different life goals
and a new appreciation of what life can mean for people at all
income levels.

The general run of men do almost no critical thinking about their
aims in life or what their world would really permit them to be
and do. If they can be stimulated to serious consideration of the
matter, we believe that many will feel the appeal of intangible
objectives and enlarged conceptions of themselves and their potential
roles. We do not intend to play down the importance of personal
success and economic gratifications but to keep them from pre-
empting all of life. It is necessary that other interests also be
aroused, so that a person's life include a wide choice of valued goals
among which he may discover ones that win his deep and enduring
commitment.

Examples of potential psychological enrichment lie both in indi-
vidualized forms of self-expression and in significant group activities.
Let us begin with the working man's spare time at home. Our
evidence on this is unambiguous: a small minority devote themselves to absorbing hobbies, largely in home workshops, but the
vast majority engage in no constructive pursuits that would yield a
sense of achievement, forward movement, and personal dignity.
Most of the men have formed no special interests or given thought
to the limitless range of things they could do to develop themselves
and enjoy the use of their talents. The striking need, trite though
the idea has become, is education for interesting, constructive use of
leisure. Above all, this presents a problem of *motivation*, of reaching
men's latent springs of action by means of effective personal discussion and concrete example. This can hardly be an achievement
beyond the powers of agencies devoted to workers' education.

If this ball once really gets rolling, workers themselves can be
counted on to exert pressure on the community to provide the
desired instruction and facilities. A constant refrain in our interviews is the lament that "you can't get anywhere without an education"—but scarcely anyone follows through to ask what he can still
do about overcoming the lack, either in respect to vocational or
avocational objectives. In this connection we would particularly
urge greater effort to expand working people's enjoyment of *intellectual* pursuits, however elementary the initial exercises may need

to be. We are convinced that much larger numbers of workers than is ordinarily supposed would eagerly respond to stimulating opportunities to "figure things out," to arrive at new insights and understandings on the basis of inquiry and thoughtful discussion. This need not imply, of course, any neglect of education and training directed to acquisition of facts, manual skills, music and fine arts, physical prowess, and every other human interest.

Apart from potential educational influences, another change may be in prospect which carries large implications for the use of leisure. We refer to the perennial proposals for joining manufacturing plants with farms and gardens in a symbiotic relationship that would permit workers to divide their time between factory work and agriculture—perhaps along with time for home industry, hobbies, study, and travel. This old dream *could* be in for rapid implementation, made feasible by advancing technology and made attractive by workers' broadening horizons regarding the good life.

However, it is in a different direction that we would place our principal hopes and emphasis. The outstanding "psychological deficit" of industrial workers as we see it in our interviews (equally perhaps of most other groups) is the paucity of meaningful social involvement and the lack of social goals. With rare exceptions, the men are wrapped up in their own very narrow private worlds. There is little evidence of devotion to the welfare and happiness of others, little activity that transcends strictly personal and family interests. This is revealed both in their restricted leisure activities and in their life aims. What would give new import and zest to their lives more than anything else, we suggest, is aroused motivation to join with their fellows in efforts to build a better world. Here lie explosive possibilities both for mental health and for significant social action.

Two questions are crucial: (1) Do working men possess latent motivation of the kind here assumed that can be tapped for such idealistic social purposes? Do they feel compassionate urges to make life better for others and to work for greater social justice? Are they prepared to seek a larger measure of self-fulfillment and meaning in their own lives through good works, personally rewarding activities, and commitment to social causes? (2) Are existing institutions and existing leadership prepared to supply the stimulation and guidance needed? And how powerful are the forces of opposition and resistance that prefer an *unaroused* working class? We do not have answers to the questions. We do have the conviction that all interested groups and persons should strenuously seek answers.

This is not the place to explore the role of the various groups and organizations that might play a leading part in pushing action programs of a kind implicit in the foregoing reflections. A comment is in order, however, in regard to labor unions since they stand out as obvious key organizations for the purpose. Under some circumstances, indeed, unions have gone far toward meeting the need for active and rewarding membership participation in imaginative social programs. This apparently occurs most notably during early enthusiastic stages of union advances and proves difficult to maintain. Generally speaking, American unionism concentrates its efforts on restricted economic gains for the members. The findings of our study, as well as a great deal of other evidence, show how shallowly these usual activities of the organization enter into the life patterns of workers and how very slightly they engender active involvement. The question we would press is whether bolder, more idealistic programs of social and economic change (in the local shop and community as well as on the national scene) might not have much stronger appeal. Perhaps unions are not now the most promising agencies; perhaps their functions and their leadership are so far committed to businesslike bargaining and institutionalized responsibility that workers must look elsewhere to find new vistas and crusading spirit of the kind suggested.

The principal issue confronting us, however, is not whether any particular organization is best suited to the task but why so little is being done by *all* organizations. If the interests of democratic social progress and the interests of individual mental health merge in the designated activities, it would seem that here is a place for educational and leadership resources of the entire community to exert their most intense efforts. Surely there are enough seriously disturbing problems to which the thought and energy of working men may valuably be directed. Many of the challenging problems, moreover, lie close at hand and are of a kind that the common man can get his teeth into if only he is encouraged to do so.

A common thread runs through all the foregoing questions and proposals. In brief, we have suggested that positive mental health depends on the total relationship between what a person wants, what he would truly like to be as a person, and what he perceives himself as actually being and becoming, the latter largely determined by what his world permits—or what he *thinks* it permits.

Individuals at every economic level have their life-long difficulties making the necessary compromises and readjustments; keeping their sights high enough to satisfy their standards of self-worth and yet not so high as to produce persistent feelings of failure and frustration. Our study shows the special difficulty of this reconciliation for the industrial worker, particularly if he is in a routine factory job. Hence we tried, in these last pages, to point to possible changes of cultural emphasis and individual life aims that might alleviate the frustrations and, hopefully, lead both to improvement of mental health and to progress toward the "good society."

Appendix A.

Interview questions

A

To start off, I'd like to ask you a little about your early life. [This question was preceded by introductory remarks and an official letter aimed at securing cooperation. Every effort was made to avoid any advance suggestion of direction or type of response desired; the stated purpose was simply "to find how things are going for the general run of people, how they feel about the way their lives are going nowadays."]

1. a. In what year were you born?
    b. Where were you born?   (City or town and state)
    c. Where did you live most of your boyhood?
    d. (If not a well-known city)   Was that on a farm _____, in a small town _____, or a medium-sized city _____?
2. Now I'd like to ask you a very big and general question.
    a. On the whole, how do you feel about your life and the way it has been working out?   (How do you mean?   In what ways? I'm interested in anything else you can tell me on how your life has been working out.)
    b. Well, I think I understand that all right.   Let's switch to some other things about how your life has been working out. How have things gone for you?
3. Now which of these statements here (show card 1) comes nearest to saying how you feel about your life in general?   Would you say you are
    _____ completely satisfied
    _____ well satisfied
    _____ neither satisfied nor dissatisfied
    _____ a little dissatisfied
    _____ very dissatisfied

293

Comments:

4. a. Do you feel that you have had good breaks in life or bad breaks?

   (If answer to a is "good breaks" or "both good and bad," ask b, then c. If answer to a is "bad breaks," ask c, then b.)

   b. In what ways have you had good breaks?

   (If says no "breaks," say: I mean in what ways have things gone well for you?)

   c. In what ways have you had bad breaks? (As in b.)

5. a. What things give you a lot of satisfaction in your life as it is now?

   b. What other kinds of things do you get a lot of satisfaction from?

6. a. Almost everybody feels sometimes that his life isn't going along just the way he wants it to. In what ways do you feel *your* life isn't just the way you'd want it to be?

   b. What other kinds of things would you say you aren't well satisfied with in your life?

   c. What things get you down most?

   d. What things do you ever worry about?

   e. (If impersonal—economic and world conditions, etc.)   What other, more *personal* things do you worry about?

7. a. What would you say you really want most out of life?

   (Will you tell me a little more about what you want?   How do you mean?)

   b. What other kinds of things do you really want in life?

   c. How do you expect things to turn out for you in the future?
   (How do you mean?   In what way?)

   d. Do you feel that you can do much to make your future what you want it to be?

   (How do you mean?   In what way?   What kinds of things do you feel you can do?)

8. Here is a list of some things people say they want in their lives. Which *three or four* of these things would you say you personally want most?   Please look at all of them before you decide.   (Show card 2.)

   1. To have people think highly of you and appreciate what you do.

   2. To have things settled and secure in your life, and not have to worry about the future.

   3. To have a lot of good friends.

4. To enjoy the work you are doing and be able to do a good job of it.
5. To have a satisfying home life.
6. To get ahead in the world and rise to a higher position and be better off.
7. To have a lot of spare time to do the things you enjoy the most.
8. To help people—to do things for other people.
9. To be treated as an independent human being, and not be pushed around and made to do things.

Which one of these things you just picked is *most* important to you?
Which one of these nine things is *least* important to you?
Comments:

B

Now I'd like to hear about your work.
1. a. What kind of work do you do? (Specific occupation. If more than one, record both and ask: Which is you *main* job?)
   b. Where do you work?
   c. How long have you worked there?
2. a. How long have you been on this job as a (specify main job named in 1a)?
   b. How did you happen to go into this kind of work rather than something else?
   c. What (else) was there about this work that made you go into it?
3. a. What do you think of your job? (In what way, etc.)
   b. What other feelings do you have about your job?
4. Would you look at this card (show card 1) and say which of these statements tells best how you feel about your job? Would you say you are
   _____completely satisfied
   _____well satisfied
   _____neither satisfied nor dissatisfied
   _____a little dissatisfied
   _____very dissatisfied
   Comments:
5. a. What things do you particularly like about the job?
   b. What other things about your job do you get satisfaction from?

6. a. What things don't you like about the job?
   b. What (other) things are there about the job that are not just the way you would like them?
7. Do you ever worry about your work?   (If yes) What do you worry about?
8. a. When you start off for work, do you usually feel that you want to go to work or that you don't want to?   (Why is that? How do you mean?)
   b. Are there any things you particularly look forward to at work each day?   (What do you look forward to?   Anything else?)
9. a. On the whole would you say that your job is (show card 3):
      (1) really interesting and enjoyable _____
      (2) or would you say that it is all right but not very interesting _____
      (3) or would you say that it is dull and monotonous? _____
   b. (If 1)   In what way is it interesting?
      (If 2)   Why isn't it interesting?
      (If 3)   What makes it dull and monotonous?
   c. Do you have to pay attention to your job all the time or can you think of other things while you are working?
   d. Would you say you think about other things most of the time _____, fairly often _____, now and then _____, or hardly ever _____?
      (Repeat the four choices immediately.)
   e. Would you say the things you think about at work are mostly happy things that you enjoy thinking about, or are they mostly on worries, troubles, and such things?
10. Would you say your job gives you a chance to use your abilities or is the job too simple to let you use your abilities   (How is that?   How do you mean?)
11. a. On your job do you feel you are doing something important, or do you feel that you are just putting in time?   (Why do you say that?)
    b. (If "important," and not answered)   In what way is it important?

Now I'd like to ask a few questions that will give me a better idea of just what your job is like.

12. a. Just what do you do on your job?   (Get clear picture of operations, tools, material, etc., enough to indicate physical strain and mental effort.)

b. Is your work the same all day _____, or do you do a variety of things _____?
   Comments:

c. How long does it take you to complete each piece of work or part of the job before you do it again? _____

   _____
   (No. of minutes in cycle or pieces per min.)

d. Is the speed of your work set by a machine or belt _____, or do you work at your own speed _____?

e. Can you work your job so that you can get ahead in the work and take a break?
   Yes_____ No_____
   (If yes)   About how long a break can you get that way?

f. In doing your job, do you work alone _____, or does someone have to work with you? _____

g. (If with others)   What do you do together?   In what way do the others work with you?

h. Are you able to talk to the other men around you while you are working?
   Yes_____ No_____

i. (If no)   Why not?

13. a. How long would it take a new man to learn the job you are on?

b. Would he then be able to do the work as well as you do it?

14. Now will you tell me just a few more things about your job?

a. How are you paid—an hourly rate, piece rate, bonus, weekly salary, or what?

b. What is your hourly rate (or weekly salary)?

c. How many hours a week do you work on the average?

d. If you had your choice, how much overtime would you like to put in on your job?

e. Why do you say that?

15. a. How do you feel about your chances for getting ahead? (How do you mean?)

b. What would you consider as getting ahead—that is, what do you mean by "getting ahead"?

c. How much do you care about chances for advancement in your work

d. Taking the general run of men on jobs like yours, what chances would you say they have for getting ahead in their work?   (How do you mean?)

16. a. How do you feel about your present wages?　Would you say you are (show card 1)
   _____completely satisfied
   _____well satisfied
   _____neither satisfied nor dissatisfied
   _____a little dissatisfied
   _____very dissatisfied
 Comments:
 b. (If not completely satisfied)　Why would it be important to you to make more money?

17. a. How do you like the people who work with you where you are now?
 b. Do you care much whether men who work with you are people you like or not?　(How do you mean?)
 c. Do you talk and kid around while you are at work?　(How do you mean?)
 d. How do you feel about talking and kidding around at work?

18. a. Is there anyone directly in charge of your work?
 b. Does he come around often to look things over or tell you what to do?
 c. What kind of a man is he to work for?

19. a. On the whole, what do you think of the company where you work?
 b. What do you think of the way they treat their employees? (Would you tell me a little more about your feelings on the way they treat employees?)

20. a. On the whole, how do you feel about what the labor union does at the company where you work?
 b. Would you tell me a little more about what you think of the union?

21. a. About how often are you absent from work?　(Approximate number of days in past year)
 b. What are the reasons you miss work?
 c. How do you feel about being absent from work?
 d. If you are absent, does it make any difference to anybody besides you?　(If yes) Who does it make a difference to? In what way?

22. a. Do you think the men where you work could turn out more work or better work if they really wanted to?　(How do you mean?)

b. (If yes) What are the reasons why they don't do as much as they could?

c. What about you—how do you feel about whether you could do more and better work yourself?

23. a. Are there times when you think about leaving the kind of work you are doing now?

Yes____ No____ Other comment:

(If *yes*, ask b to f; if *no*, ask g, etc.)

IF YES ON 23a

b. What do you think of doing?

c. Why do you want to do that?
(If not stated) In what way would that be better?

d. Why do you want to leave the kind of work you are doing?

e. Are you doing anything about plans to get into some other kind of work?

f. (If yes) What are you doing?

IF NO ON 23a

g. Why is that?

h. Have there been times in the past when you thought about leaving this kind of work?

Yes____ No____ Other comment:

(If *yes* on h, ask i to n; if *no* on h, go to Q. 24.)

i. When was it you thought of changing?

j. What did you think of doing?

k. Why did you want to do that?
(If not stated) In what way would that be better?

l. Why did you want to leave the kind of work you are doing?

m. What did you do about getting into some other kind of work at that time?

n. Why did you decide to stay on the job you're on instead of changing?

ASK ALL

24. a. How do you feel about factory work in general as compared with other kinds of work?   (How do you mean?)

b. What effects do you think production jobs have on men—does it do anything to them?   (In what way?)

c. What other effects would you say production jobs have on men?

ASK ALL PERSONS NOW IN FACTORY MANUAL JOBS

25. a. What effects do you think working in a factory has had on *you*?
    b. What other effects has factory work had on you?
26. a. What would you say it takes for people who manage industrial companies to get into those top positions?
    b. Do you think the people who manage companies actually have more brains and general ability than most employees? (Why do you say this?)
    (If answer refers to specific supervisors or managers) Well, taking management people in general, do you think that the people who manage . . . etc.   (Repeat b.)

C

Now I'd like to ask you a few more questions along a different line.

1. a. If you could have changed your parents in any way you wanted, what changes would you have liked to see in your father?
   b. What changes would you have liked to see in your mother?
2. a. Over the years there are a lot of things a man comes to learn about people. What are some of the main things you have learned about people?
   b. What would you say most people want out of life?
3. As you see it, what are the main qualities that make a man a really worthwhile person?
   What else is there about a person that would make you consider him most worthwhile—that is, a really first-rate person?
4. a. Some people push hard to change things and make their lives more like what they want; other people are content to take life as it comes. What about you—do you push hard to change things in your life, or are you content to take life as it comes?
   b. Why do you feel that way?
5. a. Do you feel that you are accomplishing the sorts of things you would like to in your life?
   b. (If yes)   What are the main things you mean?
   c. (If no)   What things aren't you accomplishing?

Now here are a few different kinds of questions about yourself.

6. Do you ever go to a doctor or clergyman or anyone like that about your personal problems, or nervousness or such things?
7. a. How has your health been over the past few years—would you say it was excellent _____, good _____, fair _____, or poor _____?
   b. It there anything at all about your health that ever bothers you? (What is it? How do you mean?)
   c. Do you ever use any special foods or tonics or anything like that to help keep you in good condition?
8. Are you ever bothered with headaches, indigestion, or any of the common ailments you see on this card? Please look at all of them and tell me which ones ever bother you. (Show card 4.)

_____headaches
_____indigestion or stomach trouble
_____constipation or diarrhea
_____sleeplessness
_____tiredness without knowing why
_____heartburn
_____backaches
_____high blood pressure

_____neuralgia
_____hemorrhoids or piles
_____nervousness
_____nose, throat, or sinus trouble
_____many colds or coughs
_____allergies
_____Do you have any other ailments like these?

9. a. Do you ever take anything for slight illnesses like headaches, upset stomach, constipation, or things like that?
   b. (If yes) About how often do you take these medicines?
   c. Have you gone to a doctor in the past few years?
   d. (If yes) How often have you gone?
   e. For what?

D

Now I'd like you to look over some other questions on this paper (show D). These are things some people say and we want to find out how other people feel about these things.

Will you please read each one and mark it to show whether you mainly agree or mainly disagree? We just want your offhand opinion.

	Agree	Disagree

1. Getting ahead in this world is mostly a matter of luck and pull.
2. In spite of what some people say, the lot of the average man is getting worse, not better.
3. These days a person doesn't really know who he can count on.
4. Generally speaking, business and industry are carried on in a very satisfactory way in this country.
5. Most people are out for themselves and don't care what happens to others.
6. The *most important* thing to teach children is absolute obedience to their parents.
7. There are two kinds of people in the world: the weak and the strong.
8. It's hardly fair to bring children into the world with the way things look for the future.
9. Any good leader should be strict with people under him in order to gain their respect.
10. There is nothing the ordinary working man can do to change the way things are run in this country even if he wanted to.
11. In general, the profits of business and industry are higher than they should be.
12. As long as the health and safety of the worker is protected, owners of factories should have the right to run the companies the way they please.
13. Nowadays a person has to live pretty much for today and let tomorrow take care of itself.
14. A few strong leaders could do more for this country than all the laws and talk.
15. There's little use in writing to public officials because often they aren't really interested in the problems of the average man.
16. Working people should have more say about how things are run in factories than they have now.

	Agree	Disagree
17. Wealthy business men have too much influence in running things in this country.	———	———
18. Labor unions have too much influence in running things in this country.	———	———
19. A labor union can't accomplish much for the working man unless it stands ready to fight the company.	———	———
20. Management and labor are really partners and there is no reason for unions and companies fighting each other.	———	———
21. Labor unions should stay out of state and national political activity altogether.	———	———
22. The government should do more about providing low-cost housing than it has done in the past.	———	———
23. The government should provide doctor and hospital care for everyone who needs it.	———	———
24. Unemployment compensation payments should be larger than they are now.	———	———

25. Who would you say is more interested in the
welfare of the working man—the heads of
your company or the union leaders?

        Heads of company————————

        Union leaders————————

This completes the first half of the interview. At this point the
interviewer expresses appreciation and states how valuable it is to
have the respondent's replies; then tactfully arranges an appointment
for a second interview to complete the needed information.

E

Last time I talked with you, you told me that you spent most of

your boyhood in ————————. Now I would like to ask you
             (name of town)

a few more questions about your early life.

  1. a. Did you live with both your mother and father when you
        were growing up, or with one of them, or someone else?

b. (If lived with *one parent or guardian*) How was that—had your (mother, father, parents) died, or were they divorced or separated or what?

c. How old were you then?

d. (If *not with either parent*) Who did you live with?   At what ages?

e. Who supported the family?

f. What was his (her) occupation?   (Specific)

g. How far did he (she) go in school?

ASK ALL

2. a. Would you tell me where your parents were born? Father_____
Mother_____

b. (If foreign born) Did they move to the U.S.? Yes_____ No_____ Other:

c. (If yes) When was that? Father_____ Mother_____

d. How far did your parents go in school Father_____ Mother_____

e. What did your father do for a living? (Just what did he do? Get specific occupation.)

f. Did your mother work outside the home? (If yes) What did she do?

3. a. Now as you think back to your childhood days, how do you feel about the way your life was then? (In what way?)

b. Taking it in general, what kind of a time would you say you had as a child? (I'm interested in anything else you could tell me about how your life was as a child.)

c. What would you say your biggest problems were as a child?

d. What fears or worries did you have as a child?

e. What were your main hopes and wishes as you grew up—what did you want to get out of life?

4. a. When you were about 12 to 14 years old, what kinds of things did you like to do most?

b. In general what things were you most interested in?

c. Did you go around with one or two close friends _____, or with a lot of other boys _____, or did you like to spend a good deal of time by yourself _____, or what?

d. How did you like the friends you had as a boy?

e. Were you usually one of the leaders, or did you leave it to others to take the lead in things?

f. What things would you say you did best compared to the other boys?

g. At home, did your family feel that you were always getting into trouble, or did they think you were well behaved?

5. a. Which one of these statements here (show card 5) best describes how happy your childhood was?

    ____completely happy

    ____very happy

    ____fairly happy

    ____a little unhappy

    ____very unhappy

b. (If completely happy) Were there any ways things were not quite as good as they might have been?

(If *not* completely happy) What things kept you from being completely happy when you were a child?

c. Would you say your parents were very happy together or not very happy?

d. Why do you say that they were very happy (not very happy)?

6. a. Did your parents make you toe the line?

b. What kind of things did they make you toe the line about?

c. Were you punished much by your parents?

d. Did you usually feel that you deserved the punishment?

7. How well off would you say your family was (the family in which you grew up)? (Show card 6.)

    ____well above average financially

    ____a little above average

    ____about average

    ____a little below average

    ____very poor

8. a. As far as you know were you a healthy child ____ or rather sickly ____?

b. (If "healthy") Would you say you were *very* healthy ____ or *fairly* healthy ____?

9. a. How far did you go in school?

b. How old were you when you left school?

c. (*H.S. graduate or more*) Did you think about going on further in school?

    d. Why didn't you go on?

    e. (*Not H.S. graduate*) What made you decide to leave school then?

ASK ALL (f to h)

    f. How did you feel about leaving school at that time?

    g. How well did you do in school—did you make very good marks _____, fairly good marks _____, or marks that weren't so good _____?

    h. Did you like school or not?

10. a. Before you started working did you have any ideas and wishes about what kind of work you wanted to do? (What kind of work did you want?)

    b. Why did you choose that kind of work?

    c. Was there any other kind of work you particularly wanted to do if you could have had a chance to get training for it?

11. a. What was your first full-time job?

    b. How old were you then?

    c. How did you get the job?

    d. How did you happen to go into that rather than some other kind of work?

    e. How did you get along on this first job?

    f. What did you like and dislike about it? (Get both likes and dislikes)

    g. How long did you work at that place?

    h. Why did you leave?

12. a. What was your next job after you left the first place you worked?

    b. How did you get that second job?

    c. Why did you go into that rather than something else?

    d. How did you like this job?

    e. How long did you stay?

    f. Why did you leave?

13. a. You told me before about the job you have now. What about the last job you had before the one you are on now—what kind of work was that?

    b. How did you get that job?

    c. How did you happen to go into that work rather than something else?

    d. How did you like that job?

    e. How long did you stay?

    f. Why did you leave?

14. a. About how many different places have you worked altogether? (Get number, not detailed listing.)

    b. What do you consider to be your *main* line of work?

    c. How many years have you been in that kind of work?

15. a. If you could go back to the age of 15, and start all over again, would you choose the same kind of work you are in now _____ or a diffrent kind of work _____?

    Comments:

    b. (If *same* kind of work) Why would you choose the same kind of work?

    c. (If *different* kind of work) Why wouldn't you choose the same kind of work again?

    d. What kind of work would you choose?

    e. In what ways would that be better than what you are in now?

16. a. Have you been unemployed much?

    b. How was that?

    c. (If not answered) In what years? For about how long?

    d. What were your feelings about the depression and unemployment in the 1930's?

F

1. a. How long have you lived in (around) Detroit?

    b. How did you happen to come here?

2. How do you feel about living in (around) Detroit? What (other) things do you particularly like or dislike about living in Detroit?

3. How long have you lived in this part of the city?

4. What do you think of this neighborhood as a place to live?

5. a. How do you usually spend your time when you're not working—what kind of things do you do, both at home and away from home?

    b. What other things do you do with your time away from work?
    What else do you do in the winter?
    What else do you do in the summer?

    c. How do you usually spend your time on weekends?
    What else do you do on your weekends in the *winter?*
    What about in the *summer?*

    d. What kinds of things do you and your wife and family do together?

6. a. Which of these statements (show card 1) comes nearest to saying how you feel about the way you spend your time when you're not working?

      _____ completely satisfied

      _____ well satisfied

      _____ neither satisfied nor dissatisfied

      _____ a little dissatisfied

      _____ very dissatisfied

  b. Are there some things you would like to do in your spare time that you don't do now? (If yes) What?

  c. Why don't you do these things?

7. a. (If not answered in 5) Do you go to sports events? How often?

  b. (If not answered in 5) Do you spend some time in bars or taverns?

  c. (If yes on b) When do you usually go?

  d. About how long do you usually stay there?

  e. Do you ever do some pretty heavy drinking? (If yes) How often?

  f. Do you do much betting, playing the horses or numbers, baseball pools, cards or dice games for money, and things like that? (If does any) About how often?

8. a. Now I'd like to talk a little about what people you see a good deal of. Do you have any relatives you get together with fairly often?

  b. How many of these relatives are there that you see often?

  c. How often do you get together?

  d. What do you do when you get together?

9. a. Do you have any specially good friends that you get together with often?

  b. How many of these specially good friends do you have?

  c. (If only one or two friends) Do you have any other good friends that you see often?
(If indefinite answer or more than six) How many of these are your *very best* friends?

  d. Are these good (very best) friends men or women or both?

  e. How did you get to know these friends?
Were there other ways that you got to know some of them?

  f. How long have you known them?

   g. What kinds of work do they do? (What other kinds of work are any of them in?)

   h. Do you get together with these friends as a group, or just one or two at a time?

   i. (If as a group or both ways) How often do you get together as a group?

   j. Where do you go and what do you do when you get together as a group?

   k. (If one or two at a time or both ways) How often do you get together with just one or two of your friends?

   l. Where do you generally go and what do you do?

10. (If not mentioned in 9e) What about the people you work with, do you spend any time with them away from work?

11. How important is it to you to have friends? (How do you mean? In what way?)

12. a. Do you read any newspapers regularly?
   b. (If yes) Which ones?
   c. What parts of the paper do you read?

13. a. How about radio and television—do you spend time that way?
   b. (If yes) How much time do you spend on radio and TV?

14. a. How about reading books or magazines?
   b. (If yes) How much time do you spend on this?
   c. What kind of things do you read?

15. a. Do you have any hobbies or other special interests?
   b. (If yes) What are they? (Get specific activities.)
   c. (For each activity) How much have you done along that line?

16. a. Do you belong to any organizations or clubs like these? (Hand respondent card 7 and ask about each item from list below:) Do you belong to any _____? (Record group *number* in column a and ask b, c, d, and e for that organization. After completing for that group, ask about each other group on list.)
   b. Get name of organization and record in column b.
   c. About how often do you go to meetings? (Record in column c.)
   d. How do you feel about belonging to this group? Do you have: (1) a *great deal* of interest in it, (2) *some* interest, or (3) *little or no* interest? (Record 1, 2, or 3 in column d and record comments in margins.)

e. Were you ever an officer or on any committee? What was it? (Record in column e)

(a) Group No.	(b) Organization's Name	(c) To Meetings	(d) Interest	(e) Offices
___	___	___	___	___
___	___	___	___	___
___	___	___	___	___
___	___	___	___	___
___	___	___	___	___

(Card 7)
1. Lodges (Elks, Moose, Masons, etc.)
2. Veterans' Organizations (VFW, Amer. Legion, etc.)
3. Church
4. Church groups
5. Parent-Teacher Association
6. Neighborhood groups
7. Sports and athletic clubs
8. Political groups
9. Labor unions
10. Social groups (dances, cards, parties, etc.)
11. Any others (nationality groups, etc.)

17. Does anyone (else) in your family belong to a union?
    Who?
    Which union?
    How does _____ feel about the union?
18. a. (If respondent does not belong to church or church group in Q. 16)
       What is your religious preference?
       P____ C____ J____ Other_____
    b. Do you go to church?
    c. About how often?
19. a. Are there certain groups or organizations you'd like to belong to that you aren't a member of now?
    b. (If yes) What ones are they?
    c. Why would you like to join?
    d. Why aren't you a member?
20. a. Are you registered to vote?
    b. How often do you vote?
    c. (If votes) What party do you usually vote for?
    d. (If doesn't vote) If you voted, what party would you vote for?
    e. (For both c and d) Why do you feel that way?

21. a. In which one of these general parts of your life would you
most like to have things different than they are?   (Show
card 8 and read.)
_____ Your spare-time activities
_____ Your friendships
_____ Your home and family
_____ Your job
_____ Your religious life
   b. Why do you pick that one?
   c. Which one of these on the card are you *best satisfied* with in
your life?
   d. Now looking at the list again, which one do you feel is *most
important* to you?
22. Now we have just a few more questions here about your home
and family.
   a. Do you rent here or do you own the house?   (Specify if rents
a room.)
   b. (If owns) Are you making payments on it?
   c. Who lives here with you?   Anyone else?
   d. Do you have a car?   Yes_____ No_____
(If yes) What make is it?_____ What year?_____
23. a. Are you single _____ or married _____?
   b. Have you ever been divorced, separated, or widowed _____?
24. a. Thinking about your family and home life as they are now,
which of these statements come nearest to saying how you
feel?   (Show card 1 and read it.)
_____ completely satisfied
_____ well satisfied
_____ neither satisfied nor dissatisfied
_____ a little dissatisfied
_____ very dissatisfied
   b. (If not completely satisfied) Would you tell me why you don't
feel completely satisfied?
25. What advice would you give a young fellow just getting married
about getting along with his wife?
26. How do you think children should be brought up—what is *most
important* for parents to teach their children?

FOR MEN NOT NOW MARRIED

27. a. As you see it now, do you expect to get married?
   b. Have you thought seriously of getting married?

    c. Why would you say you haven't married?

    d. What do you think of married women working?

28. a. Would you look a this card and tell me which of these is nearest your total income for 1952 (1953)? (Show card 9.)

_____ Under 2000		_____ 5000 to 6000
_____ 2000 to 3000		_____ 6000 to 8000
_____ 3000 to 4000		_____ 8000 to 10,000
_____ 4000 to 5000		_____ 10,000 or more

    b. Do you support other people on this income? (If yes) Who do you help support?

    c. What was your income from your main job in 1952 (1953)?

    d. (If c is less than a) Do you have any other jobs? (What other jobs?)

    e. Do you have any other kind of income? (From what source?)

FOR MEN NOW MARRIED

29. Would you say that your married life is happier than most of your friends' or not as happy as theirs?

30. a. Would you look at this card and tell me which of these is nearest your total family income in 1952 (1953)? (Hand card 9.) I mean your family living here with you.

_____ Under 2000		_____ 5000 to 6000
_____ 2000 to 3000		_____ 6000 to 8000
_____ 3000 to 4000		_____ 8000 to 10,000
_____ 4000 to 5000		_____ 10,000 or more

    b. How many are there in your family who live on this income?

    c. What was your own income *from your main job* in 1952 (1953)?

    d. (If c is *less* than a) Do you have any other jobs? (What other jobs?)

    e. Does anyone else in your family work—that is, your family living here with you? Who?

    f. Does your family have any other kind of income—that is, your family living here? (From what source?)

31. a. (If not answered in 30e) Does your wife work? Yes_____ No_____

b. (If wife works) What kind of work does your wife do?

c. How do you feel about her working?

d. (If wife does not work) Would you want her to take a job?

32. a. Do you have children?

b. (If yes) How old are they?

c. How do (did) you want their life to be different from yours? (Use "did" if *all* children are over 18)

d. (If working children) What do they do for a living (each)? How far did they go in school (each)?

G

Now we have another one of these lists of questions for you to look over. Will you please read each one and mark it to show whether it describes the way you feel or not.

Please read each question below and answer each one by putting an X under "yes" or "no"—whichever comes nearest to the way you feel.

	Yes	No
1. Do you often feel restless, wanting to be on the move doing something but not knowing what?	___	___
2. Do you wake up rested most mornings?	___	___
3. Do you feel that your children and those of your friends and neighbors have as much opportunity as they should have?	___	___
4. When things go wrong, are you usually willing to leave it to others to work matters out?	___	___
5. Do you think that young people have too much freedom nowadays?	___	___
6. Do you often blame yourself and feel bad over things you have done?	___	___
7. Do you often have a hard time making up your mind?	___	___
8. Do you think most people can be trusted?	___	___
9. Are you often worried and upset?	___	___
10. Do you sometimes boil inside yourself without letting people know about it?	___	___
11. Do you usually take things as they come without trying to do much about it?	___	___
12. Would you say you feel in good spirits almost all the time?	___	___

13. Do you have any particular physical or health problem?

14. Do you often have trouble getting to sleep or staying asleep?

15. Do you find that many people are so unreasonable that it is hard to talk to them?

16. Do you ever get so blue and discouraged that you wonder whether anything is worthwhile?

17. Do you ever feel like smashing things for no good reason?

18. Do people often hurt your feelings?

19. Do you worry much about things that might happen to you?

20. Are you ever bothered by nervousness?

21. As a boy, did you play baseball very much?

22. Did you play football very much?

23. When you were a kid were you much afraid of being left alone?

24. As a child, were you much afraid of falling off of high places?

25. Were you much afraid of being punished?

26. Were you much afraid of being laughed at by other boys?

27. When you were growing up, did you have any trouble with stuttering or stammering in your speech?

28. Do you find that you often have to tell people to mind their own business?

29. On the whole, do you usually like to be by yourself rather than with other people?

30. Would you say that you have as much chance to enjoy life as you should have?

31. Do people often get on your nerves so that you want to do just the opposite of what they want you to do?

32. So far as you know, did you ever have a nervous breakdown?

33. So far as you know, did anyone in your family ever have a breakdown?

H

Now I'd like to get your opinion on a few more questions.
1. a. In general, how do you feel about the way things are going in this country: do you want things to go along pretty much the way they are or are there some important changes you'd like to see made? (What changes do you mean?)
   b. (If no change wanted) Isn't there anything at all about the way things are going that you would like to see changed?
   c. What other changes would you like to see?
   d. (If on one track or single topic) Well now, I have your feelings about that, what *other kinds* of changes would you like to see?
2. a. In general, what people or groups are likely to feel the same way as you do about how things should be in this country? (Get clear indication of people he has in mind, e.g., "just what people do you mean?," etc.)
   b. (If answer refers to specific topic) Now thinking about how a lot of *other* things—things in general—should be in this country, what people or groups feel the same way you do?
   c. What other people or groups feel the same way you do?
   d. What people or groups are likely to feel *different than you* do about how things should be in this country? (Again, get clear indication of people he has in mind.)
   e. (If answer refers to specific topic) Now thinking about how a lot of other things—things in general—should be in this country—what persons or groups are likely to feel different than you?
3. a. Do you think the ordinary working man can do anything to make things more the way he wants them?
   b. (If yes or doubtful) What can he do?
      (If no) Why is that?
4. a. What things do you think keep people from getting ahead in the world?
   b. Who or what is to blame for this?
   c. What things do you think help people to get ahead?
5. a. How do you feel about what the government should do to see that people have better housing and medical care and that old people, unemployed, and others like that are taken care of?
   b. Should the government do more than it's now doing in helping people, or is it already doing too much?

    c. Why do you feel that the government (should do more) (is doing too much)?

6. Now I'd like you opinion about labor unions: Taking the unions as a whole, how do you feel about them and the things they do?

7. a. In disputes between companies and labor unions, do you usually side with the company or the union?

    b. Why do you feel this way?

    c. Why do you think companies and unions often disagree and have trouble getting along with each other?

    d. Some people say neither the union nor management cares much about the common worker—he gets squeezed in between. What do you think about this statement?

8. a. I'd like to ask you what think about government control over business and industry. Would you say the government has too much to say about how business and industry are run _____, just about the right amount to say _____, or that the government ought to have more to say about how business and industry are run _____?
    Comments:

    b. Would you tell me why you think (the government has *too much* to say about how business and industry are run?) (the government has *just about the right amount to say?*) (the government ought to have *more to say* about how business and industry are run?)

9. a. Should a person be allowed to speak in public for things that most people believe are completely wrong and definitely bad?

    b. Should people be allowed to speak in public against our democratic form of government?

    c. Should people be allowed to speak in public against all religion?

    d. What about colleges and universities—do you think that it is a good thing to have colleges where people study all kinds of ideas even if many of these are ideas that most of us believe are untrue and harmful?
    Why do you feel that way?

10. a. Are there any *racial, religious,* or *nationality* groups in this country that you think we would be better off without? (Which ones? Are there any others?)

    b. (If any named in "a," ask for each:) Why do you believe we would be better off without _____?

11. What you you think ought to be done about race relations in this country—that is, between whites and Negroes?   (How do you mean?   Would you make that a little clearer to me?)
12. a. What do you think should be America's position in world affairs—what should this country do about the way things are going in the rest of the world?
    b. What do you think the United States should do about working with the United Nations?   (How do you mean?   In what way?)

Appendix B.

Indexes and ratings
based on the interviews

Part I. Indexes

The various indexes referred to in the text, although constructed as crude measures without statistical refinement, are considered fully adequate for the purposes of the present exploratory study. The indexes were derived from the interview material by adding together arbitrarily assigned weights for coded responses judged to be indicative of the designated characteristic. Each set of total raw scores was then grouped into nine intervals (in some instances fewer than nine) to form the final index score.

The composition of the several indexes is shown in the following listing of questions (question numbering corresponds to that in Appendix A).

1. Index of anxiety and emotional tension
    Raw score is the sum of points assigned on 13 questions, as follows:
    0 to 2 points each—C6, C7b, C7c, C9, F7a, G2, G13, G32
    0 to 4 points each—C8, G9, G14, G19, G20
        On the whole the items are very similar to ones included in the Taylor Anxiety Scale; our Index would almost certainly correlate highly with that scale (Taylor, 1953).

2. Index of self-esteem
    Sum of points on 8 questions (or sets of questions):
    0 to 2 points each—A2 to 7 (volunteered feeling re own inadequacy), A7d, B15a (volunteered re own unfitness), C5, G6, G7, G16, G18

3. Index of hostility
    7 questions:
    0 to 2 points each—C2, G8, G10, G15, G17, G28, G31

4. Index of sociability
   10 questions:
   0 to 2 points each—C2, F8, F9b and c, F9i and k, F11, F16, D3, G4, G18
   0 to 6 points—G29
5. Index of life satisfaction
   10 questions (or sets of questions):
   0 to 2 points each—C5, G1, G6, G12, G16, G30
   0 to 4 points—A7c, F6a
   0 to 6 points—A3
   0 to 9 points—A2 to 7 (favorable versus unfavorable volunteered responses re life)
6. Index of personal morale
   9 questions:
   0 to 2 points each—D1, D2, D3, D5, D8, D13, D15, G8, G16
   This index is patterned after one originally used by Srole in a study of prejudice (Srole, 1951).
7. Index of adjustment
   Raw score is a simple sum of the final scores on preceding indexes 1 to 4. This total score was reduced to 9 intervals to form the final score for this composite index.
8. Index of mental health
   A composite index was derived from preceding component indexes 1 to 6. The actual construction is described as follows, but since it turns out that the scores derived in this slightly complicated manner correlate .95 (Pearson r) with a simple addition of the 6 component indexes, the latter procedure is to be recommended. The composite mental-health assessment used throughout the analysis is a five-degree classification which combines the adjustment scores (these are composite of indexes 1 to 4) with scores on indexes 5 and 6. The objective was to avoid placing anyone in the highest category of mental health unless he was high on all three variables (adjustment, morale, and life satisfaction) and to avoid an extremely low classification for a person who scored high on any one of the variables. The actual procedure employed a chart like that shown below in which we have indicated the final mental-health classification by the letters A to E.
   The dividing lines used to define the A to E categories were guided to some extent also by the location on the chart of 40 individual cases for whom we had obtained clinicians' estimates of mental health (see Appendix C).

Adjustment Score

	1 High	2 Above average	3 Average	4 Below average	5 Low
Life satisfaction	1 2 3 4 5	1 2 3 4 5	1 2 3 4 5	1 2 3 4 5	1 2 3 4 5
Personal morale 1	A		B	C	
2	B	B			D
3		C	C	D	
4			D		E
5	C			E	

9. Index of active life orientation
  9 questions (or sets of questions):
  0 to 2 points each—A7a and b, A8, B22c, G4, G11
  0 to 4 points—B15c, E11 to 14 compared with B1 and 2, B12a and b, B13a, B14a and b (rating of vertical job mobility)
  0 to 6 points—C4
  0 to 8 points—A7d
10. Index of job satisfaction
  11 questions (or sets of questions):
  0 to 2 points each—B8a, B9a, B10, B16a, B19, B23a, F21a, F21c
  0 to 6 points—B4
  0 to 9 points—A2 to 7 (favorable versus unfavorable comments re job), B3 to 6 (favorable versus unfavorable responses re job)
11. Index of family satisfaction
  6 questions (or sets of questions):
  0 to 2 points each—F21a, F21c, F24b
  0 to 4 points—F29
  0 to 6 points—F24a, A2 to 7 (favorable versus unfavorable comments re family)
12. Index of feelings toward coworkers
  3 questions:
  0 to 2 points each—B3 to 6 (volunteered re coworkers), B8b
  0 to 4 points—B17a
13. Index of concern re job security
  5 questions (or sets of questions):
  0 to 1 points each—A7, B7, B3 to 6 (volunteered responses re job security), H1 (volunteered responses re job security)
  0 to 2 points—A2 to 7 (volunteered comments re job security)

14. Index of prolabor orientation re unions
    4 questions (or sets of questions):
    0 to 2 points each—D18, D21, D25
    0 to 4 points—H6 and 7 (rating of attitude re unions)
15. Index of prolabor orientation re business and industry
    4 questions:
    0 to 2 points each—D11, D16, D17
    0 to 4 points—H8
16. Index of prolabor orientation re government help
    4 questions:
    0 to 2 points each—D22, D23, D24
    0 to 4 points—H5
17. Index of prolabor orientation re "working class"
    1 set of questions:
    0 to 4 points—H1 to 5, 8 (rating of identification with working-
    class versus middle-class views; see pp. 213–215).
18. Composite index of prolabor orientation
    Raw score is the total of scores on indexes 14 to 17. This total
    like the others was reduced to 9 intervals to form the final score
    for the index.
19. Index of authoritarian attitude
    6 questions:
    0 to 2 points each—D6, D7, D9, D14, G5, G15
    This index is patterned after the one developed in the
    California study of The Authoritarian Personality (Adorno et al.,
    1950) and is based more directly on the short form used by
    Fillmore Sanford (1950).
20. Index of childhood deprivation
    12 questions:
    0 to 2 points each—E1a, E1f and 2e, E1g and 2d, E2a, E2f, E3a
    to c and 5b, E6d, E8, E9e
    0 to 4 points—E5c and d, E7, E9a
21. Index of childhood anxiety
    10 questions:
    0 to 2 points each—E3a to c and 5b, E3d, E4c, E4d, E4g, G23,
    G24, G25, G26, G27
22. Index of childhood happiness
    5 questions:
    0 to 2 points each—E3a and b, E3a to c and 5b, E9f, E9h
    0 to 4 points—E5

23. Index of childhood self-confidence
    10 questions:
    0 to 2 points each—E3e, E4a and b, E9f, E10a and c, G21, G22, G23, G26
    0 to 4 points—E4e, E4f
24. Index of school success
    4 questions:
    0 to 2 points each—E9e, E9g, E9h
    0 to 4 points—E9a

Part II.   Ratings Not Included in Indexes of Part I

25. Rating of interpersonal adjustment
    A four-point rating of how well the worker relates to people (other than his family); based on all questions in section A, B, C, F of the inteview.
26. Rating of family adjustment
    A five-point rating of how good the worker's relationships are with wife, family, and home life; based on the following sets of questions: A2 to 7, F1 to 32.
27. Rating of "life style"
    A four-way classification of overall orientation to life situation based on the following sets of questions: all of sections A, B, C, F, and E11 to 16.   (See p. 257.)
28. Rating of purposefulness in work and nonwork activities
    A three-point rating of degree of purposefulness with respect to work and nonwork sectors of life separately, based on same blocks of questions as preceding rating of life style.

Appendix C.

"Validation" of the mental-health index

The validation study proceeded as follows: we selected a subsample of 40 interview reports from our files. The cases were all Detroit manual workers—20 on routine production jobs (assembly line, etc.), 10 on more varied semiskilled factory jobs, and 10 in non-factory semiskilled occupations of similar skill level. The 40 reports, divided into four approximately equivalent sets of 10 each, were submitted to our panel of clinicians for assessment. Four psychiatrists and two clinical psychologists furnished estimates, each on two sets of ten cases, to provide three ratings for each case.

The clinicians were asked to read through the entire case folder (a 44-page interview schedule, two check-response inventories, and a six-page interview with the respondent's wife) and to record, on a five-point scale, an overall estimate of "how good or satisfactory you consider the mental health of the individual rated." A short descriptive statement was given the raters to indicate the meaning attached to mental health for present purposes and in addition a briefing session was held to explain and clarify the entire procedure. The descriptive statement consisted principally of the following suggested characteristics.

Effective, mature reactions to life conditions and to people (in the light of person's opportunities and abilities)

"Adjustment" through active, reality-oriented decisions and appropriate efforts at mastery of environment (rather than solely through passive conformity)

Realistic acceptance of self, self-respect; relatively stable, consistent, integrated personality (relatively free from disrupting inner conflicts)

323

Self-reliance, zest, acceptance of responsibilities; planning ahead;
  healthy independence and emotional control
Warm, friendly interpersonal relations
Relative freedom from interfering neurotic symptoms and defensive
  reactions

In large degree, however, the clinicians remained free to utilize their
own conceptions of mental health.

The raters agree reasonably well with one another. Extremely
close agreement was not to be expected for several reasons: differing
conceptions of mental health by the raters, inadequacies of the
evidence available in the interviews, and the relative homogeneity
of the sample in the sense that extreme, readily agreed upon cases
of poor mental health were absent since all the men were well-
enough adjusted to have held their jobs for some years. On the
other hand, agreement was undoubtedly increased by the fact that
the raters based their opinions on the same body of recorded information. We have no way of knowing what agreement would have
occurred if each rater had himself independently interviewed the
workers. The present procedure is nonetheless important as a test
of the extent to which the "experts" employ common concepts of
mental health and the degree to which their judgments are similar
to the results yielded by our indexes.

Twelve measures of inter-rater agreement are available, one for
each of three pairs of raters on each of four sets of ratings (with ten
cases per set). A nonparametric measure of correlation, Kendall's
Tau, was adopted as most appropriate for these comparisons. The
twelve coefficients, aside from one negative one of —.10, range from
.22 to .77; the median of all twelve is .52. The findings indicate
very substantial agreement between most pairs of raters. Even with
the instability produced by having only ten cases for each correlation,
five of the twelve coefficients are significant at the .05 level and five
others have p's between .05 and .15. Of incidental interest, the
agreement of psychiatrists with one another was no different from
their agreement with psychologists (median Tau's of .48 and .53
respectively).

In order to derive a composite assessment for each of the 40 cases,
ratings by each rater were classified as above, below, or at the
median of ratings by that rater and were designated as +, 0, or —.
A composite rating was then assigned as follows.

$$\frac{N}{}$$

A = + by 3 raters; or + by 2 raters and 0 by the third   7
B = + by 1 rater and 0 by 2 raters; or + by 2 raters
      and − by 1 (1 case only)   8
C = 0 by 3 raters; or +, 0, − by the 3 respectively   6
D = − by 2 raters; or − by 1 and 0 by 2 (2 cases)   12
E = − by 3 raters   7
                                          40

These composite ratings were then correlated with the mental-health index. The principal results are described on pages 31–33. For the type of material in question the agreement proves decidedly good.

When assessments by the individual clinicians are examined separately, they are found also to agree consistently with the indexes. The relationships are positive in every instance and for the indexes most representative of mental health, those of anxiety and adjustment, the median Tau coefficient is .50. An example or two will illustrate how well the scores and indexes agreed in certain instances. One psychologist's assessments of his 20 cases compared with scores on the Anxiety Index as follows: 9 of the 10 persons he rated below average also received scores below average; of the 10 rated higher, only one scored below average (and that one was barely below). More typical are these results for a psychiatrist's ratings compared with Adjustment scores: of those he rated low, 7 of 10 were also low in scores; of 4 rated medium, 2 had low and 2 had high scores; of 6 rated high, all were in the high score range.

Two further points are of interest in reference to differences of results among the clinicians. (1) The raters who agree best with other raters also tend to agree best with the indexes; those agreeing least with their colleagues show least correspondence with the scores. This suggests that the indexes do represent a consensual view of mental health among the clinicians. (2) Individual clinicians differ greatly in respect to the aspects of mental health which they emphasize even when their total assessments are similar. This is illustrated, for example, by two psychiatrists who agreed equally well with the general mental-health index but A's ratings correlated much more highly than B's with certain component indexes (Tau coefficients with personal morale were .46 versus .03; with life satisfaction, .49 versus .21) but more poorly with other indexes (.40

versus .64 in respect to anxiety). Another pair of raters, again about equal in their agreement with the composite index, diverged in respect to the anxiety measure to the extent of correlations of .21 and .57 respectively. Findings of this kind reinforce the conclusion that in our present state of knowledge (or confusion) it is probably the better part of wisdom to use a shotgun approach to the measurement of mental health—that is, to include a combination of several indexes, as we have done, to tap partially diverse dimensions of the conglomerate concept.

Notes

Chapter 1.   Psychology and the Study of Working People

1. For useful reviews and evaluations of research, see Blauner (1960), Brayfield & Crockett (1955), Herzberg, Mausner, Peterson, & Capwell (1957), Scott, Dawis, England, & Lofquist (1958), Vlteles (1953), and annual reviews of research on job satisfaction in the *Personnel and Guidance Journal*. Also see varied interpretations and criticisms of research results by Argyris (1957; 1964), Bell (1947; 1956), Friedmann (1955; 1961), Inkeles (1960), Katz (1954), Katz & Kahn (1951; 1952), A. Kornhauser (1944), Mayo (1933; 1945), Mills (1951), H. C. Smith (1964), Vroom (1964), Wilensky (1964), Zander & Quinn (1962). Examples of specific research studies are Blauner (1964), Blum (1953), Centers (1948a; 1948b; 1949), Chinoy (1955), Friedmann & Havinghurst (1954), Handyside (1961), Katz, Maccoby, Gurin, & Floor (1951), Lafitte (1958), Roethlisberger & Dickson (1939), Turner & Miclette (1962), Vroom (1962), Walker & Guest (1952), Wyatt & Marriott (1958), Wyatt, Langdon, & Stock (1937), Wyatt & Langdon (1938), Zaleznik, Christensen, & Roethlisberger (1958). Other studies that deal more explicitly with adjustment and mental health of occupational groups and social classes are Fraser (1947), Gurin, Veroff, & Feld (1960), Halliday (1948), Hollingshead & Redlich (1958), Langner & Michael (1963), Leavy & Freedman (1956), Levinson, Price, Munden, Mandl, & Solley (1962), Myers & Roberts (1959), and Srole, Langner, Michael, Opler, & Rennie (1962).
2. A thoughtful historical critique of this emphasis is presented by Baritz (1960); for other critical discussions, see Bell (1947; 1956), Fromm (1955), Gomberg (1958), Koivisto (1953), A. Kornhauser (1947), and Wilensky (1957).
3. U.S. Bureau of the Census, *Historical Statistics of the U. S., Colonial Times to 1957*, Washington, D.C., 1960, p. 76.
4. For examples, see Biganne & Stewart (1963), Davis & Werling (1960), Friedmann (1955; 1961), Guest (1957), Walker (1950; 1962).

5. U.S. Bureau of the Census, *Statistical Abstract of the U.S.: 1963,* Washington, D.C., 1963, p. 231.
6. The figures are from the Secretary of Labor's report on manpower, March 1963, as presented in *Mon. Lab. Rev.,* March 1963, p. 244.
7. U.S. Bureau of the Census, *Statistical Abstract of the U. S.: 1963,* Washington, D.C., 1963, p. 224. For similar figures to May 1964, see *Mon. Lab. Rev.,* July 1964, p. 839. Figures in respect to semi-skilled "operatives" are given by M. Rutzick & S. Swerdloff, "The Occupational Structure of U.S. Employment, 1940–60," *Mon. Lab. Rev.,* November 1962, pp. 1209–1213.
8. A vast body of writing has sprung up concerning the effects of automation. We list several of the better studies, reviews, and bibliographies: Alliston (1962), American Assembly (1962), L. E. Davis (1962), Faunce (1958a; 1958b), Friedmann (1955; 1961), Hardin, Eddy, & Deutsch (1961), Jacobson & Roucek (1959), Karsh (1957), Killingsworth et al. (1959), Mann & Hoffman (1960), Shils (1963), Somers, Cushman, & Weinberg (1963), Walker (1957; 1962).
9. An opposite conclusion has been widely cited on the basis of an empirical study by Dubin (1956). In our opinion, the methods and data of that research do not all justify the conclusion that work is not of central significance for workers. What the results indicate is that workers find their *pleasures and intimate personal relationships* more in nonwork situations than at work. A clear distinction must be made between the subjective *importance* of work and the *satisfactions* it provides. Dubin defines "central life interest" to refer to *"expressed preferences"* for work relationships. Our own results, on the other hand, indicate how large the job looms in the worker's life, including its negative implications as well as the positive, and including feelings about the job's importance as a source of economic gratifications, its contribution to a sense of personal worth, and its implications regarding the worker's place in the community. For other evidence and discussion of the place of work, see Friedmann & Havighurst (1954), Morse & Weiss (1955), and the references listed in note 2, Chapter 12.
10. Examples of this treatment of motivation in relation to work are found in Gurin et al. (1960), Likert (1961), and Vroom (1962).

Chapter 2.   The Assessment of Mental Health

1. Extensive review and critical treatment of the mental-health concept, its definition and relevant evidence, with many additional references, may be found in K. Davis (1938), Eaton (1951), French (1963), French & Kahn (1962), Friedes (1960), Gurin et al. (1960), Jahoda

(1958), Rose (1955), Scott (1958a; 1958b), M. B. Smith (1959; 1961), Solley & Munden (1961), Srole et al. (1962), Szasz (1960).

2. An exposition of "relational fertility" as an extension of the validity concept is contained in McClelland (1958). For related ideas on construct validity, see Cronbach & Meehl (1955) and Peak (1953). Guidelines for systematic analysis of explanatory relationships are presented by Hyman (1955).

3. We use valuational terms with no implication that the evaluations must be accepted. "Good mental health" is merely a shorthand expression referring to an aggregate of responses which are usually considered indicative of effective, satisfying, accepted behavior in our society—but which anyone with different values and norms is free to evaluate differently if he so desires. It is not the role of the psychologist to impose his conclusions on society as to what is good mental health, but to provide knowledge on the basis of which all people can make better-informed value judgments for themselves The value problem as it pertains to mental health has been discussed in many publications. See, for example, K. Davis (1938), Eaton (1951), Friedes (1960), Jahoda (1958), M. B. Smith (1959); 1961), Szasz (1960).

4. This was a period of declining employment in Detroit. During the first half of 1953 production was at a high level with low unemployment. By late summer, however, unemployment figures were mounting. Unemployment continued to increase and remained relatively high through the winter and spring of 1953–1954.

5. Omitted from this core sample of Detroit factory workers are interviews obtained from four foremen and three full-time union stewards or committeemen. This was done in order to include only hourly paid workers actually engaged in factory jobs.

6. A copy of the interview questions is printed in full in Appendix A.

7. Most of the interviewers were graduate students or college graduates with interests in psychology, social science, education, or social work. Several were high-school social-science teachers; two were faculty members of the university psychology department. All interviewers were given special training and were required to complete supervised practice interviews.

8. For the purpose of an exploratory inquiry like the present study, we consider it more justifiable and appropriate to depend upon the consistency and meaningfulness of relationships revealed than to employ the usual technical measures of "coder reliability." Such reliability guarantees nothing in regard to the substantive value of the ratings; it may mean merely that coders have conscientiously followed arbitrary instructions of unknown relevance to the trait purportedly rated. On the other hand, to the degree that indexes of mental health and other characteristics show sizable and con-

sistent relations, this in itself attests to the "reliability" of the separate measures. When we find, for example, that our indexes of mental health correlate approximately .70 and above with clinicians' estimates based on the interviews, this is sufficient evidence that the coding which entered into the indexes was not subject to serious distorting errors. Whenever feasible, moreover, we have checked and confirmed relationships involving general indexes by the use of data from single questions, most of them unambiguous check-response items. Two further safeguards tended to reduce the danger of erroneous conclusions due to faulty coding: coders were closely supervised, with frequent spot checks of their work, and each part of the coding was carried on by several different persons, thus minimizing effects of possible constant errors by any particular coder. None of the foregoing is intended to deny that coding inaccuracies and disagreements do occur. This is one of many factors —in our opinion it is one of the less consequential—that dictate caution in drawing conclusions. Such considerations reinforce the admonition of Chapter 1 that results should be evaluated with some reference to their congruence with other knowledge and theoretical conceptions.

9. See, for example, K. Davis (1938) and Scott (1958a).

10. Correlations between pairs of indexes having one item in common do not differ from those with no identical items. The median coefficient for the former is .36, for the latter .35.

11. Still higher intercorrelations would be expected for samples of the entire population; the restriction of our sample to one part of the occupational range, and to employed men only, reduces the variability of scores and the magnitude of resulting correlations.

12. See note 2 above.

13. The four psychiatrists and two clinical psychologists were all staff members of Lafayette Clinic in Detroit. I wish to express my sincere gratitude to them for their interested, conscientious cooperation. Their help was invaluable.

14. See Scott (1958a), pp. 37–39.

Chapter 3.   The Mental Health of Automobile Workers

1. The present study deals almost solely with Detroit automobile workers. Consequently, caution must be exercised against assuming that the findings are representative for factory workers in general. Great variations undoubtedly exist between different industries, localities, and time periods. Nevertheless, the mass-production conditions and machine domination found in the automotive industry of

the 1950's are widespread enough and important enough as one typical sector of modern industrial life to give the conclusions considerable general significance. Certainly many additional studies are needed to extend existing knowledge concerning both the similarities and contrasts among industries and varied situations. A recent book by Blauner (1964) is particularly useful in underscoring the markedly dissimilar characteristics of work in several industries and the contrasting effects on working people.

2. It is to be emphasized that we do not attempt to say how many individuals are "mentally ill," "impaired," "normal," or the like; the designations "good" and "poor" mental health and "average" are arbitrarily defined positions in the total distribution of scores on the mental-health index. Our later analyses (as in Tables 3-5 and 3-6) define "high" as roughly the upper one-third of the men studied and "low" as roughly the lowest one-third. Serious unanswered problems are encountered in studies that attempt to specify per centages of the population "well" or "ill," or having "marked" or "severe" symptoms, since large variations arise in such estimates due to differences of criteria and definition of the categories. For examples and discussions of the difficulties, see Hollingshead & Redlich (1958), Langner & Michael (1963), Manis et al. (1964), Opler (1956), Srole et al. (1962).

3. Table 3-5 includes data for 46 items listed under the 6 indexes. Actually, 50 items were used in the mental-health index but 4 are omitted here, 2 because their meaning proved too ambiguous (F8 and B15), 1 because it duplicates another item (a second coding of F11), and 1 because there was almost no variation of response (G32).

4. This statement refers to the usual standards of "statistical significance" at the 5 per cent probability level. Throughout the analysis, however, we have deliberately avoided formal use of tests of statistical significance. Such tests are of extremely doubtful justification or usefulness as applied to data like ours since the assumptions of the tests are not satisfied. This is notably true in respect to the assumption of independence of the variables. Furthermore, we are not interested in testing specific hypotheses but are *exploring* for meaningful relationships. For this purpose we rely not on single "statistically significant" differences but on consistency of findings and patterns of relationships manifested in larger sets of results, particularly where the relationships "make sense"—that is, where they are congruent with accumulated knowledge and theoretical expectations. For a succinct statement of the several reasons for not employing significance tests in research of this kind, see Lipset, Trow, & Coleman (1956, pp. 427–432); more extended treatment can be found in Selvin (1957); counterarguments are presented by Kish (1959), though he, too, points to serious limitations and pitfalls.

Both these authors cite references useful to anyone wishing to pursue the matter.

5. The self-blame item is the only one on which there is a striking difference in size of percentages between young and middle-aged, the latter expressing such feeling much more frequently. Whether attributable to age, a cultural decline of "Protestant Ethic" and inner-directedness, or whatever else, the finding offers an interesting lead for further study.

6. Many studies and discussions that contribute to this picture of mental health and social attitudes of working people are included in the references listed in note 1, Chapter 1. Additional material and further references bearing on sociopolitical orientations of workers will be found in the items listed in note 1, Chapter 10.

Chapter 4.   Mental-Health Differences by Occupational Level

1. Although the occupational categories are labeled in terms of skill level, the classification represents a more general job-level hierarchy based on pay, responsibility, and variety as well. The top group of "skilled" workers consists of those in occupations that require an apprenticeship, usually of four years duration. Examples: tool maker, millwright, electrician, machine repairman, rigger, sheet-metal worker. Median hourly wage rate (1953): $2.53. "High semiskilled" jobs typically require three to six months to learn (range from a few weeks to two years); they are more varied and involve greater judgment and responsibility than the two lower categories. Examples: job setter, die setter, tool grinder, fixture welder and repairman, hi-lo mechanic (repairs), receiving inspector, salvage inspector, floorman on inspection (checks and supervises inspectors), utility man (on final assembly line), cloth cutter (for upholstery), boring mill operator, etc. Median hourly wage rate: $2.22. "Ordinary semiskilled" and "repetitive semiskilled" differ only in the degree of simplicity and repetitiveness of the job; all are specialized occupations usually learned in a few hours up to a few weeks. Median hourly wage rate is $2.02 for each of these categories. "Ordinary semiskilled" jobs are ones in which the worker does not work at a fixed pace, the task varies from time to time or, if repetitive, has a cycle of about 10 minutes to several hours, and in some instances involves moving about the shop. Examples: stock tractor (hi-lo) operator, trimmer (making convertible tops), shipping checker, assembler (truck platforms and gates, 2 hours each), tool-crib attendant, wet sander (rub down

bodies, 20 minutes each), gear grinder (machine), welder, lathe operator (specialized), oiler, stock handler (load into boxcars), repairman on special parts. "Repetitive semiskilled" jobs include mechanically paced ones ("on the line") and others that are very simple and repetitious but are not machine-paced. Examples of the former: assembly-line worker (e.g., door fitter, 1 every 2 minutes; panel buildup, 6 per minute; body paint sprayer, 2½ seconds each; valve adjuster on line, 1 every 3 minutes), punch press operator (flow of pieces, 1 per minute), inspector (of pieces on continuous conveyor). Examples of unpaced repetitive operations: centerless grinder operator (remove a piece every 20 seconds), inspector of motor parts, machine operator (drill and ream), drill-press operator (2½ minutes each, but controls own speed), automatic screw machine operator (setup by others), tube bender (machine-feeding operation), metal polisher (by machine).

    The ratio of repetitive production workers to others will doubtless appear unexpectedly small to persons whose image of an auto plant consists only of assembly lines. Although it is probable that the number would be increased if we had included Negroes and workers with less than three years seniority, the obtained figures are judged to be not far off by several men well acquainted with the industry. It seems likely, too, that the spread of automation has further decreased the proportion of routine production workers since 1953.

2. Median hourly rates of pay for the manual workers are almost identical with those of the factory groups, $2.24 compared with $2.22 for the upper semiskilled and $1.97 compared with $2.01 for the ordinary semiskilled. The white-collar median is $2.35, just about midway between the factory high semiskilled and the skilled, $2.22 and $2.53 respectively.

3. For examples of other research reports and summaries regarding psychological differences between occupational groups and between socioeconomic classes, see Anastasi & Foley (1958), Argyris (1960), Bendix & Lipset (1953), Centers (1948a; 1948b; 1949), Form & Geschwender (1962), Hollingshead & Redlich (1958), Kahl (1957), Kennedy & O'Neill (1958), A. Kornhauser (1940), Langner & Michael (1963), Lipset (1960), Lyman (1955), Reissman (1959), Srole et al. (1962), Super (1939), Warner (1953).

4. More detailed analyses and interpretations of the occupational group differences will be found in Chapters 8 to 11.

5. The composition of these indexes pertaining to childhood characteristics is more specifically described in Appendix B.

6. Examples of relationships on single objective items from the deprivation index follow. The arrangement parallels that in Table 4-5 of the text, each percentage showing the proportion of the group in that cell (N in parantheses) who have high mental health.

Young Workers

	Skilled and High Semiskilled	Ordinary Semiskilled	Repetitive Semiskilled
Country of father's birth			
United States	44% (16)	33% (27)	5% (20)
Other	69 (16)	41 (17)	22 (9)
Father's occupation			
Skilled or white collar	67% (18)	58% (12)	0% (8)
Unskilled or farmer	38 (13)	26 (31)	14 (21)
Father's education			
Eighth grade or more	64% (11)	33% (15)	10% (10)
Less than eighth grade	50 (12)	43 (14)	0 (13)

Middle-aged Workers

	Skilled	High Semiskilled	Ordinary Semiskilled	Repetitive Semiskilled
Country of father's birth				
United States	56% (27)	48% (44)	41% (37)	29% (38)
Other	56 (18)	35 (54)	37 (43)	22 (32)
Father's occupation				
Skilled or white collar	63% (16)	43% (37)	27% (30)	26% (23)
Unskilled or farmer	58 (26)	41 (54)	44 (50)	24 (41)
Father's education				
Eighth grade or more	68% (19)	41% (27)	48% (21)	27% (22)
Less than eighth grade	56 (18)	36 (39)	37 (41)	40 (20)

Chapter 5.   Job Satisfaction in Relation to Mental Health

1. See, for example, Blauner (1960; 1964), Centers (1948a; 1948b; 1949), Herzberg et al. (1957), Inkeles (1960), Katz (1954), H. C. Smith (1964), Viteles (1953), Vroom (1964).
2. The index of job satisfaction is more fully described in Appendix B.

Chapter 6.   Job-Level Characteristics That Make for Better or Poorer Mental Health

1. A possible alternative interpretation of the statistical relationships would construe the causal chain as operating in the reverse direction. That is, poor mental health would be considered a determinant of job dissatisfaction and specific complaints rather than an effect. This conception of mental health as the independent causal variable encounters two troublesome questions that, in our opinion, argue strongly against it: (1) How are observed mental-health differences between occupations to be accounted for if not by reference to job factors as determinants? The evidence examined in Chapter 4 indicates that the differences are not attributable in any great measure to prejob influences and personality characteristics. (2) If mental-health differences are determinative, how is one to explain that they affect only certain job attitudes and not others? We would expect generally healthy or unhealthy dispositions to produce pervasive favorable or unfavorable perceptions and feelings toward all aspects of the job. Actually, we find almost no relationship of mental health to some job feelings and varying degrees of association with others—and in a manner that seems to accord with theoretical expectations if the job factors are thought of as determining influences on satisfaction and mental health. Our entire analysis contributes to this conclusion and correspondingly weakens the case for the alternative type of explanation.
2. There has been a remarkable dearth of critical writing regarding the procedures and conclusions of studies that supposedly demonstrate the relative unimportance of wages. Suggestions of the serious limitations and the need for penetrating questioning may be found in Haire & Gottsdanker (1951), A. Kornhauser (1944), Viteles (1953), Vroom (1964).
3. Proportions having low mental-health scores (i.e., scores in the lowest one-third of workers, approximately) are as follows for middle-aged men.

	Abilities Used	Abilities Not Used
Skilled	12%	. . .
High semiskilled	32%	50%
Ordinary semiskilled	32%	43%
Repetitive semiskilled	18%	53%

Men in the lowest skill group who feel that their abilities are used actually have slightly *fewer* of poor mental health than is true at higher job levels (18 versus 27 per cent).

4. Research on these matters is reported in Baldamus (1961), Blauner (1964), Friedmann (1955; 1961), Turner (1955), Turner & Miclette (1962), Wyatt, Langdon, & Stock (1937), Wyatt & Langdon (1938), Walker & Guest (1952).

5. See Chapter 4, pp. 58–59.

6. Since the interview contained no direct questions on reactions to paced versus unpaced work and since spontaneous comments on this specific feature of jobs are rare and usually spread over other aspects as well, we do not have data that would enable us to relate mental-health scores to subjective feelings toward this characteristic of work.

7. See, for example, Blauner (1960), Brown (1954), Herzberg et al. (1957), Homans (1950), Seashore (1954), Viteles (1955), Whyte (1955; 1962), Zaleznik et al. (1958).

8. The generous assistance given by these busy industrial-relations experts is most gratefully acknowledged.

9. It might be thought that these relationships would be decidedly different for workers who feel that advancement is important as contrasted with those who do not care. Accordingly, we made the analysis separately for the two groups. The analysis reveals that in general the relationships shown in Table 6-3 remain essentially unchanged in both the new sets of figures. Since the number of individuals in some of the subgroups becomes extremely small, however, the results are only suggestive. One interesting variation from Table 6-3 appears in that the relatively good mental health of middle-aged repetitive workers who see chances for promotion (last sentence of the paragraph in the text) is due entirely to those who *do not care* about advancement (6 of 9 have high mental health, contrasted with only 3 of 13 men at this job level who do care and who see opportunity for advancement).

10. On the basis of a combination of men's reports of their annual earnings and their wage rates, we classified them into four levels. The

distribution of the 407 Detroit factory workers on this classification is as follows for the two age groups: young—high, 13; above average, 24; average or slightly below, 53; well below average, 19; correspondingly for the middle-aged—58, 92, 122, and 26. These figures are the totals on which percentages given in the text are based.

Chapter 7. Personal Characteristics in Relation to Mental Health

1. For evidence related to matters dealt with in this chapter, see Gurin et al. (1960), Herzberg et al. (1957), Hollingshead & Redlich (1958), Kleiner & Parker (1963), Lafitte (1958), Langner & Michael (1963), Lipset & Bendix (1959), Meier & Bell (1959), Myers & Roberts (1959), Oeser & Hammond(1954), Scott (1958h), Srole et al. (1962), Wilensky (1960; 1961).
2. Pp. 58–59. It must be recognized that the age groups differ not only in respect to variables directly dependent on age (stage of career, family condition, and so on) but also in having grown up under different historical circumstances (notably the economic depression of the 1930's). The middle-aged men ranged from 17 to 26 years of age in 1930; the young men were born between 1923 and 1932. Our data do not enable us to estimate the effects of such historical factors associated with age.
3. Chapter 4, pp. 67–69. Figures regarding education and school success on which the present paragraph is based are given in Tables 4-4 and 4-5.
4. French (1960), Kasl & French (1962), Kleiner (1959), Kleiner & Parker (1963), Meier & Bell (1959), Tuckman & Kleiner (1962), Zaleznik et al. (1958). For a comprehensive examination of relevant concepts and evidence, see Vroom (1964). A widely influential treatment of discrepancy or incongruency effects on a general theoretical level is presented by Merton (1957).
5. When we combine skilled and white-collar fathers, the obtained figures are those shown in note 6, Chapter 4. Although the number of cases remains extremely small within the young group, it appears that sons of higher-status fathers have markedly better than average mental health except among the routine semiskilled. In the middle-aged group, no clear tendencies are apparent in relation to father's occupation.
6. Analysis of our data with respect to upward or downward occupational mobility during the course of the worker's own career likewise reveals no clear or consistent relationship to mental health.
7. Chapter 4, p. 73; also see Appendix B.

8. Relevant figures are contained in Table 4-5. The present summary is based on these figures plus additional detailed comparisons, including the use of more extreme subgroups on each variable and consideration of proportions having low mental-health scores as well as high.

9. Again, certain of the results are shown in Table 4-5, but much more extensive comparisons were used as a basis for the present summary.

Chapter 8.   The Worker's Orientation to His World—
1. Relation to the Job

1. See references listed in note 1, Chapter 1, and note 1, Chapter 5.

2. For evidence and argument in support of the interpretation referred to here, see Herzberg, Mausner, & Snyderman (1959) and Herzberg & Hamlin (1961).

3. The relationships can be seen in the following percentages: among repetitive workers, 64 per cent of the job satisfied comment favorably about working conditions versus 21 per cent of the job dissatisfied; concerning wages, 58 per cent of the job satisfied are favorable versus 56 per cent of the job dissatisfied. For men in the upper three skill groups, corresponding percentages in regard to working conditions are 41 per cent of the satisfied to 28 per cent of the dissatisfied favorable; and in regard to wages, 66 per cent of the job satisfied and 51 per cent of the dissatisfied favorable.

4. In regard to working conditions the percentages are those given in the preceding note 3; by contrast, favorable comments regarding supervision show large differences between satisfied and dissatisfied both among routine workers and in upper skill groups: 82 per cent of satisfied repetitive workers comment favorably to 32 per cent of the dissatisfied; in the three higher skill groups, the difference is 75 per cent to 41 per cent.

5. Statements in this paragraph are based on the following percentage comparisons: definitely positive liking for coworkers by 84 per cent of skilled, 66 per cent of high semiskilled, 68 per cent of ordinary semiskilled, and 50 per cent of repetitive semiskilled (33 per cent of *young* repetitive workers). Of men strongly favorable toward the company, 85 per cent have high job satisfaction compared with 67 per cent of those moderately or weakly favorable to the company, and 36 per cent of those unfavorable. In respect to supervision, 72 per cent of the strongly favorable have high job satisfaction, 73 per cent of the moderately and weakly favorable, and 44 per cent of the unfavorable. Among middle-aged workers, 77 per cent of those strongly positive toward fellow workers are well satisfied with their

jobs, 70 per cent of those moderately positive, and 70 per cent of those doubtful or negative. Among young men, corresponding proportions are 73, 56, and 27 per cent.

6. These ratings are described on p. 112.

7. In important ways our results support the interpretations of Herzberg and his associates (1959; 1961), but in other ways we believe that the results run counter to conclusions they have drawn. Our findings agree in showing the vital significance of intrinsic rewards of work and opportunities for self-actualizing use of abilities—in factory employment as well as in higher-level professional and technical jobs of the kind studied by Herzberg. However, we would not assign these characteristics an exclusive place as positive motivators nor would we consign other gratifications provided by the job to either a negative or a pale neutral role. The contrast between the two views can be summarized as follows: both our empirical findings and our conceptual guidelines stress the multiplicity and variety of workers' motivations and the corresponding importance of the *many* sources of gratification and deprivation present in the job. The Herzberg view stresses the unique and indispensable role of needs for achievement, workmanship, and recognition, and the intrinsic work characteristics that satisfy these particular needs. If the job fails to offer these gratifications, the worker is unmotivated and lacks positive job satisfactions. Our contention is that whether the job is motivating and satisfying depends on the total complex balance of want gratifications, including wants for security, material well-being for self and family, social acceptance, affection, and all the other "hygiene" needs of Herzberg as well as the needs he designates as "motivators."

*Chapter 9.   The Worker's Orientation to His World—
                2. Life Away from the Job*

1. For related studies and interpretations see Anderson (1961), Clarke (1956), DeGrazia (1962), Friedmann (1961), Gurin et al. (1960), Kaplan (1960), Lafitte (1958), Oeser & Hammond (1954), Riesman (1950), Rosenberg & White (1957), Segerstedt & Lundquist (1956), Staley (1952), Wilensky (1960; 1961), Zweig (1952; 1961).

2. Questions on which the index is based are specified in Appendix B.

3. Questions on which the rating is based are specified in Appendix B.

4. Same as note 3.

5. This index is also described in Appendix B.

6. This is true even though 50 men in our sample have been, or are now, stewards, committeemen, or local officers. It is likewise noted that

3 full-time union stewards whom we excluded from our sample report no time spent on union or related activities away from work.

7. Correlations between *indexes,* where available, in place of single questions, yield essentially similar results. The question in regard to satisfaction with life in Detroit is added here as of interest though it had to be omitted from Table 9-4 since the form of question makes it not strictly comparable with the other questions in respect to size of percentages.

Chapter 10.   *The Worker's Orientation to His World—*
3.   *Sociopolitical Attitudes*

1. For related studies see Campbell, Converse, Miller & Stokes (1960), Campbell, Gurin, & Miller (1954), Centers (1948a; 1949), Christie & Jahoda (1954), Converse (1958), Ginzberg & Berman (1963), Jones (1941), Kahn (1957), Key (1958), A. Kornhouser (1940), Kornhauser, Sheppard, & Mayer (1956), W. Kornhauser (1959), Lafitte (1958), Lane (1962), Lipset (1960), Oeser & Hammond (1954), Reissman (1959), Segerstedt & Lundquist (1956), Stouffer (1955), Zweig (1952; 1961).
2. The original, widely influential studies are those of the California group (Adorno et al., 1950). For criticisms and reviews of later studies see Christie & Jahoda (1954) and Titus & Hollander (1957).
3. Questions used as a basis for the rating are specified in Appendix B.
4. For questions used in the index, see Appendix B.
5. Also in Appendix B.
6. Workers' attitudes toward their *local* union are another matter; the more job-dissatisfied workers have definitely more negative feelings about the local organization (17 per cent of the well satisfied are seriously critical of, or opposed to, the local's activities compared to 33 per cent of the dissatisfied). These relationships and the controversial question of "dual allegiance" to company and union will be treated in a later publication. For discussion of dual allegiance and further references, see Purcell (1960) and Stagner (1956).
7. This index is also described in Appendix B.
8. As the term is used by Burns (1963).
9. This relationship is found for the total labor-orientation index and for its separate components with the exception of the one measuring *pro-union* attitudes. (As stated in the text, feelings toward unions in general are not correlated, positively or negatively, with job satisfaction or life satisfaction.) The same pattern of relationships occurs in respect to mental health: prolabor sociopolitical attitudes as a whole are associated with below-average mental health but again feelings

toward unions are an exception. Apparently, support of unionism, unlike other elements of working-class orientation, appeals equally to the satisfied and the dissatisfied, the well adjusted and those less well adjusted.

Chapter 11. The Worker's Orientation to His World— 4. Attitudes toward Self and Personal Goals

1. Material related to the contents of this chapter may be found in Centers (1948b; 1949), Clark (1960), French (1963), French & Kahn (1962), Fromm (1941; 1955), Ginzberg & Berman (1963), Hyman (1953), Inkeles (1960), Knupfer, Kornhauser et al. (1956), Lane (1962), Riesman (1950), Wilensky (1964).
2. The nature of the ratings of purposiveness is indicated on p. 35 and in Appendix B.
3. This index is also explained on p. 35 and in Appendix B.
4. The size of the vote for these several goals depends to some extent, of course, on the particular wording of the choices and hence results must be interpreted with this caution in mind.
5. The questions on which the rating is based are specified in Appendix B.
6. Pp. 35 and 48–50.

Chapter 12. Conclusions

1. A vast literature has come into being that grapples with the human problems of industry. This is obviously not the place to attempt a review of thought and research in this area. The best we can do, as an aid to readers who may wish to pursue the matters touched upon in the text, is to include a sampling of references to some of the better books and articles that have appeared in recent years. These sources contain many additional references. We suggest the following: Argyris (1957; 1960; 1964), Bennis (1959; 1961), Blum (1953), Drucker (1954), Dubin (1958), Friedmann (1955; 1961), Gellerman (1963), Haire (1959), Knowles (1958), Landsberger (1958), Levinson et al. (1962), Likert (1961), McGregor (1960), Presthus (1963), H. C. Smith (1964), Strauss (1963), Warner & Martin (1959), Whyte (1955; 1962), Wilensky (1957).
2. These final pages merely nibble at the edges of enormously large and forbiddingly difficult problems. For centuries, thoughtful men and women have sought better answers to the questions raised here. Again, all we can attempt is to list a limited number of references, restricting ourselves to illustrations of modern psychological and

"behavioral science" thinking. We make no mention at all of the rich body of social-historical and philosophical writing by great thinkers of the past. Among recent publications we select a number that seem related to our present discussion—and particularly ones having a bearing on humanly oriented industrial change, the use of leisure, and more active participation in organizations and social movements. Illustratively, then, we suggest the following: Arendt (1959), Bell (1960), Brown (1954), Drucker (1950), Friedmann (1955; 1961), Fromm (1955), Kerr et al. (1960), Lerner (1957), Lipset (1960), Mayo (1933; 1945), Merton (1957), Mills (1956), Moore (1951), Presthus (1962), Riesman (1950), Staley (1952), Walker (1962), Weiss & Riesman (1961), Wilensky & Lebeaux (1958).

References

Adorno, T. W., Frenkel-Brunswik, E., Levinson, D. J., & Sanford, R. N. *The authoritarian personality.* New York: Harper, 1950.

Alliston, J. R. *Implications of automation and other technological developments, a selected bibliography.* U.S. Dept. of Labor, Bur. of Lab. Stat., 1962 (Bull. No. 1319).

American Assembly. *Automation and technological change.* Englewood Cliffs, N.J.: Prentice-Hall, 1962.

Anastasi, A., & Foley, J. P., Jr. *Differential psychology.* (3rd ed.) New York: Macmillan, 1958.

Anderson, N. *Work and Leisure.* New York: Free Press of Glencoe, 1961.

Arendt, H. *The human condition.* Chicago: Univer. of Chicago Press, 1958.

Argyris, C. *Personality and organization.* New York: Harper, 1957.

Argyris, C. Individual actualization in complex organizations. *Ment. Hyg.,* 1960, **44,** 226–237.

Argyris, C. *Integrating the individual and the organization.* New York: Wiley, 1964.

Baldamus, W. *Efficiency and effort.* London: Tavistock, 1961.

Baritz, L. *The servants of power.* Middletown, Conn.: Wesleyan Univer. Press, 1960.

Bell, D. Adjusting men to machines. *Commentary,* 1947, **3,** 79–88.

Bell, D. *Work and its discontents.* Boston: Beacon, 1956.

Bell, D. *The end of ideology.* Glencoe, Ill.: Free Press, 1960.

Bendix, R., & Lipset, S. M. (Eds.). *Class, status and power.* Glencoe, Ill.: Free Press, 1953.

Bennis, W. G. Leadership theory and administrative behavior: the problem of authority. *Admin. Sci. Quart.,* 1959, **4,** 259–301.

Bennis, W. G. Revisionist theory of leadership. *Harv. bus. Rev.,* 1961, **39**(1), 26–150 passim.

Biganne, J. F., & Stewart, P. A. *Job enlargement: a case study.* Bur. of Labor and Management, State Univer. of Iowa, 1963 (Res. Ser. No. 25).

Blauner, R. Work satisfaction and industrial trends in modern society. In W. Galenson & S. M. Lipset (Eds.), *Labor and trade unionism.* New York: Wiley, 1960. Pp. 339–360.

Blauner, R. *Alienation and freedom: the factory worker and his industry.* Chicago: Univer. of Chicago Press, 1964.

Blum, F. *Toward a democratic work process.* New York: Harper, 1953.

343

Brayfield, A. H., & Crockett, W. H. Employee attitudes and employee performance. *Psychol. Bull.*, 1955, **52**, 396–424.

Brown, J. A. C. *The social psychology of industry.* Harmondsworth, England: Penguin, 1954.

Burns, J. McG. *The deadlock of democracy: four-party politics in America.* Englewood Cliffs, N.J.: Prentice-Hall, 1963.

Campbell, A., Converse, P. E., Miller, W. E., & Stokes, D. E. *The American voter.* New York: Wiley, 1960.

Campbell, A., Gurin, G., & Miller, W. E. *The voter decides.* Evanston, Ill.: Row, Peterson, 1954.

Centers, R. Attitude and belief in relation to occupational stratification. *J. soc. Psychol.*, 1948, **27**, 159–185. (a)

Centers, R. Motivational aspects of occupational stratification. *J. soc. Psychol.*, 1948, **28**, 187–217. (b)

Centers, R. *The psychology of social classes.* Princeton, N.J.: Princeton Univer. Press, 1949.

Chinoy, E. *Automobile workers and the American dream.* Garden City, N.Y.: Doubleday, 1955.

Christie, R., & Jahoda, M. (Eds.). *Studies in the scope and method of "The authoritarian personality."* Glencoe, Ill.: Free Press, 1954.

Clark, J. V. Motivation in work groups: a tentative view. *Hum. Organization*, 1961, **19**, 199–208.

Clarke, A. C. The use of leisure and its relation to levels of occupational prestige. *Amer. sociol. Rev.*, 1956, **21**, 301–307.

Converse, P. E. The shifting role of class in political attitudes and behavior. In E. E. Maccoby, T. M. Newcomb, & E. L. Hartley (Eds.), *Readings in social psychology.* (3rd ed.) New York: Holt, 1958. Pp. 388–399.

Cronbach, L., & Meehl, P. E. Construct validity in psychological tests. *Psychol. Bull.*, 1955, **52**, 281–302.

Culpin, M., & Smith, M. The nervous temperament. *Industr. Health Res. Bd. Report No. 61.* London: H. M. Stationery Office, 1930.

Davis, K. Mental Hygiene and the class structure. *Psychiatry*, 1938, **1**, 55–65.

Davis, L. E. The effects of automation on job design. *Industr. Relat.*, 1962, **2**, 53–71.

Davis, L. E., & Werling, R. Job design factors. *Occup. Psychol.*, 1960, **34**, 109–132.

DeGrazia, S. *Of time, work, and leisure.* New York: Twentieth Century Fund, 1962.

Drucker, P. F. *The new society.* New York: Harper, 1950.

Drucker, P. F. *The practice of management.* New York: Harper, 1954.

Dubin, R. Industrial workers' worlds: a study of the central life interests of industrial workers. *Soc. Probl.*, 1956, **3**, 131–142.

Dubin, R. *The world of work.* Englewood Cliffs, N.J.: Prentice-Hall, 1958.

DuBridge, L. A. Educational and social consequences. In American Assembly, *Automation and technological change.* Englewood Cliffs, N.J.: Prentice-Hall, 1962. Pp. 26–42.

Eaton, J. W. The assessment of mental health. *Amer. J. Psychiat.*, 1951, **108**, 81–90.

Faunce, W. A. Automation and the automobile worker. *Soc. Probl.*, 1958, **6**, 68–78. (a)

Faunce, W. A. Automation in the automobile industry. *Amer. sociol. Rev.*, 1958, **23**, 401–407. (b)

Form, W. H., & Geschwender, J. A. Social reference basis of job satisfaction: the case of manual workers. *Amer. sociol. Rev.*, 1962, **27**, 228–237.

Fraser, R. The incidence of neurosis among factory workers. *Industr. Health Res. Bd. Report No. 90.* London: H. M. Stationery Office, 1947.

French, J. R. P., Jr. The effects of the industrial environment on mental health: a theoretical approach. Paper read at Amer. Psychol. Ass., Chicago, September, 1960.

French, J. R. P., Jr. The social environment and mental health. *J. soc. Issues,* 1963, **19**(4), 39–56.

French, J. R. P., Jr., & Kahn, R. L. A programmatic approach to studying the industrial environment and mental health. *J. soc. Issues,* 1962, **18**(3), 1–47.

French, J. R. P., Jr., Kahn, R. L., & Mann, F. C. (Eds.). Work, health and satisfaction. *J. soc. Issues,* 1962, **18**(3).

Friedes, D. Toward the elimination of the concept of normality. *J. consult. Psychol.*, 1960, **24**, 128–133.

Friedmann, E. A., & Havighurst, R. J. *The meaning of work and retirement.* Chicago: Univer. of Chicago Press, 1954.

Friedmann, G. *Industrial society.* Glencoe, Ill.: Free Press, 1955.

Friedmann, G. *The anatomy of work.* New York: Free Press of Glencoe, 1961.

Fromm, E. *Escape from freedom.* New York: Farrar & Rinehart, 1941.

Fromm, E. *The sane society.* New York: Rinehart, 1955.

Gellerman, S. W. *Motivation and productivity.* New York: Amer. Mgmt. Ass., 1963.

Ginzberg, E., & Berman, H. *The American workers in the twentieth century, a history through autobiographies.* New York: Free Press of Glencoe, 1963.

Gomberg, W. The use of psychology in industry: a trade union point of view. *Mgmt. Sci.*, 1957, **3**, 348–370.

Guest, R. H. Work careers and aspirations of automobile workers. *Amer. sociol. Rev.*, 1954, **19**, 155–163.

Guest, R. H. Job enlargement—a revolution in job design. *Personnel Admin.*, 1957, **20**(2), 9–16.

Gurin, G., Veroff, J., & Feld, S. *Americans view their mental health.* New York: Basic Books, 1960.

Haire, M. Psychological problems relevant to business and industry. *Psychol. Bull.*, 1959, **56**, 169–194.

Haire, M., & Gottsdanker, J. S. Factors influencing industrial morale. *Personnel*, 1951, **27**, 445–454.

Halliday, J. L. *Psychosocial medicine.* New York: Norton, 1948.

Handyside, J. D. Satisfactions and aspirations. *Occup. Psychol.*, 1961, **35**, 213–244.

Hardin, E., Eddy, W. B., & Deutsch, S. E. *Economic and social implications of automation: an annotated bibliography, 1957–1960.* East Lansing, Mich.: School of Labor & Industr. Relat., Mich. State Univer., 1961.

Hearnshaw, L. S. Attitudes to work. *Occup. Psychol.*, 1954, **28**, 129–139.

Herzberg, F., & Hamlin, R. M.   A motivation-hygiene concept of mental health. *Ment. Hyg.*, 1961, **45**, 394–401.

Herzberg, F., Mausner, B., Peterson, R., & Capwell, D.   *Job attitudes: review of research and opinion.*   Pittsburgh, Pa.: Psychological Service of Pittsburgh, 1957.

Herzberg, F., Mausner, B., & Snyderman, B. B. *The motivation to work.*   (2nd ed.) New York: Wiley, 1959.

Hollingshead, A. B., & Redlich, F. C. *Social class and mental illness.*   New York: Wiley, 1958.

Homans, G. C. *The human group.*   New York: Harcourt, Brace, 1950.

Hyman, H.   The value systems of different classes.   In R. Bendix & S. M. Lipset (Eds.), *Class, status and power.*   Glencoe, Ill.: Free Press, 1953.   Pp. 426–442.

Hyman, H. *Survey design and analysis.*   Glencoe, Ill.: Free Press, 1955.

Industrial Relations Research Association. *Research in industrial human relations.*   New York: Harper, 1957.

Inkeles, A.   Industrial man: the relation of status to experience, perception, and value. *Amer. J. Sociol.*, 1960, **66**, 1–31.

Jacobson, H. B., & Roucek, J. S. (Eds.). *Automation and society.*   New York: Philosophical Library, 1959.

Jahoda, M. *Current concepts of positive mental health.*   New York: Basic Books, 1958.

Jones, A. W. *Life, liberty, and property.*   Philadelphia: Lippincott, 1941.

Kahl, J. *The American class structure.*   New York: Rinehart, 1957.

Kaplan, M. *Leisure in America: a social inquiry.*   New York: Wiley, 1960.

Karsh, B.   The meaning of work in an age of automation. *Curr. econ. Comment*, 1957, **19**(3), 3–13.

Kasl, S. V., & French, J. R. P., Jr.   The effects of occupational status on physical and mental health. *J. soc. Issues*, 1962, **18**(3), 67–89.

Katz, D.   Satisfactions and deprivations in industrial life.   In A. Kornhauser, R. Dubin, & A. M. Ross (Eds.), *Industrial Conflict.*   New York: McGraw-Hill, 1954.   Pp. 86–106.

Katz, D., & Kahn, R. L.   Some recent findings in human-relations research in industry.   In G. E. Swanson, T. M. Newcomb, & E. L. Hartley (Eds.), *Readings in social psychology*   (2nd ed.) New York: Holt, 1952.   Pp. 650–665.

Katz, D., Maccoby, N., Gurin, G., & Floor, L. G. *Productivity, supervision and morale among railroad workers.*   Ann Arbor: Inst. for soc. Res., Univer. of Michigan, 1951.

Katzell, R. A., Barrett, R. S., & Parker, T. C.   Job satisfaction, job performance, and situational characteristics. *J. Appl. Psychol.*, 1961, **45**, 65–72.

Kennedy, J. E., & O'Neill, H. E.   Job content and workers' opinions. *J. Appl. Psychol.*, 1958, **42**, 372–375.

Kerr, C., Dunlap, J. T., Harbison, F. H., & Myers, C. A. *Industrialism and industrial man.*   Cambridge, Mass.: Harvard Univer. Press, 1960.

Key, V. O., Jr. *Public opinion and American democracy.*   New York: Knopf, 1961.

Killingsworth, C. C., et al.   Crucial problems posed by automation.   In Industr. Relat. Res. Ass., *Proceeding of the Eleventh Annual Meeting, December 1958.*   Pp. 20–75.

Kish, L. Some statistical problems in research design. *Amer. sociol. Rev.*, 1959, **24**, 328–338.

Kleiner, R. J. Status, group membership and schizophrenia. Paper read at Amer. Psychol. Ass., September, 1959.

Kleiner, R. J., & Parker, S. Goal striving, social status, and mental disorder: a research review. *Amer. sociol. Rev.*, 1963, **28**, 189–203.

Knowles, W. H. Human relations in industry: research and concepts. *California Mgmt. Rev.*, 1958, **1**, 87–105.

Knupfer, G. Portrait of the underdog. *Publ. Opin. Quart.*, 1947, **11**, 101–114.

Koivisto, W. A. Value, theory, and fact in industrial sociology. *Amer. J. Sociol.*, 1953, **58**, 564–572.

Kornhauser, A. Analysis of class structure of contemporary American society. In G. W. Hartmann & T. M. Newcomb (Eds.), *Industrial conflict.* New York: Cordon, 1940. Pp. 199–264.

Kornhauser, A. Psychological studies of employee attitudes. *J. consult. Psychol.*, 1944, **8**, 127–143.

Kornhauser, A. Industrial psychology as management technique and as social science. *Amer. Psychologist*, 1947, **2**, 224–229.

Kornhauser, A., Sheppard, H. L., & Mayer, A. J. *When labor votes.* New York: University Books, 1956.

Kornhauser, W. *The politics of mass society.* Glencoe, Ill.: Free Press, 1959.

Lafitte, P. *Social structure and personality in the factory.* London: Routledge & Paul, 1958.

Landsberger, H. A. *Hawthorne revisited.* Ithaca, N.Y.: Cornell Univer., 1958.

Lane, R. E. *Political ideology.* New York: Free Press of Glencoe, 1962.

Langner, T. S., & Michael, S. T. *Life stress and mental health.* New York: Free Press of Glencoe, 1963.

Leavy, S. A., & Freedman, L. Z. Psychoneurosis and economic life. *Soc. Probl.*, 1956, **4**, 55–67.

Lerner, M. *America as a civilization.* New York: Simon & Schuster, 1957.

Levinson, H., Price, C. R., Munden, K. J., Mandl, H. J., & Solley, C. M. *Men, management, and mental health.* Cambridge, Mass.: Harvard Univer. Press, 1962.

Likert, R. *New patterns of management.* New York: McGraw-Hill, 1961.

Lipset, S. M. *Political man.* Garden City, N.Y.: Doubleday, 1960.

Lipset, S. M., & Bendix, R. *Social mobility in industrial society.* Berkeley: Univer. of California Press, 1959.

Lipset, S. M., Trow, M. A., & Coleman, J. S. *Union democracy.* Glencoe, Ill.: Free Press, 1956.

Lyman, E. L. Occupational differences in the value attached to work. *Amer. J. Sociol.*, 1955, **61**, 138–144.

McClelland, D. C. Methods of measuring human motivation. In J. W. Atkinson (Ed.), *Motives in fantasy, action, and society.* Princeton, N.J.: Van Nostrand, 1958. Pp. 7–42.

McGregor, D. *The human side of enterprise.* New York: McGraw-Hill, 1960.

Manis, J. G., Brawer, M. J., Hunt, C. L., & Kercher, L. C. Validating a mental health scale. *Amer. sociol. Rev.*, 1963, **28**, 108–116.

Mann, F. C., & Hoffman, L. R. *Automation and the worker.* New York: Holt, 1960.

Mayo, E. *The human problems of an industrial civilization.* New York: Macmillan, 1933.

Mayo, E. *The social problems of an industrial civilization.* Boston: Grad. School of Bus. Admin., Harvard Univer., 1945.

Meier, D. L., & Bell, W. Anomie and differential access to the achievement of life goals. *Amer. sociol. Rev.*, 1959, **24**, 189–202.

Merton, R. K. *Social theory and social structure.* (2nd ed.) Glencoe, Ill.: Free Press, 1957.

Mills, C. W. *White collar.* New York: Oxford Univer. Press, 1951.

Mills, C. W. *The power elite.* New York: Oxford Univer. Press, 1956.

Moore, W. E. *Industrial relations and the social order.* (2nd ed.) New York: Macmillan, 1951.

Morse, N. C., & Weiss, R. S. The function and meaning of work and the job. *Amer. sociol. Rev.*, 1955, **20**, 191–198.

Myers, J. K., & Roberts, B. H. *Family and class dynamics in mental illness.* New York: Wiley, 1959.

Oeser, O. A., & Hammond, S. B. (Eds.). *Social structure and personality in a city.* New York: Macmillan, 1954.

Opler, M. K. *Culture, psychiatry, and human values.* Springfield, Ill.: Thomas, 1956.

Peak, H. Problems of objective observation. In L. Festinger & D. Katz (Eds.), *Research methods in the social sciences.* New York: Dryden, 1953. Pp. 243–299.

Presthus, R. *The organizational society.* New York: Knopf, 1962.

Purcell, T. V. *The worker speaks his mind on company and union.* Cambridge, Mass.: Harvard Univer. Press, 1954.

Purcell, T. V. *Blue collar man: patterns of dual allegiance in industry.* Cambridge, Mass.: Harvard Univer. Press, 1960.

Reissman, L. *Class in American society.* Glencoe, Ill.: Free Press, 1959.

Riesman, D. *The lonely crowd.* New Haven, Conn.: Yale Univer. Press, 1950.

Roethlisberger, F. J., & Dickson, W. J. *Management and the worker.* Cambridge, Mass.: Harvard Univer. Press, 1939.

Rose, A. M. (Ed.). *Mental health and mental disorder.* New York: Norton, 1955.

Rosenberg, B., & White, D. M. (Eds.). *Mass culture: the popular arts in America.* Glencoe, Ill.: Free Press, 1957.

Sanford, F. *Authoritarianism and leadership.* Philadelphia: Inst. for Res. in Hum. Relat., 1950.

Scott, T. B., Dawis, R. V., England, G. W., & Lofquist, L. H. A definition of work adjustment. *Minnesota Studies in Vocational Rehabilitation: X.* Industr. Relat. Center, Univer. of Minnesota, 1958.

Scott, W. A. Research definitions of mental health and illness. *Psychol. Bull.*, 1958, **55**, 29–45. (a)

Scott, W. A. Social psychological correlates of mental illness and mental health. *Psychol. Bull.*, 1958, **55**, 65–87. (b)

Seashore, S. *Group cohesiveness in the industrial work group.* Ann Arbor, Mich.: Inst. for Soc. Res., Univer. of Michigan, 1954.

Segerstedt, T. T., & Lundquist, A. *Man in industrialized society* (brief summary of two-volume research report). Stockholm: Industrial Council for Social and Economic Studies, 1956.

Selvin, H. C.   A critique of tests of significance in survey research.   *Amer. sociol. Rev.*, 1957, **22**, 519–527.

Shils, E. B.   *Automation and industrial relations.*   New York: Holt, Rinehart & Winston, 1963.

Smith, H. C.   *Psychology of industrial behavior.*   (2nd ed.) New York: McGraw-Hill, 1964.

Smith, M. B.   Research strategies toward a conception of positive mental health. *Amer. Psychologist*, 1959, **14**, 673–681.

Smith, M. B.   "Mental health" reconsidered: a special case of the problem of values in psychology.   *Amer. Psychologist*, 1961, **16**, 299–306.

Solley, C. M., & Munden, K. J.   Toward a description of mental health.   *Bull. Menninger Clinic*, 1962, **26**, 178–188.

Somers, G. G., Cushman, E. L., & Weinberg, N. (Eds.).   *Adjusting to technological change.*   New York: Harper & Row, 1963.

Srole, L.   Social integration and certain corollaries: an exploratory study. *Amer. sociol. Rev.*, 1956, **21**, 709–716.

Srole, L., Langner, T. S., Michael, S. T., Opler, M. K, & Rennie, T. A. C. *Mental health in the metropolis.*   New York: McGraw-Hill, 1962

Stagner, R.   *Psychology of industrial conflict.*   New York: Wiley, 1956.

Staley, E. (Ed.)   *Creating an industrial civilization.*   New York: Harper, 1952.

Stouffer, S. A.   *Communism, conformity, and civil liberties.*   New York: Doubleday, 1955.

Strauss, G.   Some notes on power equalization.   In H. G. Leavitt (Ed.), *The social science of organizations, four perspectives.*   Englewood Cliffs, N.J.: Prentice-Hall, 1963.   Pp. 41–84.

Super, D. E.   Occupational level and job satisfaction.   *J. appl. Psychol.*, 1939, **23**, 547–564.

Szasz, T. S.   The myth of mental illness.   *Amer. Psychologist*, 1960, **15**, 113–118.

Taylor, J. A.   A personality scale of manifest anxiety.   *J. abnorm. soc. Psychol.*, 1953, **48**, 285–290.

Titus, H. E., & Hollander, E. P.   The California F-scale in psychological research: 1950–1955.   *Psychol. Bull.*, 1957, **54**, 47–64.

Tuckman, J., & Kleiner, R. J.   Discrepancy between aspiration and achievement as a predictor of schizophrenia.   *Beh. Sci.*, 1962, **7**, 443–447.

Turner, A. N.   Management and the assembly line.   *Harv. bus. Rev.*, 1955, **33**(5), 40–48.

Turner, A. N., & Miclette, A. L.   Sources of satisfaction in repetitive work. *Occup. Psychol.*, 1962, **26**, 215–231.

Viteles, M. S.   *Motivation and morale in industry.*   New York: Norton, 1953.

Vroom, V. H.   Ego-involvement, job satisfaction, and job performance. *Personnel Psychol.*, 1962, **15**, 159–177.

Vroom, V. H.   *Work and Motivation.*   New York: Wiley, 1964.

Walker, C. R.   The problem of the repetitive job.   *Harv. bus. Rev.*, 1950, **28**(3), 54–58.

Walker, C. R.   *Toward the automatic factory.*   New Haven, Conn.: Yale Univer. Press, 1957.

Walker, C. R.   *Modern technology and civilization.*   New York: McGraw-Hill, 1962.

Walker, C. R., & Guest, R. H. *The man on the assembly line.* Cambridge, Mass.: Harvard Univer. Press, 1952.

Walker, J., & Marriott, R. A study of some attitudes to factory work. *Occup. Psychol.,* 1951, **25,** 181–191.

Warner, W. L., & Martin, N. H. (Eds.). *Industrial man.* New York: Harper, 1959.

Weiss, R. S., & Riesman, D. Social problems and disorganization in the world of work. In R. K. Merton & R. A. Nisbett (Eds.), *Contemporary social problems.* New York: Harcourt, Brace & World, 1961. Pp. 459–514.

Whyte, W. F. *Money and motivation.* New York: Harper, 1955.

Whyte, W. F. *Men at work.* Homewood, Ill.: Irwin-Dorsey, 1961.

Wilensky, H. L. Human relations in the workplace: an appraisal of some recent research. In Industr. Relat. Res. Ass., *Research in Industrial Human Relations.* New York: Harper, 1957. Pp. 25–50.

Wilensky, H. L. Work, careers, and social integration. *Int. Soc. Sci. J.,* 1960, **12,** 543–560.

Wilensky, H. L. Orderly careers and social participation: the impact of work history on social integration in the middle mass. *Amer. sociol. Rev.,* 1961, **26,** 521–539.

Wilensky, H. L. Varieties of work experience. In H. Borow (Ed.), *Man in a world at work.* Boston: Houghton-Mifflin, 1964. Pp. 125–154.

Wilensky, H. L., & Lebeaux, C. N. *Industrial society and social welfare.* New York: Russell Sage Foundation, 1958.

Wyatt, S., & Langdon, J. N. The machine and the worker. *Industr. Health Res. Bd. Report No. 82.* London: H. M. Stationery Office, 1938.

Wyatt, S., Langdon, J. N., & Stock, F. G. L. Fatigue and boredom in repetitive work. *Industr. Health Res. Bd. Report No. 77.* London: H. M. Stationery Office, 1937.

Wyatt, S., & Marriott, R. A study of attitudes to factory work. *Medical Res. Council Special Report Series, No. 292.* London: H. M. Stationery Office, 1956.

Zaleznik, A., Christensen, C. R., & Roethlisberger, F. J. *The motivation, productivity, and satisfaction of workers.* Boston: Grad. School of Bus. Admin., Harvard Univer., 1958.

Zander, A., & Quinn, R. The social environment and mental health: a review of past research at the Institute for Social Research. *J. soc. Issues,* 1962, **18**(3), 48–66.

Zweig, F. *The British worker.* Harmondsworth, England: Penguin, 1952.

Zweig, F. *The worker in an affluent society.* Glencoe, Ill.: Free Press, 1961.

Index

351

Frustration, relation to social attitudes, 225–231, 234
Futility, feeling of, 215–216

Gambling, relation to occupation and mental health, 203–204
Goals and values, adult, *see* Workers' goals and values
childhood, 71–75, 147–150

Hobbies, 199–203; *see also* Spare-time activities
Hostility, index of, 25, 318
relation to occupation and mental health, 27–29, 42–47, 62, 132, 135, 256–257
Human relations in industry, attitudes toward, 107–110, 178–180
management of, as influence on workers' mental health, 281–287

Income, attitudes toward, relation to mental health, 125–127
level of, in childhood, 138–139, 226–227
relation to occupation and mental health, 123–127
Indexes based on interview, description of, 318–322
Interest in work, relation to job satisfaction, 165–170
relation to mental health, 98–101
Interview, description of, 19–20
schedule of questions, 293–317

Job attitudes, *see* Attitudes, toward job
Job enlargement, 4–5
Job level, *see* Occupational level
Job satisfaction, 9–10, 78–89, 266
extent of, 157–165
index of, 84, 320
intrinsic vs. extrinsic, 165–180, 183–184
meaning of, 158–161
relation to mental health, 49–50, 52, 78–89, 158–159, 262–263
relation to nonjob satisfactions, 205–207
relation to occupational level, 84–85, 159–180, 183–185

Job satisfaction, relation to prolabor social attitudes, 225–227
Job security, attitude toward, 177–188
relation to mental health, 93–94

Labor unions, attitudes toward, 221–224
role in meeting psychological needs, 286, 291
Leisure, *see* Spare-time activities
Life satisfaction, index of, 25, 319
relation to job satisfaction, 205–207
relation to mental health, 27–29, 42–47, 62
relation to occupational level, 134 137, 186–195
relation to prolabor social attitudes, 225–227

Management, relation to workers' mental health, *see* Attitudes, toward company; Company, management's role
Mechanical pacing, 57–59, 103–105
Mental health, meaning of in present study, 11–15, 16–17
methods of assessment employed, 16–39
value problems, 17–18, 277–280, 329, 331
Mental-health differences by occupation (skill level), 55–77, 261
relation to age, 56–59
relation to education, 67–69
relation to job satisfaction, 78–89, 158–159, 262–263
relation to length of employment, 76–77
relation to occupational-level characteristics, 90–131, 263–264, 272–275
relation to prejob personal characteristics, 67–76, 261–262
selection effects vs. job effects, 66–77
urban factory workers vs. comparison groups, 59–61
Mental health of factory workers, 40–54
comparison with other groups, 59–61
differences by occupational level, 55–77

DATE DUE

11 4 '82	
AR 6 '91	
ret 3/2¢